AISB91

AISB91

PROCEEDINGS OF THE EIGHTH
CONFERENCE OF THE SOCIETY FOR
THE STUDY OF ARTIFICIAL INTELLIGENCE
AND SIMULATION OF BEHAVIOUR

16–19 APRIL 1991
UNIVERSITY OF LEEDS

EDITED BY
LUC STEELS AND BARBARA SMITH

SPRINGER-VERLAG
LONDON BERLIN HEIDELBERG NEW YORK
PARIS TOKYO HONG KONG

Luc Steels, MSc, PhD
Professor of Artificial Intelligence,
Director VUB AI Laboratory,
Vrije Universiteit Brussel,
Pleinlaan 2, 1050 Brussels, Belgium

Barbara Smith, BSc, MSc, PhD,
School of Computer Studies,
University of Leeds,
Leeds LS2 9JT, UK.

ISBN-13:978-3-540-19671-6   e-ISBN-13:978-1-4471-1852-7
DOI: 10.1007/978-1-4471-1852-7

British Library Cataloguing in Publication Data
AISB91 (Conference, University of Leeds)
AISB91: Proceedings of the 8th Conference of the Society for the Study of
Artificial Intelligence and Simulation of Behaviour, 16–19 April 1991,
University of Leeds
1. Artificial intelligence
I. Title   II. Steels, Luc   III. Smith, Barbara *1948–*
006.3

Library of Congress Cataloging-in-Publication Data
Society for the Study of Artificial Intelligence and the Simulation of
Behaviour. Conference (8th : 1991 : University of Leeds)
AISB91: Proceedings of the 8th Conference of the Society for the Study of
Artificial Intelligence and Simulation of Behaviour, 16–19 April 1991,
University of Leeds / Luc Steels and Barbara Smith.
    p.   cm.

1. Artificial intelligence – Congresses.   2. Computer simulation
– Congresses.   3. Machine learning – Congresses.   4. Reasoning –
Congresses.   I. Steels, Luc.   II. Smith, Barbara, 1948– .   III. Title.
Q334.S6315 1991   91–8041
0063–dc20   CIP

Printed and bound by Page Bros (Norwich) Ltd, Mile Cross Lane, Norwich.
34/3830–543210   Printed on acid-free paper

PREFACE

AISB91 is the eighth conference organized by the Society for the Study of Artificial Intelligence and Simulation of Behaviour. It is not only the oldest regular conference in Europe on AI – which spawned the ECAI conferences in 1982 – but it is also the conference that has a tradition for focusing on research as opposed to applications. The 1991 edition of the conference was no different in this respect. On the contrary, research, and particularly newly emerging research directions such as knowledge level expert systems research, neural networks and emergent functionality in autonomous agents, was strongly emphasised.

The conference was organized around the following sessions: distributed intelligent agents, situatedness and emergence in autonomous agents, new modes of reasoning, the knowledge level perspective, and theorem proving and machine learning. Each of these sessions is discussed below in more detail.

DISTRIBUTED INTELLIGENT AGENTS

Research in distributed AI is concerned with the problem of how multiple agents and societies of agents can be organized to co-operate and collectively solve a problem. The first paper by Chakravarty (MIT) focuses on the problem of evolving agents in the context of Minsky's society of mind theory. It addesses the question of how new agents can be formed by transforming existing ones and illustrates the theory with an example from game playing. Smieja (GMD, Germany) focuses on the problem of organizing networks of agents which consist internally of neural networks. Smieja builds upon the seminal work of Selfridge in the late fifties on the Pandemonium system. Bond (University of California) addresses the problem of regulating co-operation between agents. He seeks inspiration in sociological theory and proposes a framework based on negotiation. Finally Mamede and Martins (Technical University of Lisbon) address the problem of resource-bounded reasoning within the context of logical inference.

SITUATEDNESS AND EMERGENCE IN AUTONOMOUS AGENTS

Research on robots and autonomous agents used to be focused strongly on low level mechanisms. As such there were few connections with the core problems of AI. Recently, there has been a shift of emphasis towards the construction of complete agents. This has lead to a review of some traditional concepts, such as the hierarchical decomposition of an agent into a perception module, a decision module and an action module and it has brought robotics research back to the front of the AI stage. This session testifies to the renewed interest in the area.

The first paper, by Bersini (Free University of Brussels), is strongly within the new perspective of emphasizing situatedness and non-symbolic relations between perception and action. It discusses the trade-offs between reactive systems and goal-oriented systems. Seel (STC Technology, Harlow, UK) provides some of the formal foundations for understanding and building reactive systems. Jackson and Sharkey (University of Exeter) address the problem of symbol grounding: how signals can be related to concepts. They use a connectionist mechanism to relate spatial descriptions with results from perception. Cliff (University of Sussex) discusses an experiment in computational neuroethology.

The next paper at the conference was from the Edinburgh Really Useful Robot project which has built up a strong tradition in building autonomous mobile robots. The paper was given by Hallam (University of Edinburgh) and discussed an experiment in real-time control using toy cars. The paper was unfortunately not received in time for publication in these Proceedings. The final paper is by Kaelbling (Teleos Research, Palo Alto, California) who elaborates her proposals for principled programming of autonomous agents based on logical specifications.

At the conference, the session ended with a panel that tried to put the current work on autonomous agents into the broader perspective of AI. The panel included Smithers (University of Edinburgh), Kaelbling, Connah (Philips Research, UK), and Agre (University of Sussex).

NEW MODES OF REASONING

Reasoning remains one of the core topics of AI. This session explored some of the current work to find new forms of reasoning. The first paper by Hendler and Dickens (University of Maryland) looks at the integration of neural networks and symbolic AI in the context of a concrete example involving an underwater robot. Euzenat and Maesano (CEDIAG/Bull, Louveciennes, France) address the problem of forgetting. Pfahringer (University of Vienna) builds further on research in constraint propagation in qualitative modelling. He proposes a mechanism to improve efficiency through domain variables. Ghassem-Sani and Steel (University of Essex) extend the arsenal of methods for non-recursive planning by introducing a method derived from mathematical induction.

THE KNOWLEDGE LEVEL PERSPECTIVE

Knowledge systems (also known as expert systems or knowledge-based systems) continue to be the most successful area of AI application. The conference was not focused on applications but on foundational principles for building knowledge systems. Recently there has been an important shift of emphasis from symbol level considerations (which focus on the formalism in which a system is implemented) to knowledge level considerations. The session highlights this shift in emphasis.

The first paper by Pierret-Golbreich and Delouis (Université Paris Sud) is related to work on the generic task architectures. It proposes a framework including support tools for performing analysis of the task structure of the knowledge system. Reichgelt and Shadbolt (University of Nottingham) apply the knowledge level perspective to the problem of knowledge acquisition. Wetter and Schmidt (IBM Germany) focus on the formalization of the KADS interpretation models which is one of the major frameworks for doing knowledge level design. Finally Lackinger and Haselböck (University of Vienna) focus on domain models in knowledge systems, particularly qualitative models for simulation and control of dynamic systems.

Then there are two papers which address directly foundational issues. The first one by Van de Velde (VUB AI Lab, Brussels) clarifies the (difficult) concepts involved in knowledge level discussions of expert systems, particularly the principle of rationality. Schreiber, Akkermans and Wielinga (University of Amsterdam) critically examine the suitability of the knowledge level for expert system design.

The session ended with a panel that addressed further the question of adequacy. The panel involved Leitch (Heriot Watt University, Edinburgh), Wielinga, Van de Velde, Sticklen (Michigan State University), and Pfeifer (University of Zurich).

THEOREM PROVING AND MACHINE LEARNING

The final set of papers focuses on recent work in theorem proving and machine learning. The first paper by Giunchiglia (IRST Trento, Italy) and Walsh (University of Edinburgh) discusses how abstraction can be used in theorem proving and presents solid evidence why it is useful.

Steel (University of Essex) proposes a new inference scheme for modal logic.

Then there are two papers which represent current work on machine learning. The first one by Churchill and Young (University of Cambridge) reports on an experiment using SOAR concerned with modelling representations of device knowledge. The second paper by Elliott and Scott (University of Essex) compares instance-based and generalization-based learning procedures.

The conference also featured invited talks by Andy Clark (University of Sussex) on the philosophical foundations of the field, Rolf Pfeifer (University of Zurich) on emotion, and Tony Cohn (University of Leeds) on common sense modelling using logic. There was a closing address by the Conference Chair, Luc Steels, who speculated on the role of consciousness in artificial intelligence.

January 1991   Luc Steels
                                                                VUB AI Lab
                                                    1050 Brussels – Belgium

AISB91

PROGRAMME COMMITTEE

Luc Steels
Free University of Brussels
(Chair)

Benedict du Boulay
University of Sussex

Anthony Cohn
University of Leeds

John Hallam
University of Edinburgh

Rolf Pfeifer
University of Zurich

Tim Smithers
University of Edinburgh

Bob Wielinga
University of Amsterdam

LOCAL ORGANISER

Barbara Smith
University of Leeds

TUTORIAL ORGANISERS

Caroline Knight
Stephen Todd
Hewlett-Packard Laboratories, Bristol

SPONSORS

British Telecom Computing (Advanced Technology Group)

Digital Equipment Co. Ltd.

INVITED SPEAKERS

Andy Clark
University of Sussex
Emergence, Content and Flexibility

Anthony Cohn
University of Leeds
Logical Representations of Space and Time for Naive Physics

Rolf Pfeifer
University of Zurich
The New Age of the Fungus-Eater: Comments on AI and Emotion

CONTENTS

DISTRIBUTED INTELLIGENT AGENTS

Deriving Transformers from Knowledge Organized as a Society of Agents

Anil S. Chakravarthy
Massachusetts Institute of Technology
305 Memorial Dr. #509B, Cambridge MA 02139
e-mail: anil@athena.mit.edu

ABSTRACT

A learning program should be capable of organizing the knowledge that it acquires. This organization is necessary not only for the efficient retrieval of relevant knowledge but also for application of the knowledge to situations that are similar but not identical to the situation in which the knowledge was acquired. The "Society of Mind"[Minsky, 1988] provides a framework for organization of knowledge embodied as agents. In this paper, we describe a program that constructs *transformers* from closely related agents. A transformer abstracts the difference between two related agents. Since the transformer represents a property of the domain, it can be used under different circumstances to obtain a new agent from an existing one. These two agents are related in the same way as the two agents of the original pair. We also discuss how the same methods can be used to abstract differences between transformers to form transformer–transformers and so on. Finally, we examine the links that transformers have to other AI paradigms such as analogical reasoning, level–band theories of memory and generalization.

Keywords: Knowledge Organization, Society of Mind

1 Introduction

A learning program should be capable of organizing the knowledge that it acquires. This capability is necessary to:

- use efficiently the knowledge acquired thus far,

- use the acquired knowledge in situations similar but not identical to the original situation, and

- facilitate the assimilation of knowledge to be acquired in the future.

Many models of knowledge organization have emerged from research in Artificial Intelligence. The HACKER program[Sussman, 1975] compiled critics that detected bugs in the program proposer's code. Knowledge acquired about debugging was summarized and remembered in usable form as subroutines and patches in the Answer Library. TEIRESIAS[Davis, 1982] constructed rule models to classify rules and to expect new rules. AM[Lenat, 1983] has facets for generalizations, specializations and analogies of a concept. CYC[Lenat and Guha, 1989] defines categories of objects that abstract common properties of the underlying objects. In SOAR[Laird et al., 1986, Part 3], chunking is used as a general mechanism to encode knowledge about solutions for subgoals.

A significant theory about knowledge organization is Marvin Minsky's "Society of Mind"[Minsky, 1988]. This theory views intelligence as arising due to a (mostly hierarchical) society of relatively simple agents. It might be useful to think of such a society in terms of the following example[Minsky, 1988, page 103]. A system is trying to "understand" the concept of one "thing" being "more" than another thing. If, for example, liquids are being compared, and they are in identical containers, it is sufficient to compare their heights. Or if one group of discrete objects is being compared with another group of discrete objects, it should be enough to count them. Eventually, part of the "society" that enables the system to learn the concept of "more" could be as shown in Figure 1. We see that between the primitives and the final decision–maker, we have a number of *managers*. These managers embody the administrative ways in which the system uses what it already knows. In the Society-of-More, a manager selects advice offered by one of its subordinates. Societies may be organized in other ways as well. If a society called Builder is used to build toy towers, subordinate agents such as Find, Grasp etc. work in tandem rather than compete with each other[1].

We describe a program that acquires a society of advice–givers embodying a certain broad concept in a card game called Seahaven Towers. We will see that some advice–givers are related in the sense that they can be transformed into each other using properties of the domain. The main idea underlying the paper is that *advice–giver transformers* can be acquired if the advice–givers are organized into a society like the Society–of–More. A transformer abstracts the difference between two related advice–givers. Since the transformer represents a property of the domain, it can be used under different circumstances to obtain a new advice–giver from an existing one. These two advice–givers are related in the same way as the two advice–givers of the original pair. We will also see that the same style of organization can be used to abstract the differences between the transformers themselves to form *transformer-transformers* and so on. The process of developing transformers has significant links to other areas of AI research such as analogical reasoning, level–band theories of memory and learning by generalization.

The rest of the paper is organized as follows: Section 2 provides an introduction to Seahaven Towers. Section 3 details the methods used to learn advice–givers from specific instances and to learn transformers from advice–givers and so on. In Section 4, we discuss the relationship this learning mechanism has to other areas of AI research. Section 5 concludes the paper with a summary and possible research directions.

2 The Seahaven Towers game

Seahaven Towers is a card game similar to Solitaire. There are ten working *stacks*, four *final stacks*, and four *buffers*. Each final stack corresponds to a particular suit. Each buffer can hold at most one card. Initially, the 52 cards are distributed randomly among the stacks and the buffers. Cards can be moved in the following three ways:

1. stack or buffer to stack: A card, C, that is at the bottom of stack A or is in a buffer can be moved to another stack S if the bottom card of S is the

---

[1]To be more specific about an agent's function, we will call the agents found in societies similar to the Society–of–More as advice–givers. The term is due to Alan Ruttenberg.

successor of C. For example, (H 9) is the successor of (H 8). The empty list, nil, is considered to be the successor of a king. Hence, any king that is at the bottom of its stack or in a buffer can be moved to an empty stack if one is available. Conversely, (H 8) is the *predecessor* of (H 9). The empty list, nil, is considered to be the predecessor of every ace.

2. stack to buffer: If a buffer, B, is empty, any card, C, that is at the bottom of its stack can be moved to B.

3. stack or buffer to final-stack: A card, C, that is at the bottom of its stack or in a buffer has to be moved to its final stack if its predecessor is already on the final stack[2].

The objective of the game is to move all cards to their respective final stacks. We will represent each card by a 2-tuple. For example, the ace of hearts is (H A) while six of diamonds is (D 6).

Some experience with the game will reveal that the buffers play an important role. Any card can be moved to a buffer, and hence they are useful in getting "troublesome" cards out of the way. Also, we notice that once a card has been moved to the final stack, it need not be moved again (in fact, it cannot be). But, attaching cards to other stacks is not so benign. They may block other crucial cards, and may lead to a *deadlock* situation from which it is impossible to complete the game. There is one exception. Consider a stack that reads (from top to bottom) ((H J) (H 10) (H 9) (H 8)). Suppose we were to add (H 7) to this stack. We wouldn't be blocking any other cards, and in fact, if (H 7) is "exposed" to its final stack, all the other cards are effectively exposed as well. Let us call such a stack a *desirable list*. Finally, let us "define" a *no-cost set of moves* to be one that does not reduce the number of free buffers available or add any card to a stack that is not a desirable list. In addition, the set of moves must accomplish something useful like adding cards to some final stack or a desirable list. As we can readily see, there are so many arrangements of cards from which no-cost move-sets are possible that it is unwise to enumerate even typical examples of all of them. In fact, it is this prolificity that calls for transformers, transformer-transformers and so on.

3 Learning and Organization in the Seahaven Towers Program

In this section, we discuss the methods used to learn and to organize advice-givers and transformers. An advice-giver recognizes a stereotypical situation, and suggests a good course of action. Hence, an advice-giver is represented in a straightforward fashion as:

```
(advice-giver ag1
  :situation (STACK-A ((CARD 1) (CARD 0) OTHER-CARDS))
             (((CARD 1) NEXT-TO-IDENT-PRED (CARD 0))
             ((CARD 0) NEXT-FOR-FINAL (FINAL-STACK 0)) ((BUFFER 0) EMPTY))

  :action (((CARD 1) (BUFFER 0))
```

---

[2]If more than one card is eligible for the move, they can be moved in any order. Since this move is mandatory, it is done automatically by an internal book-keeper. That is why there might be some cards in the final stacks in the initial configuration itself.

```
    ((CARD 0) (FINAL-STACK 0)) ((CARD 1) (FINAL-STACK 0)))
)
```

The procedure that learns advice–givers takes an instance of an advice–giver as its input, and outputs an abstract characterization similar to the one shown above. A simple algorithm is used to learn advice–givers.

```
Algorithm Learn-Advice-Giver

Step 1: Identify the cards that are to be characterized
Step 2: Make an initial characterization of the cards as follows:
            If the card is involved in a king-move, i.e., it is moved to
            an empty stack at some point, characterize it as a king
            If the card's predecessor is on a final stack, F,
            characterize it as a (next-for-final F)
            If the card's successor is on a desirable list, D, characterize it
            as a (next-for-desirable D)
            If the card's predecessor, X, is one of the cards identified above,
            characterize it as a (next-to-identified-predecessor X)
            If the card's successor, Y, is one of the cards identified above,
            characterize it as a (next-to-identified-successor X)
            If none of the above apply, characterize it as arbitrary

Step 3: For each card, set the list of Previous-Characterizations to nil
Step 4: Repeat
            Test the current characterization. This is as follows:
             For each move in the action-list, see if it is
             possible under the given characterization. For example,
             a card can be moved to an empty stack only if it is
             characterized as a king.
            If all the moves are possible, the characterization is
            satisfactory and we are done. If not, single out the
            offending card, and determine what characterization it
            needs to have to make the move possible. If this belongs
            to its list of Previous-Characterizations, then form a
            conjunction of the current and the desired characterizations.
            If not, replace the current characterization by the
            desired one.
            Until the current characterization satisfies the given instance
```

How are these agents (advice–givers) organized? There are several ways in which agents might be organized under a manager. In the Society–of–More, for example, agents might be grouped under managers depending on the type of reasoning (spatial, numerical etc) they use to arrive at their conclusion. In Builder, on the other hand, the manager supervises agents that together accomplish a given task. For the Seahaven Towers program, it seems best to organize the agents depending on the property they preserve (e.g., no cards are added to any buffers or stacks by moves included in the advice). This corresponds closely to the organization of the Society–of–More because the property that characterizes the manager also identifies the line of "reasoning" that

underlies the advice. Figure 2 shows the no–cost–move society for which advice–givers
are learnt[3].

It is this organization that gives rise to transformers. The rationale is that if two
different advice–givers capture the same property of the state space, the *difference*
between the two advice–givers can probably reveal some important property of the
domain. For example, consider the transformation between the advice–giver ag1
mentioned above and the closely related advice-giver ag2 shown below:

```
(advice-giver ag2
  :situation (STACK-A ((CARD 2) (CARD 1) (CARD 0) OTHER-CARDS))
             (((CARD 2) NEXT-TO-IDENT-PRED (CARD 1))
              ((CARD 1) NEXT-TO-IDENT-PRED (CARD 0))
              ((CARD 0) NEXT-FOR-FINAL (FINAL-STACK 0))
              ((BUFFER 1) EMPTY) ((BUFFER 0) EMPTY))

  :action (((CARD 2) (BUFFER 1)) ((CARD 1) (BUFFER 0))
           ((CARD 0) (FINAL-STACK 0))
           ((CARD 1) (FINAL-STACK 0)) ((CARD 2) (FINAL-STACK 0)))
)
```

Advice–giver ag2 achieves the same effect as ag1 except that it deals with an additional
card (CARD 2) whose predecessor is (CARD 1). The transformer between these two
advice–givers is abstracted as shown below. The transformer–learning algorithm is
given in Appendix A.

```
(transformer t1
  :difference (STACK-A ((CARD 11) (CARD 2) (CARD 1)))
              (((RELATION 1) (CARD 2) (CARD 1))
               ((RELATION 1) (CARD 11) (CARD 2)))

  :action (((CARD 11) (MOVE-CORRESPONDING (RELATION 1))) ORIGINAL-MOVES
           ((CARD 11) (MOVE-CORRESPONDING (RELATION 1))))
  :documentation ''Cards 11, 12 etc denote cards
                    introduced by the transformer''
)
```

When a transformer is first created, it is "attached" to the node at which it is created (in this case, no–additions–to–buffers–or–stacks). This transformer can now be
applied to a number of advice–givers to generate new advice–givers. For example,
consider the advice–giver shown below:

```
(advice-giver ag3
  :situation (STACK-A ((CARD 1) (CARD 0) OTHER-CARDS)) ((BUFFER 1) (CARD 2))
             (((CARD 2) NEXT-TO-IDENT-PRED (CARD 0)) ((CARD 1) ARBITRARY)
              ((CARD 0) NEXT-FOR-FINAL (FINAL-STACK 0)) ((BUFFER 0) EMPTY))

  :action (((CARD 1) (BUFFER 0)) ((CARD 0) (FINAL-STACK 0))
           ((CARD 2) (FINAL-STACK 0)))
)
```

---

[3]It needs to be mentioned here that this particular choice of intermediate managers was not learnt
by the program. However, a program that is capable of discovering properties about the state space
and the operators would probably arrive at a similar organization.

This advice–giver maintains the number of empty buffers constant, but doesn't ensure that the cards in the buffers are also the same as before. In response to a given problem, transformer t1 can be applied to ag3 to generate the following advice–giver[4]:

```
(advice-giver ag4
  :situation (STACK-A ((CARD 2) (CARD 1) (CARD 0) OTHER-CARDS))
             ((BUFFER 2) (CARD 3)) ((BUFFER 3) (CARD 4))
             (((CARD 4) NEXT-TO-IDENT-PRED (CARD 3))
             ((CARD 3) NEXT-TO-IDENT-PRED (CARD 0))
             ((CARD 2) ARBITRARY) ((CARD 1) ARBITRARY)
             ((CARD 0) NEXT-FOR-FINAL (FINAL-STACK 0))
             ((BUFFER 1) EMPTY) ((BUFFER 0) EMPTY))

  :action (((CARD 2) (BUFFER 1)) ((CARD 1) (BUFFER 0))
          ((CARD 0) (FINAL-STACK 0))
          ((CARD 1) (FINAL-STACK 0)) ((CARD 2) (FINAL-STACK 0)))
)
```

As in the above example, when the program encounters a situation for which there is no advice–giver, a new advice–giver is created by looking for a transformer that can convert an existing advice–giver into the desired one. It looks for a transformer that is attached to the current node. If none are available, the search is moved up the "tree". Conversely, a transformer that is used by a node that isn't its own parent also moves up the tree, i.e., it is considered more general in its applicability[5].

Transformer–transformers are also created at nodes at which closely related transformers are formed. The difference between transformers and transformer–transformers is slight. For example, consider the transformer below:

```
(transformer t2
  :difference (STACK-A ((CARD 2) (CARD 11) (CARD 1)))
              ((NEXT-FOR-FINAL (CARD 11)))

  :action ((PART-OF-ORIGINAL-MOVES-BEFORE-OCCURENCE (CARD 1))
          ((CARD 11) CORRESPONDING-FINAL-STACK)
          (REST-OF-ORIGINAL-MOVES (CARD 1)))

  :documentation
    ''If the only difference between an advice-giver and a new
      situation is an embedded next-for-final card, the original
      advice-giver can still be used''
)
```

If the transformer t1 is applied to t2, we create a new transformer that transforms advice–givers into new versions that can work on situations that differ from existing advice–givers in that they have two embedded next-for–final cards. In fact, if t1 is applied to itself, we get transformers that work on multiple cards.

---

[4]Instantiating (RELATION 1) in a new situation is not as difficult as it first appears to be. This is because we already know what property the new advice–giver must satisfy.

[5]A transformer that moves up leaves behind a "trace", so that it is examined along with other transformers at its original node.

4 Discussion

An important field of AI research has been learning by analogy[Winston, 1980, Carbonell, 198
Indeed, [Minsky, 1988, page 238] believes that it is one of the most fundamental reasoning mechanisms in human beings. As we have seen above, transformers are like
"readymade analogies". They are able to abstract some heuristic property of the
domain that may prove useful in the generation of new advice–givers. If transformers
could be formed readily during the process of organization of the advice–givers itself,
it would be easy to explain the commonplace nature of analogical reasoning.

Another significant property of transformers (and transformer–transformers and
so on) is that they enable the program to "forget" the actual details of the individual advice–givers. As we noted in Section 3, this ability is important because
there are very many individual situations. As each new problem is encountered,
some set of transformers can be used to generate an advice–giver for the particular case (using a base case). This is essentially similar to the *level–band* theory of
memory[Minsky, 1988, page 86]. The level–band theory is the idea that a typical
mental process engages only a portion of the structure of the agency that it is operating upon. It serves to explain how the use of a frame (script) need not be limited
to the particular situation in which it was learnt. Similarly, we see how knowledge
learnt from one set of examples can be transferred to a different situation.

Although we haven't seen any examples of *censors*[Minsky, 1988, page 276] in this
paper, they constitute a very important type of advice–givers. A censor prevents the
application of a transformer or an advice-giver. Censors embody the experience that
the program has gained from the misuse of advice–givers and transformers in the
past. Censors are very general in the sense that they may pertain to transformers at
any level, and to advice–givers and managers at any level.

In the learning algorithms that have been illustrated in this paper, we find that
some heuristics have been embedded (e.g., a card is first checked to see if it can be
classified as a next–for–final before anything else). We feel that, for each manager,
the "qualification" criteria (e.g., no–additions–to–buffers–or–stacks) also provide the
clues to organize the learning algorithm. As was stated in Section 3, a discovery
system would probably be able to generate the criteria that characterize managers
and hence, provide the specifics that constitute the individual learning algorithms.

Finally, generalization itself can be viewed as a kind of transformer formation.
As a simple example, consider the fact that a beginner discovers that two (simple)
advice–givers are identical except that the first deals with cards of suit A, while the
other deals with cards of suit B. It might then be concluded that all suits are equivalent, a heuristic that is not necessarily true for all card games.

5 Conclusions

In this paper, we have presented a scheme of organization that acts in conjunction
with a society of agents. This organization enables the development of transformers that abstract the difference between related agents. If this difference reveals an
important property of the domain, it is possible to use the transformers so formed
to synthesize new agents that are applicable in previously unencountered situations.
Abstraction can be carried to higher levels by the formation of layers of transform-

ers. The creation and use of transformers is closely related to the (frequent) use of analogical reasoning, the presence of level–bands in the organization of memory, and perhaps, learning by generalization.

Much work remains to be done in several areas. Better representations are necessary for both advice–givers and transformers so that it is easy to build upon them. We need to work on how censors can be organized and how they can be applied to inhibit particular transformers. We are currently working on a discovery program to understand the kinds of in–built knowledge necessary to build such organizations. We also need to investigate how well these ideas work in other domains.

References

[Carbonell, 1983]   Jaime G. Carbonell. "Learning by Analogy," in *Machine Learning*, R. S. Michalski, J. G. Carbonell, and T. Mitchell, eds., Tioga Publishing, Palo Alto, 1983.

[Davis, 1982]   Randall Davis. "Teiresias: Application of Meta–Level Knowledge," in *Knowledge–Based Systems in Artificial Intelligence*, R. Davis and D. Lenat, Addison–Wesley, Reading, MA, 1982.

[Laird et al., 1986]   J. Laird, P. S. Rosenbloom, and A. Newell. *Universal Subgoaling and Chunking*, Kluwer Academic Publishers, Boston, MA, 1986.

[Lenat, 1983]   D. B. Lenat. "AM: Discovery in Mathematics as Heuristic Search," in *Knowledge–Based Systems in Artificial Intelligence*, R. Davis and D. Lenat, Addison–Wesley, Reading, MA, 1982.

[Lenat and Guha, 1989] D. B. Lenat and R. V. Guha. *Building Large Knowledge–Based Systems: Representation and Inference in the CYC Project*, Addison–Wesley, Reading, MA, 1989.

[Minsky, 1988]   Marvin L. Minsky. *The Society of Mind*, Simon and Schuster, New York. 1988.

[Sussman, 1975]   G. J. Sussman. *A Computer Model of Skill Acquisition*, American Elsevier, New York, 1975.

[Winston, 1980]   Patrick H. Winston. *Learning and Reasoning by Analogy*, CACM, vol. 23, no. 12, December 1980.

Appendix A: Learning Transformers

We give the transformer–learning algorithm below:

```
Algorithm Transformer-Learner(ag1, ag2)

Step 1: Assume that advice-giver ag1 has fewer cards than ag2.
        Map each card of ag1 to a corresponding card of ag2.
```

The unmapped cards of ag2 are the cards to be characterized.

Step 2: For every unmapped card do
        If card is a next-for-final or next-for-desirable, retain it
        else if its relation to card X is the same as the relation
        that X has to a mapped card, variabilize the relation
        else if the card is arbitrary, omit it from the difference

Step 3: Test to see if the characterization is able to transform between
        the two advice-givers of the given instance. If not, ''dilute''
        the characterization of the offending card and repeat.

Arbitrary cards are neglected when applying the transformer to a new advice–giver.
Transformer–transformers can be acquired by a similar generate–test–debug loop.

12

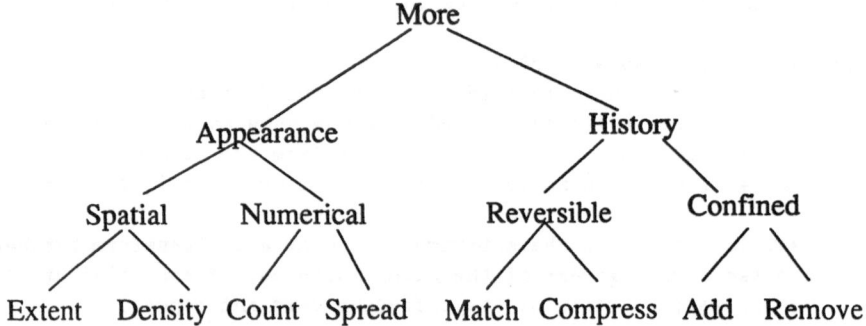

Figure 1: The Society -of-More

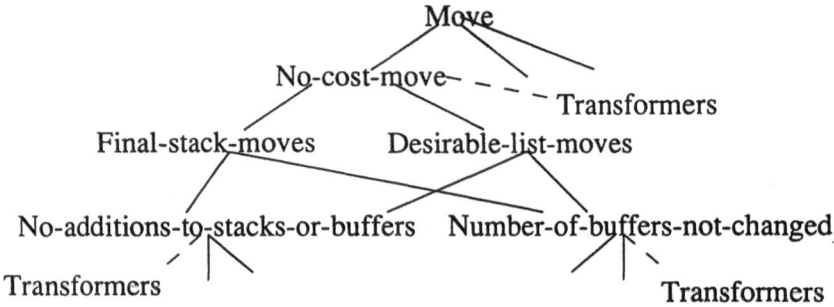

Figure 2: Organization of the no-cost-move
advice-givers

Multiple Network Systems (Minos) Modules: Task Division and Module Discrimination

F.J. Śmieja

German National Research Centre for Computer Science (GMD),
Schloß Birlinghoven, 5205 St. Augustin 1,
Germany.

ABSTRACT

It is widely considered an ultimate connectionist objective to incorporate neural networks into intelligent *systems*. These systems are intended to possess a varied repertoire of functions enabling adaptable interaction with a non-static environment. The first step in this direction is to develop various neural network algorithms and models, the second step is to combine such networks into a modular structure that might be incorporated into a workable system. In this paper we consider one aspect of the second point, namely: processing reliability and hiding of wetware details. Presented is an architecture for a type of neural expert module, named an *Authority*. An Authority consists of a number of *Minos* modules. Each of the Minos modules in an Authority has the same processing capabilities, but varies with respect to its particular *specialization* to aspects of the problem domain. The Authority employs the collection of Minoses like a panel of experts. The expert with the highest *confidence* is believed, and it is the answer and confidence quotient that are transmitted to other levels in a system hierarchy.

INTRODUCTION

The great majority of work on neural networks so far has concentrated on developing different models and observing their performance either on so-called "toy-problems" [13, 11, 19], in an attempt to improve them, or on highly preprocessed and isolated examples of aspects of real-world human processing [14, 20, 5, 12], in an attempt to demonstrate their potential. The ultimate objective is, with regard to Artificial Intelligence, to incorporate such networks into large hierarchical learning systems driven by centralized self-supervision and goal generators. We believe that only systems designed hierarchically mainly from modular neural network components will be able to solve the complex dynamic problems relevant to coping and evolving in a hostile environment. Ideally neural nets should enable the systems to adapt to new experiences in the environment, and the systems should respond in a controlled manner to new events and respond confidently to familiar ones. In order to achieve such a goal, one must first demand a degree of reliability from the constituting networks. The higher levels of the system should not need to be bothered with the low-level functioning and supervision of the basic networks, but at the same time need to *assess* responses through the receipt of some indication of the validity of an answer or memory recall obtained from lower-level modules.

We view the operation and construction of such ultimate systems in a top-down sense, based on an architecture of hierarchical and interacting *modules*, which at the lowest level are comprised of neural networks. Each module should be designed as closely as possible to a *semi-closed system*, that hides the details of the network wetware but allows interaction with other network modules and transmission of "opinions" and the *validity* of these opinions on the questions being asked it to higher processing levels of the system hierarchy. In this paper we present the design of a particular Minos network module that may form part of a group of such modules comprising an Authority. An Authority has the capability of learning difficult mapping problems, or large numbers of memories (depending on the underlying network types), through the division of subtasks among the Minoses. It generates a confidence measure together with its reply to a question (from higher up the hierarchy) based on its degree of familiarity with the question.

Another aim of the Minos generation is to be able to vary the information learnt dynamically as the environment varies, and do it in a reliable way. Normally, experiments on the different types of network are carried out with an unchanging training set of possible environment situations, and the nets are adapted to respond correctly to these, and only these. Further learning on situations exclusive of this set is however often very destructive, with the previously learnt situations degrading since they are no longer being learnt. Such degradation is equivalent to "forgetting" and is a fundamental property of neural systems. However this would be an acceptable property of the system so long as one could *distinguish* "hazy" memories from clear ones. Progressive learning clearly presents the drawback of "recency" (the more recently encountered situations are more favourably remembered) but also the advantage of being able to vary the adaptation frequency to the situations' appearance frequency in the environment. In the functioning of Minoses the above characteristics of neural systems are recognized and used to the advantage of the system. Thus, it is good if, when new situations arise in an environment, the likelihood of acting as if the old cases applied reduced and that of the new increased.

By employing neural network module decomposition of problems, Authorities adopt the "divide and conquer" approach to solving difficult mapping problems. This is a way of attacking the neural network scaling problem [7, 6]: The more difficult a mapping problem (of a fixed input space size) the more hidden units that will be necessary in order to solve it [19, 17]. Furthermore, the more difficult the mapping function to be learnt, the more training examples that will be necessary for decent generalization [18, 1]. Numbers explode with input space dimension size. Instead of scaling single networks in the way suggested by such complexity scaling, the Minos approach is to keep networks as small as possible but use arbitrary numbers of them to solve the same problem, sharing out the training set in a particular way. This is a *modular* as opposed to a *neural soup* technique of producing systems capable of solving problems of higher complexity [8]. Such division often might be rejected on generalization grounds. Indeed, if as many networks as patterns are available, then absolutely no generalization should perhaps be expected. However, if it is the possibility of being able to generalize *at all* on the training set that is *used* to divide the set among the networks, then one might expect not to lose the desired generalization.

Such assumptions about generalization are an important aspect of the Minos method of task division.

In this paper the fundamental ideas of division of tasks and module discrimination are explained, and alternative implementations discussed. First the previous influential "Pandemonium" work in this area is outlined, together with the mechanism of task division and discrimination. The need for module reliability is discussed, then improvements are proposed in the form of the Minos module, and its inclusion in an Authority system. Finally further extensions to the Authority system are briefly outlined.

PANDEMONIUM I AND II

In Selfridge's 1959 paper [15] he describes the Pandemonium system, which achieves efficiency in learning recognition problem domains through the utilization of several "demons", each of which responds in a certain way to a particular input. Thus the input to a layer of demons would be the same for each, but the weightings within the demons different, such that each demon computes different properties of the input. Thus each demon i outputs a scalar measure of the degree of "i-ness" in the input. During learning of the whole system, weights are adapted such that useful functions might be strengthened and produce larger outputs, and useless functions degraded or rejected completely. In normal operation the response of a complete Pandemonium system is that of the demon with the largest output.

In Pandemonium the demon choice criterion was related to the usefulness of the function computed by the demon in this aspect of the recognition. It is this idea that is developed in the Minos modules.

The demons of Pandemonium are really equivalent to single units in a neural net. If each demon is however replaced by a neural network one arrives at a higher-level extension of the strength in numbers policy. The idea is to reduce the learning complexity of a network working on a particular task, through sharing naturally separable members of a training set among several networks, and choosing the output of the current expert in the normal (non-learning) operation of the system.

An initial attempt at such an extension of Pandemonium was undertaken in [16] with the Pandemonium II system (see also [9]). Made available to the system was a number of feed-forward neural networks of identical structure, but different initializations. Desired was to see the system use these networks to *divide* a problem up, resulting in each network being faced with an easier mapping task. There were certain important things to consider first. Namely, *how* is the problem to be split up, *what* is going to supervise this procedure and also *what* will decide who will answer the question in normal processing mode.

In Pandemonium II it was done in the following way. An input pattern to be learnt was presented to all the nets taking part and processed. The (feed-forward) net with its output nearest to the target output associated with the input pattern, as judged by the *Taskmaster* (loosely equivalent to Selfridge's "Decision Demon"), was allocated the learning of this pattern. Learning the pattern meant performing n back-propagation [13] steps. Thus the task domain was divided up in such a way that patterns were allocated to be learnt by those nets that were most suited to this aspect of the (possibly complicated) mapping problem, at this time. The problem domain was viewed as a pool of pattern-target pairs, and these pairs converged on the system with certain probabilities. Thus the patterns would be learnt to an extent depending on their frequency of occurrence in the world of the system.

The choice of network for learning the pattern was based on a sum of squared difference measure E_α for each net α:

$$E_\alpha = \sum_i (t_i - o_{i\alpha})^2. \tag{1}$$

$o_{i\alpha}$ represents the output i of net α, and the target for the pattern in question is t_i at output i. The summation is over all the output units of the network. The choice of network for normal processing was based on a "who shouts loudest must be most confident" principle (see below).

Patterns are present in the environment and the Taskmaster effectively controls the learning of such patterns, working on a frequency of appearance principle, and allocating to the nets such that specialization develops.

In the implementation of Pandemonium II on a simple (but divisible) problem domain the two fundamental requirements of such a system become clear. They are, (1) An allocation method, and (2) A discrimination method. The Taskmaster uses the allocation method to determine by which net a particular pattern at a certain time should be learnt, and the discrimination method to determine which net should be believed in normal processing. The methods used were

1. for allocation: choose the net that produces the lowest error for this pattern. The error measure is the same as that used in the gradient descent (back-propagation) procedure (i.e. as in (1)).

2. for discrimination: In the task examined in Pandemonium II the targets consisted of only ever one output unit required to be high, and all the others at zero. Thus the correct net was deemed to be that with the highest output unit activation (which was then used to construct a binary pattern). Hence the "he who shouts loudest" term used above.

The technique was successful for this instance of Pandemonium II, but would not always be expected to be successful. It is not necessarily the case that the highest node activation for a given input pattern, among all the output nodes and nets, is the one corresponding to the target node. It may well be found that a net responds positively to an input pattern that has not been learnt, because it may share a few input node similarities with a well-learnt pattern. In such a case the output could be taken to be a *generalization* of the pattern, but there is no way of knowing whether this is happening. Indeed, such generalized patterns could produce grossly erroneous results, which would seriously undermine the performance and reliability of the entire system. A related problem was the output representation itself. In the Pandemonium II prototype the output consisted of single node activations, and not a complete n-bit pattern. In the latter case the "who shouts loudest" policy for network selection is not applicable. Required is some kind of general loudness measure so that it may be determined which network really should be believed: but there is no reason to suppose that the *intensity* of the overall output corresponds to the correctness of the response.

UPGRADING PANDEMONIUM II

In order to upgrade the simple operation of the Pandemonium II system the two conflict phases of allocation and discrimination need to be developed. They represent the two major problems confronting designers of modular systems, that can be summed up in the questions: How can I tell whether a module will be a good expert before it is trained? and: How do I know which expert to believe when I ask a question?

Shouting vs. Confidence Discriminants

Discriminating on the basis of the form or amplitude of the output may not be the wisest method. For instance, large threshold weights could cause a particular network to respond with almost boolean outputs to patterns. What is needed is not so much a measure of how the outputs look to the taskmaster, but how the *inputs* look to the networks. Thus if a network likes the look of a question, and can express this in some measurable way regardless of its actual answer, then we may more or less confidently believe its answer. So how might the Pandemonium II networks be upgraded to possess a "confidence" output? We suggest the following five ways of incorporating such a discriminator:

1. The degree of confidence in what has been learnt by the network is a function of the *number of times* the pattern in question has been presented. So this assumes the reasonable hypothesis that the net that has been chosen most often for the learning of a particular pattern should be able to give the most accurate output.

2. The degree of confidence in a particular output pattern is a function of the *sharpness* of this output pattern. i.e. given that one is always learning to map to binary targets, a net output that looks most like a binary output is taken to be indicative of closeness to the desired output.

3. There exists a separate *supervisory network* that is trained on all the patterns and learns to partition them explicitly, getting the knowledge of this decomposition from observation of the network learning allocation. In future normal processing this network is consulted (or can gate the other networks) about the suitability of each network for advice on each pattern. This idea is very similar to the first one, but employs a network with a learning instead of a counting mechanism.

4. The network monitors its own progress by employing an adjacent companion network somehow to learn to map the *current error* of patterns. In this way we know directly how accurate an answer is (assuming the mapping is achieved by this companion network).

5. The network uses an alternative companion adaptive network that indicates the degree of *familiarity* it has with the input pattern in question. This familiarity measure is dependent on the frequency with which the pattern has been allocated to the net and also the *recency* of the pattern's appearance.

Suggestion 1 is a non-neural solution, and is unappealing in that, given that a RAM is being used for every pattern to retrieve the counter, one may just as well do away with the learning net and code the answer instead of the counter. Suggestion 2 cannot work if we wish to reap the benefits of modular division of labour, for it means that not only do we wish the individual expert nets to learn well their allocated portions of the training set, but we need to ensure that they sufficiently "unlearn" sharp answers to questions not allocated. Enforcing such unlearning at this level will degrade the expertness of the modules and the effective higher complexity of the problem will degrade the scaling prospects of the networks. Suggestion 3 is a reasonably good solution to this problem, that was employed in [10] using a Kohonen net [4] to separate pattern clusters for learning among a set of modules, and the gating idea has also been employed in [3]. Such gating is viewed here as placing too great a restriction on the system as a whole. What is desired is a system consisting of a set of modules *independent* at the module level, whose learning can be affected only indirectly through target allocation, and that one may obtain reliable behaviour also when the learning task globally alters. Suggestion 4 allows such independence, and seems ideal in that it provides us with an obvious and believable confidence measure. However, when one considers learning of dynamically changing target patterns, one may also expect that the companion network might be more complex and error-prone than the other one. Thus one alleviates the strain of complex mapping learning only to be burdened by a set of complex companion network mappings.

The idea in suggestion 5 seems most appealing. It promises a variation of the monitoring of the net through degradation brought about by the reduction of a pattern's presentation frequency, and thus might be more suitable when the system is faced with a changing environment. Independence is retained by the nets. Such familiarity nets (later called "monitors"), and their integration into an Authority, will be described in the context of a Minos module.

Allocation Discriminants

In Pandemonium II there arose a problem with the allocation technique: i.e., which network should actually be chosen to do the learning. The interpretation of a fit between output and target using (1) results in a net that has been doing a little more learning than others to be automatically more suitable for learning the next pattern. To give an example, say all the networks start off with their uncommitted outputs at around 0.5. If the target values of the output are mostly going to be set to zero, then the first net that has (by chance) to learn a pattern will have an unfair advantage for all the other patterns, because most of the output nodes will be biased to the lesser side of 0.5. The next pattern to come along will then probably be best mapped by the same net.

So this kind of allocation will not lead to the automatic development of task-dependent experts. Instead the network that is by chance chosen first to do some learning will be chosen to learn the whole task domain. A rapid convergence with the vast majority of patterns being learnt by this network will certainly occur for problem domains consisting of mainly sparse target vectors (the most likely case). The problem is solved in an Authority in the following way. The absolute values of the output components from the network are not important, but their *relative values* are. An expert will be chosen on the basis of the promising state of the relative components of its output. One may look at it another way: the output vector from the module is a discretized wave; a promising undertrained output wave has a similar *form* to the desired (answer) wave.

Mathematically, the following is performed. The output vector $\vec{v}$ from a module is renormalized to $\vec{v}'$ such that its maximum component has the same value as the maximum component of the target vector $\vec{t}$, and its minimum component has the same value as the minimum component of $\vec{t}$. The module that possesses an output with the least value of $L1(\vec{t}, \vec{v}')$ (the L1 norm) is considered to be the best candidate for the expert for this pattern.

MINOS MODULES AND RELIABLE AUTHORITIES

So much for the techniques for upgrading Pandemonium II. It is appropriate at this point to discuss the objectives we have in mind, and the problems that may be attacked when such a Pandemonium II, or *Authority*, is available.

Reliability

Neural networks are notoriously unreliable. Indeed they derive their very advantages over symbol-pushing processing and RAMs from their inherent "fuzziness". That is, **generalization** on a topic of learning is a probabilistic process manifested in the neural network expressing some "leaning" towards a particular answer in preference to other possibilities. By the same token, the generalizations can be (probabilistically) very wrong—perhaps more often wrong than right. What is more, there is no way of determining whether the answer offered by the neural network to an enquiry should be strongly believed (because such an association formed part of the network's training schedule) or taken as a possible generalization (if not). Before we can hope to include sets of neural network "expert modules" in a general purpose learning system we must have some way of gleaning such critical information from these building blocks.

Thus the message is: all neural networks are in some respect unreliable, and 100% performance will like as not never be achieved from a flexible undedicated neural network module; the key is to *recognize* where the unreliability lies, gauge it and base consequent higher-level decision making on the degree of "fuzziness", or *error*, of the answer. After all, almost all decisions made by man are more or less approximate and have associated an understanding of their error, from mundane acts like walking or masticating food, to playing racket games or snooker, to the precision of scientific measurement. Once the disadvantages of the model have been recognized, or its

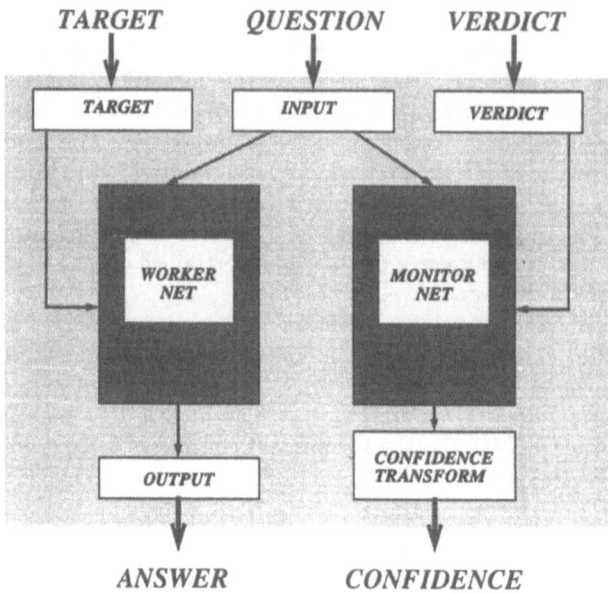

Fig. 1: The components of a Minos module.

failings, we can more confidently benefit from its advantages. This bodes too as a quicker alternative to constantly refining the performance of particular models by the odd percent.

A step in this direction is manifested in our Authority system. An Authority combines the sought-after property of a measure of confidence in the answer it provides—and through which its performance and consequently usefulness may be compared with other such Authorities—with the enticing prospect of reducing problem complexities through the Pandemonium divide-and-conquer principle.

The Minos Module

The key component of the Authority is the Minos module. It is called a module because it may be considered as a kind of black box with identifiable leads emerging from it, capable of performing a certain type of processing. Its initial design is depicted in Fig. 1. There are two networks, a *worker* and a *monitor*. The worker performs the processing and determines the capabilities of the module, while the monitor performs the job of informing one of the degree of confidence the module has in the validity of its answer, with respect to a certain input pattern. Our choice for the form of the monitor is discussed in a following section.

The inputs to a Minos are the input pattern ("question"), its actual "target" mapping (if this is necessary) and a "verdict" from the Authority (see next section); outputs include the suggested association ("answer") and its confidence.

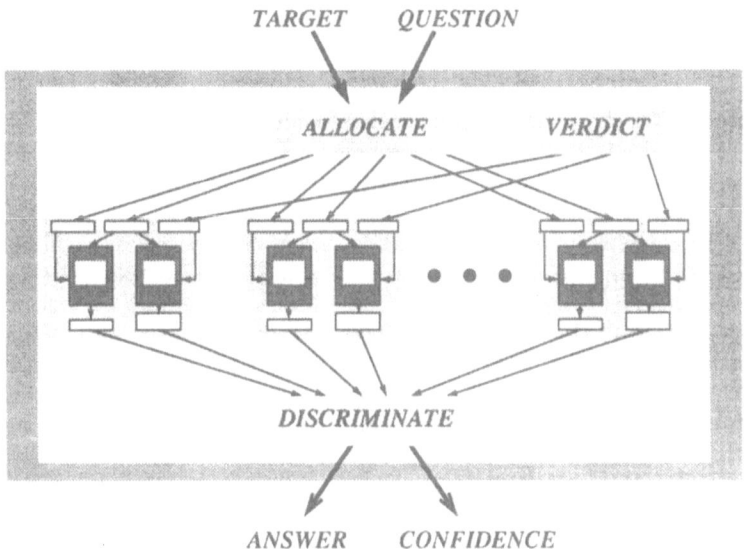

Fig. 2: The structure of an authority

Operation of an Authority

An Authority controls a number of Minoses, as depicted in Fig. 2. An Authority is also a module, and has similar leads coming in and going out.

When it receives a pattern to *learn* it allows all the Minoses to process the input, assesses their outputs (i.e. the worker net outputs, although see "Future Developments" for a refinement of this idea) based on the allocation discriminant discussed above, and *assigns* the pattern to be learnt by the Minos most successful or promising in such mappings. Of the possible learning schedules the simplest and conceptually most comfortable is for the chosen Minos now to learn this mapping (having received the target from the Authority). In our implementation we allow the Minos to learn the mapping up to *at least* a certain standard, but *no more than* a decided acceptance criterion (to prevent premature collapse of the mapping function). The monitor networks of all the Minoses simultaneously learn their mappings (see later), also to a certain standard. The Minoses receive the information of who is to learn the pattern through the "verdict" connection. If this is positive the Minos should accept a target and allow its worker and monitor to learn, if not the worker is idle and only the monitor learns.

In normal processing mode (i.e. a question/answer session) the Authority will receive the question part of the pattern and it has to output a suggested answer. It must now determine which of the expert Minoses to believe. This is simply done through choosing the Minos that has the highest confidence output. The answer and confidence are passed on to higher levels by the Authority.

THE MONITOR NETWORK

The most important property of a Minos is clearly its self-monitoring capability, without which discrimination is not possible, and upon which the assessment relies. We have chosen the simplest form for the monitor net: a YES/NO classifier network. The reasons for its choice are the following. Required is a net that can be easily taught to recognize questions that have been seen before and likewise not to recognize questions either not seen before or ones that were previously seen but have since been allocated to a better Minos. Such learning is (as our earlier experiments made clear to us) far too complex for an encoder net for example (besides, the scaling is not promising). The simplest net is going to have just the one output node, and the target for this node is easily determined by the Minos (remember we want a target that is independent of the worker target). We also insisted on a back-propagation net. The reason is merely that our experiments involved the worker net using back-propagation, and so we desired similar decay and learning speed characteristics so that the two nets might more or less keep up with one another in the learning. We may use the slow (but well generalizing) back-propagation algorithm in the worker net with a degree of confidence, since it is responsible for the monitor net learning too.

One might however envisage other forms of monitor network, such as Kohonen net [4] or ART nets [2]. One might even come up with a recurrent form for use with recurrent worker networks.

The simple confidence measure used in our initial implementations is identical to the output of the monitor net.

Thus the Minos causes every pattern question it has to learn to be mapped (to a certain standard) to 1 at the monitor network. If the question is not to be learnt then the monitor network is trained to map it to 0 (to a certain standard). We note an advantage in simultaneous learning in the worker and monitor networks: the recency effects are not eradicated in progressive learning, but accepted and manifested in higher (lower) confidences from the expert (non-expert). Furthermore, both nets should be subjected to similar decay rates for the "being-forgotten" patterns.

Note too that the complexity of a two-set classification reduces as the disparity in sizes of the the two sets increases. Thus the mapping to be learnt by the monitors becomes easier the more experts there are. This is desirable since we want to keep the monitor's job as easy as possible, given that the worker's job is alleviated through the divide-and-conquer policy anyway.

FUTURE DEVELOPMENTS

This paper is intended as a brief description of the important ideas in the construction of the Authority Minos system, and space limitations prevent detailed assessment of initial simulations. Preliminary results showed that a three Minos Authority did well in expert division for random mappings, shift experiments and handwritten digit recognition (although this latter application requires more analysis). Results will appear in a later publication. We now mention a few interesting modifications that may improve the Authority reliability further.

Inclusion of mild "unlearning" for the idle workers has been tested and seems promising (and no extra cost in parallel implementations). It involves pulling bits of the current output for the non-allocated pattern further away from the target.

Other improvement possibilities include the addition of a "rubbish" Minos module consisting of solely a monitor net to recognize the patterns that are really not very promisingly mapped by the experts. The experts would ignore this pattern because to learn it would mean probable serious disruption of the successfully learnt set of patterns by the Authority. In such an eventuality higher-level decision making processes should shift the learning to an alternative Authority system. The Authority discovers the unsuitability of this pattern through observing the monitor net output during the allocation phase. If no Minos module is terribly promising in terms of both the allocation discriminant and confidence the pattern could represent a new "concept" or task, and the Authority should be able to avoid learning the pattern and/or tell higher levels of the system.

A related development is control of the "expert decision regions". If one imagines the input space as being separated into a number of expert (Minos) regions through the monitor mappings, then one might want to prevent overlaps between monitor nets, since this will cause ambiguity in discrimination. Such occurrences are identified when there are two or more comparable top values of confidence. In order to communicate this the Authority may output an "ambiguity" measure. This is no problem. However, if the decision boundaries are too sharp the ambiguity may never be noticed. One may deal with this by constructing a "no-man's land" of ambiguity, and forbidding strong learning of mappings falling in it. These patterns may also be assigned to the rubbish net, or rejected outright by the Authority.

CONCLUSION

In this paper we have outlined the components of a neural net module that is intended to provide an environment for the multiple use of a system of networks. We have developed the idea of self-supervised Taskmaster learning from Pandemonium II, and the divide-and-conquer policy of Pandemonium I, into a more specific realization, and intend it to be used as a general mechanism for modular network system construction.

The first steps were concerned with solution of the problem of discrimination among a set of expert modules so that a Pandemonium structure might be used. In solving this another major development of allowing a confidence measure to be propagated through a hierarchical system has been achieved. Thus with these two ideas progress has been made in the direction of robust neural network components and also in the direction of problem complexity reduction, and therefore more promising scaling possibilities through divide-and-conquer among relatively independent modules.

Future steps involve sophistication of the systems and development through allowing more information to be read from the networks and shaping learning schedules and allocation among Authorities according to their current capabilities. All this should allow more intelligent use of neural network based systems such that their real advantages may overshadow their inevitable drawbacks.

REFERENCES

[1] J. Denker, D. Schwartz, B. Wittner, S. Solla, R. Howard, L. Jackel, and J. Hopfield. Large automatic learning, rule extraction and generalization. *Complex Systems*, 1(5), 1987.

[2] S. Grossberg. Adaptive pattern classification and universal recoding II: Feedback, expectation, olfaction and illusions. *Biological Cybernetics*, 23:187–202, 1976.

[3] R. A. Jacobs, M. I. Jordan, and A. G. Barto. Task decomposition through competition in a modular connectionist architecture: The what and where vision tasks. Technical Report COINS TR 90-27, Dept. of Computer & Information Science, University of Massachusetts, Amherst, MA, March 1990.

[4] T Kohonen. *Self-Organization and Associative Memory, 2nd. edition*. Springer-Verlag, Berlin, 1988.

[5] Y. le Cun. Medical diagnosis using neural networks. In *Proceedings of Cognitiva*, Paris, 1985.

[6] M. Minsky. *The Society of Mind*. Simon and Schuster, New York, 1985.

[7] M. Minsky and S. Papert. *Perceptrons*. MIT Press, 1988. see particularly the Epilogue.

[8] H. Mühlenbein. Limitations of multilayer perceptrons – steps towards genetic neural networks. *Parallel Computing*, 14(3):249–260, 1990.

[9] H. Mühlenbein and J. Kindermann. The dynamics of evolution and learning – towards genetic neural networks. In R. Pfeifer, Z. Schreter, F. Fogelman, and L. Steels, editors, *Connectionism in Perspective*, Amsterdam, 1989. Elsevier. Proceedings of the International Conference Connectionism in Perspective, University of Zürich, 10–13 October 1988.

[10] Y. Nishikawa, H. Kita, and A. Kawamura. NN/I: a neural network which divides and learns environments. In *Proceedings of the 2nd IJCNN*, Washington D.C., 1990.

[11] B.A. Pearlmutter. Learning state space trajectories in recurrent neural networks. *Neural Computation*, 1(2):263–269, 1989.

[12] N. Qian and T. J. Sejnowski. Predicting the secondary structure of globular proteins using neural network models. *Journal of Molecular Biology*, 202:865–884, 1988.

[13] D. E. Rumelhart, G. E. Hinton, and R. J. Williams. Learning internal representations by error propagation. *Nature*, 323(533), 1986.

[14] T. J. Sejnowski and C. R. Rosenberg. NETtalk: A parallel network that learns to read aloud. *Complex Systems*, 1(1), 1987.

[15] O.G. Selfridge. Pandemonium: a paradigm for learning. In *The Mechanisation of Thought Processes: Proceedings of a Symposium Held at the National Physical Laboratory, November 1958*, pages 511–527, London: HMSO, 1959.

[16] F.J. Śmieja. Evolution of intelligent systems in a changing environment: I. First steps with a structured brain. Technical report, Gesellschaft für Mathematik und Datenverarbeitung, August 1988.

[17] F.J. Śmieja. The significance of underlying correlations in the training of a layered net. In *Abstracts of the First Annual Meeting of the INNS, supplement to Neural Networks, Vol 1*, Boston, Mass., September 1988. Available as Edinburgh University preprint 88/447.

[18] F.J. Śmieja and H. Mühlenbein. The geometry of multilayer perceptron solutions. *Parallel Computing*, 14:261–275, 1990.

[19] G. Tesauro and B. Janssens. Scaling relationships in backpropagation learning. *Complex Systems*, 2:39–44, 1988.

[20] G. Tesauro and T. Sejnowski. A parallel network that learns to play backgammon. *Artificial Intelligence*, 1988. in press.

COMMITMENTS AND PROJECTS

Alan H. Bond
Department of Computer Science
4173C Engineering 1, University of California
Los Angeles, California 90024
email: bond@cs.ucla.edu

Abstract

A computational model is developed, which captures properties of relationship and organization in sets of distributed intelligent agents. The model is inspired by sociological theory, and uses centrally a concept of commitment. A formulation of the concept of commitment is proposed. The concept is propagated into notions of agent and organization. A formulation and computational model of the basic notion of commitment is given, which represents commitments as mutually agreed constraints on action, belief and world state.

A special type of organization is introduced which consists of a set of *projects*. Each project is decomposed into a set of specialized activities or problems carried out by a set of specialized agents. Projects are *elaborated*, by searching a space of subproblems. Agents share a common world, but have different views of it. They propose individual actions in their own views, and these are negotiated among the set of agents and jointly committed to. Each commitment is a constraint on the shared world being planned.

INTRODUCTION

In its present stage of development, Distributed Artificial Intelligence (Bond and Gasser, 88) is seeking new concepts which will allow DAI problems to be better expressed and better solved. To this end, we have examined the concepts of symbolic interactionism, notably the work of Strauss (Strauss et.al., 85) and Gerson (Gerson, 76), with a view to finding inspiration and insights into the description of organizations of cooperating agents. We are developing a computational system derived from the key sociological notions of *commitment, negotiation* and *organization* (Bond, 90a). Goals of our research include the development of concepts, a formal model, and an implementation of a computer system which would allow organizations of intelligent agents to be programmed. We have also studied cooperation in engineering design in manufacturing organizations (Bond, 89) (Bond and Ricci, 90).

THE CONCEPT OF COMMITMENT

The word 'commitment' originates from the Latin committere - to bring, join or combine two or more objects into one whole, to connect or unite. This to the author suggests the underlying meaning of a constraint or binding, which further is united and integrated into the world producing a change of world view.

Commitments as actions and beliefs. The constraints involved can be of various types, notably to follow a certain course of action, or to hold certain beliefs. A commitment concerns either acting in a certain way, conditional upon circumstances, or it can be a commitment to hold a certain belief. *Prospective* commitments concern the future, *retrospective* commitments concern the past. A retrospective commitment is a set of beliefs about past events. Commitments of course may be *conditional* on the state of the world, including the time. A commitment concerning another agent's action or belief will be called an *expectation*. An agent may have the expectation of some *unspecified* agent providing resources.

Commitments are social. However, a commitment is more than a constraint, it involves a trust, intention or belief. It is thus a relationship with other agents that the constraint be held to. It is also one thing to make a commitment, in the gloom of one's study, and another to make other agents aware of it. As in the denouement of Dr. Strangelove, the whole point of creating the Doomsday machine was to tell everyone about it!

Commitments as (social) goals. Further, a commitment to future action is really to a goal. Thus it is to attempt and solve the goal by performing articulation work, i.e., problem solving activity. This activity presumably is not completely unrestrained but within agreed social limits.

Commitments involve resources. Commitments for Gerson (Gerson, 76) always involve resources, they are constraints on resources. However, for him, resources involve not only basic resources and time but knowledge, sentiment and almost anything else that the agent needs. Hence, any action commits resources. A current action commits and may consume resources. A future committed action commits to the use of resources at a future time.

Commitments involve agent integrity. It seems to the author that an essential point is that agents can and do trust each other. A commitment is not just a prediction that a certain constraint, action or belief, will be adhered to, but it is an undertaking of modification of world view and of doing whatever it reasonably takes, to adhere to it. Agents must therefore satisfy some general integrity and sociability properties.

Commitment and natural language pragmatics. A discussion is given by Winograd and Flores (Winograd and Flores, 87); speech acts may be illocutionary acts which have five possible *illocutionary points*:
(i) assertives - commit the speaker to something's being the case
(ii) directives - attempt to get the hearer to do something
(iii) commissives - commit the speaker to some future course of action
(iv) expressives - express a psychological state of affairs, e.g., apologizing
(v) declarations - establish correspondence between a proposition and reality, e.g., pronouncing a couple married.

A DAI NOTION OF COMMITMENT

We now present a formal DAI notion of commitment, which we hope captures most of the sociological concept of commitment. We shall ramify the concept into a view of DAI agents and organizations of agents.

Social agents. The main idea is to program agents in terms of their commitments to each other. Thus in the description of an agent, we have (i) actions it will perform and resources needed, (ii) beliefs it will hold, (iii) expectations of actions of others and resources supplied by them, (iv) the supply of resources to others by their holding expectations. An agent has explicit representations of the resources it is generating and their benefit to others, and the resources it needs and their supply and support by others. We can formally represent a commitment as a logical formula, which can be a goal, belief or action. Associated with a formal commitment will be the specified resources for the commitment.

The Main Points

1. *Actions* can be on data or the state, or can be communication acts.

2. *Beliefs* can be about the world, about the self or about other agents.

3. *Resources* can be *basic resources*, such as storage, processor time, communication bandwidth, etc., or *knowledge*, or *results* or *commitments*.

4. A *commitment* can be an action, a belief or a goal. Each must have a specification of associated resources. Any may be conditional on the state.

5. Each action involves all the resources that it needs. Any action commits resources. A use of a resource may also consume that resource.

6. The basic activity is the *execution* of commitments. If all resources are met, then a commitment can and probably should be executed.

7. To execute an action is to perform the action, to execute a belief is to assert it, i.e., believe it, to execute a goal is to attempt it. Notably a belief can concern another agent's action.

8. A current action commits and consumes resources. A future committed action commits to the use of resources at a future time.

9. One type of action, and therefore type of commitment, is to *make* a commitment. This is usually a future commitment, but it can be the establishment of a retrospective belief.

10. One type of belief, and therefore commitment, is that a specified agent has made a specified commitment; this is an *expectation*.

11. We can thus define a concept of *agent* as
    (a) a locus of control
    (b) which makes and executes commitments.

12. The AI notion of *plan* can be generalized to be a set of related commitments which is treated as a unit of behavior. Thus a plan can be evoked, in which case the entire set of commitments which constitutes the plan comes into effect. When the plan terminates, these commitments are removed.

13. An agent has *knowledge* of methods (or theorems) which match to situations, including those involving goals, and which evoke plans. We can imagine a simple control structure similar to Planner or Prolog, but this could be changed.

14. An agent should probably communicate its commitments truthfully to affected agents, or at least respond truthfully to requests for information concerning its commitments.

15. An agent receives not only data, results, knowledge and other resources from other agents, but also commitments.

16. An agent has *integrity constraints* on its commitments; they must be consistent with each other.

17. An *organization* will be defined as a set of agents with mutual commitments.

18. In addition, there may be *global commitments*, which apply to the entire set of agents in the organization.

19. The set of commitments, held by the agents in the organization, should be integrated and consistent.

Formulating the Notion of Commitment

We shall represent commitments in the main by constraints. We believe that a wide and interesting range of systems can be described using constraints on states, actions and beliefs. This could be extended to constraints on events and constraints on commitments themselves. First, we need to define a ground or *uncommitted agent*, which has as yet made no commitments. For this, we shall take a socially uncommitted agent to also lack plans, and to behave opportunistically. Thus, a socially uncommitted agent will have: (i) a script - a set of conditional actions, (ii) a set of beliefs, and (iii) behavior which follows an opportunistic regime.

Our well-defined deterministic interpretations are straightforward. They are as follows:
1. **Commitment to act.** Add a new (conditional) action to script.
2. **Commitment to believe.** Add a new belief.
3. **Constraint on action.** (i) Before every action, test if forbidden, (ii) and in every plan, test if forbidden, (iii) and in every action which constructs a planned action, check that forbidden action is not planned.
4. **Constraint on state.** (i) Before changing state, test if forbidden (ii) and in every plan, test if states are forbidden (iii) and in every action which constructs a planned action, check that forbidden state is not planned.

Commitment is a social relationship with other agents Here we introduce some strong constraints on commitments. The computational model would ensure that they are adhered to. They are part of the semantics of the representation system we are developing.
1. Commitment is maintained by negotiation with another agent, or set of agents,

and it is labeled with this agent set.

2. Agents have knowledge of all commitments made that involve them, including knowledge of which other agents are involved.

3. Any attempt to change a commitment must be negotiated with the agents involved. A commitment cannot be changed unilaterally.

Modeling the basic constraint notion. To deal with constraints, we need at least to *enforce* them. We shall ensure that all relevant constraints for an agent are known to the agent, and, in addition, the system will enforce constraints in its interpreter. Merely enforcing constraints is not very satisfactory, and what is needed in addition are constraint *solvers*. Given constraints on action, world state and belief, the system should provide solvers which find sets of solutions for which actions, which world states and which beliefs the agent may have. Since constraints are on states, beliefs and actions, we can implement enforcement and solution using a *metainterpreter*.

Modeling the social relationship.

1. The form of a commitment includes information on the agents involved.
commitment(commitment type, actual commitment formula,{agent set})
where commitment type is action, state or belief.

2. The action of committing to a commitment is performed by the system. commit(commitment) commits the agent. Making the commit action passes this information to other agents in the agent set, and makes them aware of this commitment.

3. the action of removing a commitment. uncommit(commitment) must be received by all agents in the agent set of the commitment, and agreed by them.

PROJECTS

In describing cooperation among experts with different specialized knowledge and responsibility, we are developing a model of a special class of organization, which we briefly describe here. It has arisen in part from our study of the design of aircraft (Bond and Ricci, 90), and partly from our work on cost management (Shirley and Bond, 89). For a more conventional approach, see, e.g., (Damon and Schramm, 72). For sociological analysis of projects see (Strauss, 88).

In our study of organized design of aircraft, which was joint with Richard Ricci of Lockheed, we found that a set of about ten specialist departments designed in parallel. This activity was coordinated and given a real-time basis, by the use of *commitment steps*. Each step is specified by a set of types of constraints, including accuracies of estimates, and, during a step, agents negotiate the optimal set of joint commitments that will be made at the end of the step, within the constraints already agreed at previous steps. For related work on commitment-based approaches to project management, see (Koo, 87) (Marca, Schwartz and Cassaday, 87).

An organization will be a set of projects. Each project is decomposed into a set of specialized activities or problems carried out by a set of specialized agents. Projects are *elaborated*, by searching a space of subproblems. This is done by humans and/or by expert system rules which operate on a problem and generate new problems. Problems are also evaluated by humans and/or by rules. Agents share a common world, but have different views of it. They propose individual actions in their own views, and these are negotiated among the set of agents and jointly committed to. Each commitment is a constraint on the shared world being planned.

We shall consider a model of an organization which identifies, designs and produces products. The organization finds a business plan which includes a description of a product type, together with a market volume and target cost. It designs the product in detail and produces it to the cost and volume required. The product design has a process plan. In order to produce the product, a production plan is required, which will require the design of processes to make the product. After the design phase, there is an implementation phase in which the process and production organization are set up. Then in the production phase, units of the product are made. These four activities, designing business, product, and processes, and designing and implementing production plans, are carried out in parallel with strong interactions among them to achieve an optimal result.

In order to achieve a good optimal result and to represent real world organizations, our model
(i) represents these activities as proceeding in parallel
(ii) represents their interactions
(iii) stores the history of the project elaboration process which can be used at any time.

Here production is treated as a further elaboration of the project in which the project graph is continuously expanded as each unit is produced. The entire organization is a set of interacting projects in different phases and states of elaboration.

Activity in the General Collaboration Model

Unfortunately, space does not permit a fuller discussion or an example, which appear elsewhere (Bond, 90b). A brief outline of how the project model works is as follows:

1. Project elaboration consists of:

   - Search and plan construction
   - Implementation, for example installation of manufacturing processes, as further plan elaboration
   - Production, i.e. the manufacturing of each unit, as further continuous plan elaboration steps.

2. Problem solving occurs in the elaboration of the project.

   - The problem is detected by a failure of a goal or expectation
   - To solve the problem involves further elaboration of the goal tree
   - This may in turn evoke changes in other goal trees of collaborating agents
   - Eventually a solution may be found by activity of several collaborating agents.

3. Optimization includes:

- New product design
- New process design
- New production plan

The project elaboration tree may be continually searched and developed, perhaps initially by one agent but then collaboratively by several agents to find an improved solution. A special case is the introduction of new product type, i.e., creating a new project.

The activity of the agent is to: (i) realize the plan, i.e., elaborate it to the point of clarity or direct executability, (ii) minimize the expected total resources used and to be used. The shared total cost value being minimized is an estimate of the total project cost, and combines contributions from all agents. It is the sum of actual resources used so far and the expected use of resources up to project completion. Since there are no individual budgets, we are for the moment modeling benign cooperation of agents, by their optimizing a common total cost.

Shared Plans, Individual Goals, Commitment Steps and Negotiation

Agents mainly interact by constructing a shared world, which contains their agreed shared plan for the entire project, together with total cost estimates.

Agents search in their own individual search spaces based upon their own individual views, goals and plans. They are guided by the shared plan and cost estimates committed so far. They seek to elaborate and realize the project while minimizing its total cost. At each step, they search for the next set of commitments. A commitment made by one agent in one view will have distributed consequences for other agents in their views. We model this effect by maintaining a *rationale* for each agent which contains its search tree so far, together with its optimal solution, and reasons for choices among alternatives. Upon a commitment or proposed commitment by another agent, the individual rationales can be recomputed. We do not discuss here individual or joint search strategies, but for example, the set of commitments minimizing the total expected shared plan cost could be chosen at each commitment step.

The shared plans held by agents in our system are not the same as, but presumably have something in common with, Durfee and Lesser's Partial Global Plans (Durfee and Lesser, 89). Our shared plan is as follows:
1. Each agent has its own plan of what the entire set of agents is trying to do, and commitments made so far.
2. This is its view of the shared plan of the set of agents.
3. The plan has (at least) two dimensions, i.e., variables which characterize constituent elements: (a) level of abstraction (b) time
4. The plan consists of logical formulae constraining action and state.
5. Each commitment has an associated set of resources and real-time estimates.
6. The shared plan contains commitments which may be carried out (i.e., executed) by different agents. In the simple case, the n agents doing the planning make commitments for themselves and then carry them out.

Commitments extend the AI concept of plan since:

1. they involve beliefs about state and beliefs about belief, and not just action (and not just pre- and post-conditions on action)
2. they involve resources - their determination, allocation, planning of use and actual use
3. they combine planning and execution resources
4. they model the relationships among agents and the interrelationships of beliefs that they hold
5. they connect belief with control and behavior.

The set of commitments provides a detailed set of constraints which directs each agent's behavior:
(a) to consider relevant possibilities that are consistent with the constraints
(b) to make more accurate estimates of project costs
(c) to make more accurate assessment of the value of a design plan.

Conflict and Negotiation

The important and difficult issue of negotiation merits separate discussion (Sycara, 87). Negotiation is part of realization and optimization for each agent: (i) each agent needs joint commitments, and (ii) each agent needs information. We have limited conflict in our model by the definition of the agents as benign and altruistic, by all costs being shared, and by remaining conflicts being recast as friendly disagreement on estimated total costs, i.e., on the interpretation of the shared plan. We have described a simple approach elsewhere (Bond, 89) in which all possible conjunctions of suggested commitments are evaluated by all agents. Questions of information can be dealt with by inquiry and explanation among agents.

CONCLUSION

We have outlined how concurrent planning and design among among a distributed set of intelligent agents in an organization might be modeled and supported. The use of this class of models is as a theoretical basis for understanding, and designing support systems for, organizational activity. This model has, for the author, clarified the concept of commitment and its relation to shared problem solving, and he hopes that it may even provide feedback to research in sociological theory.

Commitment is seen as
(i) *joint*, in the context of concurrent design and production activities, and in the sense of simultaneous joint action.
(ii) *affecting*, in that commitments now form the context of planning and optimization activity of agents. Indeed, the set of commitments forms a shared plan.
(iii) *multiperspective*, the joint commitments are only understood, i.e., lead to inferences, by each agent in its own perspective.
(iv) *organizing*, commitments allow the efficient use of resources in cooperative activity.
(v) having *force*, from
      (a) the *influence* on others and the commitment of resources by others, and
      (b) *binding force* from the difficulty and expense of undoing a commitment.
(vi) having a *quantitative* measure, which can be read off the model, from the resources

required to change the commitment.

Acknowledgements

This research was supported by by the Institute for Manufacturing and Automation Research, and by the Caltech Concurrent Computation Program, directed by Professor Geoffrey Fox, to whom the author is very grateful.

REFERENCES

(Bond and Gasser, 88) Alan H. Bond and Les Gasser. *Readings in Distributed Artificial Intelligence*. Morgan Kaufmann Publishers, San Mateo, CA, 1988.

(Bond, 89) Alan H. Bond. The Cooperation of Experts in Engineering Design. In L. Gasser and M.N. Huhns, editors, *Distributed Artificial Intelligence, Volume II*, pages 462–486. Pitman/Morgan Kaufmann, London, 1989.

(Bond, 90a) Alan H. Bond. Commitment: A Computational Model for Organizations of Cooperating Intelligent Agents. In *Proceedings of the 1990 Conference on Office Information Systems, Cambridge, MA*, pages 21–30, 1990.

(Bond, 90b) Alan H. Bond. Projects: a normative model of collaboration in organizations. In *10th International Distributed Artificial Intelligence Workshop, San Antonio, Texas, October 23-27*, 1990.

(Bond and Ricci, 90) Alan H. Bond and Richard Ricci. Cooperation in aircraft design, 1990. to be published in *Research in Engineering Design*.

(Damon and Schramm, 72) Edmund H. Durfee and Victor R. Lesser. Negotiating Task Decomposition and Allocation Using Partial Global Planning. In L. Gasser and M.N. Huhns, editors, *Distributed Artificial Intelligence, Volume II*, pages 229–244. Pitman/Morgan Kaufmann, London, 1989.

(Durfee and Lesser, 89) William W. Damon and Richard Schramm. A simultaneous decision model for production. *Management Science*, 19:161–172, 1972.

(Gerson, 76) Elihu M. Gerson. On 'quality of life'. *American Sociological Review*, 41:793–806, 1976.

(Koo, 87) Charles C. Koo. *A Distributed Model for Performance Systems: Synchronizing Plans among Intelligent Agents Via Communication*. PhD thesis, Stanford University, Stanford, CA, November 1987.

(Marca, Schwartz and Cassaday, 87) David A. Marca, Steven H. Schwartz, and George Cassaday. A specification method for coordinated work. In *Proceedings of the Fourth International Workshop on Software Specification and Design*, pages 242–248, 1987.

(Shirley and Bond, 89) Gordon V. Shirley and Alan H. Bond. A Knowledge-based Cost Management System, 1989. Proposal to the Institute for Manufacturing and Automation Research.

(Strauss et.al., 85) Anselm L. Strauss, Shizuko Fagerhaugh, Barbara Suczek, and

Carolyn Wiener. *The Social Organization of Medical Work.* University of Chicago Press, Chicago, IL, 1985.

(Strauss, 88) Anselm Strauss. The articulation of project work: an organizational process. *The Sociological Quarterly*, 29:163–178, 1988.

(Sycara, 87) Ekaterini P. Sycara. *Resolving Adversarial Conflicts: An Approach Integrating Case-Based and Analytical Methods.* PhD thesis, School of Information and Computer Science, Georgia Institute of Technology, 1987.

(Winograd and Flores, 87) Terry Winograd and Ivan Flores. *Understanding Computers and Cognition.* Addison Wesley, Reading, Massachusetts, 1987.

RR — An Intelligent Resource-Bounded Reasoner

Nuno J. Mamede
njm@inesc.pt

João P. Martins
ist_1416@ptifm.bitnet

Instituto Superior Técnico
Technical University of Lisbon
Av. Rovisco Pais
1000 Lisboa, Portugal

ABSTRACT

Most of the programs developed by AI researchers, suffer from two problems: (1) they do not take into account the fact of reasoning resources are limited; (2) and they remain silent (no answer is produced) whenever a definite answer cannot be produced.

The system described in this paper combines the use of resources with the capability of producing conditional answers. A conditional answer explicitly reveals the impediments that are responsible for the lack of a definite answer.

We present RR, an intelligent resource-bounded reasoner, whose resource manipulation is flexible enough to accommodate several resource representations and resource spending strategies. Since no commitments about the way resources are spent are made *a priori*, the process of consuming resources can be used to model non-omniscient, non-exhaustive reasoners.

The concepts explored by RR are being incorporated into the SNePS, the Semantic Network Processing System, and so improving (1) the way human reasoning can be modeled, and (2) its interface with the outside world.

1 INTRODUCTION

> *"One interesting property of human reasoning is that a given inference process can be tried for a limited amount of time, then abandoned or superseded by something else."*
> [Winograd 80, p. 16]

Most of the programs developed by AI researchers suffer, among others, from two problems: (1) they do not take into account the fact of reasoning resources are bounded; (2) and they remain silent (no answer is produced) whenever a definite answer cannot be produced. Before presenting our integrated solution to these problems, we analyze the consequences of these drawbacks, and reference some of the most relevant work already done to address them.

THE OMNISCIENCE PROBLEM

Most of AI deduction systems forget that computers, like humans, do not have infinite resources and thus do not know all valid formulas, and that their knowledge is closed under implication. This was named by [Hintikka 75] the local omniscience problem. An ideal reasoner, with infinite computational power, is not appropriate for modeling human reasoning, with limited capabilities. It is necessary to recognize the fact that agents, whether human or machines, are resource bounded: they are unable to arbitrarily perform large computations in limited time. Some researchers have addressed the omniscience problem; see [Fagin and Halpern 87, pp. 40–41] for a small survey on alternative attempts to deal with it.

Few AI systems have an explicit resource mechanism to bound its inferential processes. The use of resources to limit the depth of the search was first proposed by [Bobrow and Winograd 77]. [Donlon 82] associated resources with each question, controlling the maximum computational effort that could be spent in answering it. The problem of making decisions under resource constraints has been studied by [Mutchler 86] and [Horvitz 88].

A resource can be defined as something that is consumed by an inference system when it is trying to answer a question. [Donlon 82], for example, used the operation of matching a pattern with the knowledge base as a resource unit; [Bobrow and Winograd 77] have suggested the depth of search as a criterion to bound the number of inferences that can be made.

THE SILENCE PROBLEM

When a definite answer cannot be produced, most question-answering systems return nothing, but silence. This is a burden on the user, who is left with no clues: "Is a piece of information missing?", if so "What is it necessary to assume in order to get an answer?", or "Is a piece of information mistyped?".

The only exception is KRL: *"In a case in which the processing so far has not produced a definite answer, the matcher should be able to return specific details in addition to the result of 'don't know yet'. ... As the current version, only the 'hooks' for calling these mechanisms exist, and no details have been filled in."* [Bobrow and Winograd 77, p. 26].

The justifications of a failure can be used to improve the explanation capability: *"returning reasons is at the heart of the explanation paradigm"* [Swartout 83].

AN INTEGRATED SOLUTION

Our proposal consists of combining the resources approach with the capability to produce conditional answers, i.e., answers referring to the impediments that were responsible for the absence of a definite answer.

The intention of introducing resources into the inference engine of an automatic reasoner is to allow there to be a specification of "how hard" the system can work on one inference. So, there are two reasons for a conditional answer: either some knowledge is really absent from the knowledge base or the resources are insufficient. Moreover, special care is taken with knowledge assumed as absent, but which, if introduced into the knowledge base, would generate a contradiction.

To illustrate the usefulness of this approach we briefly present RR, from Reasoning with Resources. RR is an intelligent resource-bounded reasoner, whose manipulation of resources is flexible enough to accommodate several resource representations and resource spending strategies.

RR's inference engine is supported by a logic named LORE (from LOgic and REsources) [Mamede and Martins 90b]. LORE is a four-valued logic enabling the distinction between knowing that a proposition is unknown, and not knowing whether it is known (resources were not enough). LORE expanded the capability of automatically computing the dependencies among propositions, available in SWM [Martins 83, Martins and Shapiro 88]: when the derivation of a proposition fails, LORE associates the proposition with the existing and the missing hypotheses (that blocked the derivation), that are necessary to its derivation. Each derived proposition is associated with every hypothesis used in its derivation.

For example, suppose an intelligent system only was told about $B \rightarrow A$ and that $C \rightarrow A$. Suppose also that the available resources are sufficient to know that nothing is known about C, but insufficient to know that nothing is known about B. Then, when asked if A holds, most systems return *"I don't know"*. However RR, supported on LORE, gives a more intelligent answer: *"In order to 'know' A it is necessary to accept some missing preconditions: either C (know nothing is known about it), or B (don't know if it is known or not, since the available resources were not enough)"*. This conditional answer provides information about what is missing, in order to believe in A. The concepts explored by RR enable the development of intelligent systems that can improve (1) the way human reasoning can be modeled, and (2) their interface with the outside world.

2 BASIC CONCEPTS

RR is a rule based system, whose inference engine is based on LORE. RR's *inference engine* has three components: i) the *inference rules* of LORE; ii) a *control system*, a set of strategies to direct the inference process; iii) a *resource system*, a process for regulating the amount of work performed by the inference process system.

Inference systems always include the first two components: a set of inference rules and a control system. The control system is responsible for reducing the number of inferences needed to find a problem's solution, since, in most problems, the number of possible inferences is vastly larger than the number of inferences actually used in the problem's solution.

The presence of a resource system is new, and it is based on the notions that inferences consume resources and that resources are limited. The purpose of the resource system is to control the amount of reasoning (i.e., computational effort) performed by the RR's inference engine. When RR carries out reasoning, the amount of work performed is controlled by the amount of available resources.

The possibility of restricting the amount of work performed by the inference engine gives the possibility of using RR to model non-omniscient reasoners, i.e., reasoners not capable of inferring every deducible formula, but only the formulas that can be inferred within the available resources.

In the development of the RR's inference engine the following guidelines were imposed:

1. Resources are related with the inference process;
2. The resource scheme should be flexible enough to accommodate a number of resource representations and resource strategies, i.e., no commitments should be made about the form in which resources are represented or consumed;
3. the final system should always deliver an answer when answering a query.

Despite not caring about the structures used to represent resources, RR relies on LORE being logic underlying the inference engine, which is especially suitable for this application [Mamede and Martins 90a].

The next section defines the objects the inference engine deals with. We then describe the properties of LORE that are relevant to the RR system, and describe the strategies used by the control system and the resource system to enable the achievement of the RR's properties.

3   POTENTIAL STATE

RR inference engine deals with *potential states* (PS). A PS, written [KB, RS], is a pair consisting of a *knowledge base* (KB), and a *resource scheme* (RS). Informally, the first element of a PS keeps the knowledge the reasoner has access so far, and the second element includes not only the available resources for reasoning but the spending mechanism as well.

The name "potential state" was chosen to stress that the knowledge associated with a potential state is not limited to the knowledge explicitly included in the knowledge base, but also incorporates all *future* knowledge that could be inferred using the resource scheme. A potential state holds more information than the knowledge explicitly contained in the knowledge base, except if there are no resources available, or the knowledge base is already closed under derivability.

The availability of more resources means the possibility of performing work, and so giving more potential to infer new knowledge. That is to say, the more resources the system has available, the closer it is to the omniscient situation in which all logical consequences of the known hypotheses were drawn.

3.1   KNOWLEDGE BASE

Informally the knowledge base contains propositions (written as formulas) associated with a support. The support gives an indication of the dependencies between a particular proposition and other propositions in the knowledge base.

The knowledge base is a set of *conditional supported formulas*. A conditional supported formula consists of a formula associated with an *origin tag* (OT), an *origin set* (OS), a *neither set* (NS), an *unknown set* (US) and a *contradictory set* (CS). We write $\langle A, t, o, [n, u, c] \rangle$ to denote that A is a formula with origin tag t, origin set o, neither set n, unknown set u and contradictory set c. The triple $(t, o, [n, u, c])$ is called the *conditional support* of the conditional supported formula $\langle A, t, o, [n, u, c] \rangle$.

For a particular conditional supported formula, the origin tag indicates how the that conditional supported formula was placed in the knowledge base (i.e., whether it was assumed as an hypothesis, or it was generated during inference).

The origin set, neither set, unknown set and contradictory set are sets of hypotheses. For a particular conditional supported formula, the union of these four sets determines exactly which hypotheses are needed to derive the formula: the origin set contains the hypotheses that already exist in the knowledge base; the neither set contains the hypotheses that do not exist and can not be derived; the unknown set contains the formulas which were not known to exist, or if they could be derived since the available resources were insufficient (these formulas are assumed as hypotheses);

and the contradictory set contains the hypotheses that are contradictory with another formula.

For example, considering that from the hypotheses $A{\rightarrow}B$ and A we can derive B ($\langle B, t_B, o_B, [n_B, u_B, c_B]\rangle$), these hypotheses are present in the conditional support of the formula B. $A{\rightarrow}B$ and A will be in $o_B \cup n_B \cup u_B \cup c_B$, but the sets, where they actually appear, depend on the information we have. For example, if:

- $A{\rightarrow}B$ and A are both hypotheses (information introduced by the user), then $\{A{\rightarrow}B, A\} \subset o_B$;

- $A{\rightarrow}B$ is a hypothesis and A cannot be derived in the current knowledge base, even with infinite resources, then $A{\rightarrow}B \in o_B$ and $A \in n_B$;

- $A{\rightarrow}B$ is a hypothesis and if the resources available prevent to know anything about A, then $A{\rightarrow}B \in o_B$ and $A \in u_B$;

- $A{\rightarrow}B$ is a hypothesis and if $\neg A$ is present in the knowledge base, then $A{\rightarrow}B \in o_B$ and $A \in c_B$;

- etc.

A conditional supported formula with empty NS, US, and CS must be interpreted as: the formula is a hypothesis or it has been successfully derived. If at least one of these sets is not empty, then the conditional supported formula can be interpreted as the derivation of the formula was conditional: if all the hypotheses of NS, US and CS were present then the formula would have been derived successfully and the hypotheses used to derive it would be given by the union of OS, NS, US and CS. If the CS is not empty then a contradiction may be derived.

3.2   RESOURCE SCHEME

The resource scheme, the second element of a potential state ($[\![KB, RS]\!]$), defines the available resources, and how those resources are spent. A resource scheme, written $\lll resources, R_{available?}(op), R_{consume}(op)\ggg$, is a triple where: $resources$ represents the available resources, and $R_{available?}(op)$ and $R_{consume}(op)$ are functions that manipulate the available resources $resources$. The function $R_{available?}(op)$ is used to decide if the resources available are enough to perform the operation op, and the function $R_{consume}(op)$ computes the resources remaining after the execution of the operation op. The first argument (r) of these functions is always the first element of the corresponding resource scheme.

This process of specifying a resource scheme guarantees that RR remains independent of how resources are spent and how the available resources are represented: the access to the available resources is restricted to a couple of functions, that (1) specify how resources are spent, and (2) constitute the interface between the control system and the available resources. The implementation of these functions depend on how resources are implemented, but they hide all aspects of the resources implementation from the rest of the RR framework.

Formally, $R_{available?}(op)$ receives as arguments the resources available r (the first element of the corresponding RS) and an operation op that the inference system is about to perform, and returns T just in case the available resources are enough for the operation op to be performed. The function $R_{consume}(op)$ receives as arguments the resources available r (the first element of the corresponding RS) and an operation op, and computes the resources that remain available after the execution of the operation *op*.

As an example, and perhaps the simplest one, consider that resources are represented by an integer; all operations consume one unit of resources; and the available resources are 8 units. This situation can be represented by the resource scheme: $\ll 8$, *greater-than-zero?*(r, op), *subtract-one*$(r, op)\gg$, where *greater-than-zero?*(r, op) is defined as:

$$greater\text{-}than\text{-}zero?(r, op) = \begin{cases} \text{T,} & \text{if } r > 0 \\ \text{F,} & \text{otherwise} \end{cases}$$

and *subtract-one*(r, op) is defined as:

$$subtract\text{-}one(r, op) = r - 1$$

4 THE INFERENCE ENGINE

RR's inference engine transforms potential states into potential states, i.e. $[\![\text{KB, RS}]\!]$ into $[\![KB', RS']\!]$. Figure 1 shows how the inference engine (enclosed by a doted box), is related with a potential state (enclosed by a dashed box). The set of inference rules specify the rules that can be used to add new conditional supported formulas to the knowledge base. The control system and the resource system are responsible for choosing, at each instant, the inference rule that should be used. Note that the functions $R_{available?}(op)$ and $R_{consume}(op)$ do not belong to the inference engine, but to the resource scheme.

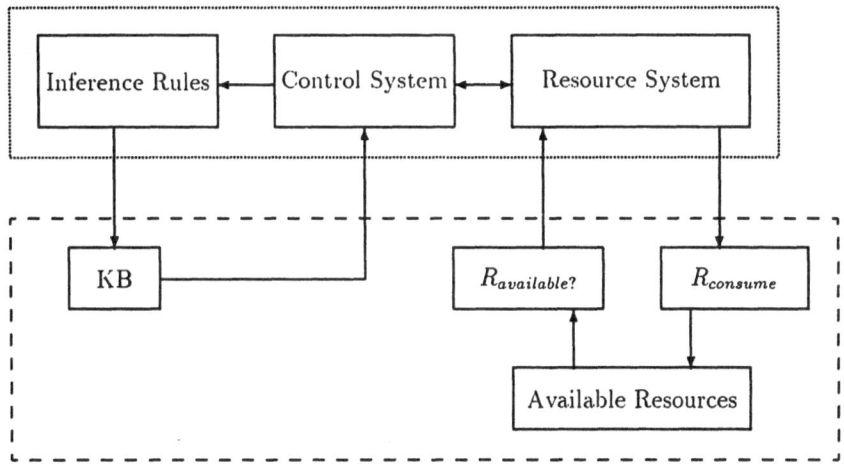

Figure 1: Blocks diagram of RR

In order to transform potential states, RR has to bring operations into action, which may consume resources. Before executing any operation, the control system has to request the resource system authorization to perform it. The function $R_{available?}(op)$ is then used to grant that authorization. So, for a specific operation $\mathcal{O}$ and a resource scheme $\ll resources$, $R_{available?}(op)$, $R_{consume}(op)\gg$, the value of the function $R_{available?}(\mathcal{O})$ indicates whether that operation can take place.

After getting authorization for performing an operation $\mathcal{O}$, the operation is applied and the old potential state $[\![KB, \ll resources, R_{available?}(op), R_{consume}(op)\gg]\!]$ gives place to a new one: $[\![KB', \ll R_{consume}(\mathcal{O}), R_{available?}(op), R_{consume}(op)\gg]\!]$. KB' is obtained after the introduction of new supported formulas into the knowledge base KB, (if the executed operation corresponds to the application of an inference rule).

Depending on the application one has in mind, different granularities of inference operations can be considered. Since RR's inference system is supported on a logic, we decided that the application of inference rules are resources consuming. However the resource consuming operations are not circumscribed to the application of inference rules, there may exist other operations with the same property. For instance, the operations of accessing (reading or writing) the knowledge base can be considered as resource consuming [Donlon 82]. We think that the set of consuming operations should include: i) the application of inference rules; ii) the search of the knowledge base (retrieving operation); iii) the operation of adding a conditional supported formula to the knowledge base as a consequence of the application of an inference rule (adding operation).

To introduce new conditional supported formulas into the knowledge base, RR exclusively uses LORE's inference rules. The next section contains a brief synopsis of LORE, presenting its properties that are relevant to RR. A complete description of LORE can be found in [Mamede and Martins 90b].

4.1 THE LOGIC LORE

LORE, the four-valued logic underlying RR, has been developed to deal with inference with limited resources. The truth values of LORE are intended as epistemic (related with an agent's knowledge or belief about a truth value), rather than ontic (the truth values are independent of anyone's knowledge of it), in character. LORE's four values are:

KT (Known True): the agent knows it has been told so;

KF (Known False): the agent knows it has been denied;

KN (Known Neither): the agent knows it has been told nothing. He has not been told it and neither has been denied it;

U (Unknown): the agent doesn't know if it has either been told, or has been denied.

The first three values (KT, KF and KN) are states of knowledge meaning that something is known, even if what is known is that nothing is known (KN). The last value (U) is a state of ignorance: it is *not known if it is either known or not known*.

The truth tables of NOT, AND, and OR connectives are consistent with the traditional connectives with respect to the values KT and KF. These connectives preserve many properties of the classical two-valued connectives. Entailment follows the relevant interpretation of [Anderson and Belnap 75], i.e. $A \rightarrow B$ means that A is relevant to B. With "relevant" one means that there must be some connection of meaning between them: A can be used to derive B. In some multi-valued logics, $A \rightarrow B$ can only be True or False [Belnap 77, Driankov 88, Garcia and Moussavi 90]. On the contrary, and due to the semantics of our truth values, we do not restrict the truth-values that can be associated with $A \rightarrow B$.

LORE deals with conditional supported formulas, written as $\langle A, t, o, [n, u, c] \rangle$, which were introduced in Section 3.1. Conditional supported formulas enable a computer system based on LORE to remember all the paths followed during an attempt to answer a question. For each path, it records the hypotheses used (the hypotheses that constitute the path), the missing hypotheses (when the path did not lead to an answer), and why they were assumed missing.

LORE's rules of inference are stated so that all the propositions derived using a particular hypothesis will have this hypothesis in their origin sets. Whenever a rule of inference is applied, the origin set of the resulting proposition is *automatically* computed from the origin sets of the parent propositions. LORE's rules of inference have inherited the same ability, the operations performed with the OSs, are now extended to the NSs, USs and CSs. The full set of LORE's inference rules include 3 rules of hypothesis, at least two rules for each connective ($\neg$, $\wedge$, $\vee$, $\rightarrow$), and two rules for each quantifier ($\forall$, $\exists$).

The association of LORE with resources is extremely profitable due to some of the LORE characteristics: i) the existence of three rules of hypothesis, the Hyp, Unkn and Neither rules; ii) inference rules use conditional supported formulas to keep hypotheses introduced with different rules of hypothesis in separate sets.

The decision to use the rules of hypothesis is the responsibility of the control system and the resource system. Since, conditional supported formulas always maintain in separate sets hypotheses introduced by a different rule of hypothesis, each rule should be associated with a different paradigm. All the three rules of hypothesis (Hyp, Neither and Unkn), are used to introduce new information in the knowledge base:

Hyp – used whenever the user wants to introduce a formula in the knowledge base.

Neither – used whenever the inference engine is allowed to conclude that neither the formula nor its negation can be derived.

Unkn – used whenever the inference engine is resource exhausted, not having the possibility to know if either the formula or its negation have already been introduced as hypotheses or can be derived. Since this rule is applied when resources are exhausted, its application should not depend on the existence of available resources, or it may never be applied.

4.2 THE CONTROL SYSTEM AND THE RESOURCE SYSTEM

The control system is responsible for focusing the choice of formulas whenever inferring new information. Our control system possesses two strategies to direct inference: backward and forward chaining. The resource system is responsible for restricting the amount of work performed throughout the duration of either a backward chaining or a forward chaining. Before explaining how this is achieved, we briefly define some notions used in the presentation.

The KB consists of rules, and non-rules called *facts*. A rule has a set of antecedents and a set of consequents, while facts do not. When a rule is involved in an inference process we say the rule is *activated*. When a rule has been activated and is conscious that all its antecedents are satisfied, the rule is *triggered*. A triggered rule is then able to *fire*, i.e. to add its consequents to the knowledge base when the consequent defines a conclusion.

BACKWARD CHAINING

Backward chaining is initiated with a query. Backward chaining can be reduced to two sequential steps: building a search tree, and then propagating results trough the tree.

Assuming the KB only contains:

$$\langle B{\rightarrow}A,\ hyp,\ \{B{\rightarrow}A\},\ [\text{-},\ \text{-},\ \text{-}]\rangle$$
$$\langle C{\wedge}D{\rightarrow}A,\ hyp,\ \{C{\wedge}D{\rightarrow}A\},\ [\text{-},\ \text{-},\ \text{-}]\rangle$$
$$\langle E{\rightarrow}D,\ hyp,\ \{E{\rightarrow}D\},\ [\text{-},\ \text{-},\ \text{-}]\rangle$$
$$\langle C,\ hyp,\ \{C\},\ [\text{-},\ \text{-},\ \text{-}]\rangle$$

whenever RR is asked about A, the following search tree is built:

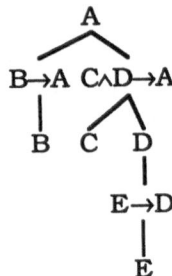

Assuming that the RS does not allow the expansion of the leaf E, different reasons justify the non-expansion of the leafs C, B, and E:

- a leaf matches an unconditional formula in the KB (the leaf C) or,

- a leaf does not match anything (B), or

- the resources available are exhausted (E).

In the first case a required piece of information is found, and the propagation step is initiated. The other two situations occur when the potential state does not hold the information required to answer a query. Either the lack of information is at the KB level (leaf B), or resources are exhausted and the the lack of information is at the RS level (leaf E).

In traditional inference systems, backward inference fails whenever the propagation of results do not reach the top of the tree, i.e., the knowledge base does not hold enough information. RR does not remain silent in these situations; it always gives an answer. RR assures the generation of at least one answer for each path of the search-tree, allowing us to state that RR's backward inference never fails.

The introduction of the missing information is sanctioned by the Neither and Unkn inference rules. When a leaf node does not match anything, meaning the inference engine is not able to find an answer to a query (in the positive or negative), the Neither rule is used:

$$\langle B,\ hyp,\ \text{-},\ [\{B\},\ \text{-},\ \text{-}]\rangle$$

When the reason for not expanding a leaf node is associated with the lack of resources the rule used is the Unkn rule:

$$\langle E, \; hyp, \; \text{-}, \; [\text{-}, \; \{E\}, \; \text{-}] \rangle$$

The propagation step can then be initiated, and since the hypotheses introduced with the Neither and Unkn rule do not get confused with the other hypotheses or between themselves, whenever an answer is produced, it is possible to know what information is necessary but, either is missing, or the available resources did not allow to certify of its existence in the knowledge base. In the present case the following conditional supported formulas are derived:

$$\langle D, \; der, \; \{E \to D\}, \; [\text{-}, \; E, \; \text{-}] \rangle$$
$$\langle A, \; der, \; \{C, E \to D, C \wedge D \to A\}, \; [\text{-}, \; E, \; \text{-}] \rangle$$
$$\langle A, \; der, \; \{B \to A\}, \; [B, \; \text{-}, \; \text{-}] \rangle$$

Note that, since the inference engine assures that all queries and subqueries are answered, we have to reduce the available resources, not when an inference rule is applied, but when it is known that an inference rule is going to be applied: when a deduction rule is activated.

Resuming, when a "traditional" answer cannot be found, meaning the potential state does not contain enough information, RR gives a weaker or *conditional answer*. A conditional answer contains the information that is missing and is responsible for the lack of existence of a definite answer. RR produces a conditional answer whenever (i) any relevant piece of information is absent from the knowledge base or (ii) the available resources are not enough to produce a traditional answer.

FORWARD CHAINING

Contrary to the backward chaining, forward chaining is modeled by a single step process. In forward chaining, whenever new data is added to the knowledge base, the data is matched against all antecedents of all deduction rules. If the data matches an antecedent of a deduction rule that rule is activated, if not already activated. Whenever all the antecedents of an activated rule are satisfied the rule is triggered and fired. When a deduction rule fires, the consequents that are added to the knowledge base are treated as new data and matched against antecedents, which may cause additional rules to be activated and to be triggered.

The resource system is used to bound the number of inferences that should be done with the conditional supported formula just introduced in the knowledge base. When the resources are exhausted, the resource system disables all rule firing, stopping forward chaining. Note that forward chaining never produces conditional answers, since the objective of the inference engine is not specific (as is the case when performing backward chaining).

CONCLUSION AND FUTURE WORK

A program that accesses a knowledge base should be able to perform certain useful inferences in order to respond a query. Since the retrieval process must be guaranteed to terminate, and terminate quickly, we have introduced resources. We presented a high-level specification of a resource-bounded reasoner, whose major role is to constrain the amount of reasoning that must be done. Given identical sets of propositions and the same inference task, RR may come to different conclusions, depending on the resource availability.

Many real world knowledge are incomplete because not all information needed for an inference is available at a particular time. In these situations most of the present system remain silent. RR, the framework presented herein, memorizes the missing information and returns a conditional answer (conditional to the presence of the missing information).

The conditional answers returned by RR can also be regarded as being abductive answers. RR has the ability to generate abductive inferences by a backward chaining mechanism which terminates with leaves of the search tree that cannot be further expanded. The same approach is followed by [Reiter and de Kleer 87]. In our case, the incapability of expanding a leaf can be two fold: either it is not a hypothesis and it cannot be derived (as in Reiter and de Kleer's approach) or resources are exhausted. Our approach has the advantage of getting the depth of the abductive explanation under control through the specification of the available resources [Mamede and Martins 90c].

RR also exhibits potentialities to perform hypothetical reasoning, to perform the planning of inference, to perform default reasoning, and, perhaps most importantly, to enable the development of friendly interfaces.

The existence of inference rules capable of updating the conditional supports when new hypotheses are introduced, and the implementation of the RR system in the SNePS environment constitute work in progress.

ACKNOWLEDGEMENT

Many thanks to Maria Cravo, Ernesto Morgado, Rui Neves, Vasco Pedro, Carlos Pinto-Ferreira, and Richard Wyatt for their general discussions while the research was in progress. This work was partially supported by Grant 87-107 of Junta Nacional de Investigação Científica e Tecnológica (JNICT).

References

[Anderson and Belnap 75] A. Anderson and N. Belnap, *Entailment: The Logic of Relevance and Necessity 1* (Princeton University Press, Princeton, NJ, 1975).

[Belnap 77] N. Belnap, A useful four-valued logic, in: G. Epstein and J. Dunn, eds., *Modern Uses of Multiple-Valued Logic* (D. Reidel, Dordrecht, The Netherlands, 1977) 8–37.

[Bobrow and Winograd 77] D. Bobrow and T. Winograd, An overview of KRL, a knowledge representation language, *Cognitive Science* 1 (1) (1977) 3–46.

[Donlon 82] G. Donlon, *Using resource limited inference in SNePS*, SNeRG Technical Note 10, Department of Computer Science, State University of New York at Buffalo, Buffalo, NY, 1982.

[Driankov 88] D. Driankov, Towards a many-valued logic of quantified belief, Ph.D. Thesis, Thesis 192, Department of Computer and Information Science, Linköping University, Linköping, Sweden, 1988.

[Fagin and Halpern 87] R. Fagin and J. Halpern, Belief, awareness, and limited reasoning, *Artificial Intelligence* 34 (1) (1987) 39–76.

[Garcia and Moussavi 90] O. Garcia and M. Moussavi, A six-valued logic for representing incomplete knowledge, in: *Proceedings 20th International Symposium on Multiple-Valued Logic*, Charlotte, NC (IEEE, 1990) 110-114.

[Hintikka 75] J. Hintikka, Impossible possible worlds vindicated, *Journal of Philosophical Logic* **4** (1975) 475–484.

[Horvitz 88] E. Horvitz, Reasoning under a varying and uncertain resource constraints, in: *Proceedings AAAI-88*, Saint Paul, MN (1988) 111–116.

[Mamede and Martins 90a] N. Mamede and J. Martins, Expanding SNePS capabilities with LORE, in: D. Kumar , ed., *Proceedings First Annual SNePS Workshop* Buffalo, NY (Springer-Verlag, Berlin, 1990) 27–39.

[Mamede and Martins 90b] N. Mamede and J. Martins, Bringing resources into logic, in: *Proceedings 20th International Symposium on Multiple-Valued Logic*, Charlotte, NC (IEEE, 1990) 220-227.

[Mamede and Martins 90c] N. Mamede and J. Martins, Resource-bounded abduction, GIA Technical Report 90/4, Technical University of Lisbon, Lisbon, Portugal, 1990.

[Martins 83] J. Martins, *Reasoning in multiple belief spaces*, Ph.D. Thesis, Technical Report 203, Department of Computer Science, State University of New York at Buffalo, Buffalo, NY, 1983.

[Martins and Shapiro 88] J. Martins and S. Shapiro, A model for belief revision, *Artificial Intelligence* **35** (1) (1988) 25–79.

[Minicozzi and Reiter 72] E. Minicozzi and R. Reiter, A note on linear resolution strategies in consequence-finding, *Artificial Intelligence* **3** (1–4) (1972) 175–180.

[Mutchler 86] D. Mutchler, Optimal allocation of very limited search resources, in: *Proceedings AAAI-86*, Philadelphia, PA (1986) 467–471.

[Reiter and de Kleer 87] Reiter R. and J. de Kleer, Foundations of assumption-based truth maintenance systems: Preliminary Report, in: *Proceedings AAAI-87*, Seattle, WA (1987) 183–188.

[Slagle, Chang and Lee 69] J. Slagle, C. Chang and R. Lee, Completeness theorems for semantic resolution in consequence-finding in: *Proceedings IJCAI-69*, Washington, D.C. (1969) 281-285.

[Swartout 83] W. Swartout, XPLAIN A system for creating and explaining expert consulting programs, *Artificial Intelligence* **21** (3) (1983) 285–325.

[Winograd 80] T. Winograd, Extended inference modes in reasoning by computer systems, *Artificial Intelligence* **13** (1) (1980) 5–26.

SITUATEDNESS AND EMERGENCE IN AUTONOMOUS AGENTS

A COGNITIVE MODEL OF GOAL-ORIENTED AUTOMATISMS AND BREAKDOWNS

Hugues Bersini
Iridia - Université libre de Bruxelles
50, Av. Franklin Roosevelt CP 194/6
1050 Bruxelles-Belgium[1]

Abstract

Before being someone who plans, man is someone who acts. Because planning often intervenes in case of uncertainty or failures in activity, the planning process must be understood as an intermediary intermittent contribution to the success of actions unfolding. An important part of man behaviour does not need any symbolic mental representation beyond the "just-perceived-environment" with which man interacts. Breakdowns are cognitive occurrences due to sudden ruptures in sensory-motor automatisms that are usually adapted to a situation. They constitute a preliminary way to understand in what circumstances an actor is really engaged in symbolic problem solving. This symbolic thinking however is entirely dependent on the breakdown context. In the cognitive model proposed in this paper, what happens before a breakdown is based on a PDP matching with automatic scripts followed by a procedural execution of the selected automatic script. Concerning the PDP developments, a simple model grounded in a multi-layer architecture architecture and capable of bottom-up and top-down inferences will replicate the deductive and inductive mechanisms of recognition processes. Concerning the execution of the automatic scripts, we will try to justify why a hierarchical goal-oriented structure is still needed. The major part of this paper discusses the simulation of six types of breakdowns and analyses the motivations for such an enterprise both from a cognitive and an AI perspective.

1. INTRODUCTION

"One of the most fundamental aspect of Heidegger's discourse is his emphasis on the state of throwness as a condition of being-in-the-world. We do at time engage in conscious reflexion and systematic thought but they are secondary to the pre-reflexive experience of being thrown in a situation in which we are always already acting (...) Objects and properties come into existence only when there is an unreadiness or breakdown (...) A breakdown is an interrupted moment of our habitual, standard, confortable "being-in-the-world" (...) A design must contribute to an interpretation of breakdown and a committed attempt to anticipate future breakdowns." Winograd and Flores (1986)

Except for long-term planning or for the thinking of symbolic activity, an important part of human behaviour does not need any mental representation beyond the perception of the environment with which he interacts. For this behavioural spectrum, the whole representation required for achieving a certain project is totally dependent and elaborated from the environmental stimuli. The actor does not "mentally project" any view of his environment in order to test and appreciate in this internal view the pursuit of his current attitudes. Such behaviours consist of adapted reactions to the world, triggered by specific situation features and by implicit goals or needs. It relies on simple pattern matching, from perception, or perception+intentions, to actions without intermediary reflexive problem solving or planning steps. Breakdowns are cognitive occurrences characterized by surprise and/or uncertainty and/or apprehension. They are due to sudden ruptures in sensory-motor automatisms that are usually adapted to a situation. They provoke an uncoupling of man and his environment which is reinforced by the emergence of explicit

---

[1] This research is supported by the Belgian National incentive-program for fundamental research in AI initiated by the Belgian State - Prime Minister's Office - Science Policy Programming.

representations of the world with which man interacts, and the reasons for such an interaction. Depending entirely on the nature and context of the breakdown, these representations allow to review mentally the last actions, to remember previous similar situations and to anticipate or project further plans (instead of straighforwardly implementing these plans). If expertise is gained by a gradual "compilation" of originally declarative knowledge (Anderson, 1983) into a more procedural form, a breakdown is responsible for an opposite phenomenon. This paper intends to clarify and formalize the notion of breakdown, to emphasize the need for an adequate modeling and to present the basic elements of the model.

Philosophically, the notion of breakdown is a phenomenological concept largely present in Heidegger's and Merleau-Ponty's works which were introduced into cognitive sciences by Dreyfus (1972) and further exploited by Winograd and Flores (1986). An important school of sociology i.e ethnomethodology studies the intimate coupling of man with his physical and social environment (Suchman, 1986; Coulter, 1989). What is strongly questioned is the necessity inherent in cognitive sciences that some environmental symbolic representation characterizes the actor's mental state prior to the act. The environment is "taken for granted" and does not denote a mental state but something outside of our heads that, precisely because it is non-problematic there, we do not need to think about it. In cognitive sciences, breakdown is a well known phenomenon. It is patent when Gregory (1988) hazards himself to postulate that consciousness is always associated with some surprise. Minsky (1986) emphasizes the inverse relation between the success of our actions and the degree of consciousness involved in their execution. To some extent, breakdowns appear in Schank's discussion (1982) of dynamic memory based on expectation failure (one of the six types of breakdowns exposed later). An important literature treats the problem of expectation failures which interrupt automatisms, initiate explicit reasoning, demand low level replanning (Sacerdoti, 1975; Wilkins, 1985; Firby, 1987) and contribute to the learning and the indexing of episodic memory (Schank, 1982). A meaningful distinction has been drawn between expectation failure and the larger concept of surprise (related to other types of breakdown) (Ortony at al., 1987). Finally a lot of AI practicians have admitted the key responsibility of breakdowns for understanding the switching from sub-cognitive to cognitive behaviours (Mitchell, 1990; Chapman et Agre, 1987; Hammond, 1990; Malcolm and Smithers, 1990).

However, the different works integrating the notion of breakdown often lack a satisfactory cognitive realism. Their approach, following the Newell's symbolic paradigm, is supported by a propositional or quasi-linguistic mental representation of the world, by an explicit definition of the goals and the world transformation operators and by a set of problem solving strategies. Concerning the simulation of cognitive automatisms, these approaches can only claim to mirror the "thinking" or the "communicating" of these automatisms that precede or follow but never "accompany" them. Because of its inherent implicitness, parallelism, adaptive capabilities and neuronal inspiration, connectionism allows to handle the pre-breakdown pattern-matching processes in a more adequate way (Bersini, 1989a). Insofar as connectionism enables to construct the ladder anchored at perception models (Smolensky, 1986) joining higher cognitive processes, it is the appropriate methodology for simulating the first next rung: the automatic perception ---> action mechanisms. On the other hand, the cognitive processes resulting from a breakdown such as diagnosing and planning a recovery strategy, are of a more symbolic and sequential type. Breakdown should therefore primarily allows for a better understanding of the relation between connectionist and symbolic types of cognitive processes. This could play some part in current hybrid attempts (Hendler, 1987; Day, 1987; Clark, 1989).

Another related interest for simulating breakdowns is to better understand the toing and froing between the two extremities of the action-planning axe. These two extremities are 1) situated activity which consist in an arbitrary function from the set of possible situations into the set of possible actions (Schoppers, 1987, see the compilation of works in (Maes, 1990)) and 2) strategic planning which tries, in an as exhaustive as possible preliminary step, to construct the whole sequence of actions which will be implemented in a second separated step. Certainly, the frontiers between purely reactive behaviours and purely planning are fuzzy and movable (Firby, 1987; Malcolm and Smithers, 1990). The imbrication of planning interludes in the unfolding of actions is nothing precise. Very vaguely, planning generally compensates for acting weakness. As a straight consequence, the cognitive fuzziness of these frontiers will not disappear during the transposing of this cognitive/sub-cognitive hybridizing in AI systems. Then the robot designers will have to tolerate and account for breakdown occurrences even in nearly optimum systems. On the other hand, breakdown analysis will help to reformulate the "qualification problem" (Mc Carthy, 1980; Pylyshyn, 1986). It is that part of the "frame problem" facing the impossibility of an exhaustive consideration of any relevant pre-condition necessary for the success of a plan, from the first to the last action. For human behaviour, an important set of these pre-conditions are generally accounted for not a priori but a posteriori i.e following a breakdown. Finally, in the same vein of expectation-failure based learning, a better understanding of breakdown will contribute to the learning of learning and of memory indexing.

The next chapter introduces the modelling global framework including the "before breakdown" connectionist and procedural parts and the simulation of six types of breakdown. The connectionist part of the model is responsible for the matching between the environmental data and the implicit goals on one side and the indexing elements of the automatic scripts on the other side. A differentiation between three types of intention (and deriving from Searle's distinction between intention-in-action and prior-intention) is proposed. A simple recognition model grounded in a multi-layer architecture and capable of bottom-up and top-down inferences is presented and discussed. It is the connectionist simplistic version of diagnostic systems based on production rules processed deductively and inductively. The automatic scripts indexed by the situations are modules of goal-oriented hierarchy. Despite today existence of a lot of behaviour-based approaches where the behaviour modules are just elementary actions, the modules considered here are small, independent and pre-compiled networks of actions. Moreover, goal-hierarchy must still exist somewhere in order to understand the processing of actions feedback, essential in human behaviour. The last chapter describes the simulation of six type of breakdowns. In previous publications (Bersini, 1989b), the "after breakdown" cognitive processes are discussed and modelling attempts are sketched largely influenced by works on case-based planning. Here the description is limited to the "pre-breakdown" behaviour.

2. THE MODELING GLOBAL FRAMEWORK

2.1 The basic architecture

The model basic architecture is shown in fig.1. It is composed of three essential components:1) a library of automatic scripts indexable by environment data and implicit intentions 2) a PDP net for realizing the matching between the environment data and the automatic scripts 3) an intentional network whose elements are connected with the nodes of the scripts in an excitatory or inhibitory ways. The model, following in the footsteps of Searle (1980) differentiates three types of intentions: explicit prior-intentions, implicit prior-intentions and goals-for-feedback. The explicit prior-intentions will not be described in this paper (they are discussed in (Bersini, 1987; 1989b) except by saying that they are the classical cognitive materials of "after breakdown" symbolic planning processes. The implicit prior-intentions are the elements of the intentional network. Being linked to the nodes of the automatic scripts, they are involved in their activation and constitute the goal-oriented part (still necessary even if neglected in a lot of situation-oriented behaviour-based approaches (Maes, 1989)) of the behavior triggering. On the other hand, the presence of the inhibitory links explains the anticipated-risk breakdown described latter. The goals-for-feedback are akin to the Searle's intentions-in-action. Their role in the automatisms execution is to indicate the moments of intensive sensibility to the actions feedback. Their presence explain the expectation-failure breakdown described latter.

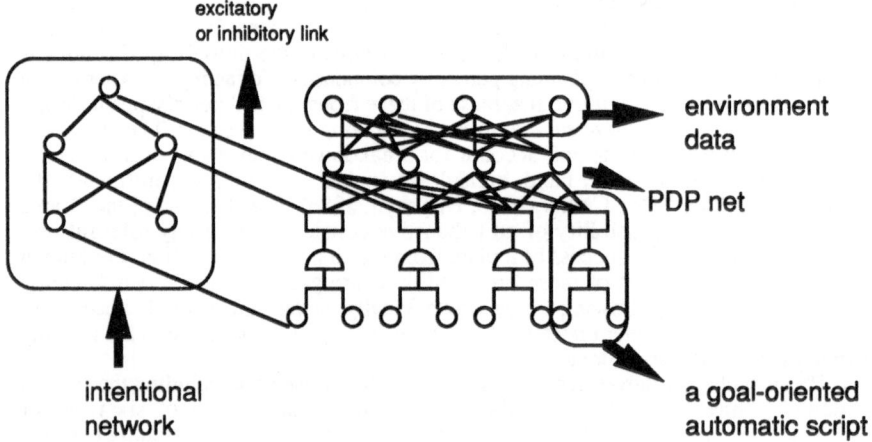

fig.1 : the basic architecture

2.2 The goal-oriented automatic scripts

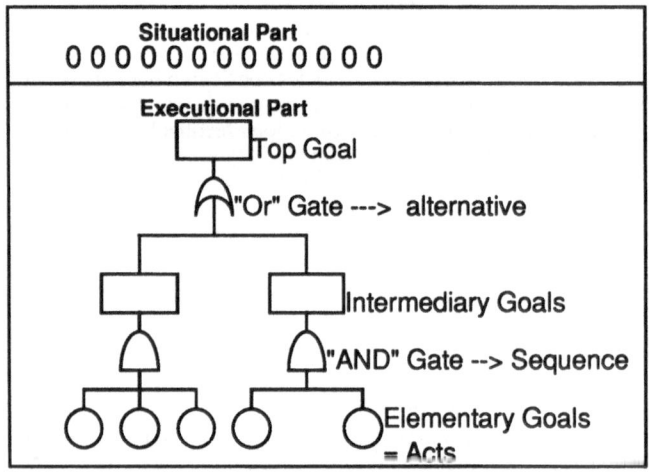

fig.2 : A goal-oriented automatic script

The automatic script is schematized in fig.2. It contains a "situational" part and an "executional" one. The situational part is simply a set of elementary features of the situation which straighforwardly match environment data. The executional part is an AND/OR hierarchical tree of goals and sub-goals (the goals-for-feedback). The tree is composed of the Top-Goal, of intermediary sub-goals and, at the lowest level, of elementary goals or real actions to execute in the world. The role of OR-gates and the checking of the actions feedback will be discussed in a next chapter. AND-gates indicate that the whole sequence of sub-goals below the gate must be executed in order to satisfy the higher goal. For each goal of the tree, a degree of priority expresses the measure of sequentiality among goals and enables, in a top down way, to determine the chronological order of the elementary goals to execute. At each level of the tree, the sub-goal with the highest degree of priority is executed. The environment data and (possibly but not necessarily) some intentions index the automatic scripts. For basic automatisms, no intention activation is required, observations are enough for triggering an automatic script and the sequential execution of its elementary goals. In other less automatised cases, the activation of one or various intentions (the implicit prior-intentions) can contribute to the triggering of a specific script. The elements of the intention network are connected to the nodes of the automatic scripts. Then any node of the goal-tree can be involved in a script indexing. In case of sub-goal (rather than top-goal indexing), only the sub-script leading to the sub-goal satisfaction will be executed.

Ballard et al. (1988) are achieving a connectionist version of the execution of AND/OR goal-tree.They are exploiting recurrent networks for the generation of temporal sequences of goals and actions. Until now, in our approach, the execution of the tree was done by classical programming. However, we are currently investigating the connectionist alternative with great attention because such a transformation could allow a complete and homogeneous connectionist model.

2.3 The Connectionist Developments

Because of the conjunction of various cognitive prerogatives which are the parallelism and speed, the content-addressability of memory, the resistance to damages and noises, the inferential implicitness, the neuronal inspiration, the generalization and approximated performances, and the adaptive capabilities (Bersini, 1989a), connectionism has been exploited for simulating the sensory-based memory retrieval of the automatic scripts. In fig.1, the connectionist net is a PDP net. The input layer receives the environment data. The output layer represents all the possible situations, each situation leading to the automatic execution of a script as indicated in fig.1. Then this PDP application is a classical diagnostic process. Using a connectionist network made possible to reproduce the Reason's two basic cognitive mechanisms: the Similarity-Matching (SM) and the Frequency-Gambling (FG) (Reason, 1986; Bersini et al., 1987). The SM is the name of the matching process performed by the network between the environment data and the scripts indexing elements. The FG intervenes in case of conflict among possible candidates matching environment data not enough discriminatory. The selection will rely on frequency and recency criteria implemented by adequate connectionist learning strategies which enable to graduate the statistical correlation between input and output. If a script has been learned a larger number of times or has been more recently learned than another one, both the PDP and cognitive tendency are either to execute straightforwardly this script (with the highest activation) or at least to try to confirm its adequacy by means of an inductive strategy.

The trick for keeping only one situation in output is to increase the threshold of the output units. This technic allows easily to reproduce the FG mechanism and to conserve only one schema to act or to perform the following schema-driven behaviours. In fact, the only originality of our connectionist application resides in the network capability to reason in a top-down way. That means the network can discover good questions concerning the attribute to test even if the learning was performed only in one direction: from the attributes to the situations. This is a basic advantage when we know that cognition processes in both ways: from environmental data to mental schema and inversely. In order to achieve this ability, the technique we adopt is trivial: just propagating the network activations from the output to the input units in the same manner than in the forward "normal" sense (from the input to the output). Then in case it becomes necessary like for the multiple-paths breakdown, we make the network perform its diagnostic in a closed-loop fashion as indicated fig.3. The network is involved in a deductive-inductive mechanism: making first hypothesis based on data and trying in a following step to confirm or reject these hypothesis (for a more detailed description see (Bersini and Decossaux, 1990). Such an bi-directional approach for diagnosis has already been realized in the Fukushima's neo-cognitron (1988) and the Grossberg's ART methodology (1988) but both require different links for bottom-up and top-down processing as well as separated learning. Nothing has been previously done in such an immediate and elementary way.

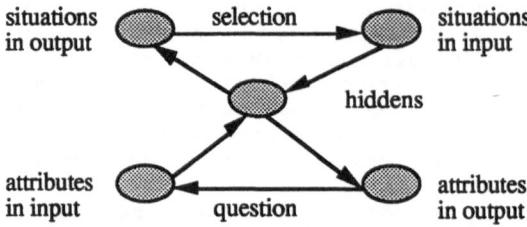

fig.3: The closed-loop diagnosis

3. SIX TYPES OF BREAKDOWN

The six types of breakdowns are: the no-script, the multiple-paths, the sequence-obstruction, the expectation-failure, the absolute-surprise and the anticipated-risk. They overlap to some extend. First, they provoke psychological manifestations and recovery strategies that are not entirely dissimilar. Their modeling share various basic aspects. However, the original mechanisms that generate each of them are distinct and justify a separate treatment. Everyday examples will be given; their modeling as well as some related works will be briefly exposed.

3.1 The no-script and the multiple-paths breakdowns

The no-script breakdown occurs when no automatism can be executed to handle a certain situation. The actor realizes the novelty of the situation and must initiate a planning process. In the model, this situation occurs if no script is activated above the selection threshold. Mitchell (1990) has realised a model which incorporates planning, execution and learning and which just reacts when it can and plans when no pre-compiled reaction is available. His model is able to learn (by explanation-based learning) new stimuli-response rules resulting from the recovery planning process.

The multiple-paths breakdown occurs during a sequential execution if, at a certain step of the sequence, more than one alternative appear suddenly possible. There is a selection problem: a decision must be taken in an uncertain and partly unfamiliar context. These breakdowns can occur during a recognition process, for example, during a diagnosis, when the expert still hesitates among two or more hypotheses. They can also occur during the execution of daily routines : "the traffic light switches to orange", "two telephones rings simultaneously". Modeling this type of breakdown is easy. It occurs when the activation value of more than one output of the connectionist matching is greater than the selection threshold. In case of stress due to shortage of time and in spite of the uncertainty, the FG mechanism makes the difference in selecting the most frequently or recently met candidate: "you never respect the traffic light in this particular place". If more time is available, the selection involves reflexive processes.

In case of recognition ambiguity the classical recovery strategy is to look for complementary observations in order to force the selection. It becomes a schema-driven generate-and-test mechanism implemented by a separated processing structure. The candidate with the highest FG remains activated and the model tries either to confirm or to reject it, looking for typical associated observations. The process becomes linear: the alternatives are tested one by one till the most satisfactory is selected. In the previous chapter, we describe how this two-stages view of recognition - from a "pre-attentive" mode, in which simple features are processed rapidly and in parallel, to a second "attentive" mode, more directed to particular features (Ullman, 1987), was simply implemented in a PDP net. PENGI (Chapman et Agre, 1987) is also capable of this oriented vision for discriminating among several paths. Other authors (Kaelbling, 1986) have stressed the importance of an oriented perception where the perception is subject-based and not environment-based, dependent on the internal state of the cognitive system in terms of current understanding as well as motivation and affect aspects.

The multiple-paths breakdown can occur during the execution of a motor process. The situation is perfectly identified (for example, in the traffic light case), but the problem lies in deciding which course of action to execute. The environment data match perfectly (and not approximately as in the recognition case) the situational part of various scripts. The recovery implies a transfer into the working memory of the information required for performing a classical planning. This information is a description of the situation, of the plan and its associated desirable and side effects, of the goals to satisfy and the constraints to respect. When the different plans are projected and selected in function of the constraints and goal satisfaction, a meta-planning takes place. In case of goal conflict, "diplomatic" strategies (like merging plans; Wilensky, 1983) are possible for satisfying totally or partially the conflicting goals.

3.2   The sequence-obstruction and the expectation-failure breakdowns

A sequence-obstruction breakdown appears when, in the goal hierarchical tree, the sub-goal(i) is an absolute pre-condition of the sub-goal(i+1) (i.e the following sub-goal can not be executed if the previous one is not attained), and when the sub-goal(i) cannot be satisfied. Some examples are : a door impossible to open, a lift that never comes, unsuccessful log-in in a computer or Dennet's example (1984) of the beer glass being glued to the shelf. The breakdown occurs because the non-satisfaction of sub-goal(i) prevents the actor from physically carrying on with his plan. Ortony et al. (1987) distinguish a deducible expectation-failure from a not-deducible one. In the case of the closed door or the glass of beer, the expectation is not an explicit conscious manifestation but rather an embodied unconscious expectation i.e the feedback of a physical homeostatic loop. The model described in this paper obviously does not claim to simulate these physical breakdowns very faithfully. The trick consists in preventing the realization of the sub-goal and then the continuation of the plan execution in the modeling of the situation. The successful result of sub-goal(i) becomes a kind of obligatory expectation. Even though the sequence-obstruction and the expectation-failure breakdowns appear to be modeled in a similar way, they have different psychological origins.

Indeed, a sub-goal(i) can be essential to the top-goal but not to the execution of the following sub-goals. For instance, to play a record, you have to switch on the amplifier, the turn-table, then put the record on and enjoy the music. The success of the sub-goal: "switch on the amplifier" is not a necessary condition for carrying on with the first following sub-goals of your plan. A sub-goal(i) can even be not necessary at all for the satisfaction of a top-goal and be in the tree simply by automatism, from force of habit: locking the door of the car when you leave it, or pulling the chain when you leave the lavatory.

For simulating the expectation-failure, each elementary goal or action can be associated with the checking of some higher goals expectations. For any goal of the tree, the result of its execution can be associated with indications which enable the actor to check whether the goal obtains i.e to compare what happens with the previous expectations. What is important to understand is that these expectations explicitly indicated in the automatic script does not pretend to reproduce a similar explicit expectation in the actor's mind. It only indicates that the actor expects something rather precise to occur in his environment, even if this expectation is tacit and absolutely not "mentally represented". The environment has to filled a case in the actor's mind. When you pull the chain you don't explicitly wait for the waterfall noise, however if nothing happens, you'll be surprised. It is this surprise phenomenon that we try to grasp in the model. Indeed, following the execution of a certain action, the model compares with the current situation the expectation it has for the goals associated with the action.

58

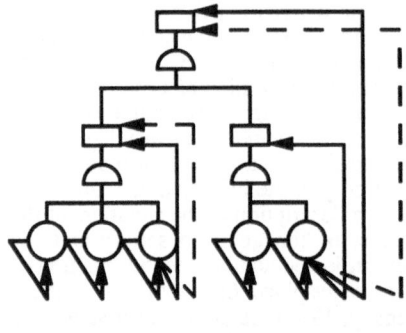

————————————> : normative checking
- - - - - - - - - > : descriptive checking

fig.4 : Checking the expectations

In fig.4, (for clarity, the goal-tree is only composed of AND-gates), the normative "checking behaviour" should be the one indicated by the bold arrows. The real motivation to ground execution process in a goal-hierarchy is this "checking behaviour". Each node of the tree is a moment of high sensibility to the actions feedback. However, man does not check the satisfaction of every intermediary goal present in the tree; a more realistic (descriptive) behaviour could be the one indicated by the dotted arrows. Checking the satisfaction of a sub-goal can be an active behaviour : you really go and check it (as with the case of the amplifier light). However, it can be a more passive one: you don't really go and check it, but the indications of goal success are so salient that you realize immediately when the goal is not successful (you pull the chain and nothing occurs). That will depend on the degree of "expectiveness" and the degree of supervisory attention you allow to the script execution. These two cases, the active and the more passive one, demand a same modelling for the breakdown occurrence. Following the execution of the required actions, whenever the goal is not attained, the actor realizes that the expectation associated with the goal is not satisfied

Determining which intermediary sub-goals the model checks during the execution of the script mainly depends on two factors :

- the perceptual "strength" or saliency of the indications associated with the realization of the goal. A fortiori, when there are no possible indications for the goal, there are no expectation.

- the importance of the goal for other subsequent or higher goals. If a sub-goal is a pre-condition of the following sub-goal, we are back in the sequence-obstruction type.

In the AI planning field and even more in reactive planning, many authors have regarded it as essential to give their system the opportunity to monitor and check the results of the execution steps, and, in case of expectation-failure, to recover from the problem (Sacerdoti, 1975; Wilkins, 1985; Firby, 1987). It is clear that the more the planning system tends to be reactive, the more these monitoring and verifying tasks have an important part to play. Avoiding heavy computations during the initial planning step may merely postpone the need to plan which will arise when a breakdown, due to situation conditions not considered at the beginning, occurs. This allocation puzzle is related to the "qualification problem". In cognitive reactive planning, in order to recover a plan that is failing, a lot of pre-conditions are considered, not a priori, but after the breakdown. In daily life, man is better for adapting than for foreseeing. To what extend should it be the case for an AI system?

The possible recovery strategies for the sequence-obstruction and for the expectation-failure differ in their cognitive demands. The first one is the automatised alternative and its simulation is the role of the OR-gate in the goal tree. When a sub-goal is not satisfied and there is an OR-gate below this sub-goal, the execution model just switches to another branch. Various alternatives can appear possible for a same sub-goal. Their degree of priority depends on their position at their level of the tree (from left to right). The OR-gates can be distributed at different levels of the tree enabling the model to backtrack. If the model has no more automatised alternative, a classical planning process, based on a symbolic type of reasoning, follows the breakdown.

3.3 The absolute-surprise and the anticipated-risk breakdowns

Referring to Ortony et al. (1987) : *"there is much more to surprisingness than expectation failure"*. The absolute-surprise breakdown consists in the occurrence of something completely surprising that could absolutely not be expected a priori. It is fundamentally different in its intimate nature from the previous four types of breakdowns. It includes salient events such as a stone hitting your head or crashing through a window or even an erotic paragraph in a book on modal logic. The saliency of an event depends on contextual and psychological factors. Indeed, the saliency and the probability of drawing attention are function of the sudden discrepancy between what happens and what is perceived as usually happening. It is an interruption of a "perceptual cognitive equilibrium". The anticipated-risk breakdown is characterized by a sudden apprehension. You see somebody crossing the road just in front of your car (or you notice a level crossing): it is salient because you "feel", without the need to represent it, that merely carrying on with your behaviour something undesired maybe unpleasant will occur. The apprehension arouses due to an immediate very short term projection of the current behaviour. The breakdown occurs because this prediction violates some background tacit intentions that manifest themselves only when they are violated or expected to be violated. It is the interaction of the situation and the current plan with the violated tacit intention that makes these various aspects emerge in consciousness.

The data-driven component of the matching process, which is continuously fed with and filters external stimuli, deals with the simulation of the absolute-surprise. Independently of the recognition or execution schema-driven component, salient stimuli get directly into the set of environment data to process. The simulation of the anticipated-risk is more delicate. As the description of the basic architecture has shown, the model integrates an intentional network whose elements can be connected in an inhibitory way with nodes of the automatic scripts. If one of the tacit intention is about to be violated by the current actions, it inhibits the execution of the plan. Then, more attention gets on the situation and the plan. Indeed, the recovery of these two last types of breakdowns depends on the resolution of a data-driven / current-schema-driven conflict. If the new data do not force a replacement of the current schema (i.e if no results of the connectionist matching are greater than a certain threshold), the actor can carry on with his actions as if nothing had occurred. But in an opposite case, the new event provokes the emergence of a new plan which satisfies a new goal. In the case of time-stress, the model can automatically switch to another plan taking immediately the control of the sensory-motor processors (as will be the case if somebody crosses the road in front of your car). In less urgent cases, when intermediary reflexive steps appear possible, the new data lead to the development of meta-planning strategies which organize and conciliate the different goals. In her theory of action selection, Maes (1989) accounts for the anticipated-risk breakdown, when a short prediction of the actions sequence violates pre-conditions of goals to satisfy.

4. RELATED WORKS AND CONCLUSION

Some related works have been realized in order to simulate the pre-breakdown type of reactive and automatic cognitive processes (Maes, 1989, 1990; Schoppers, 1988; Ballard,

1988; Mitchell, 1989). A closely related work is the development of PENGI (Chapman and Agre, 1987) which plays a video-game in a continuous and interactive manner. The authors do not pay too much attention to the breakdown simulation except to the multiple-paths one, when the player has to select among different possible actions. The selection relies on further observations determined in a top-down fashion. Indeed, the power of Pengi relies on a collaboration of a central and a visual systems, which together selectively throw away most of the information present in the visual scene. The reasons for neglecting the other types of breakdown are obvious. In the Pengi environment, nothing really unexpected can occur. The methodology of Maes (1989) takes the extremist road of reducing the behaviour modules to simple and totally distributed actions rather than compiled structures of actions. She does not really tackle the problem of breakdowns even if her work shows a lot of interesting and unique potentialities like the "planning ahead" capability.

For the reasons mentioned previously, some works on reactive planning pay a lot of attention to various kinds of breakdowns such as: the no-script, the expectation-failure and the multiple-path (Firby, 1987; Georgeff, 1989). These occurrences are responsible for higher decisional process on what to do next. The Georgeff's AI reactive planner share with our work a lot of features as - the use of some sort of automatic scripts which can be evoked in a goal-directed as well as in a situation-directed fashion - and the fast-backtracking process for activating alternative goals. In line with our work, various planning studies envisage the global integration of a simulation of pre-breakdown sub-cognitive behaviour with a simulation of post-breakdown cognitive one (Mitchell, 1990; Day, 1987; Malcolm and Smithers, 1990; Hammond, 1990).

In the close future, AI will have to implement a lot of automatised, sub-cognitive behaviours, extending thus perception models to motor models. An important problem will be to clearly understand to what extend these automatisms can simulate the behaviour. At a recent connectionist conference, Margaret Boden claimed that a crucial problem with this methodology was its opacity. No one would ever admit that an intelligent black box might one day be responsible for the ultimate decision : to press or not the button. This paper contributes to show that, as long as the network will have some alternative (multiple-paths) and realizes the dramatic humanitarian consequences of its decision (anticipated-risk), it will think about it in a transparent way. But when no more alternative will appear possible and if the network does not care about the humanity survival ....

References

Anderson, J.R. (1983) : *The architecture of Cognition*. Cambridge, Mass: Harvard University Press.

Ballard, D and S.D. Whitehead (1988): Connectionist Design on Planning. In *Connectionist Models Summer School Proceedings* - Touretzky, Hinton, Sejnowski (Eds) - Morgan Kaufmann.

Bersini, H., Cacciabue, P.C. and G. Mancini (1987) : A Cognitive Model for Representing Knowledge, Intentions and Actions of Process Plant Operators. In *Proceedings of the First European Meeting on Cognitive Science Approaches to Process Control*. Marcoussis (France), October 19-20, 1987.

Bersini, H. (1989a): Connectionism vs GOFAI for modelling and supporting process plant operators: a brief critical analysis. in *Proceedings of 2nd European Meeting on Cognitive Science Approaches to Process Control*.

Bersini, H. (1989b): Before and after breakdowns. in *Proceedings of the 4ème colloque de l'ARC: Progrès de la recherche cognitive*.

Bersini, H. and Decossaux, E. (1990): Exploitation of connectionist systems for deductive and inductive diagnosis. *IRIDIA internal report*.

Chapman, D. and P.E. Agre (1986): Abstract Reasoning as Emergent from Concrete Activity. *In Procedings of the 1986 workshop on Reasoning about Actions and Plans - Georgeff and Lansky (Eds.)*

Chapman, D. and P.E. Agre (1987) : Pengi : An implementation of a theory of activity, in *Proceedings of the Sixth National Conference On Artificial Intelligence*, American Association for Artificial Intelligence, Seattle, Wash..

Clark, A. (1989): Connectionism and the multiplicity of mind. *Artificial Intelligence Review*. Vol. 3 - 1

Coulter, J. (1989): *Mind in Action*. Polity Press.

Day, D.S. (1987) : JANUS: an architecture for integrating automatic and controlled problem solving, in *Proceedings of the Ninth Annual Conference of the Cognitive Science Society*, Seattle, Wash.

Dennet, D. (1984) : Cognitive Wheels : the frame problem of AI. In C. Hookway (Ed.) *Minds, Machines and Evolution. New* York, Cambridge University Press.

Dreyfus, H. (1972) : *What Computers can't do; A Critique of Artificial Reason.* New York: Harper & Row.

Firby, R.J. (1987) : An investigation into reactive planning in complex domains, in *Proceedings of the Sixth National Conference on Artificial Intelligence,* Morgan Kaufmann, Seattle, Washington.

Fukushima, K. (1988): A Neural Network for Visual Pattern Recognition. *IEEE Computer,* March.

Georgeff, M.P. and F.F. Ingrand (1989): Decision Making in an Embedded Reasoning System. In *Proceedings of the 11th IJCAI Conference.*

Gregory, R.L. (1988): Consciousness in science and philosophy: conscience and con-science. *Consciousness in Contemporary Science* - A.J. Marcel and E. Bisiach (Eds.) - Oxford Science Publications.

Grossberg, S. (Eds) (1988): *Neural Networks and Natural Intelligence.* MIT Press, Cambridge Mass.

Hammond, K.J. (1990) : Integrating Planning and Acting in a Case-Based Framework. In *Proceedings of the 8th AAAI Conference.*

Hendler, J.A. (1987) : Marker-Passing and Microfeatures. In *Proceedings of the Tenth International Joint Conference on Artificial Intelligence.* Milan, August 23-28.Maes, P. (1989) : The Dynamics of Action Selection. In *Proceedings of the 11th IJCAI Conference.*

Kaelbling, L. (1986): An architecture for Intelligent Reactive Systems. *In Procedings of the 1986 workshop on Reasoning about Actions and Plans - Georgeff and Lansky (Eds.)*

Maes, P. (1989): The Dynamics of Action Selection. *In proceedings of the 11th IJCAI Conference.*

Maes, P. (eds.) (1990): Designing Autonomous Agents - *Robotics and Autonomous Systems* 6 - North-Holland.

Malcolm, C. and T, Smithers (1990): Symbol Grounding via a Hybrid Architecture in an Autonomous Assembly System. in *Robotics an Autonomous Systems* - 6.

Mc Carthy, J.M. and P.J. Hayes (1981) : Some philosophical problems from the stand-point of artificial intelligence, in : *Readings in Artificial Intelligence.* Tioga, Palo Alto, CA.

Minsky, M. (1986) : *The Society of Mind.* A Touchstone Book. Published by Simon & Schuster Inc.

Mitchell, T. (1990): Becoming Increasingly Reactive. In *proceedings of the 8Th AAAI.*

Ortony, A. and D. Partridge (1987) : Surprisingness and Expectation Failure : What's the Difference ? In *Proceedings of the Tenth International Joint Conference on Artificial Intelligence.* Milan, August 23-28.

Pylyshyn, Z.W. (Ed) (1986) : *The Robot's Dilemma.* Ablex, Norwood, NJ.

Reason, J (1986) : Intentions, Errors and Machines : A Cognitive Science Perspective. *Conference on Aspects of Consciousness and Awareness.* Bielefeld, W. Germany, 1-3 December.

Sacerdoti, E.D. (1977) : *A Structure for plans and Behaviour.* Elsevier-North Holland, Amsterdam.

Schank, R.C. (1982) : *Dynamic memory.* New York : Cambridge University Press.

Schoppers, M.J. (1987): Universal Plans for Reactive Robots in Unpredictable Domains. In *Proceedings of the tenth IJCAI Conference.*

Searle, J.R. (1980) : The intentionality of intention and action. *Cognitive Science,* No 4.

Smolensky, P. (1986): Information Processing in dynamical systems : foundations of harmony theory. In *Parallel Distributed Processing: Explorations in the Microstructure of Cognition. Vol.1 : foundations* (eds D.E. Rumelhart, J.L. Mc Clelland & the PDP Research Group) MIT Press/Bradford Books, Cambridge, MA, USA.

Suchman, L. (1987): *Plans and Situated Actions. The Problem of Human/Machine communications.* Cambridge University Press.

Ullman, S. and C. Koch (1987): Shifts in Selective Visual Attention: Towards the Underlying Neural Circuitry. In L.M. Vaina (ed) *Matters of Intelligence* - D. Reidel Publishing Company.

Wilensky, R. (1983) : *Planning and Understanding.* Addison-Wesley, Reading, Mass.

Wilkins, D.E. (1985) : Recovering from execution errors in SIPE. *Computational Intelligence,* 1 (1), February.

Winograd, T. and F. Flores (1987) : *Understanding computers and cognitions.* Ablex Publ.

THE 'LOGICAL OMNISCIENCE' OF REACTIVE SYSTEMS

Nigel Seel, STC Technology Ltd, London Road, Harlow, Essex CM17 9NA.
Tel: +44-279-429531; fax: +44-279-451-434; email: nrs@stl.stc.co.uk

ABSTRACT

The problem of 'logical omniscience' continues to engage attention in AI. In this paper it is argued that the problem arises from interpreting formal properties of epistemic logics into agent performance domains, where agent cognition is taken to incorporate formula-manipulation, which then mirrors inference in the logic. The case of Reactive Systems is examined, where some such systems eschew such formula-manipulation in favour of fast-acting mechanisms. A formal account of such agents' knowledge states can still be given, but the 'problem' of logical omniscience re-emerges in a new light.

1. INTRODUCTION

The *phenomenon* of 'logical omniscience' is a technical one, which occurs within certain formal systems which attempt to capture notions of 'knowledge'[1]. It is usual to formalise the notion that an agent 'knows ϕ' where ϕ is some proposition, by defining an operator such as 'K' and writing syntactically: 'Kϕ'. K cannot be an ordinary propositional operator such as '*not*', ('$\neg$'), because it is not truth functional (eg. if ϕ is contingently true, then nothing special can be said of the truth value of Kϕ).

The standard approach is to treat K as a modal operator, and to treat the analysis of epistemics as a particular interpretation of standard modal logic with possible worlds semantics. A story is then told as follows. Agents are not omniscient about the contingent facts of the world they inhabit: there are many possible ways the world could be, that an agent cannot distinguish between. Thus in each situation (world) we associate a number of 'accessible worlds' with the agent, capturing the space of possibilities within which the agent considers its actual situation to be. The things an agent is sure about reflect commonalities between these worlds; the things an agent is agnostic about take distinct forms in different worlds. Note that the agent's *lack of knowledge* prevents it from identifying which of the possible worlds is to be considered actual, while if it has *incorrect beliefs*, then none of the accessible worlds will be the real one.

In such a semantics, the following axiom, called 'K', is valid:

K. $K\phi \wedge K(\phi \rightarrow \psi) \rightarrow K\psi$

Axiom 'K' is valid because in every world in which ϕ and ($\phi \rightarrow \psi$) hold, ψ has to hold too, by the meaning of the implies operator '$\rightarrow$' (Chellas, 1980, p. 7), and the notion of satisfaction relation used.

---

[1] The notion of logical omniscience is orthogonal to distinctions between knowledge and belief. Notions of 'knowledge' and 'belief' intermix freely in this paper.

In a similar fashion, logically necessary formulae, which could not be false, must be true in every possible world, and therefore must be 'known'. So we have the inference rule called Necessitation, (Chellas, ibid, p. 14):

$$RN: \quad \frac{\vdash \phi}{\vdash K\phi}$$

To sum up, on the standard modal logic account axiom K is valid and inference rule RN is sound.

These facts, not necessarily controversial in the context of modal logic, become problematic when epistemic logic is interpreted into the real-world domain of agents which are said to know things. It seems to follow that such an agent knows all the consequences of the things it knows (by axiom 'K' and modus ponens), and knows all necessary truths (presumably including all of mathematics) by inference rule RN. The trouble is, these conclusions are felt to violate our intuitions about how knowledge and belief actually work (in people). More precisely, our intuitions encompass a performance model of knowing and believing, in which people, when asked, fail to give satisfactory answers where the theory would suggest they ought: (eg "Is 'Fermat's Last Theorem'[2] actually a theorem of Peano Arithmetic ?").

In this paper I first survey recent attempts to address the 'problem' of logical omniscience. This is followed by a discussion which focuses more on agents 'in the world', reactive systems, and in particular what it means for a reactive system to know something. Finally, I discuss whether considering *situated agent-environment interaction* as the primary phenomenon might shed new light on the 'problem' of logical omniscience: for example, by establishing it as an artifactual problem.

2. THE PROBLEM OF LOGICAL OMNISCIENCE

As Hintikka (1962) observed, it is possible to 'get round' the *problem* of logical omniscience by assuming that the K operator does not refer to what is explicitly believed by a person, but instead refers to what is implicit in those beliefs - what would have to be the case if those beliefs were true. Another proposed interpretation is that we are dealing with 'idealised reasoners', which in some sense do not suffer from ordinary limitations.

Even if these suggestions were acceptable, there still remains the problem of dealing with agents which are presumed not to believe all the consequences of their beliefs, and not all necessary truths. What is the nature of the assumed fallibility of such agents ? Four limitations have been discussed in the literature, (Levesque, 1984; Fagin & Halpern 1985, 1988; Konolige, 1986).

1. The agent lacks awareness of a concept (syntactically, the predicate naming the concept is 'missing' in some sense from the agent's lexicon, or semantically, it lacks a valuation).

2. The agent undertakes some actions equivalent to theorem-proving - by applying transformation rules to tokens, but is resource-

---
[2] See (Mendelson, 1987, p. 117).

bounded, so that tokens requiring more than some number of applications of the rules are not derived.

3. The agent is as (2), but some transformation rules which are needed for completeness are contingently omitted.

4. The agent maintains a number of contexts for reasoning, which are applied in different situations. These contexts need not be the same, or even consistent with each other.

Assuming we wish to model some or all of these epistemic fallibilities, the strategy runs as follows. First we introduce a new operator, B say, which aims to capture *explicit* belief - the beliefs actually attributable to the epistemically-fallible agent. The kinds of beliefs which are closed under logical consequence, include all valid formulae etc are then called *implicit* beliefs, and given a different operator, say ⊡.

Secondly, some axioms are then given which characterise the nature of the agent's epistemic limitations: for example we might want to make

(1) $\neg B(\phi \vee \neg\phi)$

satisfiable, where a necessary truth is not believed in the case where the agent has never heard of ϕ. Similarly,

(2) $B\phi \wedge B(\phi \rightarrow \psi) \wedge \neg B\psi$

may be satisfiable, showing a failure to draw logical consequences.

Finally, some mathematical structures are derived which provide a suitable class of models for the proposed logic, and which make the axioms come out valid. This last step may be more or less difficult.

An early example of this procedure was Levesque's use of partial and incoherent worlds, called situations after the similar constructions in Situation Theory, (Barwise & Perry, 1983). Partial situations do not provide valuations for all the sentence letters of the language of the logic, which permits lack of awareness to be modelled as in (1) above; incoherent situations permit simultaneously supported contradictory valuations of sentence letters, resulting in the failure of closure of explicit belief under implication as in (2) above.

Although it appears that there is nothing wrong with Levesque's treatment from a formal point of view, there are some questions as to whether it adequately addresses the problems it sets itself. Thus as Vardi (1986) points out, Levesque's agents are perfect reasoners in the constrained framework of relevance logic: "Unfortunately, it does not seem that agents can reason perfectly in relevance logic any more than in classical logic" (p. 294). The esoteric nature of incoherent worlds also raises some problems. In interpreting the semantics into the actual world, what could they be?

In (Fagin & Halpern, 1985, 1988) a number of logics are presented which attempt to model one or other of the epistemic fallibilities mentioned above, while avoiding Levesque's difficulties. Levesque's logic is re-engineered into a 'Logic of Awareness', which restores the general setting of total possible worlds semantics (abandoning partial and incoherent situations), but associates with each world an (agent-indexed) 'awareness set' of propositional tokens which the agent is aware of at that world. Under the semantics given, all of Levesque's axioms are valid.

By extending the 'awareness set' to formulae in general (not just propositional tokens), properties of Levesque's operators such as failure of consequential closure can be reproduced, and by choosing the contents of the 'awareness sets' with care (by computability properties), resource-bounded reasoning can be modelled.

As Konolige (1986) observes, however, the superposition of a basic possible worlds model together with arbitrary syntactic restrictions at worlds leads to a rather clumsy hybrid system. The system is neither elegant, not does it provide good support for intuitions about resource-bounded reasoning. In particular, the technical apparatus can be re-expressed more coherently in purely sentential terms.

Fagin and Halpern's final logic supports a notion of 'local reasoning'. Here, each agent in a given state is associated with a collection of sets of possible worlds. Each of these sets constitutes a 'context of belief'. Hence the satisfiability of (2) above can follow from the agent believing ϕ in one context, $\phi \rightarrow \psi$ in another, but never putting these two contexts together to believe ψ.

To sum up, these approaches to handling the 'logical omniscience' problem all exhibit a common theme: a movement from (1) to (3) thus, (see figure 1 below).

(1) The identification of a concept of 'knowledge' or 'belief', abstracted from human affairs.

(2) A formalisation of the concept by operators, (K's or B's), which take the concept, as a *category*, to be unproblematic. This is then followed by the exploration of its properties through various candidate axiomatisations as we have seen above.

(3) The search for a simple, elegant mathematical structure capable of providing a semantics for the axiomatisation.

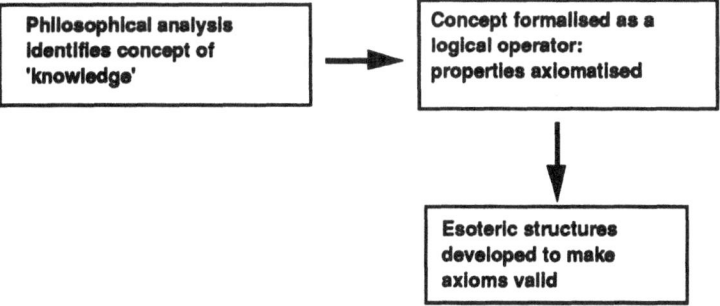

Figure 1. The primacy of the reified category of 'knowledge'.

Looking at reactive systems forces us to break with this reified view of 'knowledge' as a thing in itself, and restores the primacy of the situated epistemic subject engaged in practical relationships with its environment.

3. REACTIVE SYSTEMS

In most areas of AI, it is impossible to define the key concepts (eg knowledge-based system, blackboard architecture) with any precision. Things are no different with reactive systems, as can be seen from this preliminary attempt at definition, adapted from (Pnuelli, 1986).

Definition: Reactive System

A reactive system is an entity which interacts in a systematic way with its environment.

This however fails to capture the main intuitions of workers in this area: (eg Brooks, 1986; Kaelbling, 1986; Agre & Chapman, 1987) that:

* the environment is taken to be complex and hard to perceive,

* the environment is unpredictable in the large, and continually sets novel contexts for the system to which it has to respond,

and perhaps the most important intuition:

* the environment requires (often, always ?) a very <u>fast</u> response from the system.

Designers of reactive systems have therefore emphasised

* rapid response procedures, which take input (in some more or less 'raw' form) and optionally, state-information maintained by the system; and return output (in some more or less 'raw' form) and optionally updated state;

* a taxonomisation of required agent behaviours: *most important* ⇒ *least important*, which can be factored into concurrent task-achieving modules in the system architecture, plus some scheduling mechanism (cf Brooks, Kaelbling ibid).

Designers have de-emphasised/rejected suggestions that reactive systems should support explicit world-models + declarative reasoning about world and agent behaviour, in favour of <u>any</u> mechanisms which will permit the agent to respond appropriately (including *fast enough*) in a situated fashion. So although in principle a reactive system (according to the definition) *could* maintain a 'formulae database' world-model as a causal factor in its behaviour, it *need* not, and in what follows I assume it *does* not.

Now, if the notion of an agent's 'having knowledge' crucially depends upon the existence of such a formulae database, then one is in some epistemic trouble with reactive systems. But perhaps epistemic notions are not, after all, architectural, but are instead a fine-grained way of describing agent *behaviour*?

In (Seel, 1989) I described in detail a reactive agent in a Skinner box environment, and proved some properties of it using a temporal logic. In (Seel, 1990 a, b) I extended the logic with an epistemic operator, and showed how it captured fine-grained agent behaviour in the environment, such as making mistakes, and learning. I will briefly restate the approach to the epistemic modelling of reactive systems outlined there, and then consider the implications for the 'logical omniscience' of reactive systems.

4. HOW CAN A REACTIVE SYSTEM KNOW SOMETHING?

I will summarise the epistemic treatment of reactive systems in nine theses.

1. Consider the agent as an automaton-object (not necessarily finite-state). Consider the other entities constituting the agent's environment as also automata-objects (not necessarily finite-state). Let a collection comprising an agent plus the other objects constituting its environment, each in a definite state, be called a **scene**. Agent and environment objects are deterministic.

2. Scenes can be executed, so that as each object's next state function is applied, each object in the scene updates itself to its next state: collectively the next scene is constructed. Call the infinite sequence: [initial-scene; next scene; one after that; ...] a **history**. Note that the behaviour of objects defined in an initial scene is entirely determinate - the notion of history is well-defined.

3. Each object has both private and public state. An object cannot access another object's private state (it can access its own private state + other objects' external states as part of its own next-state computation). Assume an **observer** who looks at scenes from 'outside'. The observer also can only 'see' the objects' external states. This means that on the information available to the observer, the evolution of scenes as a history unfolds may *not* be determinate.

4. The behaviour of the agent and environment is not arbitrary but is constrained by rules. These rules have a conditional and temporal character:

if such and such has happened then subsequently the environment will behave thus;

if such and such has happened then subsequently the agent will behave thus.

These rules state conditions on the external states of objects, they are assumed to be known to both the agent designer and to the observer. Conditionality imposes on the agent designer that the agent must determine at 'run time' the specifics of the rules which actually hold. The resulting learning task provides the conditions for non-trivial epistemic description of the agent.

5. The observer starts by looking at an initial scene, scene zero. There are many possible histories which would look the same to the observer at scene zero, (differing in objects' private states, and next state functions). The observer collects these together and calls them the *possible histories* at scene zero. As the actual history unfolds, scene by scene, perfectly definite events occur, registered in the changing external states of the objects. The observer prunes from the possible histories all the ones which differ in their early

scenes from what has actually happened in the history being watched.

As the actual history unfolds, and evidence accumulates, certain of the rules have their antecedents satisfied, 'kick in' and constrain the pattern of future events. All the histories which don't fit these patterns get removed from the possible histories as well.

6. Suppose we have now reached scene n of the actual history. As the observer looks at the possible histories, it may be the case that they all agree on what the agent (or environment) will do in scene (n+1) - (and maybe (n+2), (n+3) etc). Since the actual history is certainly one of the possible histories, then it is predictable what the agent (or environment) will do next.

7. If the different histories in the space of possible histories tell different stories about what the agent (or environment) will do next, then the observer cannot predict exactly what will happen next, only that some choice from amongst those in the possible histories will be found to occur in the actual history.

8. Since the agent itself may have no more information than the observer (recall the designer's ignorance mentioned above), then it may also find itself in an informational state as in (6), in which case it may be said to act appropriately, or (7) in which case it may, by "guessing wrong", be said to act in error.

9. Given a certain adequacy of the rules (thought of as specifications), there may come a point where in certain types of scene, the possible histories always agree on what the agent should do next. If that was not previously the case, the observer may say that the agent has learned to behave appropriately in these scenes.

Now, all this may seem a creative use of conditional rules to compensate for lack of information about private states on the part of the observer, and so it is. But when it is formalised properly, the changing structure of possible histories over 'time' turns out to replicate the Kripke semantics underlying a logic of knowledge and time. So if we wish, we can stop talking about *possible histories*, and instead introduce talk about the agent's **knowledge**. Since the semantics is in place (it induces a KT45 axiomatisation for the knowledge operator) we can prove theorems about perception, knowledge and action[3].

Needless to say, the agent itself need have none of this: it only needs to change some internal structures to align its response behaviour correctly to the incoming stimuli from the environment, in the best reactive tradition.

5. REVISITING LOGICAL OMNISCIENCE

Notice how the above treatment dramatically modifies the way the problem of 'logical omniscience' is posed. Unlike in figure 1 above, we are no longer trying to exemplify some abstract, platonic notion of 'pure knowledge'. Such conceptual analysis is replaced by an attempt to reason correctly about a highly situated agent-environment interaction (figure 2).

---

[3] See (Seel 1990, a, b) for details of the formalisation, proofs and discussion.

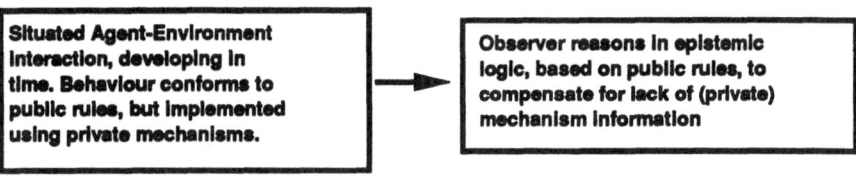

Figure 2: The primacy of the concrete situation.

So what are the properties of the formal epistemic theory which, generated by the observer, is attributed to the agent? The most obvious feature is the restriction of the lexicon of the logic to the naming of the interaction-relevant events in the 'life' of the agent. There is no attempt to start talking about number theory or stock-exchange prices. (And why should there be? These are problems within some localised regions of *human* social life - another, but different concrete situation.) Hence the notion of 'limited awareness' here arises as a natural consequence of the specificity of the agent-environment mathematical model.

As regards the other issues flagged as problems above, (resource-boundedness, consequential closure and the knowing of all valid formulae), it is certainly true that the observer's epistemic theory has axiom 'K' as valid, and supports the Rule of Necessitation. But this is beside the point because there are no performance implications to these facts.

The agent is not concerned because it is not computing with the logic, merely being a reactive mechanism. Resource-boundedness may be a problem for the observer reasoning in the logic, as it is for all users of formalised theories, but not for the agent, which merely acts. In some sense, the logic 'makes contact' with the agent at perception and action: in between, the observer may undertake arbitrarily long chains of reasoning, and deduce all kinds of valid formulae; the agent simply operates as a mechanism according to its design, using its *private state* and various observable public states to produce its next output. To sum up, the agent (in its environment) <u>satisfies</u> the logic, but doesn't <u>use</u> it. Hence for the agent, the proof-theoretic properties of the logic which are called 'logical omniscience' (and which get dressed up with all kinds of performance implications to worry us), simply don't apply.

The reader is likely to be left uneasy by this conclusion. "Sure, you can cut the problem down to size for the dumb beasts, which is what reactive systems really are, but it's cheating - the problem is really meant to be people !"

Well, no and yes. It <u>is</u> an achievement to base a concept of knowledge on a thoroughly behavioural analysis of agent behaviour in an environment - it's <u>not</u> cheating. And yes, the real problem <u>is</u> people (and not logic !).

This suggests that a more compelling resolution of the classical difficulties will emerge from formalised sociological *theories*, modelling the situated formation of social constructs such as mathematics by human communities. Difficult as this may seem, it holds out more hope of success than those approaches which reify the problem as one of *logic* design.

6. CONCLUSION

The problem of 'logical omniscience' in its traditional guise was outlined, and some recent attempts to address it were surveyed. Attention was then focussed on the agents themselves which traditionally are meant to suffer the 'problem'.

In the case of reactive systems, it was argued that a perfectly coherent behaviour-based notion of agent-knowledge is possible, without any assumption that the agent has to conduct logical reasoning of any kind. In this case, the problem of logical omniscience, which at root is a performance problem, simply vanishes as a real problem. It is suggested that the task of adequately modelling *human* 'beliefs' and cultural accomplishments, such as mathematics and the formalised sciences, belongs more properly to yet-to-be-developed formal social theories rather than logic per se.

ACKNOWLEDGEMENTS

Although disagreeing with their conclusions, I found (Reichgelt & Shadbolt, 1990) a useful source of ideas.

REFERENCES

Agre, P. E. & Chapman, D. (1987). Pengi: an implementation of a theory of activity. In *Proceedings of the Sixth National Conference on Artificial Intelligence*, pp 268-272.

Barwise, J & Perry, J. (1983). *Situations and Attitudes*. Bradford Books/MIT Press.

Brooks, R. A. (1986). A Robust Layered Control System for a Mobile Robot. *IEEE Journal of Robotics and Automation*, Volume RA-2, Number 1, pp 14-23.

Chellas, B. (1980). *Modal Logic: An Introduction*. Cambridge University Press.

Fagin, R. & Halpern, J.Y, (1985). Belief, Awareness, and Limited Reasoning: Preliminary Report. In *Proceedings of the Ninth International Joint Conference on Artificial Intelligence, (IJCAI-85)* , pp 491-501.

Fagin, R. & Halpern, J. Y (1988). Belief, Awareness and Limited Reasoning. In *Artificial Intelligence* 34.

Hintikka, J. (1962). *Knowledge and Belief*. Cornell University Press.

Kaelbling, L. P. (1986). An Architecture for Intelligent Reactive Systems. In Georgeff M. P. & Lansky A. L. (Eds.), *Reasoning about Actions and Plans*. Morgan Kaufmann.

Konolige, K. (1986). What Awareness Isn't: A Sentential View of Implicit and Explicit Belief. In J. Y. Halpern (Ed.), *Theoretical Aspects of Reasoning About Knowledge: Proceedings of the 1986 Conference*. Morgan Kaufmann.

Levesque, H. J. (1984). A Logic of Implicit and Explicit Belief. In *Proceedings of the National Conference on Artificial Intelligence*, (AAAI-84), pp 198-202.

Mendelson, E. (1987). *Introduction to Mathematical Logic*. Wadsworth & Brooks.

Pnuelli, A. (1986). Specification and Development of Reactive Systems. *Information processing 86 (IFIP)*. Elsevier Science.

Reichgelt, H. & Shadbolt, N. R. (1990). *Logical Omniscience as a Control Problem*. Paper, Department of Psychology, Nottingham University.

Seel, N. R. (1989). A Logic for Reactive System Design. *Proceedings of the Seventh Conference of the Society for the Study of Artificial Intelligence and the Simulation of Behaviour*, pp 201-211.

Seel, N. R. (1990a). Intentional Description of Reactive Systems. In Y. Demazeau & J-P. Muller (Eds.), *Proceedings of the Second European Workshop on Modelling Autonomous Agents in a Multi-Agent World*. Elsevier Science. (To appear).

Seel, N. R. (1990b). *Formalising First-Order Intentional Systems Theory*. Technical Report. STC Technology Ltd.

Vardi, M. (1986). On Epistemic Logic and Logical Omniscience. In J. Y. Halpern (Ed.), *Theoretical Aspects of Reasoning About Knowledge: Proceedings of the 1986 Conference*. Morgan Kaufmann.

A Connectionist Semantics for Spatial Descriptions

Stuart A. Jackson & Noel E. Sharkey
Department of Computer Science,
University of Exeter

ABSTRACT

One of the most important considerations in designing a model of spatial
cognition involves finding a way to specify the meanings of the terms,
such as *left* and *front* and so on, that the model is to interpret. Such a
specification is difficult using the componential-based microfeature encoding that many connectionist systems employ. The approach taken in this
paper involves training a network to map linguistic spatial assertions onto
a *task enviroment*, such that the meanings of the assertions become
encoded in terms of how the system has processed them. By analogy with
Classical computation, such meanings can be referred to as *procedural*.
Cluster analyses of weights and activations are employed to investigate
how such procedural meanings might be implemented in a connectionist
system. Results of two simulations are discussed using the theoretical
vocabulary of model-theoretic and procedural semantics.

INTRODUCTION

Consider the spatial assertion 'A is on the left of B'. An individual is
readily able to comprehend such a sentence, yet will have extreme
difficulty in explaining the meaning of the word *left* when it occurs in isolation. This curious phenomena is the province of lexical semantics, which
attempts to provide an account of how word meanings are computed by
the language user. Two of the most enduring ideas used in formulating
theories of such computation are the twin notions of semantic primitive
and compositionality, whereby the meaning of a word is regarded as a
compositional function of a given set of semantic primitives (eg. Katz &
Fodor 1963; Wilks 1975; Schank & Abelson 1977).

In connectionist research, the notion of semantic primitive is most
closely related to the notion of *microfeature*. Like semantic primitives in
linguistic theory, microfeatures are the atomic elements of connectionist
distributed representations. However, connectionist researchers use the

term microfeature in two different ways.

Some authors, for example McClelland & Kawamoto (1986), use the term to refer to elements which are themselves semantically interpretable. These are equivalent to the earlier featural representations, but without the theoretical overtones of generative semantics. We will call such semantically interpretable microfeatures *symbolic* primitives. Other authors however, for example Hinton (1981) and Smolensky (1988), discuss microfeatures in terms of semantically *un*interpretable entities. In this case, no one individual microfeature refers to a property of the world. Instead, reference to such properties emerges from a pattern of activation across many microfeatures. We will call such semantically uninterpretable microfeatures *subsymbolic* primitives (see Sharkey, 1990a, for a review of these terms).

For a connectionist system to cope with the semantics of most natural language words, employing symbolic primitives is adequate. For spatial terms such as *left* and *front* however, their employment is inadequate. This is because such terms are themselves natural language primitives, ie. it is not possible to define the word *left* in terms of other natural words, where those words are serving as putative symbolic primitives. This problem does not arise if the connectionist employs subsymbolic primitives to specify the meanings of spatial terms. Adopting this approach would usually amount to coding a semantically uninterpretable feature set over input activations.

However, a different way of thinking about subsymbolic primitives is as procedural entities, that are not encoded over input activations, but which, instead, are contained in the weights evolved after a given period of learning. This approach can be assimilated to what is referred to in Classical computation as procedural semantics (Davies & Isard, 1972; Winograd, 1972). In procedural semantics, the meaning of a word is regarded as some entity that constrains the nature of the representation constructed by a given computational system when the word is encountered in the course of comprehension.

The aim of this paper is to report on preliminary results from connectionist simulations inspired by the notion of procedural semantics. The two simulations reported here were trained on a simple spatial task. Employing symbolic or subsymbolic primitives to specify the semantics of the terms *left* and *front* would usually amount to coding the semantics of these words as vectors of activations over input units. However, the current simulations used no such encoding. Instead, they were designed with the idea in mind that the meaning of a word like *left* would become encoded in terms of how the network actually processed it. That is, in terms of weights and activations over hidden units. Given that such a task has been learned, analyses should reveal the nature of the procedural meanings that the two networks have come to embody.

SIMULATION 1 : LANGUAGE TO THE WORLD

A 12-10-20 network was trained using the standard back-propogation learning algorithm (Rumelhart, Hinton & Williams, 1986), with momentum = 0.9, learning rate = 0.05. The network was trained on 1000 passes through the training set and was adjugded to have learned the task satisfactorily when the global error tolerance = 0.05.

The Spatial Task

This can be characterized essentially as a mapping from language to the world. Given an input, coding a representation of a natural language assertion, the network was asked to perform a mapping to an output, coding a representation of a very simplified world or *task enviroment*. The set of input vectors code assertions of the form 'A is on the left of B', using two spatial terms, **left** and **front**, and five symbols, **A, B, C, D** and **E**. A given input can be conceptually broken down into three fields : The **op** field (containing two units) codes for the spatial terms, and the **arg1** and **arg2** fields (each containing five units) code for the symbols. For example, the vector **01 00100 00001** codes the assertion 'C is in front of E'. The set of output vectors code for the task enviroment to which the input assertions refer. This enviroment can be conceptuallly broken down into four fields, and visualized as a cross, with the **left** and **right** fields on the horizontal axis, and the **front** and **behind** fields on the vertical axis. Each field contains five units, and each symbol can be identified by its position within that field. For example, the vector **00010 10000 00000 00000** codes for the task enviroment in which D is on the left of A. Using two spatial terms and five symbols yields an exhaustive training set of forty assertions. Ten of these assertions were removed from the corpus, and reserved to test for network generalization. Each symbol was omitted four times, and each spatial term five times. This left a training corpus of thirty assertions.

RESULTS

The network exhibited 90% generalization to the test set, using an activation of > 0.35 as criteria. The analysis of the learned network was broken down into three components : (*i*) input to hidden weights; (*ii*) hidden unit activations; (*iii*) hidden to output weights. A heirarchical cluster analysis of the weights and activations of this simulation used the Ward method.

Fig 1 : Projective weights of input. The numbers after the symbols refer to which field the symbol occupied in a given input, either **arg1** or **arg2** fields.

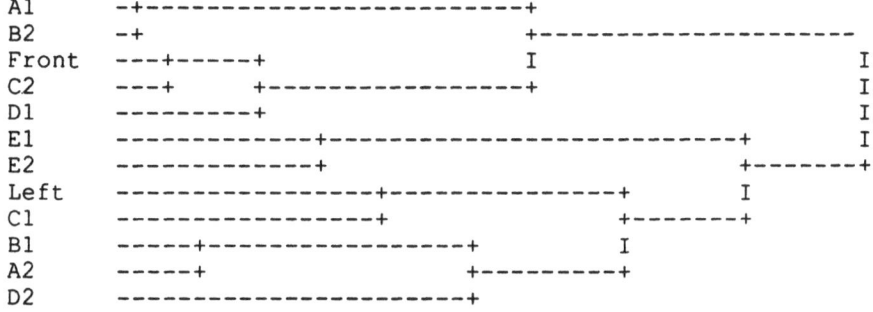

```
A1       -+------------------------+
B2       -+                        +---------------------
Front    ---+-----+                I                    I
C2       ---+     +----------------+                    I
D1       ---------+                                     I
E1       ------------+-------------------------------+  I
E2       ------------+                            +-------+
Left     -----------------+---------------+       I
C1       -----------------+            +-------+
B1       -----+---------------+        I
A2       -----+              +---------+
D2       ----------------------+
```

The dendogram in Fig 1 shows that the constituent weights have been divided into two major clusters. The first includes the vector of weights associated with the input unit coding for the **front** operator, and the second, the vector of weights associated with the the input unit coding for the **left** operator. The two clusters are thus determined by the two spatial operators of the input assertion. The two arguments, **arg1** and **arg2** are distributed uniformly in the n-dimensional space around the vectors of weights for the two operators. This is because there is no principled reason why the argument weights should show any systematic clustering, as all of them were combined an equal number of times with each operator during learning. The fact that the division of the constituent weights uses the two operators as the determining factor is borne out by an examination of a cluster analysis of the hidden unit activations, shown below in Fig 2.

Fig 2 : Hidden unit activations. For example, LAC means 'A is on the left of C', and refers to the particular input assertion that gave rise to the hidden unit representation.

```
LCA     -+--------------+
LBC     -+                +--------------------+
LDC     ---+-----------+                       I
LDE     ---+           I                       I
LAE     -----+-----+   I                       I
LBE     -----+     +---+                       I
LCE     -----------+                +-----------+
LCD     -+---------+                I           I
LED     -+           +----------------+         I           I
LAD     -------+---+                  I         I           I
LBD     -------+                      I         I           I
LBA     -+---+                        +-------+ I
LCA     -+   +----------------------+ I         I
LDA     ---+-+                      I I         I
LEA     ---+                        +-+         I
LEB     -----+-----------+          I           I
LEC     -----+           +---------+            I
LAB     -------+-+       I                       I
LCB     -------+ +-------+                       I
LDB     ---------+                               I
FBC     -+------------------+                    I
FBE     -+                    +------------+     I
FDA     -+-----------+        I            I     I
FDB     -+           +-------+             I     I
FDC     ---------+---+                     I     I
FDE     ---------+                         +--------------+
FAB     ---+---------------+               I
FEB     ---+                +----------+   I
FAC     ---+-------+        I          I   I
FAE     ---+       +-------+           I   I
FEC     -----------+                   +---+
FBA     -+----------------+            I
FCA     -+                +---------+  I
FCD     ---+-----+        I         I  I
FCE     ---+     +---+             +-------+
FCB     ---------+       I
FAD     -----+---------------------+ I
FBD     -----+                       +-+.
FEA     -------+-------------+
FED     -------+
```

The dendogram in Fig 2 shows that the hidden units take on two clearly distinguishable classes of activation. One representing the generic class of **left** patterns and the second representing the generic class of **front** patterns. Once again, the arguments appear to be uniformly distributed within the two clusters determined by the spatial operators.

Fig 3 : Receptive weights of output. For example, **D-behind** refers to the output unit coding for D in the behind field of the output vector.

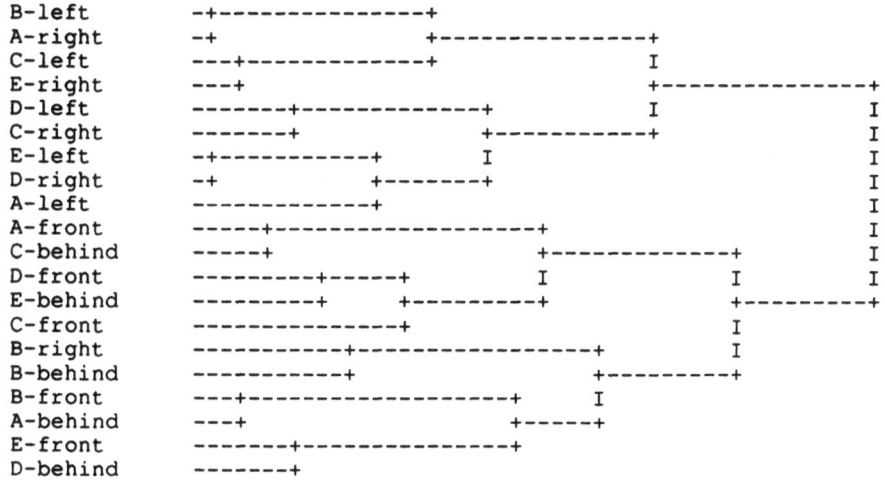

```
B-left      -+----------------+
A-right     -+                    +----------------+
C-left      ---+-------------+                      I
E-right     ---+                         +---------------+
D-left      -------+-------------+       I                  I
C-right     -------+                +-----------+           I
E-left      -+-----------+     I                            I
D-right     -+           +-------+                          I
A-left      ------------+                                   I
A-front     ----+-------------------+                       I
C-behind    -----+                    +-------------+       I
D-front     ---------+-----+       I               I       I
E-behind    ---------+     +---------+             +---------+
C-front     ---------------+                    I
B-right     -----------+----------------+       I
B-behind    -----------+                +---------+
B-front     ---+-------------------+     I
A-behind    ---+                    +-----+
E-front     -------+---------------+
D-behind    -------+
```

The dendogram in Fig 3 shows two major clusters. One includes the vectors of weights associated with output units coding for arguments in the **left** and **right** positions of the task enviroment, which corrosponds to the horizontal axis of the cross. The second includes the vectors of weights associated with output units coding for arguments in the **front** and **behind** positions of the microworld, corresponding to the vertical axis of the cross. There is one abberant data point, the vector of weights associated with the unit coding for **B** in the right position, which can be explained using the raw coefficient data of the cluster analysis. We found this vector to be closer, in terms of squared Euclidean distance, to the vector of weights associated with the output unit coding for **B** in the behind position. Why this should be remains unclear.

SIMULATION 2 : LANGUAGE TO A MORE COMPLEX WORLD

The task enviroment for simulation 1 was limited in that it could only represent spatial relations between two arguments at any one time. If the output coding were made *richer* in some respect, then this limitation could be overcome, and the spatial relations bewteen many arguments could be represented simultaneously. Simulation 2 was designed with this goal, of increasing the richness of the task enviroment, in mind. A 12-40-25 architecture, with recurrent connections from both hidden and output units, of the sort used by Stolcke (1990), was trained using the standard back-propogation algorithm (ibid), with momentum set to 0.9 and the learning rate to 0.05. The network was trained to tau = 0.1 on 983 cycles.

The Spatial Task

The essence of the input/output coding remained the same as that used in the first simulation. The set of input vectors code for assertions of the form "B is in front of D" (**01 01000 00010**), using the same two operators and the same five symbols. Instead of mapping single assertions however, training was conducted using sequences of four input assertions, comprising a **left** assertion followed by a **front** assertion, followed by a second **left** assertion followed by a second **front** assertion. The set of output vectors code for the task enviroment, the richness of which has been increased by the addition of a fifth conceptual field, corrosponding to a *centre* position of the cross described earlier for simulation 1. The network was provided with a target vector for each individual assertion of a given sequence, illustrated below in table 1.

Table 1. Sequence of input assertions and their associated target vectors

Input Assertion	Task Enviroment Target
LAB	A B
FBC	C A B
LBD	C A B D
FEB	C A B D E

In this way, the network is being asked to intergrate a *subsequent* assertion with the task enviroment representation of a *consequent* assertion.

The training set consisted of 60 such sequences, composed from 30 of the possible 40 single assertions. Each such training assertion occured six times within the training set. The 60 sequences themselves represented precisely half of the possible 120 configurations that the task enviroment (representing all five symbols at once) was able to assume. The test set also consisted of 60 sequences, this time including the 10 novel assertions it had not previously seen

RESULTS

The network exhibited 75% generalization to the test set as a whole, using an activation of > 0.35 as "on", and < 0.35 as "off". However, the test set also included (by necessity) some assertions from the training set. Taking these into account, the measure of generalization on the truly novel assertions falls to just above 20%, which is a disappointing figure. In many cases, this lack of generalization was due to other units in the task enviroment becoming activated to a greater extent than the correct unit, rather than the correct unit not being activated at all. As yet, we have conducted no further analyses of this net.

DISCUSSION

On the Notion of Semantic Theory

The species of procedural semantics that inspired this simulation is detailed in Johnson-Laird (1983), which in turn was grounded in model-theoretic semantics (MTS). MTS provides a semantic interpretation for natural language with respect not to the real world, but to a **model**. A model in this sense is an abtract concept, consisting of a function from the syntactically well formed expressions of the language to some specified *model structure* (an arbitary set of entities).

In such a model, the property that an expression such as *on the left of* captures - ie., its **intension** - is treated as a primitive and unanalysed function. That is, MTS assumes that there are *interpretation functions* that directly provide each such expression with an interpretation in the model structure

MTS allows a theorist to distinguish between truth conditions and semantic relations. The *truth conditions* (meaning) of a descriptive sentence determine the set of situations of which that sentence could be a correct description. In MTS, an expression such as 'on the left of' is said to make a *contribution* to the truth conditions of the sentences in which it occurs. This contribution is specified by the interpretation function, which provides the ordered set of entities in the model structure between which the relation holds.

In this way, MTS finesses the problem of lexical semantics by taking the intensions of lexical items and expressions as unanalysed functions. Computationally, the question one must ask is what is in the 'body' of the function corresponding to the intension of the expression. That is, what must be computed in order to specify the entities possesing the property. Procedural semantics is concerned with precisely this question. That is, the truth conditions (meaning) of an expression such as 'on the left of' in procedural semantics is its contribution to the truth conditions (meaning) of the sentence in which it occurs.

On the Notion of Procedural Meaning

This section will explore the extent to which the theoretical vocabulary of MTS, such as interpretation function, truth conditions and so on, can be assimilated to the behaviour of these two simulations. Let us begin, though, by looking at the first layer of weights of simulation 1, from input-to-hidden, and the hidden unit activations.

The *composing function* (see Sharkey, 1990b) over the first layer of weights serves to map an input assertion onto a hidden unit representation. This representation is not a compressed version of the input, and is specifically *not* encoding a (weight mediated function of) a semantically interpretable set of symbolic primitives.

Cluster analysis of the hidden unit activations shows that a hyperplane divides the hidden unit space into **left** and **front** patterns. This is due firstly to the fact that each argument occurs equally with each operator during learning, and secondly to the fact that in the structure of the task, the *only* regularity that the hidden unit activations could reflect was in the seperation of the operators.

Given this pattern of clustering, we can characterize the hidden unit representations as serving as a *task model*, in the sense that they have come to encode information that allows the hidden-to-output weights and composing function over them to perform the task entailed in the input assertion. By analogy with MTS, the input assertions are interpreted with respect to this hidden unit task model

Now, what about the second layer of weights, from hidden-to-output? Let us begin by restating what we know. (i) A descriptive sentence, such as 'A is on the left of B', has truth conditions ; (ii) Those truth conditions determine the (set of) situation(s) of which that sentence is a correct description ; (iii) The interpretation function, mapping from syntactically well formed expressions of the language to the model structure, gives a full account of truth conditions.

One of the most important idealizations that MTS makes is to treat the intensions of basic lexical items and expressions as unanalysed functions. As stated above, computationally, one would want to know just how such functions work. What, in this simulation, might correspond to such unanalysed interpretation functions?

The answer, we beleive, is in the weights. That is, the weights can be characterized as (distinctly connectionist) procedures, specifying *how* the mapping performed by the interpretation function from language to the world is being carried out. Given this conjecture, it follows that the weights evolved by back propogation have come to encode truth conditions. That is, truth conditions for the whole training set. These weight-encoded truth conditions then determine the set of vectors of activation across the task enviroment of which any given input assertion is a correct description.

However, things are not quite so simple. This is because as well as encoding the truth conditions for whole assertions, there is also - buried in amongst them - some aspect of the hidden-to-output weights which have encoded the *contribution* to truth conditions made by each spatial operator to the input assertions in which it occurs.

Precisely how one goes about disassembling a weight matrix to get at such a contribution is a question that has received little attention in the literature (but see McMillan & Smolensky, 1988; Sharkey, 1990b). However, assuming that this is done, the result would be the isolation of *procedural primitives* underlying the meanings of the spatial operators used in the simulation. Such primitives would not simply be symbolic (or subsymbolic) microfeatures, nor would they corrospond closely to the Classical conception of procedure. Rather, they would be a new type of semantic primitive, a connectionist procedural primitive.

Given that the weights have encoded truth conditions, the network has also got to be able to *use* those truth conditions. That is, the network has to use the meaning of the spatial operators that the weights have encoded in terms of truth conditions to perform the spatial task asked of it. This is where the composing function comes in. The composing function over the hidden-to-output weights takes the information contained in the task model, and uses that information to instantiate a vector of activation over the task enviroment that *satisfies* the truth conditions encoded in the weights. Or put another way, the composing function is manipulating the task enviroment on the basis of what is known about the truth conditions of the assertion.

The argument advanced above was developed to explain how simulation 1 had accomplished the task asked of it, but it also applies equally well to the second simulation. The temporally extended processing characteristics of a recurrent network do, obviously, complicate a network analysis. However, the weights of a trained recurrent net are as invariant as the weights of a trained feed-forward net, and as such are open to matrix decomposition. Accordingly, the isolation of connectionist procedural primitives is still viable.

CONCLUDING REMARKS

This paper details the research conducted to date on developing a notion of connectionist semantics for spatial terms. The notion can be most readily assimilated to the Classical conception of procedural semantics. We would stress that this assimilation is more useful, in terms of explanation and elucidation, than strictly accurate.

We have argued that the weights of these two simulations can be characterized as encoding a quantity analagous to the theoretical truth conditions found in MTS. Which is to say, they serve as *constraints* on the possible form of the output enviroment.

We have also noted that the meanings of the spatial terms used in the two simulations are, in a sense, *buried* in the weights. That is, there is some aspect of the weight matrix that captures the contribution that the spatial operators make to the truth conditions of the input assertions in which they occur. A suitable analyses should reveal precisely which aspects this involves. When such analyses is complete, we will have isolated the procedural primitives that underly the meanings of the spatial operators in both simulations. These primitives are, we believe, a new type of theoretical entity, far removed from either Connectionist microfeatures or indeed Classical procedures.

REFERENCES

Davies, D.J.M. & Isard, S.D. (1972) Utterances as programs. In D.Mitchie (ed) *Machine Intelligence*, Vol 7. Edinburgh : Edinburgh University Press.

Hinton, G. (1981) Implementing semantic nets in parallel hardware. In G.E.Hinton & J.A.Anderson (eds) *Parallel Models of Associative Memory*.P.161-188. Hillsdale, NJ : Erlbaum.

Johnson-Laird, P.N. (1983) *Mental Models*. Cambridge : Cambridge University Press.

Katz, & Fodor (1963) The structure of a semantic theory. *Language*, **39**, 170-210.

McClelland, J.L. & Kawamoto, A.H. (1986) Mechanisms of sentence processing : Assigning roles to constituents. In D.E.Rumelhart & J.L.McClelland (eds) *Parallel Distributed Processing : Explorations in the Microstructure of Cognition*, Vol 1. Cambridge, Massachusetts : MIT Press.

McMillan, C, & Smolensky, P. (1988) Analysing a connectionist model as a system of soft rules. Technical report CU-CS-393-88. University of Colorado, Boulder.

Rumelhart, D.E., Hinton, G.E & Williams, R.J. (1986) Learning internal representations by error propogation. In D.E.Rumelhart & J.L.McClelland (eds) *Parallel Distributed Processing : Explorations in the Microstructure of Cognition*, Vol 1. Cambridge, MA : MIT Press.

Schank, R.C. & Abelson, R.P. (1977) *Scripts, Plans, Goals and Understanding*. Hillsdale, NJ : Erlbaum.

Sharkey, N.E. (1990a) Connectionist representations for natural language : Old and New. In Georg Dorffner (Ed) *Konnektionisimus in AI in Kognitionsforschung*. Springer Verlag : Heidelberg.

Sharkey, N.E. (1990b) Implementing soft preferences for structural disambiguation. In Georg Dorffner (Ed) *Konnektionisimus in AI in Kognitionsforschung*. Springer Verlag : Heidelberg.

Smolensky, P (1988) On the proper treatment of connectionism. *Behavioral and Brain Sciences*, **11**, 1-74.

Stolcke, A. (1990) Learning Feature-Based Semantics with Simple Recurrent Networks. ISCI Tec Report TR-90-015

Wilks, Y. (1975) A preferential, pattern-seeking semantics for natural language interface. *Artificial Intelligence*, Vol 6, P.53-74.

Winograd, T. (1972) Understanding Natural Language *Cognitive Psychology*, *3*, 1-191.

Neural Networks and Visual Behaviour: Flies; Panned Eyes; and Statistics

Dave Cliff

School of Cognitive and Computing Sciences, University of Sussex, Brighton BN1 9QN, England, UK. Email: `davec@cogs.sussex.ac.uk`

ABSTRACT

Computer vision researchers have only comparatively recently begun to acknowledge the behavioural contexts of vision. So-called *animate vision* has a number of advantages over the inanimate paradigm. This paper reviews an ongoing project in animate vision using neural networks. The project has a novel context: it involves the simulation of a hoverfly, with the neural network acting as a closed-loop controller for the simulated fly. The underlying thesis of this work is that most neural network models which do not recognise the behavioural contexts of neural computation are of limited interest. This stance places the model within the domain of "computational neuroethology", rather than "computational neuroscience".

1 INTRODUCTION

Over the past few years, computer vision research has witnessed an explosion of interest in so-called "neural network"[1] models of processing. More recently, a new research paradigm known as *animate vision* has emerged, which recognises the behavioural contexts of vision. The research summarised here is an exploration of issues arising in applying neural network techniques to aspects of low-level animate vision. The study is pursued in a novel context: the visual processing performed by an airborne insect; specifically, the hoverfly *Syritta pipiens* L.

The focus on insects is not a novelty aspect of the work: rather, it is a result of the philosophy underlying the project. The project is an experiment in *computational neuroethology*. Briefly, computational neuroethology is the study of the neural basis of behaviour, using computational modelling techniques. This should not be confused with "computational neuroscience" (the branch of neural network research that aims for a scientific analysis of real neural systems [33]), despite some similarity in the methods involved.

The style of computational neuroethology advocated in this project is particularly extreme: it is argued that the only fruitful path to the understanding of cognition (or, more tentatively, intelligence) is to study it at its roots. That is, we should first aim to understand animals at the bottom of the evolutionary scale, before we attempt to study animals (such as humans) that have evolved to an advanced state. The justification for this extreme position is based on a critical appraisal of the methodology of current computational neuroscience, summarised in the last section of this paper.

This paper briefly reviews the background literature for the project, and then gives an overview of the work in progress. The work is at an early stage, and the

---

[1]For the purposes of this paper, "neural network" models are synonymous with "connectionist" and "parallel distributed processing" (PDP) models.

most significant result to date is the generation of the view through the fly's eyes. The paper concludes with further discussion of computational neuroethology.

2 BACKGROUND

2.1 Animate Vision and Nonuniform Sampling

These notes on animate vision are based on the publications of Ballard (e.g. [3, 4]) and Brown (e.g. [6]), concerning the Rochester Robot [7]. The definition of animate vision given below is, however, my own interpretation and therefore possibly not wholly representative of the Rochester view.

The term "animate vision" denotes visual processing performed in circumstances where the image-formation apparatus is a subsystem under dynamic control of the overall visual processing system. Note that the definition allows for a distinction between natural and artificial animate vision (NAV and AAV respectively). In NAV, the image-formation apparatus consists usually of two eyes, linked to musculature allowing for dynamic resampling of the optic array, i.e. seeing creatures are capable of looking around. Essentially it is the capability of looking around that distinguishes AAV from previous work in computer vision, where degrees of freedom associated with the camera (e.g. focus, position in space) are rarely under dynamic control.

The rationale underlying animate vision is that one should first question *why* we want to use vision. That is, "... *animate vision* argues that vision is more readily understood in the context of the visual *behaviors* that the system is engaged in, and that these behaviors may not require elaborate categorical representations of the 3-D world." [4, p.1635, original emphasis].

The several computational savings offered by animate vision include the ability to use visual search rather than algorithmic search, and the natural establishment of coordinate systems invariant with respect to observer motion [4, pp.1636–1637].

Furthermore, the overwhelming majority of work in computer vision employs uniform-resolution image acquisition (URIA), where the imaging resolution of all pixels in the image is assumed to be identical. Nevertheless, interest is growing in non-URIA approaches [36, 38, 39], where the imaging resolution is in inverse proportion to the distance from the central point of the image. Young's work indicates that there are significant computational advantages to be gained when using such a scheme, but that the restricted area of high resolution requires an animate vision component to provide a resampling mechanism.

2.2 The Antianthropocentric Context

The animate and non-URIA paradigms share a common feature: they draw inspiration from biological studies of human (or more generally, primate) visual processing. This marked preference towards human visual processing is, however, an unfounded bias: visual processes at the levels addressed by these paradigms are not species-specific. Thus the anthropocentricity of these theories cannot be justified.

Specifically, there is a functional isomorphism between the visual behaviours of humans and certain arthropods, e.g. flies. This isomorphism was described by Land [22], his argument centred on studies of the hoverfly *Syritta pipiens* [16]. The crucial point is that *Syritta*-NAV is a good analogue of human-NAV, but with fewer degrees of freedom: because *Syritta*'s eyes cannot be moved independently of the rest of the body, gaze control is effected solely by body reorientation.

Syritta's eyes are aligned to give an area of binocular overlap in the frontal part of the field of view, and more importantly they produce non-URIA images, with the central resolution approximately three times higher than that at the periphery.

Finally, the number of photoreceptors in *Syritta*'s eyes is less than half the 65536 pixels in a 256 × 256 image, whereas the human eye has about 127 million receptors [8, p.25].

All of these factors (especially the small number of receptors) make *Syritta* particularly suitable for the study of low-level non-URIA animate vision, via simulation. Ballard rejects a simulation approach because of the difficulty of achieving real-time performance, but surely this is a problem of engineering, not science.

3 APPROACH

3.1 Flies

The project relies on the construction of a simulator system. This involves modelling biological data concerning the anatomy and optics of *Syritta*, thereby allowing conventional computer graphics ray-tracing techniques (e.g. [19, p.291ff.]) to be employed in generating synthesized images of the view through *Syritta*'s eyes.

These images are then operated on by processes modelling the massively parallel transformations occuring in the first few layers of nervous tissue in *Syritta*.

The transformed images are used as input to a neural network which acts as a flight control system (FCS). The output of the FCS network represents the degrees of freedom of flight used in gaze-control by hoverflies. The intention is to create trained networks which can replicate, to some degree of accuracy, the classic optomotor reflex and target-tracking behaviour of real flies [16, 14]. Trained FCS networks can operate as closed-loop servo controllers in the hoverfly simulator. For this reason, the outputs of the FCS network (i.e. movement commands) at time t affect the input to the network (i.e. the retinal image) at time $t + \Delta t$.

This provision of sensorimotor feedback through the environment in which the simulated fly exists is the most important aspect of the simulator, and is necessary in order to give the model a meaningful semantics. This point is discussed in greater detail in the section below on computational neuroethology. The use of such "closed-environment simulators" is not common in neural network modelling, but a few other researchers do employ such techniques [29]. Closed-environment simulation allows for direct objective comparison with natural hoverfly activity: an unusual feature in research of this type.

The simulated fly is referred to as *Syritta computatrix*, the computational hoverfly, after Arbib's *Rana computatrix* [2]. To avoid confusion, *Syritta* is used only as an abbreviation for *S. pipiens*; *S. computatrix* is abbreviated to SYCO.

3.2 Panned Eyes

The simulator is currently being used to study the optomotor response. The optomotor response is a simple visual reflex that has been investigated in detail by biologists. Basically, the optomotor response helps maintain flight in a desired direction: it corrects against undesired rotations caused by winds or turbulence.

The standard experimental apparatus in optomotor studies (see Figure 1) involves tethering a fly in the centre of a cylinder. The cylinder has vertical stripes painted on the inside, and it can rotate under motor control. As the cylinder rotates, the fly turns in the same direction and at approximately the same speed as the cylinder, thereby minimising the movement of the retinal image (i.e. optic flow). This operation is much like 'panning' with a movie camera, where the camera is rotated about a single axis so as to follow a subject moving along the ground; the same principle applies to panned eyes.

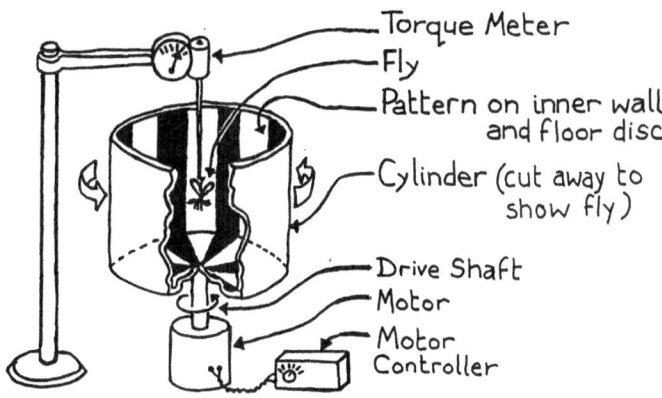

Figure 1: A typical optomotor experiment.

Such an experimental environment is simulated for SYCO. Figure 2 shows an image from inside the cylinder, while Figure 3 illustrates a similar view, the difference being that the second image has been ray-traced using an eye-model based on the anatomy and optics of *Syritta*. This is, as far as I'm aware, the first synthetic view through the eyes of the hoverfly. Figure 3 illustrates well the binocular and foveal aspects of *Syritta*'s vision.

Current research is concentrating on the flight control system (FCS). The intention is to construct a network model capable of replicating optomotor behaviour. This requires two theories. First, a theory of visual motion detection is required, because SYCO must be capable of perceiving the direction and speed of movements in the retinal image. Second, a theory is required that accounts for how the motion information is used in order to generate the required movement of the fly; this is a theory of the control architecture of the fly.

Briefly, the theory of motion detection being developed is not based on a Reichardtian motion detector (e.g. [35]). Rather, motion detection using spatial gradient in $x - y - t$ space [1] is being investigated; recent experimental evidence [27] indicates that the human visual system employs gradient detectors. The control architecture is also relatively novel. Rather than employ the standard hierarchical *efference copy hypothesis* model of visual feedback control (e.g. [9, p.342ff.]), a heterarchical control architecture (e.g. [8, pp.248–251]) is being investigated, using Brooks's *subsumption architecture* [5]. All of this work is at an early stage, and currently there are no significant results to report. Further details of this work are given in [10, 13].

Dynamic Frame: TICK=0000000001   TIME=00:00:00.02

Figure 2: View from inside the cylinder, about one third of a radius from the centre and at an altitude about one quarter of the vertical extent of the cylinder. The angle of view corresponds approximately to that given by a 17mm lens on a 35mm camera.

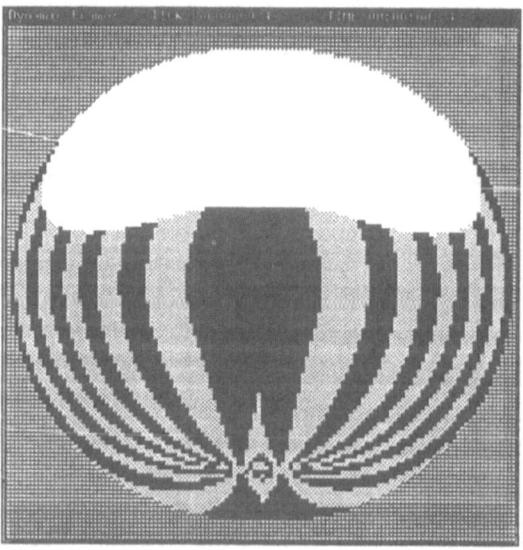

Figure 3: View through the SYCO eye-model; location in cylinder is similar to that of the previous figure. Resolution of this image is approximately that of *Syritta*'s eyes. The centre of the floor disc appears twice because it is within the binocular area of the field of view. The increased resolution towards the centre of the image leads to the 'bulging' appearance of the walls.

3.3   Statistics

A variety of techniques are being employed in the construction of the FCS. Early work involved attempting to use established neural network techniques, such as back-propagation [32], to make a 'blank' FCS network learn to perform the task. This approach proved to be impracticable. Essentially, the necessary network size (and hence the amount of training data needed) would require vast computational and storage resources. There is also an increasing body of anecdotal evidence that techniques such as back-propagation suffer badly from scaling problems.

Current work is concentrating on the use of established statistical techniques which either underly conventional neural-network research [37], or are more efficient [25].

Recent neural network literature shows a growing shift towards explaining network learning in statistical terms (e.g. [20, 23, 24]), and experimental evidence is also being accounted for by statistical models (e.g. [30, 34]).

The move to statistical techniques is a response to the *ad hoc* nature of much neural network research. Too many advocates of neural networks show a minimal understanding of the mechanisms underlying the techniques they employ; this failing is often obscured by the difficulty of interpreting the distributed representations found in neural networks[2]. At the other extreme, there appears to be a sizeable number of neural network researchers who suffer from a "physics mentality", believing in the primacy of reducing neural activity to a neat set of equations. Researchers with a physics mentality run the risk of being seduced by maths at the cost of biological feasibility: in the limit, they create elegant models with no explanatory power [17, 11, 12].

No claims of biological validity are attempted in justifying the use of statistical methods. They are just more efficient network learning techniques, searching for high-order correlations in the input-space of the network (cf. [31]). It is the final, trained, networks that are of interest. Units in the trained networks will be compared to known neurological data concerning visual guidance of flight in flies (e.g. [15]).

4   COMPUTATIONAL NEUROETHOLOGY

Two aspects of this work are notably different from the majority of neural network research: the focus on a primitive animal such as the hoverfly; and the embedding, via a sensorimotor system, of the simulated neural system within an environment.

These aspects are not incidental. They allow for the study of simulated neural systems, but in a manner that differs markedly from conventional computational neuroscience: the outputs of the model are expressed in terms of behaviour of the simulated animal.

In this respect, the work does not belong to mainstream "computational neuroscience" [33], but is more akin to "computational neuroethology" [11, 12]. Neuroethology is the study of the neural basis of behaviour (e.g. [9, 21]). There are few instances of computational neuroethology in the literature other than Arbib's [2] work.

---

[2]For example, at a major European conference in 1989, only one connectionist paper was accepted. This paper employed back-propagation to create a network. Both the author and the referees missed the fact that the network was underconstrained and was merely performing table-lookup. Simple algebra from network statistics explicit in the paper would have revealed this. No names, no pack-drill.

This type of model offers an important advantage, which conventional neural network models do not have: results from a closed-environment simulator are *observed*, not *interpreted*.

In conventional computational neuroscience, the activation values of units in the network are normally assigned an interpretation (or "meaning") by the person who designs the network. Outside a sensorimotor context, there are no constraints on the assignment of meaning: in the final analysis, the semantics of the system are arbitrary because they are dependent on the intentions of the network designer. The symbols in the system (i.e. activation levels) are not grounded (cf. [18]), and so the results require *subjective* interpretation.

This is not the case if the network is connected to a sensorimotor system, because the meaning of a unit's activation value in the network depends on that unit's interaction with the sensorimotor system, and hence with the environment. In this sense, the symbols in a sensorimotor neural network are grounded by the environmental linkage, and so results from the network can simply be observed: there is less requirement for interpretation; and the semantics of the system are no longer arbitrary.

Essentially, it is the above argument that forms the case for computational neuroethology: it is an attempt to eliminate the arbitrary semantic nature characteristic of many neural network simulations within the computational neuroscience canon. This was only a cursory overview of the argument. For further details see [11, 12].

A requirement of this style of computational neuroethology is therefore that the model neural network has full sensorimotor linkage to an environment (which can be either the real world or a simulated one). This entails a need for a continuous path through the model network from sensory input to motor output. A manifest implication of this is that studying aspects of human (or even mammalian) cognition will require very large model networks indeed.

For this reason, I advocate an evolutionist approach, where animals at the bottom of the phylogenetic hierarchy are studied before we attempt to understand more highly developed creatures, such as ourselves. The style of computational neuroethology advocated here is particularly extreme. A slogan for this approach might be *insects first, people later*. By definition, the general principles of intelligence and cognition will be those that are shared between a large number of species.

For vision research at least, it seems strange that (post-Marr [26]) few people question the "intellectually bottom-up" approach, where low-level function, such as edge detection or depth perception, is studied before high-level function such as the appreciation of abstract art. Yet few researchers question the naive arrogance of attempting to understand the human visual system at the neuronal level before we even have an understanding of the neural basis of (e.g.) visual function in honeybees.

Such an approach is not without precedent, (geneticists spent decades studying a small fruitfly, *Drosophila Melanogaster*), and is rapidly gaining support (the first international conference on artificial animals, SAB90 [28], attracted over 160 participants). This approach has serious implications for the study of the neural basis of language, but that's another story [11, 12].

5   CONCLUSIONS

The work aims to contribute to the fields of motion detection, and network-level control theories for non-URIA AAV. Additionally, it is intended to further the development of computational neuroethology as a distinct research paradigm. Currently the main practical result is the generation of the view through SYCO's eyes, but the philosophy underlying this project is just as important: the meaning of the SYCO network models will not be arbitrary. Study cognition in lower animals before tackling the most developed animals of all, for surely the simple animals will be understood first. We should walk before we run.

References

[1] E. H. Adelson and J. R. Bergen. Spatiotemporal energy models for the perception of motion. *J. Opt. Soc. Am. A*, 2(2):284–299, February 1985.

[2] M. A. Arbib. Levels of modelling of mechanisms of visually guided behaviour. *The Behavioral and Brain Sciences*, 10:407–465, 1987.

[3] D. H. Ballard. Eye movements and spatial cognition. TR 218, University of Rochester Computer Science Department, November 1987.

[4] D. H. Ballard. Reference frames for animate vision. In *Proc. IJCAI*, pages 1635–1641, 1989.

[5] R. A. Brooks. A robust layered control system for a mobile robot. A.I. Memo 864, M.I.T. A.I. Lab, September 1985.

[6] C. M. Brown. Predictive gaze control. In *Proceedings of the Fifth Alvey Vision Conference*, pages 103–108, 1989.

[7] C. M. Brown, editor. The Rochester Robot. TR 257, University of Rochester Computer Science Department, August 1988.

[8] V. Bruce and P. R. Green. *Visual Perception: physiology, psychology and ecology*. Lawrence Erlbaum Associates, London, 1985.

[9] J. M. Camhi. *Neuroethology: Nerve Cells and the Natural Behaviour of Animals*. Sinauer Associates Inc., Sunderland, Mass., 1984.

[10] D. T. Cliff. The computational hoverfly; a study in computational neuroethology. In J.-A. Meyer and S. W. Wilson, editors, *From Animals to Animats: Proceedings of the First International Conference on the Simulation of Adaptive Behaviour*, Cambridge MA, 1990. M.I.T. Press — Bradford Books.

[11] D. T. Cliff. Computational neuroethology: A provisional manifesto. CSRP 162, University of Sussex School of Cognitive and Computing Sciences, May 1990.

[12] D. T. Cliff. Computational neuroethology: A provisional manifesto. In J.-A. Meyer and S. W. Wilson, editors, *From Animals to Animats: Proceedings of the First International Conference on the Simulation of Adaptive Behaviour*, Cambridge MA, 1990. M.I.T. Press — Bradford Books.

[13] D. T. Cliff. Network control for animate vision with nonuniform sampling. CSRP 163, University of Sussex School of Cognitive and Computing Sciences, 1990. Forthcoming.

[14] T. S. Collett. Some operating rules for the optomotor system of a hoverfly during voluntary flight. *Journal of Comparative Physiology A*, 138:271–282, 1980.

[15] T. S. Collett and A. J. King. Vision during flight. In G. A. Horridge, editor, *The compound eye and vision of insects*, pages 437–466. Clarendon, Oxford, 1975.

[16] T. S. Collett and M. F. Land. Visual control of flight behaviour in the hoverfly, *Syritta pipiens* L. *Journal of Comparative Physiology*, 99:1–66, 1975.

[17] F. Crick. The recent excitement about neural networks. *Nature*, 337:129–132, January 1989.

[18] S. Harnad. The symbol grounding problem. In *CNLS Conference on Emergent Computation*, Los Alamos, May 1989. Submitted to Physica D.

[19] D. Hearn and P. M. Baker. *Computer Graphics*. Prentice Hall International, Englewood Cliffs NJ, 1986.

[20] G. E. Hinton and S. Becker. An unsupervised learning procedure that discovers surfaces in random-dot stereograms. In *International Joint Conference on Neural Networks*, Washington DC, January 1990.

[21] G. Hoyle. The scope of neuroethology. *The Behavioral and Brain Sciences*, 7:367–412, 1984.

[22] M. F. Land. Similarities in the visual behaviour of arthropods and men. In M. S. Gazzaniga and C. Blakemore, editors, *Handbook of Psychobiology*, pages 49–72. Academic Press, New York, 1975.

[23] R. Linsker. Designing a sensory processing system: What can be learned from principle component analysis? Research Report RC 14983, I.B.M. T. J. Watson Research Centre, Yorktown Heights, NY, September 1989.

[24] R. Linsker. How to generate ordered maps by maximising the mutual information between input and output signals. Research Report RC 14624, I.B.M. T. J. Watson Research Centre, Yorktown Heights, NY, May 1989.

[25] M. R. Lynch and P. J. Rayner. The properties and implementation of the non-linear vector space connectionist model. In *First IEE International Conference on Artificial Neural Networks*, pages 186–190, London, October 1989. IEE.

[26] D. Marr. *Vision*. W. H. Freeman, New York, 1982.

[27] G. Mather, B. Moulden, and A. O'Halloran. Polarity specific adaptation to motion: evidence for gradient detectors, 1990. preprint.

[28] J.-A. Meyer and S. W. Wilson, editors. *From Animals to Animats: Proceedings of the First International Conference on the Simulation of Adaptive Behaviour*. M.I.T. Press — Bradford Books, Cambridge MA, 1990.

[29] D. Parisi, F. Cecconi, and S. Nolfi. Econets: Neural networks that learn in an environment. *Network*, 1:149–168, 1990.

[30] M. G. Paulin, M. E. Nelson, and J. M. Bower. Dynamics of compensatory eye movement control: An optimal estimation analysis of the vestibulo-ocular reflex. *International Journal of Neural Systems*, 1(1):23–29, 1989.

[31] T. Poggio and F. Girosi. A theory of networks for approximation and learning. A.I. Memo 1140, M.I.T. A.I. Lab, July 1989.

[32] D. E. Rumelhart, G. E. Hinton, and R. J. Williams. Learning internal representations by error propagation. In D. E. Rumelhart and J. L. McClelland, editors, *Parallel Distributed Processing, Volume 1: Foundations*, pages 318–362. M.I.T. Press — Bradford Books, Cambridge MA, 1986.

[33] T. J. Sejnowski, C. Koch, and P. S. Churchland. Computational neuroscience. *Science*, 241:1299–1306, September 1988.

[34] M. V. Srinivasan, S. B. Laughlin, and A. Dubs. Predictive coding: a fresh view of inhibition in the retina. *Proc. R. Soc. Lond. B*, 216:427–459, 1982.

[35] J. P. H. van Santen and G. Sperling. Elaborated Reichardt detectors. *Journal of the Optical Society of America A*, 2(2):300–320, February 1985.

[36] A. B. Watson. Detection and recognition of simple spatial forms. In O. J. Braddick and A. C. Sleigh, editors, *Physical and Biological Processing of Images*, pages 100–114. Springer-Verlag, Berlin, 1983.

[37] H. White. Learning in artificial networks: A statistical perspective. *Neural Computation*, 1:415–424, 1989.

[38] S. W. Wilson. Adaptive "cortical" pattern recognition. In *Proceedings of the International Conference on Genetic Algorithms and Their Application*, Pittsburg, PA, July 1985.

[39] D. S. Young. Logarithmic sampling of images for computer vision. In A. G. Cohn, editor, *Proceedings of the Seventh conference of the Society for the Study of Artificial Intelligence and Simulation of Behaviour*, pages 145–150, London, April 1989. Pitman/Morgan Kaufmann.

Specifying Complex Behavior for Computer Agents

Leslie Pack Kaelbling*
Teleos Research
576 Middlefield Road
Palo Alto, California, 94301 USA

ABSTRACT

It is very difficult to specify behaviors for agents that must operate in complex environments. A variety of formalisms have been developed for specifying behaviors for computer agents, including the general paradigms of "classical planning" and "reactive behavior." These formalisms represent points in a complexity space that has as two of its most important dimensions (1) ease of expression of complex action strategies by the human programmer, and (2) efficiency of execution of formal behavioral specification by the agent. This paper will focus on three different methods for specifying behaviors for agents: direct programming, operator descriptions, and goal reduction rules. These will serve as example formalisms and form a basis for discussion of the ease of human programming, the ease of automatic execution, and the value of compilation.

1 INTRODUCTION

Consider the problem of programming computer-controlled agents to behave in complex environments. These agents might be robot arms that assemble cars, household assistants that do the laundry and take out the trash, or database agents that schedule appointments and keep computer files up to date. Such agents must interact with a world that is dynamic and is predictable in some respects but highly unpredictable in others.

---

*This work was supported in part by the Air Force Office of Scientific Research under contract F49620-89-C-0055DEF, in part by the National Aeronautics and Space Administration under Cooperative Agreement NCC-2-494 through Stanford University subcontract PR-6359, and by the Defense Advanced Research Projects Agency through NASA contract NAS2-13229.

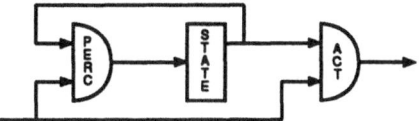

Figure 1: Framework for embedded computation, divided into perception and action functions.

In recent years, a wide range of formalisms have been developed for specifying behaviors for computer agents, including the general paradigms of "classical planning" and "reactive behavior." These formalisms represent points in a complexity space that has as two of its most important dimensions

- ease of expression of complex action strategies by the human programmer

- efficiency of execution of formal behavioral specification by the agent

There is no single formalism that is most appropriate for all problems of agent behavior specification. By studying the properties of various behavior-specification formalisms and of the settings of particular problems, we can choose formalisms appropriately.

This paper will focus on three different methods for specifying behaviors for agents: direct programming, operator descriptions, and goal reduction rules. These will serve as example formalisms that will allow us to discuss ease of human programming, ease of automatic execution, and the value of compilation.

2   FRAMEWORK

In order to make the following discussion precise, we must assume a concrete model of the agent's interaction with its environment. This discussion will be based on a model of computation in which an agent is seen to perform a finite transduction from a stream of input data into a stream of output data (this model also forms the foundation of *situated-automata theory* [Rosenschein, 1985, Rosenschein and Kaelbling, 1986]). The agent receives an input from the environment, updates its internal state as a function of the input and the state value, then outputs that action, effecting the world. This cycle happens at regular intervals that are timed in a way that allows the agent to keep pace with the important events in its environment (this pace may vary from 100 cycles per second in an automatic-pilot system to 1 cycle per day in a system that does inventory management in a store).

The job of an agent designer, then, is to specify the state-update and output functions, which make up the agent's program. We shall refer to them as the *perception* and *action* functions, as shown in Figure 1. We require the computation time of these functions to have a finite upper bound. This bound will guarantee that the agent can react with appropriate speed to external events by having a bounded delay between the arrival of any given input and the generation of an output that depends on that input. This paper is primarily concerned with the specification of the action function.

Another popular computational model for embedded agents is one of many concurrent processes. Typically, one process runs with a guaranteed fixed cycle time, and its outputs can be influenced by the results of other processes as they are completed. This is a useful model, especially appropriate for machines with coarse-grained processor parallelism, but it makes the semantic analysis of the computation performed by the agent quite difficult. The exact meaning of the result of any computation depends crucially on how much time has passed since the inputs to the computation were sensed by the agent; this is more difficult to measure and keep track of in a concurrent-process model than in the simple circuit model of Figure 1.

One important thing to note is that, in this framework, "perceptual actions" that are performed to gain information are not distinguished from actions in general. One reason for treating all actions uniformly is that perceptual actions may be externally indistinguishable from other actions and use the same resources: a robot may put its hand on a table to steady the table or to find out if it is clear. We must, then, consider all actions together in attempting to determine which one is most appropriate to execute.

This paper considers different ways in which programmers can specify the mapping from an agent's perceptual state (current values of the internal state and input vectors) into an action; we shall refer to this mapping as the *action map*.

3   SPECIFYING ACTION MAPS

There is a wide variety of formalisms that may be used by a human programmer to specify the action map for an agent. It is widely held to be easier for humans to program in formalisms that allow a modular, declarative expression of the program, rather than a direct procedural account. This point is discussed at length by Winograd [Winograd, 1985] in connection with the general knowledge-representation problem. This section will address the use of three different types of formalisms for specifying actions maps, leaving issues of executability for discussion in the following section.

3.1   Direct programming

The most traditional method of supplying the action map for an agent is to use the standard methods of computer programming. Using a functional or procedural programming language, the programmer can specify the function that should be computed to generate each new action.

In simple domains, especially those to which the methods of control theory can be applied, this approach is quite adequate. In many domains, for example, there is a simple numerical functional relationship between output values and input values, which can be easily specified in a traditional programming language.

Another situation for which this method is appropriate is when the programmer has complete information about the initial state of the world and about the effects of the agent's actions on the world. In this case, the agent's program can typically be written as a list of actions, which the agent executes one-by-one, ignoring the input values from the world. Domains that are this benevolent and understandable are rare, but the approach has been used successfully for "sequencing" unmanned space missions and for programming highly constrained robotic assembly tasks.

In most other cases, the actions that an agent should take are highly conditional on the perceptual state, requiring a large and complex computer program. Of course, any action map can be specified this way, but direct programming can become very tedious and difficult for the programmer.

3.2 Classical Operator Descriptions

The standard artificial intelligence (AI) technique for specifying an action map is to give a description of the abilities of the agent, a description of a desired goal state of the world, and a description of the initial state of the world. From this information and the assumption that the agent should act in such a way as to cause the world to satisfy the goal-state description, it is possible to derive the next action that should be taken by the agent by finding a string of actions that, if executed starting in any state satisfying the initial state description, will cause the world to be in some state satisfying the goal state description. The agent's abilities are typically described using an operator description language. In this language, each possible action of the agent is characterized by a set of preconditions and a set of postconditions. If the preconditions are true in the world and the agent performs the action, then the postconditions will be true in the world. The descriptions of the initial and goal states of the world do necessarily correspond to completely individuated perceptual states. In general, they can be arbitrarily general or specific. If the initial state description is *true*, then the agent must act without assuming anything about the initial state of the world. This process is typically referred to as "planning" and has a large related literature [Allen *et al.*, 1990].

Using operator descriptions to specify action maps is very appealing. It allows the programmer to write a declarative specification in terms of facts about the world and the abilities of the agent; this makes the task less like regular programming and (theoretically) easier for non-professionals. Another benefit is that, once the agent's abilities have been described in the operator description language, generating a new action map amounts to specifying new initial state and goal state descriptions. Finally, this finite description of the operators and the initial and goal states may engender behaviors of arbitrary complexity; there is no bound on the number of actions that can be strung together to achieve the goal.

This approach has a number of drawbacks, as well.

First, the semantics of the operator descriptions can rarely be satisfied in the real world. The effects of low-level operations, such as sending a voltage to a wheel in a mobile robot, cannot be modeled reliably at a level of abstraction for which planning is appropriate. Higher level actions that have non-deterministic results might be usefully modeled with probabilistic operator descriptions.

In addition, operator-description languages are typically oriented toward single goals of achievement, but it is often useful to supply a goal of maintenance like "don't spill the milk." Goals of maintenance could be added to such a framework by adding a third component to operator descriptions describing which conditions are maintained. Although this extension is theoretically possible, it gives rise to an explicit version of the frame problem [Hayes, 1990], in which a possibly infinite number of maintained conditions would have to be specified for each operation.

3.3 Goal Reduction Rules

There are many formalisms that lie between direct programming and operator descriptions on the procedural-declarative spectrum. One is goal reduction rules.

Gapps [Kaelbling, 1988] is a declarative language in which the programmer writes a set of instantaneous goal-reduction rules. These rules, together with a top-level goal description, specify an action map for the agent. The goal-reduction rules specify how to take the top-level goal and, depending on the current state of the world, reduce it to another top-level goal. Eventually the reduction process bottoms out in an action that is correct to execute given the current state of the world.

The use of goal-reduction rules moves some of the burden of "plan synthesis" from the agent to the programmer, but allows easy expression of many kinds of action strategies that are difficult to encode using operator descriptions. Take, as an example, the strategy of hammering in a nail until it is flush with a board. It might be possible to describe an operator *hit-the-nail* that has as its post-condition that the nail is some fraction of an inch farther into the board than it was, or one called *probably-hit-the-nail* that 10% of the time has as its postcondition that the nail is flush with the board. Both of these uses of operator descriptions require fairly sophisticated plan synthesis methods. The simple goal-reduction rule captures the commonsense knowledge that if your goal is to have the nail be flush with the board and the nail is not yet flush with the board, you should hit the nail.

```
(defgoalr (ach nail-flush-with-board)
    (if (nail-not-flush-with-board)
        (do hit-the-nail)
        (do anything)))
```

Rather than saying exactly what the effects of an operation are, the user specifies under which environmental conditions an action is appropriately performed. In the goal-reduction approach, the initial condition of the world need not be specified; instead, the world is monitored as the agent interacts with it, and each action is selected on the basis of the currently perceived state of the world rather than on its predicted state. This makes it easy to specify action mappings for domains in which the effects of individual actions are quite unreliable.

One drawback of goal-reduction rules in comparison with operator descriptions is that the programmer must provide a reduction rule for any primitive goal that might occur. This is in contrast to the operator-description approach, in which any formula in the formal language used to specify the domain could, potentially be used as a goal.

4 EXECUTING ACTION MAPS

Once the programmer has specified an action map, it must be executed by the agent. The degree of difficulty of this execution depends on the nature of the language used to specify the map. It can vary from trivial to nearly impossible. This section considers the computational aspects of executing specifications written in each of the specification languages discussed above.

4.1 Direct programming

Languages used for direct programming are designed to be compiled and executed directly by the agent's computer. In using such languages, it is incumbent upon the programmer to guarantee that the computation time for the state-update and action functions is bounded. This problem can be avoided by using a language, such as Rex [Kaelbling, 1987b] or a more standard real-time programming language and operating system, that guarantees response time.

4.2 Operator Descriptions

Operator description languages are not directly executable by an agent. The standard execution model is to search for a sequence of actions that will take the agent from any state satisfying the initial state description to some state satisfying the goal state description. Having found this sequence, the agent should take the first action. In order to avoid repeating this work, this process is often divided into two phases: planning and execution. In the planning phase, the search is done and the chain of actions stored. In the execution phase, the actions are simply emitted in sequence with no regard to the state of the world. More sophisticated systems of this type perform "execution monitoring" in which the planning phase records the expected state of the world between the actions. The execution phase then monitors the execution of the plan, making sure that the world satisfies the descriptions of the expected intermediate states. If it does not, the system reverts to the planning phase with a description of the current state of the world as the initial state.

Chapman has shown that the planning phase in such a system is, in the general case, undecidable [Chapman, 1987]; for very restricted operator-description languages, it is merely intractable, with the time it takes to find a plan increasing exponentially in the number of operators. Because the agent must complete the planning phase before it takes its first action, this sort of execution of operator descriptions does not satisfy the requirements of having a constant bound on the reaction time of the agent. Additionally, an advantage that we cited of operator-description languages, that a small description could generate an arbitrarily long program, is a detriment for execution, because arbitrarily long programs take exponentially more time to generate.

Also, if it takes too long to perform the planning phase, the information upon which it was based, especially the initial state description, may change, invalidating the entire plan. A good execution monitoring system might notice this before any wrong action was taken and cause the planning phase to be re-entered, but this kind of behavior makes the reaction time even worse.

Despite the apparent intractability of executing operator descriptions, there are at least two ways to limit the total expressiveness of the language and make the execution compatible with a requirement for guaranteed reaction time.

4.2.1 Using Space

If we are willing to limit the scope of planning to plans of a fixed length, it is possible to do the search to that depth in an amount of time that is bounded by a constant. This can be thought of as expanding the search tree in parallel to a fixed depth all at once; hence, "using space." This process can be made even more efficient (but no longer strictly correct) if a beam search is used, assuming that at each level of the search all but a certain number of candidate plans can be pruned.

In this formulation of the planning problem, just the first step of the plan is executed. The next time the action function is called, the computation is repeated and, again, the first step is executed. This planning and execution style does no caching of plans and is, therefore, not in danger of diverging from the expected execution path in the world. The disadvantage is that the time-constant required to do this computation may be too large for many systems (on current hardware) to keep up with their environment.

4.2.2 Using Time

An alternative to computing a fixed-length plan on every cycle is to express the planning process as an incremental computation, which is carried out over the course of many calls to the action function. This method of "using time" requires that state be used in the computation of the action. On each call to the action function, the planning process generates an output, but it may be one that means "I don't have an answer yet." After some number of cycles (depending on the size of the planning problem) the planner will generate a real result. This result might be cached and executed as in a traditional system, or the agent might simply take the first action and wait for the planner to generate a new plan.

One advantage of organizing the computation this way is that it allows the programmer to specify a hierarchical action map. It may be that the best actions for the agent to take are those specified in the operator description language (because it is easiest for the human programmer to come to grips with the complexity of the domain in this language), but that certain instantaneous reflexive reactions can be specified in a more direct way. The agent can then execute the planner and the reflex program in parallel, performing the action suggested by the planner when there is one, and otherwise heeding its reflexes. This need not happen on just two levels; the general organization of such a system with many levels is described by Kaelbling [Kaelbling, 1987a].

We must still take care that the plan generated by the planner, given that time has passed since it began its task, is appropriate for the situation in which it is finished. This can be guaranteed if the planner monitors the conditions in the world upon which the correctness of its plan depends. If any of these conditions goes false, the planner can begin again. This is correct behavior, with the planner continuously emitting the "I don't know" output and allowing the agent to react reflexively to its environment if necessary.

Such a planner might generate a plan in the form of a linear sequence of actions or a set of condition-action rules. It is important to be able to evaluate the validity of a plan as time passes, so that the planner may be reinvoked if the execution of the plan does not take place as expected. One useful and robust way to provide a validity test is to generate a directly executable action map for some small part of the input space that the agent is likely to find itself in as it traverses a path from the current state to a goal state. The plan becomes invalid when the world enters a state for which the plan provides no action. Triangle tables [Nilsson, 1985] were a solution of this type, but they assumed that the likely deviations of the world from the intended solution path would be, themselves, to other states on that path. More general plans could be constructed by making their scope (the number of situations for which they have a reaction) somewhat larger. How large they should be depends on the nature of the domain and how likely the operators are to do what they are expected to do. Given probabilistic characterizations of the operators' effects, it is possible to generate an action map such that if the agent were to act according to the map it would, with high probability, arrive in a goal state before finding itself outside the domain of the map (a planning algorithm with similar characteristics has been developed by Drummond and Bresina [Drummond and Bresina, 1990]).

The kind of planner discussed above is a form of an anytime algorithm [Dean and Boddy, 1988]. An anytime algorithm always has an answer, but the answer improves over time. In the example given above, the answer is useless for a while, then improves in one big jump. It might be useful to have planning algorithms that improve more gradually. Such algorithms exist for certain kinds of path planning, for instance, in which some path is returned at the beginning, but the algorithm works to make the path shorter or more efficient. There is still a difficult decision to be made, however, about whether to take the first step on a plan that is known to be non-optimal or to plan for a while longer.

4.3   Goal Reduction Rules

Given a set of goal-reduction rules, an action map is specified by a top-level goal for the agent. The rules can be "executed" by using them, on each call to the action function, to reduce the top-level goal to a primitive action that is suitable for the currently-perceived state of the world. If the reduction rules are not recursive, execution time has a bound linear in the number and size of the reduction rules. If they are recursive, the goal-reduction process may not terminate, so bounded reaction time cannot be guaranteed.

5   COMPILATION

We have seen that the high-level languages in which it is convenient for human programmers to specify action maps are often intractable for an agent to execute. Conversely, languages that can be efficiently executed tend to be tedious for human programmers to use. It is possible to bridge this gap, to some degree, by adding a compilation stage in which the language used by the programmer to specify the action map is translated into another language for execution by the agent. This section discusses the compilation of action maps specified as operator descriptions and as goal reduction rules, then considers when it is desirable to perform this compilation.[1]

5.1   Compiling operator descriptions

Operator descriptions can be compiled into a directly executable language. If the initial state description and the goal state description are known at compile time *and* the world is completely deterministic and the operator descriptions absolutely correct, then compilation can simply be planning. The result would be a list of actions to be taken by the agent. This is a very limited approach, because it assumes that the agent has some fixed goal of achievement (unless the planner is a very sophisticated one, capable of synthesizing plans with loops and conditionals, a goal of maintenance would require an infinite list of actions).

---

[1]In the terms used by Russell to discuss knowledge compilation [Russell, 1989], the methods described in this section perform heterogeneous compilation, mapping knowledge of types A, B, and F into knowledge of type D.

When a description of the goal state is known, but the initial state is not known or when the operator descriptions are not completely reliable, descriptions of the goal and the operators can be compiled into an action map specified by a set of condition-action rules. The rules map every possible situation into an action that, according to the operator descriptions, is a useful step toward the goal.

Schoppers' algorithm for synthesizing universal plans [Schoppers, 1989] performs compilation of this sort, although the reaction time of the compiled code may not have a constant bound on execution time.

A disadvantage of compiling operator descriptions into condition-action rules is that very large program structures can result, and although they are as robust as possible, the majority of the program will never be consulted. Additionally, the top-level goal is frozen into the compiled structure.

5.2 Compiling goal-reduction rules

The Gapps language includes an algorithm for compiling a set of goal-reduction rules and a top-level goal into a set of condition-action rules. Whereas the goal-reduction rules could not, in general, be executed by the agent in bounded time, the condition action rules are efficiently executable. To enable this compilation, the top-level goal must be fixed at compile time. It is still possible for the compiled program to respond to externally specified run-time goals, but the goal-reduction mechanism cannot be used at run time [Kaelbling, 1988].

The Gapps compilation procedure described above can be used, in conjunction with standard operators described in terms of a regression function, to compile a set of operator descriptions and a top-level goal into a set of condition-action rules. This compilation method requires that the operator descriptions be used to define a function (regress p alpha), which returns the weakest condition in the world such that, if operator alpha is executed, p will be true.

```
(defgoalr (ach p)
    (if (regress p alpha)
        (do alpha)
        (ach (regress p alpha)))))
```

This goal-reduction rule says that the goal of achieving a condition p can be reduced to performing some action alpha if that action will cause p to be true in one step (the condition denoted by (regress p alpha)); otherwise, it can be reduced to the condition of being one step away from p. If the Gapps compiler is modified to have a depth bound, so that only plans of finite length may be considered, it will generate a partial action map that has an action for every situation from which the goal can be achieved in a number of steps that is less than the depth bound.

5.3 Online versus Offline Compilation

There is a middle ground between compiling all of the declarative structure and flexibility away and performing large search computations on each action step. When the agent can encounter a wide range of goals or initial states at run time, it may be more efficient to retain a compact declarative description of the agent's abilities in terms of operator descriptions or goal-reduction rules and use them to derive actions at run time. This approach is an instance of a space versus time trade-off. It would always be possible to do the complete compilation in advance, but storing the result could take a huge amount of space. In addition, we have already seen that complete direct execution of the declarative specification is intractable. Thus, for each world, agent, and task specification there is an appropriate degree of compilation.

An agent's behavior usually stems from the requirements of a number of constraints. They may be ever-present constraints, such as not running out of power or avoiding running into walls; they may be reflex constraints, such as pulling away from touching a hot object; or they may be dynamic goal constraints, such as going to the store to get a sandwich because someone asked you to. An intuitively reasonable place to divide compilation from run-time interpretation is according to when the constraints are known. Thus, all of the agent's background and reflex constraints might be compiled into a program that is intersected with a program obtained by run-time interpretation associated with a particular dynamic goal that has been received by the agent. Another intuitive dividing line would be to compile those parts of the agent's behavior that are appropriate for the situations in which it is most likely to find itself. If the agent finds itself without a compiled response to a particular situation, it can fall back on dynamic interpretation of high-level structures.

Blythe and Mitchell have explored incremental compilation methods in a mobile robot [Blythe and Mitchell, 1989]. The robot uses a traditional planner to solve problems initially, but it caches the results of the planning as situation-action rules. Whenever the robot re-encounters a situation, it can act reactively. This is a relatively simple but reliable way to ensure that the agent can react quickly to common occurrences.

6 CONCLUSION

The selection of a formalism for specifying the action map of an embedded agent is much the same as the selection of a programming language for a conventional programming project. Two important considerations are the ease of use of the formalism for the agent's designer and the efficiency of execution of the formalism by the agent. These two considerations are often in direct conflict, but that conflict can be mediated very successfully by a variety of compilation methods. It is an important research direction to develop new compilation methods, exploring the trade-offs between efficiency of the compiler and efficiency of the compiled code and between online and offline compilation.

Acknowledgments

Many of these ideas are a result of joint work with Stan Rosenschein. This paper was also influenced by helpful discussions with David Chapman on action formalisms as programming languages.

References

[Allen *et al.*, 1990] James Allen, James Hendler, and Austin Tate, editors. *Readings in Planning*. Morgan Kaufmann, San Mateo, California, 1990.

[Blythe and Mitchell, 1989] Jim Blythe and Tom M. Mitchell. On becoming reactive. In *Proceedings of the Sixth International Workshop on Machine Learning*, pages 255–257, Ithaca, New York, 1989. Morgan Kaufmann.

[Chapman, 1987] David Chapman. Planning for conjunctive goals. *Artificial Intelligence*, 32(3):333–378, 1987.

[Dean and Boddy, 1988] Thomas Dean and Mark Boddy. An analysis of time-dependent planning. In *Proceedings of the Seventh National Conference on Artificial Intelligence*, Minneapolis-St. Paul, Minnesota, 1988.

[Drummond and Bresina, 1990] Mark Drummond and John Bresina. Anytime synthetic projection. In *Proceedings of the Eighth National Conference on Artificial Intelligence*, pages 138–144, Boston, Massachusetts, 1990. Morgan Kaufmann.

[Hayes, 1990] Patrick J. Hayes. The frame problem and related problems in artificial intelligence. In James Allen, James Hendler, and Austin Tate, editors, *Readings in Planning*. Morgan Kaufmann, San Mateo, California, 1990.

[Kaelbling, 1987a] Leslie Pack Kaelbling. An architecture for intelligent reactive systems. In Michael P. Georgeff and Amy L. Lansky, editors, *Reasoning About Actions and Plans*, pages 395–410. Morgan Kaufmann, 1987. Reprinted in *Readings in Planning*, J. Allen, J. Hendler, and A. Tate, eds., Morgan Kaufmann, 1990.

[Kaelbling, 1987b] Leslie Pack Kaelbling. Rex: A symbolic language for the design and parallel implementation of embedded systems. In *Proceedings of the AIAA Conference on Computers in Aerospace*, Wakefield, Massachusetts, 1987.

[Kaelbling, 1988] Leslie Pack Kaelbling. Goals as parallel program specifications. In *Proceedings of the Seventh National Conference on Artificial Intelligence*, Minneapolis-St. Paul, Minnesota, 1988.

[Nilsson, 1985] Nils J. Nilsson. Triangle tables: A proposal for a robot programming language. Technical Report 347, Artificial Intelligence Center, SRI International, Menlo Park, California, 1985.

[Rosenschein and Kaelbling, 1986] Stanley J. Rosenschein and Leslie Pack Kaelbling. The synthesis of digital machines with provable epistemic properties. In Joseph Halpern, editor, *Proceedings of the Conference on Theoretical Aspects of Reasoning About Knowledge*, pages 83–98. Morgan Kaufmann, 1986. An updated version appears as Technical Note 412, Artificial Intelligence Center, SRI International, Menlo Park, California.

[Rosenschein, 1985] Stanley J. Rosenschein. Formal theories of knowledge in AI and robotics. *New Generation Computing*, 3(4):345–357, 1985.

[Russell, 1989] Stuart J. Russell. Execution architectures and compilation. In *Proceedings of the Eleventh International Joint Conference on Artificial Intelligence*, pages 15–20, Detroit, Michigan, 1989. Morgan Kaufmann.

[Schoppers, 1989] Marcel J. Schoppers. *Representation and Automatic Synthesis of Reaction Plans*. PhD thesis, University of Illinois at Urbana-Champaign, Urbana, Illinois, 1989.

[Winograd, 1985] Terry Winograd. Frame representations and the declarative/procedural controversy. In Ronald J. Brachman and Hector J. Levesque, editors, *Readings in Knowledge Representation*. Morgan Kaufmann, 1985.

NEW MODES OF REASONING

Integrating Neural Network and Expert Reasoning: An Example

James Hendler[1]
Leonard Dickens

Department of Computer Science
University of Maryland
College Park, MD 20742

ABSTRACT

In this paper we describe a shell which has been developed to allow an integration of neural network and expert systems technology. The system, SCRuFFy, is based on an analysis of the different abilities and time courses of NN and AI systems. Critical to the processing of this system is a temporal pattern matcher which is used to mediate between the two subsystems, providing a "signal to symbol" mapping. This mapping allows the expert system to reason about the time course of signals which are classified by a connectionist network which is trained via classical back-propagation of error during a separate training phase. An example of the simulated control of the temperature of an underwater welding robot is presented to demonstrate these capabilities.

INTRODUCTION

Steels (1989) has pointed out that connectionist networks can perform heuristic classification tasks in a matter different than, but comparable to, the heuristic classification used in many expert systems. He argues that the distinction of which to use should be based on an analysis of features of the domain, rather than based on pre-theoretical biases. In addition he outlines a set of criteria to determine those situations in which a statistically-based classification method (such as the connectionist back-propagation algorithm) can be used: the cost of observation should be low, the features of the class may or may not all be present, the set of classes is known prior to classification time, the categorizations are based on statistical criteria, and hierarchical structure of the classes is either not necessary or used in only a limited manner.

One type of operation fitting these criteria is the categorization of sensor signals into classes. Typically, sensor data is obtained cheaply at a high rate of speed, features of the class may be underdetermined (necessitating a learning algorithm), classification of the signals is desired to match known categories, classification is based on high-order statistical correlations between features in the signal, and no hierarchical categorization of the signals is typically performed. Thus, it is no surprise that one of the greatest successes of connectionist models is in the classification of sensor signals.

Making intelligent decisions based on signals received from sensors,however,

[1]e-mail: hendler@cs.umd.edu. Dr. Hendler is supported in part by ONR grant N00014-88-K-0560 and NSF grant IRI-8907890 and by the UM Systems Research Center.

does not fit these criteria at all. Such decisions may require merging a long time history of sensor results, all features of a situation may need to be present before expensive corrective operations would be authorized, the set of all possible problems may not be known, the recognition of a problem is often context dependent, and hierarchical structure is often used in the decision making processes. Thus, the connectionist approach seems less suited to such tasks than to the classification tasks themselves, and such decision making remains the domain of traditional AI systems.

Unfortunately, this dichotomy of utility leads to a major problem for those who wish to work in domains such as those for the control of mechanical systems in which sensor feedback is needed to monitor the status of ongoing processes. For example, given an automated robot working in a hostile domain (for example an underwater welder or space based system), the controller needs to interpret sensor signals to determine whether normal operating conditions are being observed, or whether some error condition is occuring. If the latter, corrective action needs to be taken – perhaps adjusting the system or even shutting it down to prevent serious damage. As argued above, this sort of application requires the classification of sensor signals, deliverable using the connectionist framework, and symbolic decision making, not well suited to that approach.

The differences in the computing metaphors underlying symbolic AI and connectionist systems have led researchers to conclude that these approaches are either separate paradigms (Smolenksy, 1990) or fill different computational niches (Dyer, 1988). Faced with developing systems needing multiple capabilities, research has generally focused on drastically extending the capabilities of one sort of reasoning or the other. This includes efforts to produce symbolic reasoning using connectionist systems (cf. Shastri, 1985) or to use traditional AI techniques to handle the sorts of perceptual tasks currently solved most successfully by connectionist networks[2].

In this paper we describe an alternative: a system which integrates a connectionist classifier and a symbolic reasoner. Based on an analysis of the differing criteria for heuristic classifiers and complex decision makers, we have targeted a hybrid system as the best way of developing applications such as the sensor-based control systems described above. To facilitate the near-term development of such systems we have been working on the development of an applications-oriented shell providing an integration of a connectionist back propagation learning network with an OPS5-based expert system development language. In this paper we describe the architecture of our system, give a simple example of its use, and describe extensions to the prototype shell which are currently uderway.

THE *SCRuFFy* HYBRID SYSTEM SHELL

We have developed the SCRuFFy[3] system as a prototype shell for the development of applications which require the merging of connectionist and symbolic techniques, such as the control systems described in the introduction. A diagram

---

[2]As an example of this, consider the work in AI models of machine vision, which often involve pushing symbolic reasoning to the pixel level (cf. Canning et.al., 1987).

[3]SCRuFFy: *S*ignals *C*onnections and *Ru*les - *F*un *F*or every*y*one.

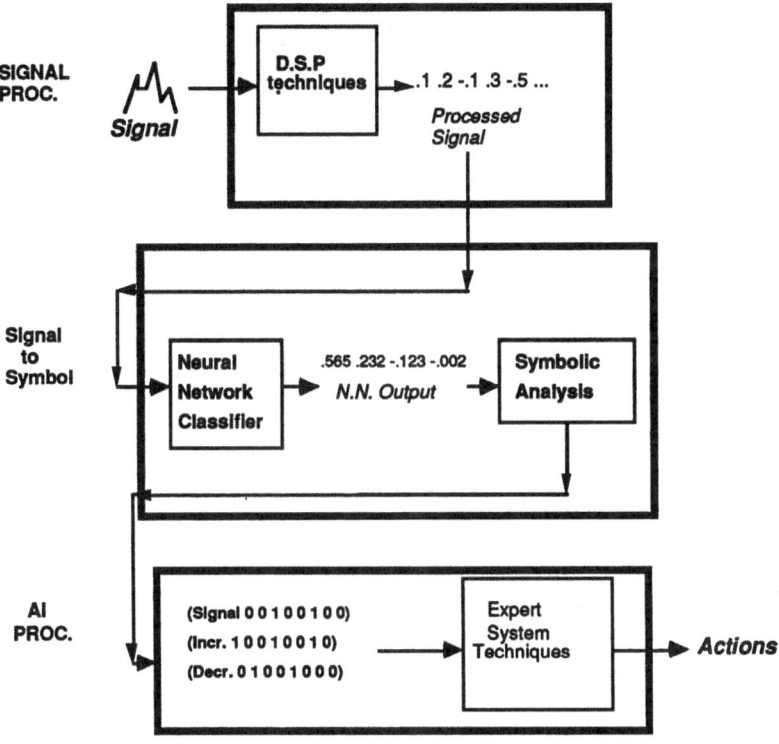

Figure 1: Flow of Control in SCRuFFy

of the flow of control in the system is shown in Figure 1. A sensor signal feeds through a digital signal processing program which converts it into a vector of discrete values. A set of known signals is gathered, and these are used to train a back propagation network to perform the signal classification task. Once the network is trained, the flow of control is for a new signal to be received, to be sampled, and to be classified using the connectionist network. The output of this process is then fed into a symbolic analysis program – a program which tracks the changes in signal classification over time and produces symbolic information describing the time course of the signal. This symbolic information is put onto a blackboard (or working memory) and thus a traditional blackboard-based expert reasoning system can make control decisions based on this information.

The heart of the SCRuFFy system is a "temporal pattern matcher", which provides an interface between the continuous signal sampling and classification, provided by the analog connectionist system, and the expert system used in making the control decisions. The pattern matcher is based on the observation that the particular activation patterns from the connectionist component for a given signal will usually be less interesting to the expert system-based reasoning than will the pattern of a set of signals over time. For example, in a simple application, we might have 10 outputs coming from the connectionist system. Two of these might be indicators of normal operation, while the 8 others represent different kinds of errors. If a controller takes no action until one of the error signals is the highest output, then this may result in drastic corrective actions needing to be taken. However, a recognition that one of the errors is increasing over time, even though it is not currently the highest value, could allow a less drastic response.

We have based our patterns on the temporal relations discussed by Allen and Koomen (1983). These include relations such as "before, after, during, etc." which are specified for temporal intervals. These patterns are used to reason about the time course of a set of signal samples, rather than a single input. The heart of the matcher is an array, which keeps track of sample values for each of the outputs produced by the connectionist classifier. (The number of past outputs stored is a user specifiable parameter.) The matcher then examines its rules to see if any of them have conditions which are satisfied[4].

Rules for the matcher are specified over intervals using predicates. For example, a rule can check for the predicate "increasing" over an interval of time. When the set of predicates are all matched, a set of associated actions can be taken. Variables can be bound, thus providing a standard production-rule-like method for associating the patterns and actions. In addition, the actions taken can include posting items on the blackboard used by the expert system. For example, the rule:

```
(R carbon-leakage
   (highest SIGNAL-B)
   (decreasing (recent ?Sigtype))
   (not (eq ?Sigtype SIGNAL-B))
 -->
   (format t "~%Carbon leakage noted!")
   (post-to-blackboard NOTED CARBON-LEAKAGE <current-time>))
```

could be used to recognize a situation where the connectionist network produces a set of outputs where signal type "B" is the highest, but a "non-B" signal is decreasing over a small set of samples[5]. When this is recognized two actions are taken: a message is printed out, and a working memory element indicating carbon leakage is posted for the expert system.

EXAMPLE

As an example of the use of SCRuFFy, we have developed a very simple expert system for the control of an underwater welding robot using information from an acoustic sensor. The system is fed an acoustic signal (which is randomly supplied via a simulator which uses actual signals sampled from a 1MHz sensor). This acoustic signal is analyzed by the back propagation network to produce a four element vector, representing the relative classification strengths of normal welding and three known error conditions. When the system notices an increasing strength in one of the error signals, even if it is not the highest component of the classification vector, it can suggest repair actions to be taken, such as reducing the temperature or shutting down the welder. Actual control of a complex system has

---

[4]A Rete-like algorithm can be used for efficiency, although our current implementation uses a simpler matching procedure.

[5]The interval "recent" is used to indicate a number of samples set by the user as a parameter.

not yet been attempted, instead, diagnostic messages describing what is occuring and what actions are suggested are the outputs of the system.

The following is an example of SCRuFFy running on acoustic data. Comments are indicated in *italics*, output from the expert system component (i.e. system control decisions) are indicated by SMALL UPPERCASE text. The example uses signals from a simulator designed to show particular behaviors. In this case, we see SCRuFFy taking actions to control "streaming," a particular error condition arising in the welding.

; The expert system is initialized

********** INITIALIZING EXPERT SYSTEM
********** INPUT WATER TEMPERATURE: *021*
********** INPUT WATER DEPTH: *030*
; the context information provided by water depth and temperature
; is used by the SCRuFFy's expert system component.
==
; the first signal is sampled
Signal (after DSP) is:

0.727 0.672 0.508 0.738 0.56 0.633 0.144 0.429 0.196 0.554 0.658 0.483
0.602 0.41 0.371 0.955 0.225 0.796 0.021 0.922 0.447 0.255 0.549 0.855
0.97 0.807 0.77 6 0.641 0.834 0.674 0.581 0.726 0.005 0.716 0.073
0.664 0.69 0.191 0.905 0.367 0.427 0.844 0.783 0.078 0.403 0.453 0.775
0.989 0.292 0.726 0.355 0.335 0.61 0.12 0.723 0.629 0.857 0.889 0.864
0.63 0.369 0.406 0.246 0.617 0.552 0.014 0.09 3 0.633 0.704 0.682
0.592 0.615 0.769 0.945 0.893 0.512 0.68 0.587 0.473 0.681 0.732 0.475
0.956 0.142 0.986 0.947 0.827 0.82 0.602 0.764 0.209 0.884 0.788 0.208
0.301 0.036 0.304 0.351 0.347 0.249 0.124 0.352 0.922 0.272 0.618
0.768 0.92 7 0.554 0.925 0.057 0.321 0.09 0.171 0.527 0.86 0.231
0.768 0.111 0.798 0.78 0.891 0.786 0.905 0.678 0.751 0.981 0.957 0.732
; This signal is input to the pre-trained connectionist network
Output from Connectionist network is:
.9296 .0145 .0759 .0465
; And the output is recorded for use by the temporal pattern matcher

The temporal pattern matcher finds any patterns that match
Output from temporal pattern matcher:
  Normal operation.
  A is highest, and no increasing minors
; Control is then transferred to the expert systems
Transferring control to Expert System:

********** NORMAL OPERATION OF WELDER
; and diagnostic or control messages are produced
==
... *; Several normal signals are omitted*
==
; another signal is sampled
Signal (after DSP) is:
  ... *; signals are deleted to save space*
Output from Connectionist network is:
  .9405 .0323 0.005 .2729
Output from temporal pattern matcher:
  Normal operation.

A is highest, but increasing error signal B
; *this time, a temporal pattern fires representing an increase in*
; *an error signal*
Transferring control to Expert System:

********** EVIDENCE OF STREAMING INCREASING
********** CONTROL: NO ACTION TO BE TAKEN AT THIS TIME
; *Given the error rates of neural network processing, it is*
; *possible that this is network error, so we wait for another*
; *signal to confirm the error.*
==
; *The next signal*
Signal (after DSP) is:

  . . .

Output from Connectionist network is:
.9227 .2279 .0311 .0148
Output from temporal pattern matcher:
  Normal operation.
  A is highest, but increasing error signal B
Transferring control to Expert System:

********** EVIDENCE OF STREAMING INCREASING PERSISTENTLY
********** CONTROL: DECREASE TEMPERATURE (MINOR = .2)
********** CHANGING WELDING TEMPERATURE: WAS 40 – NOW 39.8
;*this time, an action is taken, since the error is repeated.*
==
Signal (after DSP) is:

  . . .

Output from Connectionist network is:
.4158 .5424 .2176 .0037
Output from temporal pattern matcher:
  Time 1010:
  Channel B is highest.
Transferring control to Expert System:

********** NON-OPERATING SIGNAL TYPE STREAMING ENCOUNTERED
********** ERROR OCCURS AFTER INCREASE
  ; *it is recognized that this is not a transient - since previous*
  ; *action was taken for this type of error.*
********** CONTROL: DECREASE TEMPERATURE (MAJOR = 2.5)
********** CHANGING WELDING TEMPERATURE: WAS 39.8 – NOW 37.3
  , *so a more drastic control measure is suggested by the*
  ; *expert reasoner.*
==

FUTURE WORK

The hybrid system described in this paper is based primarily on an analysis of the
differing capabilities of the connectionist and symbolic approaches, and on the different temporal properties of continuous and discrete systems. The temporal pattern matcher provides an interface between these components, allowing a smooth
integration. Such components are clearly necessary to any systems integration of
these technologies. In the longer term, however, the design of our current system,
providing only a "feed-forward" model of computation (no feedback loops) is con-

sidered to be quite a limitation. The overall system is a "loosely-coupled" hybrid model[6] and cannot take self-modifying actions.

The current system provides a mapping from signals through to "control" actions proposed by the expert system reasoning component. There is no reason that these control actions could not be self-modifying, that is, changing the various parameters and rules used by the system itself. Thus, in addition to control of an external system, the current model can be extended for self control. The major forms of self-modification we are currently examining include:

- Changing the temporal patterns: Upon the receipt of external information (or via internal decisions), the system can modify the set of temporal patterns of interest.

- Changing network parameters and/or output multipliers: Neural networks are governed by a set of parameters (learning rate, momentum, etc.). Controlling these parameters dynamically is an area just starting to be explored. As control models are developed, "intelligent" control (using the expert system) can be implemented, and experimented with, in this framework.

- Changing network configuration: Certain sorts of network models (such as Hopfield networks for minimal cost paths) have structural constraints depending on external information (path cost between nodes, etc.) When information is discovered during processing, it may reflect a change in this information, and thus necessitate dynamic reconfiguration of the network.

In addition, the current model provides for a single network reporting to a single temporal pattern-matcher. However, the blackboard architecture on which SCRuFFy is based provides a natural mechanism for the integration of multiple knowledge sources. A hierarchical model of the temporal patterns (in which patterns found for a given network can be compared with other patterns for other networks) can provide for a merging of the data from various sensors. By exploring the use of such patterns, coupled with the parameter changes described above, we believe this framework will allow for experimentation with varying models of multi-sensor systems.

CONCLUSIONS

In this paper we have described a shell which was developed to allow an integration of neural network and expert systems technology. The system, SCRuFFy, is based on an analysis of the different abilities and time courses of neural network and AI systems. Critical to the processing of this system is a temporal pattern matcher which is used to mediate between the two subsystems, providing a "signal to symbol" mapping. This mapping allows the expert system to reason about the time course of signals which are classified by a connectionist network which is trained via classical back-propagation of error during a separate training phase. An example of the simulated control of the temperature of an underwater welding robot was presented to demonstrate these capabilities.

---

[6]See (Hendler, 1989b) for a discussion of loosely and tightly coupled hybrid models.

As a final, more "philosophical" note, we wish to point out that the design and motivation of the SCRuFFy system derives largely from a careful analyis of the problem-solving exhibited by connectionist and symbolic systems (Steels, 1989; Hendler, 1989b). The techniques used in this analysis were not special to either approach, but rather derived from examining the information processing features of the two so-called paradigms. Such an analysis, common in the expert systems community, but often ignored by neural network developers, enables the strengths and weaknesses of the approaches to be identified, and allows the design of component based systems, such as SCRuFFy, which can exploit the appropriate technologies for the particular aspects of problems which are being solved. Thus, in short, we agree strongly with Steels in his contention that "when this analysis is made ... the differences between expert systems and connectionist problem solving are relatively marginal as far as operation is concerned." By viewing the technologies in this light, it is easier to see that they can be viewed as cooperating, rather than competing, approaches.

REFERENCES

[1] Allen, J.F. and Koomen, J.A. Planning using a temporal world model *Proceedings of the Eighth International Joint Conference on Artificial Intelligence,* 1983.

[2] Canning, J., Kim, J., and Rosenfeld, A. Symbolic pixel labeling for curvilinear feature detection, *Proc. DARPA Image Understanding Workshop,* Morgan Kaufmann Publishers, Feb., 1987.

[3] Dyer, M. *Symbolic NeuroEngineering for Natural Language Processing: A Multilevel Research Approach* Technical Report UCLA-AI-88-14,Computer Science Dept., University of California, Los Angeles 1988.

[4] Hendler, J.Marker-passing over microfeatures: Towards a hybrid symbolic/connectionist model *Cognitive Science,* 13(1), March, 1989a.

[5] Hendler, J. Problem Solving and Reasoning: A Connectionist Perspective, in *Connectionism in Perspective,* R. Pfeifer, Z. Schreter, and L. Steels (eds.) Amsterdam: Elsevier, 1989b.

[6] Smolensky, P. Connectionist AI, Symbolic AI, and the Brain. *AI Review,* 1990.

[7] Shastri, L. *Evidential Reasoning in Semantic Networks: A formal theory and its parallel implementation* Doctoral Dissertation, Computer Science Department, University of Rochester, Sept., 1985.

[8] Steels, L. Connectionist Problem Solving – An AI Perspective, in *Connectionism in Perspective,* R. Pfeifer, Z. Schreter, and L. Steels (eds.) Amsterdam: Elsevier, 1989.

An architecture for selective forgetting

Jérôme Euzenat[1], Libero Maesano[2]

(1) Sherpa project, Laboratoire ARTEMIS/IMAG, BP53X, F-38041 GRENOBLE
(2) CEDIAG/Bull, 68 route de Versailles, F-78430 LOUVECIENNES

ABSTRACT

Some knowledge based systems will have to deal with increasing amount of knowledge. In order to avoid memory overflow, it is necessary to clean memory of useless data. Here is a first step toward an intelligent automatic forgetting scheme. The problem of the close relation between forgetting and inferring is addressed, and a general solution is proposed. It is implemented as invalidation operators for reasoning maintenance system dependency graphs. This results in a general architecture for selective forgetting which is presented in the framework of the Sachem system.

INTRODUCTION

The generalized computerization of the organizations leads to a worrying amount of stored data. The problem of forgetting is an old one: it is simply the ability to avoid memory overflow by freeing it. Moreover, freeing memory do not only care for memory overflow but also insures good performances of data retrieving procedures. So, this problem is critical for data management. Computer systems are yet able to exhibit forgetting skills. In several programming languages, the programmer can use some instructions in order to free the occupied memory. In more evolved languages, a garbage collection mechanism is able to find out unworkable data that can be discarded from memory. Concerning secondary storage, every operating system provides "remove file" commands and every data base management system "remove record" ones. It is possible to go ahead in the mechanization of forgetting and to put forth intelligent forgetting tools.

It is possible to consider simple forgetting scheme (with or without archive of forgotten data) for the future database systems. It can be a very basic system (banks must keep information on transactions for ten years) or a more sophisticated and intelligent one.

Intelligent forgetting capabilities will be studied in a knowledge based system context for reasons of declarativity of the knowledge expressed and of availability of exploitation tools. The relations between forgetting and inferring will be especially accounted for: rather than being a problem, they allow building a smarter forgetting scheme taking advantage of inferences. It will be demonstrated through a real world application in which these ideas were experienced. This study will not distinguish between primary and secondary storage memory because it is concerned with very large applications that must reside in databases.

Forgetting will be considered together with knowledge base systems, and so, will meet the problem of the relations between inferring and forgetting. These relations will be dealt with through two attitudes: consolidation and abstraction.

Reasoning maintenance systems will be introduced in order to demonstrate the implementation of these two attitudes. This will lead to the presentation of a complete architecture for selective forgetting, together with a proposal enabling to determine what to forget. This is presented through its application to a knowledge based system which monitors a blast furnace process: Sachem.

It is worth noting that this work concerns artificial systems, and so, is not preoccupied by psychological plausibility. Nevertheless, it obviously can and should be related with psychological studies and psychological preoccupation in computer science. This will be addressed in the last section.

FORGETTING AND INFERRING

When considering knowledge based systems, forgetting some datum must be considered in connection with every other part of the base it is connected with. The problem to be faced is that of the attitude toward the relation after forgetting: discarding relations or discarding the related item (and so on…). Moreover, the relations can be of two sorts:

- *Explicit relations* can be found as references from an object to another. Knowledge representations and, among them, object based knowledge representations allow for a wide range of relations to be introduced in the base and a rich semantics associated with each kind of relation (Kim & al., 1989; Escamilla & Jean, 1990).
- *Implicit relations* need computation in order to be established. This is the case for the relations from classes to instances through the inheritance mechanism but also for every deductive inference mechanism.

Only the relations between forgetting and inferring are discussed here. This will lead to a safe and generic solution for this relation. A deductive relationship between datum to forget and other data is twofold: a backward relation with other data that enabled to infer it and a forward relation with data it allowed to infer. Both sides of the relation are discussed below.

Backward references

Forgetting is not of logical concern. Logic tells us what interpretation can be given to a set of facts while forgetting changes the set of facts considered. So, as for other problems (reasoning maintenance for example), the justification of forgetting is to be found in reasoning rather than logic. However, in order to insure a sound behavior of the system, we want it to have a semantics that warrants that every item which can be inferred is indeed. For that purpose, an inference system is required to infer every formula that is inferable from a set of facts. So, the problem to be faced is that of the meaning of forgetting inferred knowledge: the facts introduced into the database by the inference system. In fact, after forgetting an item, it should be legitimate for the reasoner to infer it again, perhaps *ad infinitum*. Moreover, forgetting the conclusions while the premises remains is not appropriate: usually, the inference process is oriented toward inferring gradually more relevant data, so, it is better to preserve relevant data while forgetting rough and less relevant data.

Our choice, consists in forgetting only what is called initial knowledge (i.e. knowledge that the logical interpretation of the base considers as axioms). This is the price to be paid for insuring a logical behavior of the system.

This accords with the observation that only more abstract data is inferred (through true abstraction or aggregation): it is a suitable approach to forget initial knowledge rather than more abstract knowledge. In fact, if the system is dedicated to infer abstract knowledge (and this is mainly how does the Sachem system behaves), it seems curious to forget abstract knowledge while keeping at hand the initial knowledge that generated it.

Forward references

On the other hand, if one wants to forget initial data, (s)he may want to forget what that data allowed to infer. In fact, there are two possible attitudes:
- Forgetting data while leaving everything else unaltered, which will be called *consolidation*. This can be used in order to forget initial data while preserving relevant consequences of those data.
- Forgetting data while leaving everything else as if the forgotten datum was in a particular state (usually valid or invalid), which will be called *abstraction*.

It is noteworthy that the latter does not rely on a current state while the former does. But those two possibilities are not independent: the former can be expressed by the latter with the state conditioned by the actual state of the datum, the latter can be expressed by changing the state of the datum before applying consolidation. Both attitudes allow for logical interpretation: the forgotten data, which was axioms are not any more, and so their consequences are invalid or become axioms in turn. However, the presented attitudes have been stated in a very abstract fashion: even the forward references are not mentioned. It must be instantiated in particular deductive systems.

These forgetting primitives are very interesting and must be provided, but their implementation is not straightforward because axioms and consequences are not usually explicitly related. The architecture presented below deals with such a problem, but first, the implementation of the operators is introduced.

REASONING MAINTENANCE SYSTEMS

Reason maintenance systems (RMS) are aimed at managing a knowledge base considering different kinds of reasoning. Such a system is connected to a reasoner (or problem solver) which communicates every inference made. The RMS has in charge the maintenance of the reasoner's current belief base. Reasoning maintenance systems' dependency graph will form the basis on which the operators can be implemented. So reasoning maintenance systems are first exposed before showing how to implement forgetting operators.

Dependency graph

RMSes record each inference in a *justification* that relates *nodes* representing propositional formulas plus a special atom ($\perp$) representing contradiction. The system accepts non monotonic inferences so the justifications have an appropriate structure: a justification $(<\{i_1,...i_n\} \{o_1,...o_m\}>: c)$ is made of an IN-list ($\{i_1,...i_n\}$) and an OUT-list ($\{o_1,...o_m\}$). Such a justification is said to be valid if and only if all the nodes in the IN-list are known to hold while those in the OUT-list are not; a node, in turn, is known to hold if and only if it is the consequent (c) of a valid justification. The recursion of the definition is stopped by nodes without justification and by axioms that are nodes with a justification containing empty IN- and OUT-lists.

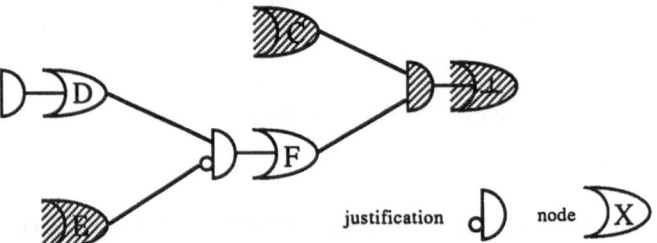

Fig. 1. A dependency graph is here represented as a boolean circuit where or-gates are nodes and and-gates are justifications where the nodes in the IN-list come directly while nodes in the OUT-list come through a not-gate. Nodes that have a justification whose IN- and OUT-lists are empty (e.g. D) represent true formulas because they do not need to be inferred. White nodes and justifications are considered valid while hatched ones are invalid. Of course, the value propagation satisfies the rules implied by the circuit components. So, the formulas in the base are insured to have a valid justification (i.e. corresponding to a valid inference).

TMS and ATMS

Jon Doyle's TMS (for "truth maintenance system"; Doyle, 1979) proceeds by labelling the nodes of the graph with IN and OUT tags which reflect whether they are known to hold or not. A labelling respecting the constraints stated above is an admissible labelling and a labelling which labels the node $\perp$ OUT is a consistent labelling. The TMS algorithm finds a (weakly) founded labelling, i.e. a consistent admissible labelling which rely on no circular argument. The main work of the TMS occurs when it receives a new justification. It then has to integrate the justification in the graph and, if this changes the validity of the formula, it must propagate this validity: all the nodes that could be IN-ed because of the justified node and all those which could be OUT-ed are examined and updated. If an inconsistency occurs following the addition of a justification, the system backtracks on the justifications in order to invalidate an hypothesis — a formula inferred non monotonically — which supports the inconsistency.

Johan De Kleer's assumption-based TMS (Martins & Shapiro 1988; De Kleer, 1986) is rather different. This system considers only monotonic inferences (with only IN-list: $<\{i_1,...i_n\}>$: c), but it deals with several contexts at a time. It considers initial formulas called hypotheses; so, the user can generate and test hypotheses with great efficiency. A set of hypotheses is called an environment and the set of all the environments constitute a complete lattice structured by the "includes" relation (cf. Fig. 2). Instead of labelling absolutely a node (with IN or OUT tags), each node has a label consisting of the set of environments under which it is known to hold. An environment is consistent if $\perp$ is not known to hold in it and the computed labels are minimal in the sense that they do not contain comparable environments. After each inference, the system computes the set of environments that support the inference, inserts it in the label of the inferred node and propagate it through the graph. Then, in order to know if a formula is valid, it compares the current hypothesis set with the label of the node.

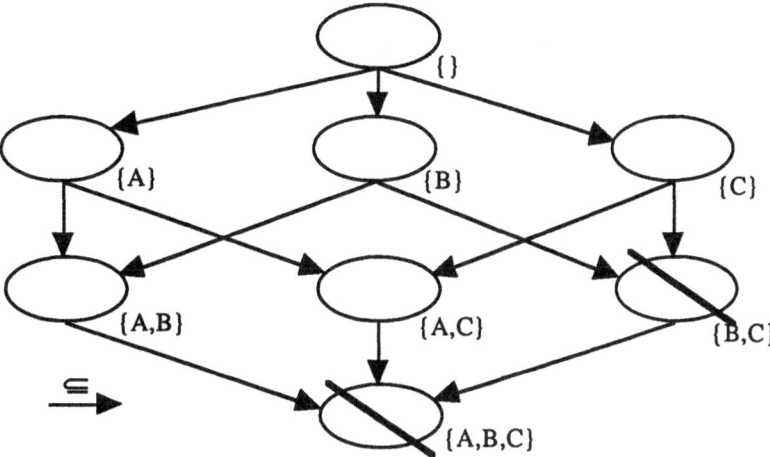

Fig. 2. The environment lattice constructed with the hypotheses A, B and C in which the environment {B, C} is known as inconsistent.

As a summary, the TMS handles non monotonic inferences and is able to maintain the set of deduced formulas with regard to an axiom set. The axiom deletion, while not explicitly described by Jon Doyle, is trivial to implement. The ATMS, for its part, cannot accept non monotonic inferences, but is able to consider several contexts simultaneously.

Specialized graph operators

Reasoning maintenance systems record every inference, but, independently of TMSes, the dependency graph constitutes a picture of the reasoning process and every manipulation of this graph can be seen as meta-reasoning. It is then possible, for other utilities, to take advantage of the graph. This is the case for:
* explanation generation,
* automatic inconsistency recovery (the task of backtracking),
* forgetting.

The forgetting primitives will be implemented, at a low level, as dependency graph procedures called *inferential* and *influential invalidation* that are run against a TMS node and a justification in which it appears. The former, enable forgetting the justification, and, the latter, forgets the effects of the node on the justification. Influential invalidation consists in replacing the justification in which the node appears (in IN- or OUT-list) by another in which the node no longer appears. Inferential invalidation suppresses the justification in which the node appears. Then, the reasoning maintenance propagation process is run in order to account for the change in the rest of the graph.

This last operation is not native in the ATMS (because it is a monotonic system), but if the forgotten fact is an hypothesis the result of the propagation will consist in a simple operation on the labels. Two logical concepts, called *universal* and *existential abstraction*, have been established at the Bull research center (Coudert & Madre, 1990) and are the simple quantification of boolean formulas by some variable (which ranges over 0 and 1). If applied to the labels, considered as formulas in disjunctive form, these operators formalize, in sentential calculus, the two possible operations of forgetting a fact with or without taking care of its consequences. So, the propagation phase of these operators are implemented by applying the relevant operator with the hypothesis to each consequence of the hypothesis.

Example

If a node X has for label {{A,B},{B,C},{A,D}} which can be expressed in sentential calculus
by (A∧B)∨(B∧C)∨(A∧D) then

∀B (A∧B)∨(B∧C)∨(A∧D) (universal abstraction)

= [(A∧D)]∧[(A)∨(C)∨(A∧D)]

= (A∧D): {{A,D}} is its OUT-abstraction after B's forgetting and

∃B (A∧B)∨(B∧C)∨(A∧D) (existential abstraction)

= [(A∧D)]∨[(A)∨(C)∨(A∧D)]

= (A∨C): {{A},{C}} is its IN-abstraction after B's forgetting.

Invalidation operators are far away from the consolidation and abstraction that were introduced previously. Here is sketched their implementation in term of invalidation. The consolidation is not explained provided that it is straightforwardly adapted from abstraction.

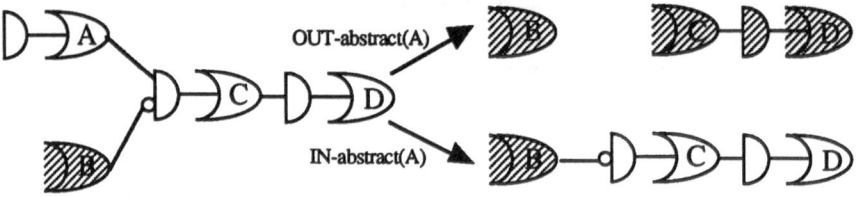

Fig. 3. Effect of abstraction on the dependency graph through invalidation operators.

The IN- or OUT-abstraction operators first check for the validity of the operation: the data must be an axiom (or an hypothesis), i.e. it cannot have been inferred. Then, the invalidation operators are called against the justifications in which the node appear. For IN-abstraction, the influential invalidation is called against the justification in which the node is in the IN-list and inferential invalidation against those in which it appears in the OUT-list. For OUT-abstraction, it is exactly the opposite. At last, the node can be suppressed from the node base.

Nevertheless, the invalidation operators are very powerless since they only allow the forgetting of one node at a time. So, two additional procedures are provided that are called recursive invalidation. They recursively apply invalidation to the consequences of the initial fact, provided that the operation is also valid (the consequence has become in turn an initial fact). It is noteworthy that these new operations necessitate only one propagation because the additional operations respect the current logical interpretation.

SACHEM FORGETTING PROCESS

This approach to forgetting stems from a large real-time knowledge-based system in which data comes from 800 sensors. This system diagnoses failures in the process of a blast furnace. It must infer from rough data (coming from the sensors) higher level representation of the process. From this representation, the system is able to make several diagnostics. They are represented by assumptions of failure. The system will then observe (or focus) on precise data in order to confirm, infirm or invalidate these hypotheses. Since it works in real time, it must also decide how to act in order to recover from the failure. These decisions take into account the irreversibility and the range of such actions and the plausibility of the hypotheses that support them.

The application is written in the object oriented language KOOL (Lacroix, 1989) enhanced with reasoning maintenance capabilities (Euzenat, 1989a). It uses objects for representing data and hypotheses and rules for reasoning. The tasks of the system and their schedule is described in Fig. 4.

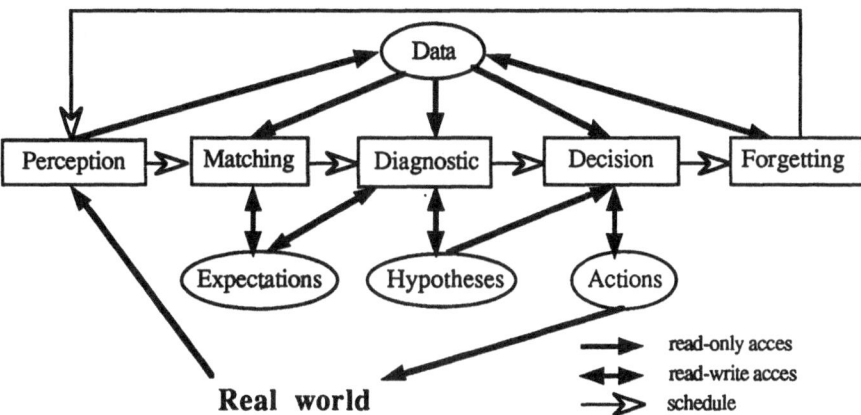

Fig. 4. Sachem general process.

The system receives large amount of data, and also constructs large amounts. This leads to important storage requirements and forces forgetting a part of this data in order to not overflow memory. The real-time constraint rules out the possibility of stopping the system in order to clean memory. But, it is loose enough so it is possible to run a system that will decide what to forget and thus free memory.

"What to forget?" versus "What to remember?"

There are two ways of achieving forgetting: the first one provides forgetting operators to the user who has in charge the explicit liberation of space, the second one, close to the garbage collector approach, uses a supervisor in order to decide what and when to forget. Of course, the supervisor can be driven by specific rules. We decided to use the second approach as shown by Sachem's main cycle.

When required to free memory, computer systems are usually able to do it, if they are told which places or which items to free. So, the whole problem of automating forgetting is to tell the computer what to forget. The problem of finding "what to forget" has been pointed out, but one can address the dual problem of "what to remember". Both answers are suitable in order to determine what to forget. The latter has been chosen for Sachem. It consists of establishing a set of relevant data (called the focus of attention) and forgetting everything which is not related to that set of data.

However, the problem of circumscribing that focus of attention is not solved. There is no all-purpose method. The solutions can be some automatic methods such as declaring initial data older than some date to be irrelevant, or heuristic methods, using inference upon the current state of the process in order to decide what to remember.

In Sachem, both methods are used. Validity duration of data and hypotheses leads to discarding them after some time or not discarding them before another time. The focus of attention is also used; it is based on a numeric comparison of the concurrent diagnostic hypothesis. They are affected a plausibility factor which can change during their lifetime.

There is a bound under which an hypothesis is considered as no relevant any more: such an hypothesis will not appear any more in the focus of attention, and equally for the initial data that led to propose this hypothesis. Another approach, more domain dependent, is under investigation: it consists of imitating the way an expert manage its own focus of attention and necessitate special expert knowledge.

However, this problem is still open and a lot of different solutions can be considered. Now, will be presented the architecture which allows a close integration of the mechanisms provided so far. It is a general architecture and protocol that enable forgetting in knowledge based systems.

A knowledge-based system architecture for forgetting

The software architecture of Sachem is made of three levels (Euzenat, 1989b). The upper level is the fact base on which the inference methods can be run: this the the KOOL object level. The medium level is a reasoning maintenance dependency graph, representing each formula manipulated by the inference methods as a node and relating them by justifications which represent inferences. The lower level is made of the data structures of the implementation programming language (Lisp in this case). The novelty of the architecture stems from the way it is used for forgetting.

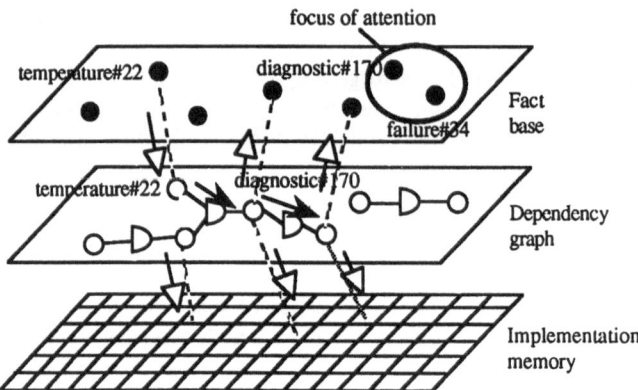

Fig. 5. The three level architecture of Sachem. The arrows represent the propagation of forgetting: from high level representations to lower levels (white arrows), from raw to more abstract data (black arrows).

This architecture leads to a simple protocol for forgetting. The forgetting process, as said above, is a high level mechanism, so it begins at the higher level by determining the focus of attention. Every item that has to be forgotten is then discarded from the fact base and a query for discarding it at the medium level is emitted. At the reasoning maintenance level, the invalidation operators are provided which discards recursively the concerned facts and their references from other structures. At the implementation language level, the garbage collector is able to collect the free memory. Of course, the reasoning maintenance level tells the knowledge base level to discard the consequences it has identified.

FORGETTING AS AN OPTIMIZATION PROCESS

Up to know, our preoccupations only relate to the computer implementation of reasoning systems. But this work can be compared with more general ideas and theories such as those on human cognitive forgetting.

Psychological insight

Psychology works distinguish between short term and long term memory (LMT). The analogy with the work presented here can only be done with LTM. There are two main models of retrieval in memory that account for forgetting (Tiberghein, 1987):
- Interference theory in which the item to be found is inhibited by a reorganization of memory (due to new information arrival).
- Context theory in which the storage context is so different to the retrieval context that the retrieval procedures are unable to find the item.

Generally, psychological models of forgetting, more than storage failure, emphasize retrieval failure. Storage failure, as opposed to retrieval failure, is non reversible and thus more difficult to test safely. But, such models show that forgetting reveals the optimization of the retrieval process: forgetting is the price to pay for retrieving quickly, almost every time. The view of forgetting presented here, while it differs from the ones above, is also an optimization, but a storage optimization. It also has its shortcomings: sometimes, items that had been known by the systems are no longer remembered. While the current psychological theories account for cognitive economy of processing, our forgetting proposal concerns cognitive economy of storage (Lenat & al., 1979).

However, studies in psychology should be interesting for artificial intelligence if they can show how workable part of memory is circumscribed: this could bring new ideas about how to forget while insuring coherency of considered data.

Abstraction

There is previous work in artificial intelligence which uses psychological models in order to build memory systems. For example, Roger Schank (Schank, 1982) considers that forgetting of individual data is the consequence of its integration in a more general scheme (in his case it was more general instances of scripts). This is also true in the psychological context theory of forgetting that observe that if something is learned under a wide range of contexts, the context does not matter anymore: the learned item is abstracted from the context.

The abstraction concept can take this into account. Moreover, that concept can be found in each context where a forgetting tool can be useful:
- In reasoning, it is possible to forget initial data which allowed to infer more synthetic and pertinent data. This approach can be related with the actual work on deepness level of reasoning (Bonté & al., 1988) which can help to determine what can/must be forgotten or not.
- In a scientific discovery perspective, every fact that is singular and contradictory with the current theory is very active in memory because it has to be explained. When explained with the help of a new theory, the abstraction, that the new theory represents, remains while the singular fact is forgotten because it is not singular any more (it is just an instance of the abstraction).

- In computer vision, pixels that constitute the input of the system are forgotten for the benefit of edges which are themselves forgotten in objects' advantage...
- In symbolic machine learning, when minimal and maximal representations of the concept to learn are acquired, examples and counter-examples from which they are built can be forgotten (this is the case of the restaurant-script example of Schank).

All of these categories can be taken into account in order to help choosing the items to forget. For example, Sachem's reasoning goes through several abstraction levels. The possibility of several different forgetting politics tied to the different levels are currently under study.

Of course, all these forgetting actions must only be processed when the infered/extracted/learned abstractions are strong enough. The forgetting action disables the explanation of the abstraction processes. So the choice of the items to be forgotten must be very careful.

As a conclusion, several concepts constructed for psychological purposes can be confronted with the forgetting ability described here. While not inspired from them, the contexts of ATMS share the same purpose with psychological contexts theory: reducing the search space. Schank abstraction is the same as that which is used here. Moreover, the understanding of forgetting schemes as an optimization can open some interesting artificial intelligence perspectives such as using encoding and decoding schemes inspired of those provided by psychological research (this is, of course, yet true for the computationalistic part of psychology, e.g. (Anderson, 1976)).

CONCLUSION

An "attitude" toward the relations between forgetting and inferring in knowledge based systems has been presented. Through abstraction and consolidation operators, forgetting can be safely dealt with. Moreover, it is possible, with the help of a reasoning maintenance system, to implement those operators. This leads to a proposal for a generic architecture which is suited to the purpose of forgetting and which has been implemented for the Sachem application prototype.

The forgetting operators meet the meta-reasoning activity which is the work of the reasoning maintenance system. At first sight, the action of forgetting can be seen as antithetic with reasoning maintenance systems which recall every inference produced in view to support defeasible reasoning. Moreover, reasoning maintenance systems seemed to burden large applications with too much data. But, at last, they turned out to be of major relevance when discarding an item must be propagated to its consequences.

The architecture presented here is a very generic one. Currently, many systems based on the object principle are developed, including object-oriented databases. There is discussions in order to know if these systems will be provided with garbage collectors or explicit freeing operators. Our claim is that garbage collectors are better, but not as they are currently understood. Classic garbage collectors are too low level tools for objects. In the most part of object applications, each object is connected with the entire base and have a lot of connections. So, it is not suited to ground the destruction operation on the lack of connections that which will not be achieved often. It is necessary to define the criteria that made an object "garbageable". For that purpose, a generic system that has in charge to apply the criteria to the objects in order to determine which object must be forgotten is proposed. This is done, in Sachem, through the determination of the focus of attention.

Farther than deductive implicit relations, explicit relations such as those that are definable in object based knowledge representations are actually under investigation. The taxonomy of these relations will control the spreading effect of forgetting (e.g. relation of composition or class-membership should lead to specialized forgetting policies).

Our architecture is designed for forgetting in a reasoning system. As mentioned above, forgetting is useful in several contexts. We think that this architecture can be generalized. In particular, reasoning maintenance systems can be applied, for several reasons, to learning systems.

Forgetting is a major concern as far as data and inference memorization is used in large applications. The starting research on that topic, especially if the efforts take into account the yet available and foregoing results of psychology and logic, should lead to very useful methodological tools.

ACKNOWLEDGEMENT

This work was initiated when the first author was with CEDIAG. The authors are grateful to Martin Strecker who pointed out some shortcomings in the first formulation of these ideas. Of course, remaining ones are under authors responsibility.

REFERENCES

Anderson J. R. (1976), Language, memory and thought, Lawrence Erlbaum associates, Hillsdale

Bonté E., Castaing J., Grandemange P., Grumbach S., Kayser D., Lévy F. (1988), Description succincte d'un raisonneur à profondeur variable, proc. 8ièmes journées internationnales sur les systèmes experts et leurs applications, EC2, Avignon, 117-132

Coudert O., Madre J.-C. (1990), Logic over finite domain of interpretation: proof and resolution procedures, Bull research center, Louveciennes (Research report)

De Kleer J. (1986), An assumption-based TMS, *Artificial intelligence* 28(2):127-162

Doyle J. (1979), A truth maintenance system, *Artificial intelligence* 12(3):231-272

Escamilla J., Jean P. (1990), Relationships in an object knowledge representation model, proc. IEEE Conference on tools for artificial intelligence, Herndon, 632-638

Euzenat J. (1989a), Connexion KOOL/RMS, spécifications, CEDIAG/Bull, Louveciennes (Internal report Sachem JE004)

Euzenat J. (1989b), Démonstrateur B: architecture et fonctionnement, CEDIAG/Bull, Louveciennes (Internal report Sachem JE007)

Kim W., Bertino E., Garza J. (1989), Composite objects revisited, *SIGMOD records* 18(2):337-347

Lacroix V. (1989), KOOL: a reflexive representation language, proc. TOOLS 89, Paris, 309-321

Lenat D., Hayes-Roth F., Klahr P. (1979), Cognitive economy, Stanford university, Stanford (Research report HPP-79-15)

Martins J., Shapiro S. (1988), A model for belief revision, *Artificial intelligence* 35(1):25-79

Schank R. (1982), Dynamic memory, a theory of reminding and learning in computers and people, Cambridge university press, Cambridge

Tiberghein G. (1987), Introduction aux concepts contemporains dans l'étude de la mémoire chez l'homme, in: Martial Van Der Linden, Raymond Bruyer (eds.), proc. conference sur la neuropsychologie de la mémoire humaine, Société de Neuropsychologie de Langue Française, 2-31

Constraintpropagation in Qualitative Modelling: Domain Variables Improve Diagnostic Efficiency

Bernhard Pfahringer
(email: bernhard@ai-vie.uucp)

Department of Medical Cybernetics and AI
University of Vienna, and
Austrian Research Institute for Artificial Intelligence
Freyung 6, A-1010 Vienna, Austria

September, 1990

ABSTRACT

This paper shows how a specific constraint propagation technique - namely *domain variables* - can speed up qualitative diagnosis considerably. We are using the KARDIO system, a qualitative simulation model of the electrical activity of the heart, to exemplify our points. Furthermore we describe how the domain handling mechanism itself can be implemented in PROLOG efficiently. For a class of applications, where the constraint solver only performs a minor part of the computation our approach is comparable to or better than specialised constraint logic programming systems with regard to overall runtime. Additionally we gain the benefit of being able to specify all of the system in a single language.

1 INTRODUCTION

This paper shows how a specific constraint propagation technique - namely *domain variables* [van Hentenryck & Dincbas, 1986] - can speed up qualitative diagnosis considerably. We are using the KARDIO system [Bratko et al, 1989], a qualitative simulation model of the electrical activity of the heart, to exemplify our points. Given a state of the heart (some combination of arrhythmias) the KARDIO model can be used to compute possible ECG patterns and vice versa. The design of the model influences efficiency heavily: simulation (going from arrhythmias to ECG patterns) is fast whereas diagnosis (going from ECG patterns to arrhythmias) is slow. By introducing domain variables the latter can be sped up without changing the structure of the model. Furthermore we will show how to implement all constraint handling in PROLOG itself with good results regarding absolute runtimes.

This paper is outlined as follows: Section 2 introduces the KARDIO model. Section 3 defines domain variables. In section 4 we first show a (naive) implementation in standard PROLOG and then introduce some improvements. Section 5 discusses the results and compares our solution to other approaches.

2 THE KARDIO MODEL

The KARDIO expert system models the electrical activity of the heart in a qualitative way. We will just briefly sketch the model, an extensive description of KARDIO can be found in [Bratko et al, 1989]. Overly simplified, the heart works electrically as follows: certain generators supply electrical impulses which are in turn conducted and combined through specific pathways. These resultant impulses allow the model to predict possible ECG patterns.

The current version of KARDIO relates 943 different combinations of basic arrhythmias to 3096 different ECG patterns yielding a total of 5240 arrhythmia-ECG pairs. Simulation is very efficient: running on an Apollo DN 3000 using compiled QUINTUS PROLOG computing all possible ECGs for a given arrhythmia takes 0.024 seconds on the average. Diagnosis is much slower: computing all possible arrhythmias for a given ECG takes 8.6 seconds on the average. In the following we show how to improve diagnostic efficiency by introducing and combining several constraint propagation techniques.

3 DOMAIN VARIABLES

In this section we briefly introduce *Domain Variables*, a more thorough discussion can be found in [van Hentenryck & Dincbas, 1986]. The main idea is simple. Sometimes it is known in advance that a certain variable in a clause should only be bound to one of several possible values. Using standard PROLOG there are just two ways of specifying such knowledge. Either correctness can be tested after the variable has received a value or the set of legal values can be enumerated via backtracking. Both solutions can lead to combinatorial explosion in involved computations. Domain variables allow the variable to be explicitly augmented with the set of legal values, its *domain*. Of course, unification has to be extended to handle such augmented variables. In the following we restrict ourselves to domains consisting solely of atomic values. Furthermore assume that domain variables are represented via a term:

domain(FutureValue, LegalValues)

Unification has to properly handle three different cases: (1) Unifying a domain variable with a standard variable simply succeeds in binding the standard variable to the domain variable. (2) Unification of a domain variable with an atomic value succeeds with the variable bound to the value, iff the value is legal. (3) The interesting case is unifying two domain variables: both domains have to be intersected to yield the new restricted domain. If the resultant domain contains just one value, the variable can be bound directly to this value. Lastly, if the intersection is empty, unification will simply fail.

Some (experimental) PROLOG systems already support either domains directly [van Hentenryck, 1989], whereas others (like Metaprolog [Holzbaur, 1990]) allow for user-defined extensions of the unification algorithm. The latter was available to us, so some test-runs were performed. As the latest version of the KARDIO model was written with domains in mind [Mozetic, 1990], porting to Metaprolog turned out to be rather simple. Extension of unification for domains can be defined as follows in Metaprolog:

```
:- metafunctor( domain/2 ).

metatermunify( domain(X,Values), X ) :- member( X, Values).

metametaunify( domain(X,V1), domain(X,V2) ) :-
   intersection( V1, V2, V3 ),
   new_domain( V3, X).

new_domain( [SingleValue], SingleValue) :- !.
new_domain( [X|L], domain(_,[X|L]) ).
```

First domain/2 is declared to be a special functor with regard to unification, then u-nifying a domain variable with a term and unifying two domain variables is specified by appropriate clauses for metatermunify/2 and metametaunify/2. Unification of standard variables with domain variables is handled by the Metaprolog kernel itself. Note that unification of domain variables can result in chains of domain variables. The KARDIO model required just one modification to incorporate domain variables; the original clauses of mem/2:

```
mem( X, [X|_]).
mem( X, [_|L]) :- mem( X,L).
```

were replaced by the following clause:

```
mem( X, L) :- X = domain(_,L).
```

The first result - 61 seconds/ECG - was rather discouraging, but should not come as a surprise. Metaprolog is essentially a modified version of the CPROLOG interpreter, whereas the above mentioned average 8.6 seconds were obtained from compiled code. A closer inspection of the way the model is stated revealed that reversing the order of subgoals in the toplevel predicate heart4 could possibly yield a speed up. For the original (compiled) KARDIO model this hope fails, 22.5 seconds are needed per ECG pattern (see chapter 3.1.4 of [Bratko et al, 1989] for an explanation), but with the advantage of (interpreted) domains to reduce unnecessary backtracking efforts, efficiency is improved to 12.1 seconds/ECG.

The benefit of using domains can also be seen clearly from the total number of subgoal calls (summed up for all 3096 ECG patterns), which is reduced by a bit more than one order of magnitude, from 69 millions down to 4.7 millions. But still absolute runtime is larger for running diagnosis interpreted with domains (12.1 seconds) than running diagnosis compiled without domains (8.6 seconds).

4 IMPLEMENTING DOMAIN VARIABLES IN VANILLA PROLOG

The standard way of adding to PROLOG extensions which are themselves implemented in PROLOG is building a meta-interpreter. This technique could of course be used to extend unification by domain variables. But as unification is such a basic operation for a logic programming language, runtime would increase intolerably. Nonetheless we can partially evaluate the application of meta-interpreter to the KARDIO model. To cope with the overwhelming increase in source code size, we have identified three common call patterns that need explicit handling of unification. Before introducing the appropriate predicates to handle these cases, we first show the result of partially evaluating a simple clause which is part of the KARDIO knowledge base:

```
ret_reg_4( _, reg(Loc, _, Rate), reg(Loc, none, zero)) :-
    mem( Rate, [zero, between_250_350, over_350] ).
```

is transformed to:

```
ret_reg_4( _, reg(L1, _, Rate1), reg(L2, Rhythm, Rate2)) :-
    Rhythm := none,
    Rate1 := zero,
    Rate2 <= [zero, between_250_350, over_350],
    L1 :=: L2.
```

This example clause fortunately covers all three cases. Unification of an arbitrary argument (possibly a domain variable) with an atomic value is handled by :=, unification of an arbitrary argument with a list of possible legal values is handled by <=, and lastly, unification of two arbitrary arguments is handled by :=:. The predicate :=/2 is defined as follows:

```
V := Atom :-
    deref( V, Vd ),
    ( var( Vd ) ->
        Vd = Atom
    ;
        atomic( Vd ) ->
            Vd = Atom
    ;
            Vd = domain( Atom, Values ),
            memberchk( Atom, Values )
    ).
```

First, the arbitrary term V is dereferenced, as it could be the starting point of a chain of domain variables. Next, dispatching takes place according to the type of the dereferenced value: an unbound variable will get bound to Atom, an atom will be tested for equality, and a domain variable will get bound in the case when membership-testing succeeds. Dereferencing is done by the predicate deref/2, which is defined as follows:

```
deref( X, Value) :-
    nonvar( X ), X = domain( Link, _), nonvar( Link),
    !,
    deref( Link, Value).
deref( Value, Value).
```

The first clause detects bound domain variables and dereferences them recursively. The second clause catches all other cases.

The above mentioned predicates `<=/2` and `:=:/2` are defined in a similar s-traightforward fashion. With these definitions runtime is 7.2 seconds/ECG, a neglegible improvement in efficiency compared to 8.6 seconds/ECG as mentioned in section two. This result can be explained as follows: backtracking is considerably reduced, but only at the expense of a lot of runtime spent for explicitly unifying terms. After identifying the culprit, remedies can be taken. One well-known principle in computer science is special-case coding of frequently encountered, but easily handled situations. Some statistics gathering revealed the following: most of the time `:=/2`, `<=/2`, and `:=:/2` are called with either unbound variables or atomic values as arguments and not with domain variables. So these predicates had to be modified accordingly to take these special cases into account early. As an example the new definition of `:=/2` is given:

```
V := Atom :-
   ( var(V) ->
       V = Atom
   ;
     atomic(V) ->
       V = Atom
   ;
       deref( V, Vd),
       ( atomic( Vd) ->
           Vd = Atom
       ;
           Vd = domain(Atom,Values),
           memberchk(Atom,Values)
       )
   ).
```

The argument is first of all checked for both of the special cases and if necessary dealt with appropriately, and only then dereferencing and standard dispatching takes place. The other predicates were modified accordingly. This simple and small modification yielded a speedup of a factor of two: 3.4 seconds/ECG.

The next step we undertook was kind of a flow analysis done by hand revealing the following: certain attributes of impulses are never instantiated to or compared with domain variables, namely the rhythm of regular impulses and the focus of ectopic impulses. The same turned out to be true for most of the variables depicting states of different parts of the heart. Therefore unifications involving only such attributes or variables could be handled safely and much faster by the builtin unification mechanisms of the underlying PROLOG system. Thus the model was once more automatically transformed to a form as exemplified by our running example `ret_reg_4`:

```
ret_reg_4( _, reg(Loc1, _, Rate1), reg(Loc2, none, Rate2)) :-
   Rate1 := zero,
   Rate2 <= [zero, between_250_350, over_350],
   Loc1 :=: Loc2.
```

Unification of Rhythm to none is now implicit in the head of the clause. Roughly one third of the number of calls to :=/2, <=/2, and :=:/2 were eliminated by this transformation, and the gained efficiency mirrored this figure nicely: runtime per ECG pattern was now down to 2.3 seconds on the average.

So far all the reported transformations were domain-independent, principled ways of improving efficiency. Yet some analysis of the KARDIO model, especially of the toplevel structure, reveals one more source of unnecessary backtracking. When starting from given ECG attributes to generate impulses non-deterministically, these impulses cause backtracking a considerable number of times when fed into the predicates representing the impulse generators of the heart. Chronological backtracking clearly looses in such situations where choices made several subgoals earlier need to be reconsidered. Simple solutions like static or dynamic reordering of subgoal calls did not perform well, either. The former encountered to much interdependencies whereas the latter encurred to much runtime cost. Still there is a simple domain-specific solution to the basic problem. Backtracking efforts can be reduced by supplying minimum constraints for certain impulses beforehand. To stay on principled grounds, all these four impulses were selected, which are directly produced by the generators. For each impulse all solutions were computed (which were few, usually between 5 and 10). Forming the least general generalisation for each solution set yielded constraints on the impulses like the following:

```
ImpSA = form( reg( sa_node, _,
                   domain(_,[zero,under_60,between_60_100,
                            between_100_250] )),
              ect( sa_node,no))
```

When incorporating these constraints on the four basic impulses, the gained speedup is an additional factor of almost two: 1.26 seconds/ECG. The following table shortly summarises the results. *Runtime* is the time needed to find all arrhythmias measured in seconds/ECG, *Calls* is the total number of subgoal calls measured in millions, and *Speedup* is the ratio of the runtimes:

Approach	Runtime	Calls	Speedup
1. Reverse Order	22.54	69.0	1
2. 1 + Domains	7.20	4.7	3
3. 1 + Improved Domains	3.40	4.7	7
4. 3 + Flow Analysis	2.30	4.7	10
5. 4 + Constrained Impulses	1.26	2.5	18

5 DISCUSSION

The following is a comparison of our approach to other possible approaches. Most of the literature on constraint logic programming either argues for, or implicitly assumes that special builtin predicates are necessary for yielding appropriate performance. Therefore available CLP systems are usually prototype PROLOG implementations equipped with extended builtin unification mechanisms like [Jaffar, 1990] or with additional builtin predicates like [van Hentenryck, 1989]. The provided functionality is *opaque* to the user, meaning that the supplied constraint solving method(s) can only be used as is, there is no chance of inspecting, modifying or extending them. And there is a price to be paid: usually execution of the standard PROLOG part of such specialised systems is inferior to commercially available PROLOG systems.

Our example clearly shows that at least one constraint solving technique - *domain variables* - can be implemented in PROLOG itself and still yields results comparable to or better than specialised systems. This should be true not only for the KARDIO model, but also for a larger class of applications exhibiting similar properties. The relatively small domains and their quick reduction to atomic values eliminates the need for special-purpose builtin representation and handling of domains, like what is provided in CHIP [van Hentenryck, 1989]. If mechanisms for extending unification as proposed by [Holzbaur, 1990] or [Neumerkel, 1990] find their way into commercial systems, the more elegant approach of section 3 will possibly be more efficient, too. But till then, our preprocessing way of amalgamating PROLOG and domain variables is better off for applications like the KARDIO system.

ACKNOWLEDGEMENTS

I am indebted to Igor Mozetic for providing the KARDIO model, to Christian Holzbaur for providing Metaprolog, to both of them for discussions on the topic, and especially to Robert Trappl for creating a very special working environment. This work was supported by the Austrian Federal Ministry of Science and Research.

REFERENCES

Bratko I., Mozetic I., Lavrac N.: *Kardio - A Study in Deep and Qualitative Knowledge for Expert Systems*, MIT Press, Cambridge, MA, 1989.

Hentenryck P.van, Dincbas M.: Domains in Logic Programming, in *Proceedings of the Fifth National Conference on Artificial Intelligence (AAAI-86)*, Morgan Kaufmann, Los Altos, CA, 1986.

Hentenryck P.van: *Constraint Satisfaction in Logic Programming*, MIT Press, Cambridge, MA, 1989.

Holzbaur C.: *Realization of Forward Checking in Logic Programming through Extended Unification*, TR-90-11, Oesterreichisches Forschungsinstitut fuer Artificial Intelligence, Wien, 1990.

Jaffar J.: *CLP(R) Version 1.0 Reference Manual*, IBM Research Division, T.J. Watson Research Center, Yorktown Heights, N.Y. 10598, 1990.

Mozetic I.: *Diagnostic Efficiency of Deep and Surface Knowledge in KARDIO*, in Artificial Intelligence in Medicine, 2(2), pp.67-83, 1990.

Neumerkel U.: *Extensible Unification by Metastructures*, Proc. META90, 1990.

Recursive Plans

G.R. Ghassem-Sani and S.W.D. Steel

Computer Science Department
  University of Essex
  Colchester, CO4 3SQ

ABSTRACT

It is generally agreed that a planner should be able to reason with uncertain and iterative behaviours because many actions in real world have such behaviours. Some of
earlier non-linear planners have approached these issues, nevertheless, the way that
they handle the problem has not been logically derived. We introduce a new type of
non-linear plans, *Recursive Plans*, which can be used to solve a class of conditional
and recursive problems. The idea, which has been implemented, is based on
mathematical induction.

1. INTRODUCTION

A planner should be able to reason with uncertain and iterative behaviours
because many actions in real world have such behaviours. Some of earlier non-linear
planners have approached these issues, nevertheless, the way that they handle the problem has not been logically derived. For instance, in Warplan-C (Warren, 1976) the
issue of uncertainty was tackled by planning all branches of a conditional action which
led to a redundant tree-structured plan. NOAH (Sacerdoti, 1977), the first implemented non-linear planner, can model an iterative action as a single entity. Actions in
SIPE (Wilkins, 1984) are allowed to loop over a list of objects. However, these
planners work only where the number of objects on which the iteration is to be performed is known; whilst the most important application of iteration is where we are
not certain about the number of iterations. Steel (1988) has also proposed a solution
to the iteration issue which is analogous to the FOR constructs in structured programming languages and has been partially implemented (Ghassem-sani, 1988). The proposal works on the assumption that there is a constant function from numbers to objects.
Another approach to iteration is plan nets (Drummond, 1986). Plan nets are more
expressive than the conventional procedural nets, used by non-linear planners, because
they permit representation of the loops. However, the problem is that it seems much
more difficult to implement a planner to generate plan nets. Furthermore, termination
of a plan net may not be provable. Manna and Waldinger's deductive synthesis
method (Manna & Waldinger, 1980) is another approach to the issues of uncertainty
and iteration. They have mostly used their method to synthesize programs rather than
plans. Recently, however, they introduced a slightly different version of situational
calculus (McCarthy, 1963), plan theory, and applied their method to planning (Manna
& Waldinger, 1986). Their method is sound and general but fairly complicated. Note
that we are particularly interested in control of the search process. We have chosen
the framework of non-linear planning because it is well-understood and a relatively
easily controllable process. Manna and Waldinger's deductive method is general but
hard to control. Therefore, we are prepared to sacrifice the generality for the sake of
controllability.

It is agreed that the rules of or-elimination and induction (in theorem proving) are related to conditionals and recursive statements (in program synthesis), respectively. Our aim has been to incorporate these rules in non-linear planning. Having preserved the principle of non-linear planning, we introduce a new strategy, *Recursive Non-linear Planning*, which can be used to solve a class of conditional and iterative problems. The main idea, which has been inspired by (Manna & Waldinger, 1986) on one hand and (Boyer & Moore, 1979) on the other hand, is based on mathematical induction. We have also implemented a planning system to generate recursive plans. The system is currently running on several different problems.

2. BOYER AND MOORE'S INDUCTION PRINCIPLE

It seems that the Boyer and Moore's theorem prover (Boyer & Moore, 1979) is so far the most powerful system in which the induction principle has been extensively used. Using a slightly different notation, their definition of the induction principle is as follows:
Suppose that

   (a) P and Q are predicates;
   (b) < denotes a well-founded relation;
   (c) f is a function;
   (d) x is a variable;
   (e) $P(x) \rightarrow f(x) < x$ is a theorem.

Then in order to prove that Q(x) is a theorem, it is sufficient to prove:

   (1) $\tilde{}P(x) \rightarrow Q(x)$ (i.e. the base case) and;
   (2) $(P(x) \& Q(f(x))) \rightarrow Q(x)$ (i.e. the step case) are theorems,

in which Q(f(x)) is the so-called induction hypothesis. The above definition is sufficient for the simple cases in which there are only one base case and one step case. In general, however, it might be necessary to prove several base and step cases. We do not present their definition of general case here.

3. RECURSIVE NON-LINEAR PLANS

Similar to an ordinary non-linear plan, a recursive plan is a partially ordered set of nodes. Each node in a recursive plan is identified by a unique integer code. All nodes have also their own pre- and postconditions. Postconditions of the unique node *begin* (code 1) represents the initial state and preconditions of the unique node *end* (code 2) represents the goal state. The so-called ranges, which are 3-ary tuples <Producer, User, Condition> represented by '===...===', are to protect certain conditions at certain parts of plans. Actions are 4-ary tuples of form <Name, Preconds, Effects, Delete-list>. Although a recursive plan and an ordinary non-linear plan are very similar, there are three new type of nodes that may appear only in a recursive plan. These nodes are called CASE, PROC, and CALL which are analogous to the CASE, PROCEDURE, and CALL statements in programming languages.

3.1. CASE Nodes

Each CASE node in a recursive plan has a number of internal plan. Internal plans of a CASE node have different initial states, but all have the same goal state. Preconditions of node *begin* in internal plans act as labels. During the execution depending on the state of the world at the time of choosing an internal plan, any internal plan whose label is true in the world can be chosen to be executed.

The following figure shows a typical CASE node.

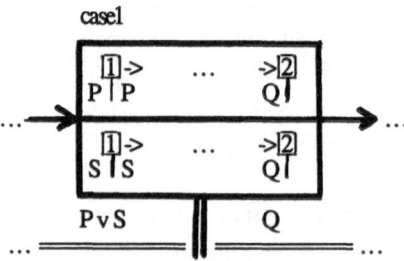

Note that we assume all labels in CASE nodes are testable. Therefore, we do not consider the problem of 'monkey, bomb, and banana' mentioned by (Manna & Waldiger, 1986).

From outside, a CASE node is like an ordinary node with its own pre- and postconditions. The disjunction of labels of the internal plans form preconditions of CASE nodes; and the postcondition of a CASE node is equal to the goal states of its internal plans. Each internal plan is itself a recursive plan, which means it might comprise a number of CASE nodes. However, the innermost internal plans comprise no CASE node.

In general, there are two situations where we add a CASE node to a recursive plan. First if there is an unsupported precondition P and there is either a node in the plan or an action in the repertoire with postconditions including a disjunctive sentence of form '... v P v ...', then a CASE node is generated to support P. The second situation where a CASE node is generated corresponds to the case analysis of an inductive proof and has been adopted from Boyer and Moore (1979) who say:

> "To apply the principle of induction to a conjecture, we must invent a case analysis, together with some substitution, a variable n-tuple, a measure, and a well-founded relation. We must prove the conjecture under each of the cases."

By analogy and in non-linear terms we claim that to apply the principle of induction to a goal we should generate a CASE node whose internal plans correspond to the appropriate case analysis. How one could achieve a goal by a CASE node, is discussed in section (4).

Finally, after a CASE node is generated, it will be added to the action repertoire (with a similar format to that of ordinary actions) as a new action, which could be later used to create CALL nodes.

3.2. PROC Nodes

PROC nodes in recursive plans are analogous to a special case of sub-procedures in programming languages. A PROC node, here, is essentially a CASE node. To be more precise, if a generated CASE node is invoked by a CALL node (discussed next), it will be tactically renamed into a PROC node. There are two reasons behind renaming some of CASE nodes into PROC nodes. First to keep the analogy between recursive plans and imperative programs as much as possible; and, more importantly, to prepare recursive plans for the task of detecting and, if necessary, resolving conflicts. Since PROC nodes (together with CALL nodes) form recursion, detecting conflicts involving internal plans of a PROC node is both different from and more difficult than for a CASE node. Therefore, from now on, we refer to any CASE node which is invoked by a CALL node as a PROC node.

3.3. CALL Nodes

· A CALL node in our system is very similar to procedure invocation in imperative languages. A CALL node in a recursive plan invokes a PROC node. Although it is not very likely, there might be several different CALL nodes calling the same PROC node. Similarly to other type of nodes, a CALL node has its own pre- and postconditions. There is always a relation between postconditions of a CALL node and postconditions of the invoked PROC node. Preconditions of a CALL node and the invoked PROC node have exactly the same relation as their postconditions have. The following figure shows a recursive plan in which the main goal is to make the base of a tower of blocks (i.e. 'a' here) clear. In this plan node 5 is a CALL, 4 an ordinary, and 3 a PROC node. (hat(a) designates the block directly on top of a, hat(hat(a)) the block directly on top of hat(a), etc.) In section (4) we explain how such a recursive plan is generated.

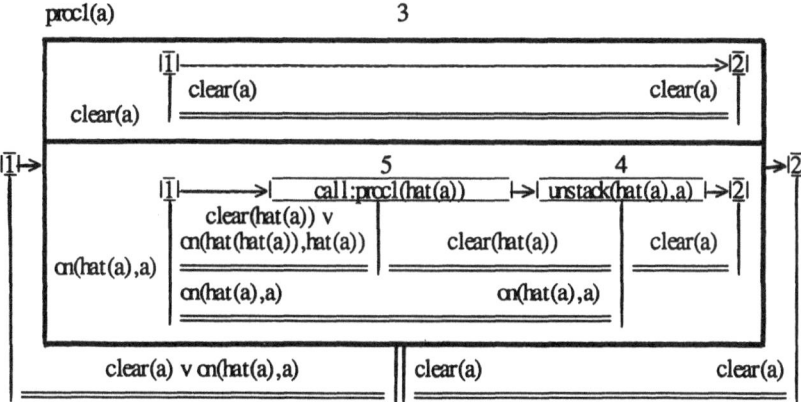

3.4. Relation between Recursive Plans and Induction Principle

It was earlier said that recursive plans are based on the Boyer and Moore's induction principle. The following figure shows their induction principle in contrast with a general form of a simple recursive plan.

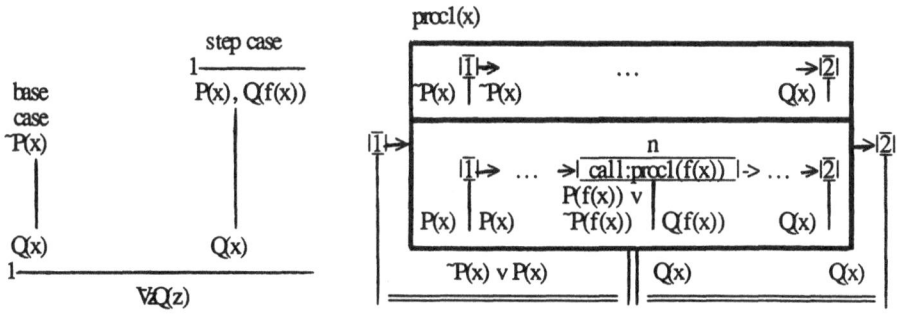

induction principle   recursive plan

The first internal plan of *procl* corresponds to the base case of the induction principle and the second internal plan to its step case.

4. PLANNING PROCESS

4.1. Overview

Before explaining the planning process, let us call our system RNP (Recursive Non-linear Planner). Conventional operations, by which non-linear planners achieve a subgoal in order to modify an incomplete plan, are linking to an old node, and adding a new node to the plan. Apart from conventional operations, RNP can improve an incomplete plan by two new operations: creating a CALL node, and generating a CASE node. (Note that PROC nodes are produced by renaming those CASE nodes which are invoked by CALL nodes. Therefore, RNP does not have a separate operation to generate PROC nodes). RNP applies its modification operations to an incomplete plan in the following order:

(1): linking to an old node,
(2): creating a CALL node,
(3): adding a new (ordinary) node,
(4): generating a CASE node.

Why have we chosen the above order? The last three of the above operations add a new node to an incomplete plan. Each time that a new node is added to a plan, the node's preconditions will be appended to the list of unsupported preconditions which must be achieved. The first operation (i.e. linking to an old node) should have a higher priority than that of the other three, because it appends nothing to the list of unsupported preconditions. Among the last three operations, generating a CASE node is more time consuming and complicated than the others; because, unlike the others, it involves generating a number of internal plans. Thus, generating a CASE node should have the least priority of these operations. Finally, creating a CALL node should be tried before adding a new simple node, because otherwise the planner is likely to be trapped in a loop. Consider, for instance, the following action:

$$\overset{\boxed{A}}{P(f(X))\,\big|\,P(X)}$$

Suppose that the planner is to achieve the subgoal P(a). It improves the plan by action A and then P(f(a)) will be its new subgoal. If, at that stage, the planner applied the operation (3) before (2), it would choose action A again and then P(f(f(a))) would be the next new subgoal. Had the planning process continued this way, the planner would have never tried to create a CALL node; whilst, as we later see, the planner should in fact try to achieve P(f(a)) by a CALL node.

4.2. Generating CASE Nodes

Generating a CASE node is the last resort by which RNP tries to improves an incomplete plan. However, we explain it first for the sake of simplicity and providing some information for the subsequent sub-sections. We do not explain conventional operations (1) and (3) above. Consider the following partial plan:

$$\boxed{1}\!\!\mapsto \quad \dots \quad \to\!\boxed{6}\qquad \boxed{5}\!\!\mapsto\!\boxed{4}\!\!\mapsto\!\boxed{3}\!\!\mapsto\!\boxed{2}$$
$$\underset{}{\big|}\qquad\qquad\underset{P\vee S}{\big|}\qquad \underset{\underline{\underline{}}}{P}\;\underset{\underline{\underline{}}}{Q}\;\underset{\underline{\underline{}}}{R}\;\underset{\underline{}}{G}$$

Suppose that the planner is trying to achieve the subgoal P of node 5. Let us call node 5, the user. If RNP fails to achieve P by either conventional operations (1 and 3 above) or by adding a CALL node (discussed later), it will try to achieve P by generating a CASE node. In order to generate a CASE node, RNP searches for a node in the plan (or an action in the repertoire) with postconditions including a disjunctive sentence of the form '... v P v ...'. Let us call such a node the producer. If RNP fails to find such a producer, it will add the sentence '~P v P' (equivalent to truth) to the postconditions of node *begin* (code 1) and regard node *begin* as the producer. RNP then adds a CASE node to the plan to link the producer (eg. node 6) and the user (eg. node 5). The following figure shows the above partial plan after adding a CASE node.

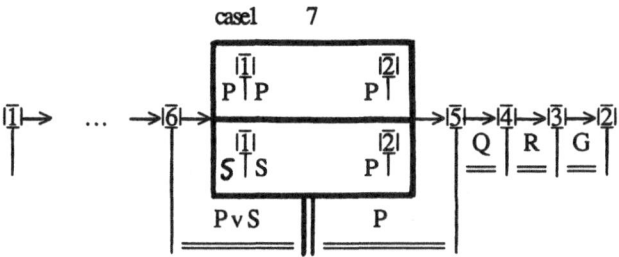

Now RNP has to generate the internal plans of the CASE node. Note that generating the first internal plan of the above CASE node is trivial. If RNP fails to generate any of these internal plans, the CASE node will be replaced by backtracking by another one as shown in the following figure. The new CASE node differs from the previous one mainly in the goal states of its internal plans.

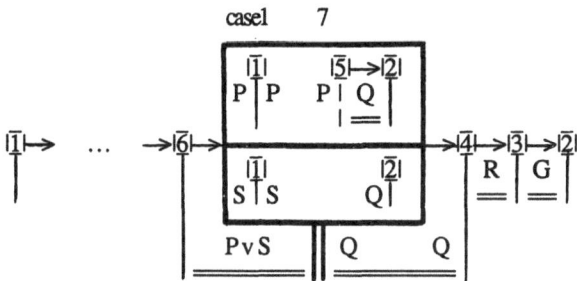

Backtracking may continue and each time a new CASE node, of which mostly the goal states of the internal plans change, would be tried, until finally RNP succeeds in generating all the internal plans of a CASE node. How does RNP choose the goal states of the internal plans in each try? Consider the above partial plan before adding *case1*, and suppose again that RNP is trying to achieve the subgoal P. RNP first finds all paths from node 5 to the node *end* (code 2). We use the PROLOG (Bratko, 1987) list notation, '[...]', to show a path. In this example there is only one such a path, [5, 4, 3, 2] (Members of a path are integer codes of nodes). In each try, RNP chooses one node of this path. Let us call this node the user. The preconditions of the user in each try form the goal states of the internal plans. Although in this example there is only one path between node 5 and node 2, in general there might exist several such paths. After all members of a path have been tried as the user, if backtracking continues, RNP will nominate the first member of another path as the new user.

Those nodes that precede the user in the path will be removed from the main plan. For example, if node 5 is chosen to be the user, nothing will be removed from the main plan because nothing precede node 5 in the path; but if, for instance after backtracking, node 4 is chosen to be the user, node 5 will be removed from the main plan. The intuition behind removing this part of the main plan is that this part will be included in one of the internal plans of the CASE node.

4.3. Creating CALL Nodes

4.3.1. Similar Subgoals

In order to create a CALL node, one needs to be able to recognise the appropriate time to do so. A similarity between a subgoal and a top level goal indicates the possibility of achieving the subgoal by recursion. Thus the problem is how to recognise the similarity between a subgoal and a top level goal. In general, a subgoal of form $Q(f(x))$ and a goal of form $Q(x)$, where x is a variable tuple, are similar; but how could one detect such similarity? It is clear that the similarity here does not mean being unifiable by the first order unification algorithm (Robinson, 1965). However, one can identify the similarity between such terms using typed-lambda unification algorithm (Huet, 1974). For this purpose we try to solve the following equation, in which '?...' indicates a variable and '==' means lambda unifiable:

$$\text{top level goal} == ?Q(?x), \text{ and subgoal} == ?Q(?f(?x)) \qquad (1)$$

The above equation is solved by finding substitutions S1 and [?f:= ...] such that:

$$\text{top level goal} = ?Q(?x)S1, \text{ and subgoal} = (?Q(?f(?x))S1)[?f:= ...] \quad (2)$$

Having found such substitutions, one can conclude that the subgoal is similar to the top level goal. In the tower-clearing recursive plan shown in section 3.3, for instance, the subgoal clear(hat(a)) of node 4 (inside *proc1*) and the top level goal clear(a) of node 2 (outside *proc1*) are similar; because if we solve the equation (1) for these two goals, we will get the substitutions [?x:=a, ?Q:=clear] and [?f:=λ?z.hat(?z)] such that:

$$\text{clear(a)} = ?Q(?x)[?x:=a, ?Q:=clear], \text{ and}$$
$$\text{clear(hat(a))} = (?Q(?f(?x)))[?x:=a, ?Q:=clear])[?f:=λ?z.hat(?z)]$$

Definition 1:

A subgoal SG is similar to a top level goal TG if and only if there exist S1 and F such that: $TG = ?Q(?x)S1$, and $SG = (?Q(?f(?x))S1)[?f:= F]$ in which S1 is a substitution for the variables ?x and ?Q.

4.3.2. Termination Condition

The similarity between a subgoal and a top level goal, though necessary, is not sufficient for RNP to create a CALL node. Let us call this other precondition, which guarantees that recursive plans terminate, the termination condition. The condition corresponds to the precondition (e) of the induction principle explained in section 2. For a subgoal $Q(f(x))$ similar to a goal $Q(x)$, the condition has the form of $P(x) \to f(x) < x$, in which P is a predicate, and < a well-founded relation. Roughly speaking, the termination condition ensures that the subgoal is a reduced (or simpler) form of the top level goal. Satisfiability of the termination condition is determined by looking up a table which is part of RNP's knowledge base. The table comprise, for instance, the following statements:

$$\tilde{}\,clear\_block(?x) \to hat(?x) < ?x,$$
$$\tilde{}\,empty\_list(?x) \to tail(?x) < ?x.$$

Definition 2:

A subgoal Q(f(x)) is a reduced form of a top level goal Q(x) if and only if there exist a predicate P and a well-founded relation < such that:
P(x) → f(x) < x.

4.3.3. Case Analysis

After a subgoal Q(f(x)) has been proved to be a reduced form of a top level goal Q(x), RNP will try to achieve the subgoal by creating a CALL node invoking a suitable PROC node. But what is a suitable PROC node? A PROC node is suitable to be invoked by a CALL node to achieve Q(f(x)), if the PROC node produces Q(x) and its internal plans cover the base and step cases of the corresponding inductive proof. For instance, the following figure shows the general form of a suitable PROC node in the simplest case, where the proof has only one base and one step case.

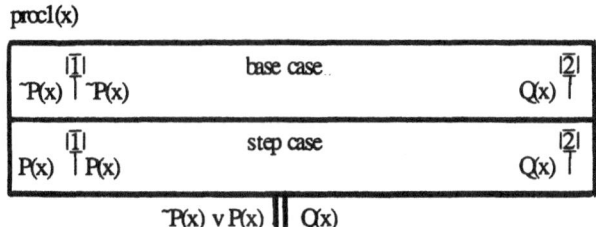

Therefore, if there is a suitable PROC node such as *procl(x)* above, a CALL node *call:procl(f(x))* of the following form will be added to the developing plan, to achieve the subgoal Q(f(x)).

$$¬P(f(x)) \vee P(f(x)) \mid Q(f(x))$$

But what if there is not such a PROC node? Having failed to find a suitable PROC node, RNP will try to generate one. Consider, for instance, the following partial plan.

$$Q(f(x)) \qquad \overline{|c|}\text{->}...\text{->}|\overline{b}|\text{--->}|\overline{a}|\text{->}... \qquad Q(x)$$

In situations such as the above partial plan, after failing to find a suitable PROC node, RNP would first try to generate a PROC node (i.e. generating and renaming a CASE node) to produce Q(x), and then create a CALL node invoking the PROC node to achieve Q(f(x)). Next figure shows the above partial plan after generating a PROC node.

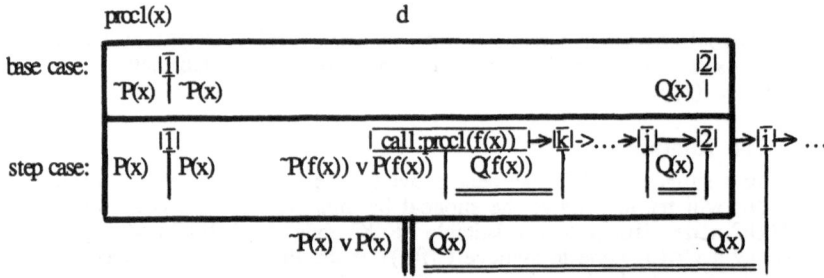

Note that some part of the original partial plan is now included in the PROC node. In order to complete the process of generating *procl(x)*, RNP has to generate an internal plan for the base-case branch, and complete the step-case branch. Achieving subgoals '~P(x) v P(x)' and '~P(f(x)) v P(f(x)))', which are equivalent to truth, is trivial.

4.4. Detecting & Resolving Conflicts

One of important tasks of a non-linear planner is the task of detecting and, if necessary, resolving conflicts. Apart from conflicts involving only ordinary nodes, in a recursive plan, we may also face conflicts involving CASE, PROC, or CALL nodes. RNP Detects conflicts involving CASE and PROC nodes by performing the following stages:

(1) replacing all CASE (and PROC) nodes by one of their internal plans, which transforms a recursive plan into a CASE-PROC-free non-linear plan (i.e. a plan without any CASE or PROC node),

(2) detecting conflicts of the CASE-PROC-free plan as an ordinary non-linear plan.

RNP then repeats this process for all combinations of internal plans of CASE (and PROC) nodes.

Although a CASE-PROC-free plan is treated like an ordinary non-linear plan, some of its nodes which originally belong to a PROC node (eg. CALL nodes) need a special conflict detection strategy. The fact that PROC nodes might be executed several times implies that there might exist a conflict involving only certain cycles of executing the PROC node. In general, a recursive plan is independent of the number of operands on which the plan may be executed. For instance, the tower-clearing plan, shown in section 3.3, can be used to clear the base of any tower consisting of any number of blocks. This makes the task of detecting conflicts involving PROC nodes difficult, because during the planning process it is not known how many times a PROC node might be executed. Nevertheless, we can predict the possibility of some conflicts (occurring in the execution time) during the planning process; because although one cannot forecast how many times a PROC node would be called, it is known that in each call all ranges inside the PROC node are a reduced form of that of the previous call (according to some well-founded relation and toward a base element). Now if there is a node (outside a PROC node) denying a condition which is a reduced form of a range inside the PROC node, there is the possibility of a conflict occurring in execution of the PROC node. For instance, if we assume there is a node N outside *procl(a)* of the tower-clearing plan with the postcondition ~clear(hat(hat(a))), there would be such a possible conflict between range <5, 4, clear(hat(a))> (in the second internal plan of *procl*) and node N, because node N denies clear(hat(hat(a))) which is a reduced form of clear(hat(a)).

For a more rigorous definition of conflicts involving PROC nodes and a detailed account of RNP's conflict resolution strategy, the interested reader may refer to the complete version of this paper (Ghassem-sani & Steel, forthcoming).

5. DEFICIENCIES

Although our planner (RNP) is currently running on several different problems, there are still a number of improvement that we need to make. For example, RNP cannot generate a plan for the problem of building a tower, which is a recursive problem (One of difficulties with this problem is how one should represent the main goal statement). Furthermore, RNP cannot generate a plan for problems similar to the so-called quick-sort, which involves multiple recursion. Another obvious improvement is that to be able to generate recursive plans for inductive proofs involving more than only one base and one step cases. The difficulty, here, is to determine the appropriate initial states of internal plans corresponding to the base and step cases.

6. CONCLUSION

There are many actions in real world which have conditional and/or iterative behaviour. It is essential for a planning system to be able to model such actions. Contemporary non-linear planners, however, do not have such an ability. We have introduced and implemented a new strategy, *Recursive Non-linear Planning*, which enables a non-linear planner to handle a class of conditional and recursive problems. The process of generating these plans, which comprise a few new modification rule besides conventional rules used in ordinary non-linear planning, is based on mathematical induction.

REFERENCES

Boyer, R. S. and Moore, J. S. (1979)
ACM monograph series, A Computational Logic, Academic Press, INC. London

Bratko, I. (1987)
Prolog Programming for Artificial Intelligence, Academic Press, INC. London

Drummond, M. (1986)
A representation of action and belief for automatic planning systems, in: (Georgeff, M. and Lansky, A.), Morgan Kauffman

Ghassem-Sani, G. R. (1988)
Iterative actions in non-linear planners, M.Sc. Thesis, Department of Computer Science, University of Essex

Ghassem-Sani, G. R. and Steel, S. W. D. (forthcoming)
Recursive Plans, Internal Report, University of Essex

Huet, G. P. (1974)
A unification algorithm for typed lambda-calculus, note de travial A 055, Institute de Recherche d'Informatique et d'Automatique

Manna, Z. and Waldinger, R. (1980)
A deductive approach to programme synthesis, ACM Transactions on Programming Languages and Systems, 2(1), PP. 90-121

Manna, Z. and Waldinger, R. (1986)

A Theory of plans, in: (Georgeff, M. and Lansky, A.), Morgan Kauffman

McCarthy J. (1963)

Situations, actions, and causal laws, Technical report, Stanford university, Stanford, Calf.

Robinson, J. A. (1965)

A machine oriented logic based on the resolution principle, J. ACM 12, No 1, PP. 23-41

Sacerdoti, E. D. (1977)

A Structure for Plans and Behaviour, American Elsevier North-Holland, New York

Steel, S. W. D. (1988)

An iterative construct for non-linear precedence planners, Proc. Seventh Biennial Conference of the Canadian Society for the Computational Study of Intelligence, PP. 227-233

Warren, D. H. D. (1976)

Generating Conditional Plans and Programmes, In Proceedings of the AISB summer conference, PP. 344-354

Wilkins, D. E. (1984)

Domain-independent Planning: Representation and Plan Generation, Artificial Intelligence 22(3), PP. 269-301

THE KNOWLEDGE LEVEL PERSPECTIVE

TASK CENTERED REPRESENTATION FOR EXPERT SYSTEMS AT THE KNOWLEDGE LEVEL

Christine PIERRET-GOLBREICH & Isabelle DELOUIS

Laboratoire de Recherche en Informatique
Equipe Intelligence Artificielle et Systèmes d'Inférences
Université Paris Sud, 91405 Orsay Cedex, FRANCE

Email: pierret @lri.lri.fr

ABSTRACT

This work comes within the framework of current research on the development of functional architectures for second generation expert systems. The aim is to propose a model that allows the elicitation of a problem solving process at a "more appropriate" level of abstraction. The TASK model being developed has been specified in such a way as to offer the possibility of expressing the specificity of the semantics and the control structures implicit in certain clearly recognized reasoning modules whatever the level of abstraction is (generic tasks relating to a high-level cognitive activity or more specific tasks involved in solving a particular problem). This model is based on the key concept of "task", a data structure which makes it possible to clearly reflect all the conceptual operations involved in the type of reasoning to be modelled. TASK denotes at one and the same time a representation model and the general architecture supporting task based system.

1. INTRODUCTION

The need to go beyond the limits of first-generation expert systems has led to a series of works on the abstraction level of the modelling of the reasoning involved. A restropective analysis of first generation systems indeed shows that the direct transcription of expertise at the level of current implementation languages brings about a loss of information relating to knowledge of the field: either the semantics or control of the reasoning. This loss of information is detrimental to the quality of answers to such questions as the elicitation of the reasoning, the knowledge acquisition, explanation, debugging, maintenance, etc. The solutions found at an implementation level (e.g., weighting rules, organization into packets, contexts definition, meta-rules, etc.) are inevitably dependent both on the application and the implementation model. The proposed answers are local, and difficult to extend or reproduce. Faced with such a situation, a new approach has been appearing over the last few years : the development of functional architectures for knowledge-based systems. The work presented comes within this perspective. The aim is to offer a model which allows, at a high level, the elicitation of the nature of the reasoning and strategies involved in solving complex problems. The model being developed has been specified in such a way as to offer the possibility of explaining both the specificity of the semantics and the control structures implicit in certain clearly identified reasoning modules whatever their levels of abstraction (generic tasks, related to high-level cognitive activity or more specific tasks used to solve individual problems). The model is based on the key concept of "task".
We shall firstly define the concept of "task" before giving a detailed presentation of the TASK model. We shall finally present an example of a problem representation and resolution using TASK.

2. MOTIVATIONS AND OBJECTIVES

The motivating factors that led to this work are akin to the motivations of Task Specific architecture [Chandrasekaran 1987]: First Generation Expert Systems had got a lot of trouble to tackle problems of knowledge-based systems construction and debugging, knowledge acquisition process, explanation and maintenance. The analysis of these systems [Chandrasekaran 1987] [Clancey 1985], [Steels 1989] brought to light that two levels of analysis are often confused about the problem solving process : the computational level, the knowledge level :

At the computational level, the term of problem solving process refers to the kind of activity of the system dynamic part (Shell) i.e. the organization and the way of invocating some predefined inference mechanisms (e.g. hypothesis and match for rules, unification, clause selection and theorem proving for logic, inheritance and demons for frames) according to the system's own control strategy.

At the "knowledge level" [Newell 1982], it refers to a problem solving method, regardless of the implementation, i.e. a decomposition of the problem into sub-problems whatever the type. This decomposition can be described in domain specific terms and the solving strategy linked to the domain (cf. the inference structure of SACON [Bennet & 1984] : Investigate numeric stress and deflection magnitudes of each load component, Find composite numeric stress and deflection estimates of each loading, etc.). It can also be domain independent but connected to an abstract type of task (for instance, generic solving strategy associated to heuristic classification: data-abstraction, heuristic match, refinement [Clancey 1985]). This latter knowledge about the solving method cannot be captured and is in fact embedded with the former.

This confusion is ineluctable because no representation structures are available to explicit the problem solving process at the right level of abstraction. Therefore, the objective of this work is to provide representations structures with suited mechanisms operating on these structures that make it possible to elicite reasoning at the knowledge level in a declarative fashion.

3. THE TASK CENTERED REPRESENTATION PARADIGM

3.1. Task-centered representation vs object-centered representation

Object-based models are particularly well-suited to modelling *factual* knowledge (i.e. objects in the universe). On the other hand, these models are less suited, at least in their present state of development, to modelling the *dynamical* knowledge of the problem solving process. When dealing with these types of knowledge, object-based models generally make use of other formalisms (procedural languages in the Object Oriented Languages, or rule formalisms in the hybrid systems). Thus, in order to avoid losing the problem solving knowledge through its scattering among a knowledge base (often split up, for example, in a rule base or swamped in the system's control mechanisms), the idea of task-centered representations is to propose a formalism which allows the elicitation of such knowledge. The goal of the task-centered representation proposed with TASK, is to provide data structures (called Tasks) which make it possible to reflect the globality of the conceptual operations involved in the reasoning process to be modelled at a "better" level of abstraction. Task-centered representations and object-centered representations are complementary as concerns offering a knowledge representation environment that is based on the notion of syntactic unit of representation whose goal is to allow the elicitation of both structural knowledge (objects) and reasoning knowledge (tasks).

3.2. The Task concept

"Task" must be understood in the broadest sense of the term. Regarding to the different authors terminologies and the different existing systems, the term "task" can cover the notions of module, step, plan, specialist, procedure, function, work, etc. It may for instance be applied to a numerical or symbolic procedure (Hessien's computation procedure,

procedure of derivation), a numerical resolution method (a quasi-Newton method), a user task corresponding to a user operational level ("drawing up a report"), a system task at the system operational level ("unstack the current task"), a generic task corresponding to a specific and clearly identified high-level cognitive activity (design, planning), a problem-task, a solution-task (instance of a problem-task) or a problem solving strategy. Thus a task is the level of granularity used to represent knowledge relating to any problem solving module.

> A Task is a structured entity gathering all the informations involved in a problem resolution, in the form of a [CONTEXT / PROCESS] association, (whatever the problem abstraction or structural level is : generic or particular type, complex or elementary structure).

3.3. Typology of tasks according to their genericity

Tasks can be listed from the more abstract to the most particular level:

- . **Very High level Tasks** (VHT) which correspond to so called "primitive Inference Making Functions" [Wielinga & 1988], or "conceptual operations" by other authors i.e. universal reasoning mechanisms which are independent of the domain type (e.g. Abstraction, Particularization, Matching)
- . **High level Tasks** (HT) which correspond to the "generic tasks" of Chandrasekaran, i.e. generic reasoning modules, which are independant of the domain but characterize a problem type (e.g. Planning, Diagnosis, Heuristic Classification etc.). Thus they are domain independant but type of problem dependant.
- . **Domain Tasks** (DT) which correspond to real tasks involved in a specific application. They are particularizations of the HTs on a specific domain. Thus they are domain dependant but solving case independant (e.g. The Hanoï Task is an instantiation of the Planning task on a specific domain).
- . **Realization Tasks** (RT) represent a particular problem under resolution and thus are case specific).

4. THE TASK SYSTEM

TASK originates from a number of previous works [Pierret 1988], [Scapin & 1989], [Pierret & 1989], [Pierret & 1990]. Other authors have suggested task description formalisms, for instance in the field of design, [Montalban 1987], [Mittal & 1986], [Frayman & 1987], [Fajon & 1988], and knowledge acquisition [Dieng 1988].

4.1 The "*Task*" data structure:

A *Task* is composed of three parts :

> *A Contextual part* characterized by a
>
> - **Initial-state** : types of input data to be provided to the *Task*
>   preconditions : constraints on the Initial .State
> - **Final-state** : types of output data provided by the *Task*
>   postconditions : constraints on the Final.State
> - **Goal** : subset of the I.S. and F.S. eliciting the aim of the *Task*
> - **Parameters** : parameters of the *Task*
>
> *An Executive part* characterized by a
> - **Body** : operating level describing how the *Task* can be achieved
>
> *A Relational part* characterized by
> - **Super** : list of the known super-tasks of the *Task*
> - **Spec**: list of the known specializations of the *Task*

Each variable in the description of the initial and final states is defined by a data couple including a name and a type. The type defines the object class to which the field value must belong. The name is either a formal object (called generic instance) that behaves like a universal variable and can be replaced during execution by any concrete object from the application domain since it is of correct type, or by a particular concrete object that behaves then like a constant.

A specific data structure is also proposed to explicitly represent each condition as a conventional tree where the leaves represent the elementary relations, and the nodes are the connectors.

4.2. Typology of tasks regarding to their body structure

The methods used to solve problems in expert systems are partly deductive, but can also be partly algorithmic. The fields where the conjunction between these two types of knowledge is particularly prevalent are design ([Mostow 1985], [Neveu 1987] [Montalban 1987] for CAD), diagnosis in engineering applications [David & 1989], assistance in scientific computing and technical diagnosis. Problem-solving modules are often clearly identified and invariable(e.g. "Situation Recognition, Data Abstraction, Diagnosis Development" modules in DIVA [David & 1989]). However other phases of the solving process may rely on other types of reasoning mechanisms: logical inferences or external procedures. For these two different types of reasoning to coexist, TASK can accommodate static tasks chainings that can be defined using elementary control structures with dynamic task chainings, which are calculated according to a context or strategy. Thus, specific data structures have been defined such as for instance *Sequence-task, Iterative-task* to represent procedural parts of reasoning while *Alternative* or *Abstract tasks* are used for deductive parts.

There are three types of task according to their body structure :
- **Elementary tasks**, whose operational level is distinguished by an indivisible procedural entity that points towards a process exterior to the model, e.g., LISP function, user action, FORTRAN programs, etc. Even though these processes may be complex procedures capable of solving a non-trivial problem, within the TASK modelling level, they are considered as elementary processes. Elementary tasks are the problem solving modules that correspond to primitive problems.
- **Composite tasks**, whose operational level is a combination of sub-tasks. The basic notion is that of decomposition: composite tasks are associated with problems whose solution can be reached by solving several sub-problems :

   solve Pb <= solve OP (Sp1, Sp2, ...,Spn) , where OP is a composition operator

   There are two types of composite tasks, depending on whether the combination expresses a static or dynamic chaining of sub-tasks :

   The so-called "fixed" tasks are used to elicit complex problems solving methods by a static chaining of sub-tasks. Thus, fixed tasks enable invariable and well-known task chainings to be explicitly describe. Fixed tasks make it possible to define chainings that frequently occur in the reasoning process for problems such as :

   solve Pb <= solve AND (Sp1, Sp2, ...,Spn)
   solve Pb <= solve WHILE (cond, Sp)

   Structured sub-task chainings are defined using the andpar, andseq, loop and if operators. **Andpar** is used to define a chaining of tasks that can be executed in any order, or even at the same time. **Andseq** is used to define a chaining of tasks that must be executed in sequence. **Loop** is used to define iterative tasks, such as "while", "until", "for". **If** is used to define conditional task.

   The so-called "alternative" tasks are used to elicit the complex problems solving methods by a dynamic chaining of sub-tasks. These tasks correspond to problems whose exact decomposition is not previously known, but for which different alternative decompositions are available:

   solve Pb <= solve OR (Sp1, Sp2, ...,Spn)

   The different alternatives must be tried in parallel. Choosing an alternative is not deterministic but relies on notions of heuristics or strategy.
- **Abstract tasks** have an indeterminate executive part. These tasks correspond to problems whose operational level can be elicited neither by a primitive process nor by a

combination of sub-tasks. These tasks are used to bring together in a single entity the common characteristics of more specific tasks. An abstract task describes a general problem to be solved by eliciting the task context (general type of objects involved, preconditions, goal, etc) but not the means of solving the problem. The process can be inferred by replacing the abstract task with another that is chosen according to the context or strategy.

Abstract tasks are used to represent problems for which no solving method is predefined; while it is frequently impossible to define the general method of achieving a given goal, a specific method of reaching the same goal can be found for individual contexts. In other words, while a process cannot be defined for a general problem, nevertheless a process may be associated with more specific situations, thus it is possible to define specialized tasks T1, T2, etc., Tn that describe valid and known situation-process combinations. In this case, an abstract task T can be used to describe the common characteristics relating to the set Ti of more specific tasks. These tasks are then defined as specializations of the general task T, which is the root of a task Ti hierarchy. To solve a given problem, it is first necessary to select a process that is suited to the given situation. The process can be inferred by applying a classification mechanism to the hierarchy. The mechanism selects from the task base a specialization whose context matches the context of the given situation (matching input objects in the task, preconditions, etc.).

An abstract task T provides a specific spec field in order to refer to the different tasks T1, T2, etc., Tn which enable the goal defined in the abstract task T to be reached

Thus, *Elementary* tasks and *Fixed* tasks describe solving modules corresponding to static knowledge about the reasoning, while *Alternative* and *Abstract* tasks correspond to tasks requiring dynamic calculation of the sub-tasks chaining.

4.3. Examples of tasks

There is no isomorphism between the two above typologies. For instance, a HT can be represented by a *Fixed* task and a DT can be represented by an *Abstract* task. Thus different types of tasks can be represented with the TASK formalism whatever the level of abstraction or the structure is :

- *A High Level Task :* e.g. "Hierarchical classification"

```
{Hierarchical-Classification
   init      :    [(Hierarchy $H), (Node $N)]¹
   final     :    [possible -l, impossible-l, sure-l]
   goal      :       - - -
   body      :    (SEQUENCE
                         {Establishment
                            - - -
                         body    :  (SEQUENCE
                                          {K.Dir.Inf.Passing
                                              --                              }
                                          {Hyp  Matching
                                              ---                            }}
                         {Refinement
                            ---                          )       )        }
```

Figure 1 : A High level task represented by a *Fixed* Task

---

[1]   (Type $v) is the syntax used in TASK for a generic variable $v of type Type. For instance (Process $P) represents a process whose value is named $T but is unknown

- *A DomainTask* e.g. "Hanoï"

The general Hanoï problem, which consists in moving $n disks from tower $t1 to tower $t2, is a DT represented by an *Abstract* task that specifies the context (initial, final states, etc)

[Displace		
parameters	:	[(Integer $n), (Tower $t1), (Tower $t2)]
init:	:	[(Tower $t1), (Tower $t2), (Tower $t3)]
final	:	[(Tower $t1), (Tower $t2), (Tower $t3)]
body	:	[Process $P]
spec	:	Displace-1 Displace≠1]

Figure 2 : A Domain Task represented by an *Abstract* Task

- *A Realization task*

Each particular Hanoi problem is a Realization task, represented by an *Abstract* Task instance of the generic Displace task, (while the solution is represented by a *CT*)

[Pb1		
is-a	:	Displace
parametres	:	(3, A, B)
init:	:	(A, B, C)
final	:	(A, B, C)
body	:	[Process $P]]

Figure 3 : A Realization Task represented by an *Abstract* Task T

4.4. General organization

A task-centered knowledge base system includes the following modules :
  . a knowledge base containing the structural and expert knowledge that are represented by objects and tasks respectively;
  . a knowledge management system having tasks, objects, a specification and procedures as arguments;
  . an engine that executes the tasks.

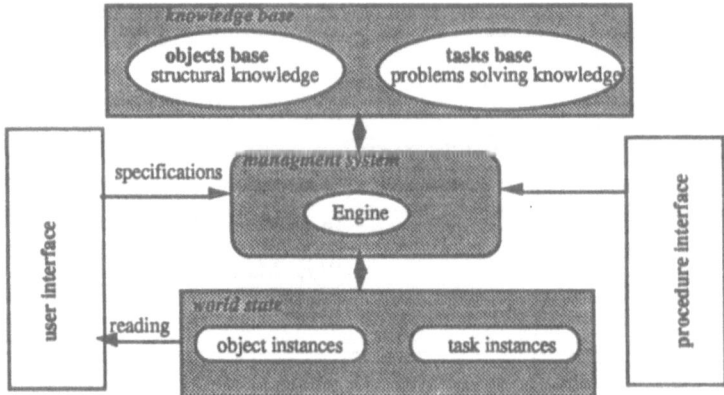

Figure 4: General architecture of a Task-centered knowledge system

The problem to be solved is specified by means of an instance of the problem-task class that models the problem to be solved, and instances that describe the objects involved in the task description. The system then asks questions about these instances. The instances are usually incomplete, and some slots have not been assigned values. The role of the inference mechanisms is precisely to infer these values.

4.5 Coherence control and inference mechanisms

4.5.1. Fixed Tasks. The suggested formalism is used to define the Fixed tasks by composing the Elementary tasks using operators. The Fixed tasks are managed by a set of coherence constraints that depend on the type of operator used to compound the sub-tasks.

. Sequence tasks: $T = ANDSEQ(T1,T2)$

If task T is made up of two tasks, T1 and T2, connected by the ANDSEQ operator, then, the task T inputs set is the union of T1 and T2 inputs, with inputs bearing the same name being merged. The T outputs set is the union of T1 and T2 outputs. If an output of T2 has the same name as an output of T1, the output of T1 is masked. The outputs of T1 are connected to the inputs of T2.

. Parallel tasks: $T = ANDPAR(T1,T2)$

If task T is decomposed into two tasks, T1 and T2, connected by the ANDPAR operator then,

T1 and T2 must not have any outputs of the same name. Further, the task T inputs set is the union of T1 and T2 inputs, with inputs bearing the same name being merged. The T outputs set is the union of T1 and T2 outputs

. Iterative tasks: $T := WHILE (<cond> , T1)$, or $T = UNTIL (<cond>, T1)$

If T is an iterative task built on task T1, which has inputs (ai) that are also task outputs, then the values sent by the ai outputs are 'consumed' by inputs with same name. The output that is looped back to the input of the same name masks this input.

4.5.2. Specialization and inference by inheritance. Specialization between tasks corresponds to the notion of more specific task. If certain individual tasks share common characteristics, they are grouped together in a single category within the general task to which they belong.

The specialization of a task inherits the same slots as its super-task on the next highest level, and can also bring into play new slots. The inherited slots are either of the same type or are a specialization of the types on a higher level.

If a task T' is a specialization of a super-task T, then:

. task T' has the same inputs and outputs as T, possibly with one or several additional objects. With inherited inputs or outputs, the types of input or output objects of the task T' are specializations of the types of inputs or outputs of T.

. task T' has the same preconditions or postconditions as T, possibly with one or two additional conditions. With inherited conditions, the types of predicate in the task T' are a specialization of the types of predicate of task T.

. if T is a composite task, then task T' has the same sub-tasks that are defined in T, or some specializations of these sub-tasks. The operator is either identical or is of a more specific type. In any case, the constraints related to the coherence of the structure, and particularly those that manage the transfer of parameters from the composite task to the sub-tasks, must be obeyed. Specializations of composite sub-tasks are "isomorphous" in structure with the sub-task itself and only differ by the types of objects involved in the different components, the preconditions and postconditions, or the type of operator used.

. If T is an abstract task, no constraints are applied to the body of its specialization T', whose value may be any decomposition into sub-tasks or an elementary procedure.

5. THE HANOI PROBLEM RESOLUTION WITH TASK

The Hanoï problem consists in finding a plan to progress from a given initial state (e.g. 3 disks on tower A) to a final state (3 disks on tower B) . While a general method of solving a Displace problem cannot be defined, it can be specified for specific cases : for n disks $(n \neq 1)$, one possible strategy is to sequentially chain three Displace sub-tasks while for 1 disk, simply execute the "move-1-disq"method.

Thus two specializations of the Displace task have been defined respectively called Displace-1 and Displace≠1. For instance, the specific problem of displacing n disks $(n \neq 1)$ from tower Ti to tower Tj is represented by the generic Fixed task, Displace≠1:

```
{Displace≠1
      kind-of : Displace
      body :    (ANDSEQ
                    (Displace
                              parameters      <- ($n - 1, $t1, $t3)
                              initial state   <- ($t1, $t2, $t3)
                              final state     -> ($t1, $t2, $t3))
                    (Displace-1
                              parameters      <- (1, $t1, $t2)
                              initial state   <- ($t1, $t2, $t3)
                              final state     -> ($t1, $t2, $t3))
                    (Displace
                              parameters      <- ($n - 1, $t3, $t2)
                              initial state   <- ($t1, $t2, $t3)
                              final state     -> ($t1, $t2, $t3) }
```

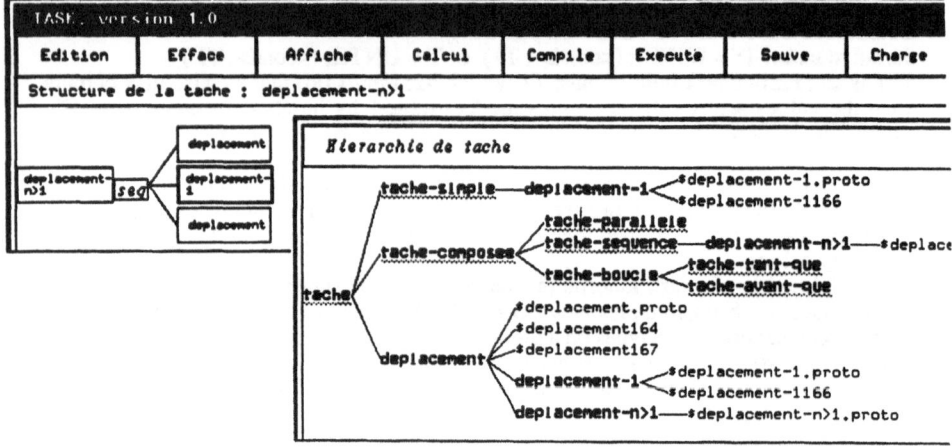

Figure 5: Task specialization and Task decomposition hierarchies
First window: the Displace≠1 Task decomposition hierarchy
Second window: the Task specialization hierarchy (classes in bold, instances in normal type)

The TASK system uses the description of knowledge contained in the Displace task and its specializations to automatically generate the solution plan suited to solve a particular Hanoi problem. By way of example, in order to "Displace 3 disks from tower A to tower C using tower B", the solution plan is inferred by the system as follows: a Displace Task instance is created that models the problem (Fig. 3). The system seeks to infer the final state on the basis of the context of this Task. Since the "body" field of the Displace task is empty, the task is replaced by one of its specializations that is inferred using the classification mechanism. In view of the context in this example (n=3), the task Displace≠1 is selected and performed. The definition of Displace≠1 indicates that this problem task can be decomposed into three sub-problems: Displace, Displace-1, and Displace:
- The first sub-problem (SP1.1) consists in "Displacing 2 disks from tower A to tower B using Tower C". To solve this last problem, the Displace task is again replaced by a Displace≠1 type task since the context is (n=2). This task can be decomposed into three further sub-problems:
. the first (SP1.1.1) consists in "Displacing 1 disk from tower A to tower C using tower B". This sub-problem is modelled by an instance of the Displace task. The classification inference mechanism is called and this instance is tied to the simple Displace-1 task, which points to the "move one disk" action;

. the second (SP1.1.2) is modelled by an instance of the Displace-1 task;
. the third (SP1.1.3) consists in "Displacing 1 disk from tower C to tower B using tower A". This sub-problem is modelled by an instance of the Displace task. The process then continues like SP1.1.1.
- The second sub-problem (SP1.2) is modelled by an instance of the Displace-1 task.
- The last sub-problem (SP1.3) consists in "Displacing 2 disks from tower C to tower B". The process is identical to SP1.1.

TASK's inference mechanisms build up the following solution trees (Fig 6).

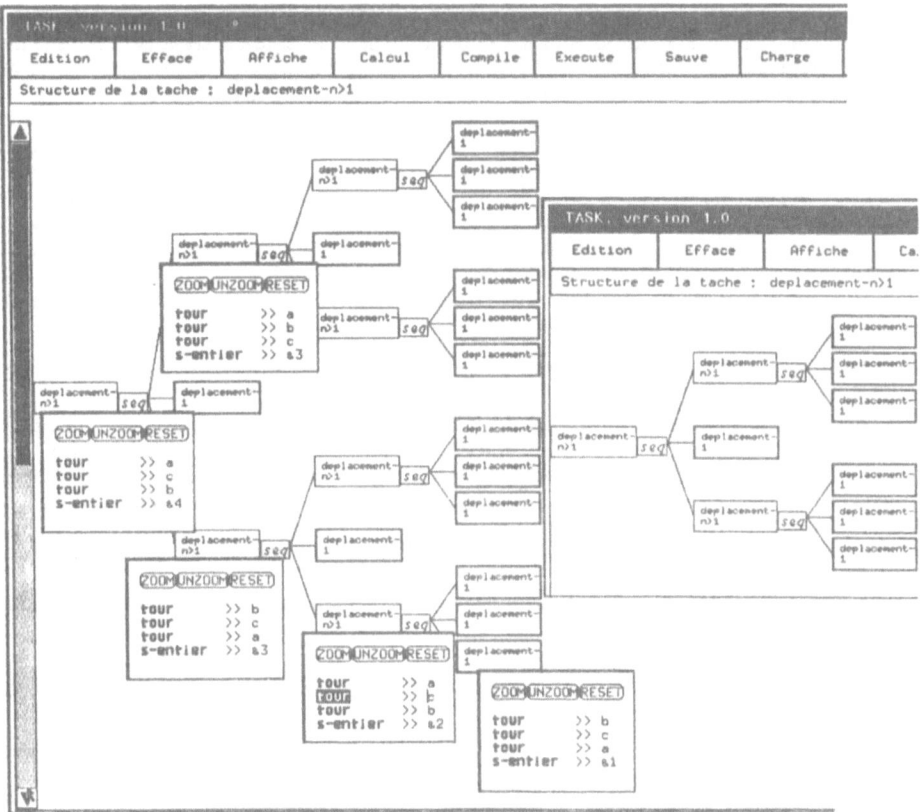

Figure 6: Plan for the Hanoi problem
a) Displace 4 disks from A to C
b) Displace 3 disks from A to C

The TASK system was implemented in the Lelisp environment.using SHIRKA a knowledge base management system [Rechenmann 1988] and the AIDA, MASAI graphic interface managers. Within this implementation some problems araised such as parameters passing for which a technical solution has been proposed based on the notion of prototypical instance [Pierret 1989].

6. CONCLUSION

A new architecture based on the task centered representation paradigm is proposed to facilitate expert systems construction.

This paradigm wants to allow the elicitation of the solving process of a problem at a "better" level of abstraction.

The knowledge base of Task-centered knowledge based systems is compounded of two parts : the Objects base which models structural knowledge by use of objects organized in a specialization hierarchy way, and the Tasks base which models the problem solving knowledge by use of tasks classes organized in specialization and decomposition hierarchies. Each task within the base is a functional unit, intended for solving an information processing problem using specific knowledge forms and inference mechanisms that are appropriate. The aim purchased in defining such a representation paradigm is the development of Task Specific Architectures allowing knowledge based systems to be constructed according to the specificities of the problematic issue involved.

The control in this architecture is hybrid. An important problem encountered with Task Specific Architectures, was the integration and cooperation of GTs within a given application. The solutions to this problem were more practical than theoritical (for instance, the responsability for the formulation and calls between the different problems solvers were left to the knowledge engineer). Other solutions have been recently explored for instance in TIPS [Punch & 90]. TASK's uniform representation and hybrid control seems to be an interesting avenue of future investigation for such new solutions.

TASK will include at the same time a representation model and a library of prototypical Tasks (themselves encoded in TASK 's formalism).

TASK representation formalism will be tested trough different abstraction level tasks. It will be experimented with :
. generic tasks such as those defined in [Chandrasekaran 1988], for instance diagnosis specific architecture will be defined on the basis of a Diagnostic Generic Task whose body is associated to a dynamically calculated chaining of generic building Tasks such as "hierarchical classification", "hypothesis matchers", "abductive assembly" and "knowledge-directed data abstraction and inference".
. specific tasks involved in a real application concerning the assistance in the planning of electric power networks;
. system tasks: all the inference mechanisms in the TASK system will be modelled using Tasks.

The actual perspectives of the work concern the control problem, and the prototypical Tasks library realization.

References :

Bennet, J.S. and Engelmore, R.S. *Experience using NEOMYCIN* in *Rule Based Expert Systems*, Buchanan and Shortliffe , Reading : Addison Wesley Pub. Comp. 1984

Chandrasekaran, B. (1987) *Towards a Functional Architecture for Intelligence Based on Generic Information Processing Tasks.*, IJCAI Vol 2, 1987.

Chandrasekaran, B. (1988) *Generic tasks as building blocks for knowledge-based systems : the diagnosis and routine design examples*, The Knowledge Engineering Review, September 1988, 3 (3):pp183-219.

Clancey, W.J. (1985) *Heuristic Classification* Artificial Intelligence, 27, 1985, pp 289-350

David, J.M. et Krivine, J.P. (1989) *Designing Knowledge-Based Systems within Functional Architecture: the DIVA experiment*, IEEE Conference on AI Applications, Miami, mars 1989.

Dieng, R. and Trousse, B. (1988) *3DKAT, A dependency-driven dynamic-knowledge acquisition tool*, Third Symposium on Knowledge Engineering, Madrid Espagne, 1988.

Fajon M., Corby O.(1988) *ERASME: entretien routier par systeme multi-expert, 8 ème journées Internationales* "Les systèmes experts et leurs applications", Avignon, Mai 1988.

Frayman, F. and Mittal, S. (1987) *COSSACK: a constraint-based expert system for configuration tasks*, Proceedings of the 2nd International Conference on Appl. of Artificial Intelligence in Engineering, Cambridge, M.A., U.S.A., August 1987.

MASAI, (1989) *MASAI Version 1.0: L'outil de développement interactif d'interfaces graphiques*, ILOG, Mai 1989.

Mittal, S., Dym, C.L. and Morjaria M. (1986) *PRIDE: an expert system for the design of paper handling system*, IEEE 1986, pp102-114.

Montalban, M. (1987) *Prise en compte de spécifications en Ingéniérie, application aux systèmes experts de conception*, Thèse Informatique, Université de Nice, 17 Novembre 1987.

Mostow, J. (1985) *Toward Better Models of The Design Process*, The AI Magazine, Spring 1985.

Neveu, B. (1987) *EXPORT: an expert system in breakwater design*, 5th National Conference on Artificial Intelligence, Philadelphia, 1986.

Newell, A. (1982) *"The knowledge level"*, A.I., 18(1), 87-128.

Pierret, C. (1988) *Vers un système à base de connaissances centrées objets pour la modélisation de systèmes dynamique en biologie*, Thèse de doctorat à l'Université de Compiègne, nov 1988.

Pierret, C., Delouis, I. and Scapin, D. (1989) *Un outil d'acquisition et de représentation des tâches orienté-objet*, Rapport de Recherche INRIA 1063.

Pierret, C., Delouis, I.(1990) *TASK: Task Architecture for Structuring Knowledge*, General Conference Second Generation Expert Systems, Tenth International Workshop Expert Systems & their Applications, Avignon , May 28-June 1st, 1990

Punch F., Chandrasekaran B.(1990) *An investigation of the roles of problem-solving methods in diagnosis*, General Conference Second Generation Expert Systems, Tenth International Workshop Expert Systems & their Applications, Avignon , May 28-June 1st, 1990

Rechenmann, F (1988) *SHIRKA : Système de gestion de bases de connaissances centrées-objet*, Manuel d'utilisation 1988.

Scapin, D. and Pierret, C. (1988) *Une Méthode Analytique de Description des tâches*, Colloque sur l'ingénierie des interfaces homme-machine, Mai 1989, Cargèse.

Smeci, (1988) *SMECI Version 1.4, Manuel de Référence*, ILOG, Gentilly.

Wielinga, B., Bredeweg, B., Breuker, J. (1988) Knowledge acquisition for expert systems, in R. Nossum (ed) Proceedings of the ACAI'87, Berlin, Springer

Knowledgeable knowledge acquisition

Han Reichgelt and Nigel Shadbolt[1]
Artificial Intelligence Group
Department of Psychology
University of Nottingham
Nottingham NG7 2RD

Abstract

In this paper we describe a system aimed at providing software support for the process of knowledge acquisition. Such support comprises a workbench incorporating a number of knowledge acquisition tools; knowledge elicitation techniques such as sorting and rating methods, together with machine learning techniques. The paper discusses the various problems raised by this work. These include; defining an adequate view of the general acquisition process, developing an appropriate implementation architecture, directing knowledge acquisition via knowledge level models and producing a sufficiently powerful representation language to integrate the results of acquisition. Finally we describe the limitations of our current system and future developments in our work.

1 INTRODUCTION

The acquisition of knowledge remains the critical phase of expert system development. Recently a number of software support tools have appeared that provide for the analysis, refinement and integration of knowledge from diverse sources; texts, manuals, verbal transcripts, cases, and the experts themselves.

Consideration of these systems reveals three broad classes of support tool (Shadbolt and Wielinga, 1990). One class provides support for acquisition in specific domains. A second consists of computer implementations of particular knowledge acquisition (KA) techniques and are as such domain independent. The third class we might refer to as *loosely integrated* systems.

Each of these types of support system is restricted in scope. The aim of ESPRIT II Project (P2576) ACKnowledge is to achieve integration between a wide range of acquisition techniques, and to combine the best features of current support tools. The goal is the construction of a knowledge engineering workbench (KEW). KEW would implement a range of elicitation techniques, incorporate machine learning methods, apply across domains, and embody a principled or knowledgable approach to the entire acquisition process. To build such a workbench would require that we effectively build a knowledge based system for knowledge engineering.

As part of the ACKnowledge work a number of prototype systems have been developed. In this paper we describe ProtoKEW, a system developed at the University of Nottingham. A substantially more detailed account of ProtoKEW is provided in Reichgelt and Shadbolt (In press).

The structure of this paper will be as follows. In the next section we will present our view of the KA process. In Section 3 we describe an architecture sufficient to implement the concept of an integrated and active acquisition workbench. Section 4 shows how control of the

---

[1] We would like to thank Nigel Major for his help in implementing aspects of ProtoKEW, to Peter Terpstra of the University of Amsterdam and GEC Marconi Research Centre who made available software for inclusion in ProtoKEW. Thanks also to Anjo Anjewierden who commented on an earlier version of this paper. This research was carried out, in part, under the auspices of ESPRIT P2576 ACKnowledge. The ACKnowledge consortium comprises: Cap Sesa Innovation, Marconi Command and Control Systems, GEC-Marconi Research Centre, Telefonica, Computas Expert Systems, Veritas Research, the University of Amsterdam, Sintef, and the University of Nottingham

KA process is effected within this architecture. Section 5 describes the underlying knowledge representation language that allows for the integration of results in the workbench. In section 6 we briefly describe the subset of tools chosen for inclusion in ProtoKEW. Section 7 examines an example of how ProtoKEW translates and integrates the outputs of tools. Section 8 discusses the substantial issues that remain to be investigated.

2 THE KNOWLEDGE ACQUISITION PROCESS

Within our project we regard acquisition as both a *constructive* and *interpretive* process. In any acquisition process we attempt to *model* the application domain and associated problem solving expertise. A model of an object, device, process or procedure is an abstraction of selected characteristics. The decision as to which characteristics at what level of detail to use in the model are subjectively determined. They are judged in terms of the intentions and purposes which users and designers of the system have in mind.

The models so produced are clearly *knowledge level* in the sense that Newell (1982) uses the term. They say nothing about how this knowledge might be implemented in a run time program. Within our work we follow the KADS (Breuker, 1989) approach of distinguishing four knowledge levels. The first of these is *domain* knowledge and describes the domain concepts, elements and their relations. A second type is *task* knowledge. This has to do with how goals and sub-goals, tasks and sub-tasks should be performed. A third sort of knowledge is referred to as *strategic*. This is used to monitor and control problem solving. Finally, we distinguish *inference level* knowledge. This has to do with how the components of problem solving and expertise are to be organised and used in the overall system. The inference level is sometimes used to discriminate different classes of expert system; diagnostic from planning systems and so on.

Considerable research is underway to understand expertise in terms of models of various knowledge levels; problem solving, task models and domain representations (Steels, 1990). The hope is that by understanding the content and form of these models we can use them to inform acquisition.

Breuker and Wielinga (1989) advocate the use of models of problem solving. These so-called interpretation models are knowledge constructs — they indicate how components of expertise are organised and used in problem solving. An alternative approach is to build task level representations (Bylander and Chandrasekaran, 1988; Clancey, 1985). Here the aim is to use general, invariant features of a task to guide KA. Finally, a number of researchers exploit the fact that many KBS applications are built in similar, if not nearly identical domains (Eshelman, 1989; Marcus, 1988). In this case one attempts to build reusable domain descriptions.

Knowledge acquisition itself can be viewed as a cyclic process, figure 1. Data are collected, interpreted, integrated within existing knowledge, and plans for a new cycle are made. This process can occur at different phases of the life cycle of KBS development and maintenance. Moreover, the emphasis on any aspect may vary.

Figure 1 The KA activity cycle

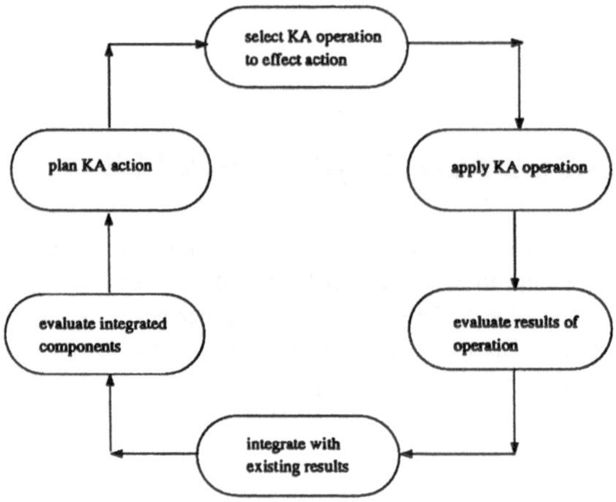

In order to support this activity, our KBS for KA would need a variety of knowledge sources. Firstly, knowledge about the KA process itself. This would comprise advice and guidance about what to do when. It would be sensitive to our position in the activity cycle as postulated in Figure 1.

A second source of knowledge is the use of *models* in the broadest sense of the term. This could be knowledge resident in the system about classes of problem solving, epistemological categories, domain structures and so on.

Knowledge about the KA tools themselves constitutes a third component in any KBS for KA. These tools make assumptions about data, how it is represented and analysed. The system and knowledge engineer should have explicit command and use of this knowledge.

A fourth element has to do with our theory and account of how to transform and integrate the knowledge acquired from different tools into a consistent and evolving application knowledge base.

Finally the emerging application KB needs to be evaluated. Knowledge concerning effective evaluation of the results of KA is the final component in our system.

Each of these types of knowledge is important in the implementation of the KA KBS we envisage. In the sections that follow we attempt to show how these various components feature in ProtoKEW.

3 ARCHITECTURE FOR PROTOKEW

ProtoKEW has been implemented in CommonLisp and PCE (Anjewierden and Wielemaker, 1989), a high-level object-oriented graphics language. In this section we describe the global architecture of ProtoKEW, figure 2.

Figure 2 The architecture of ProtoKEW

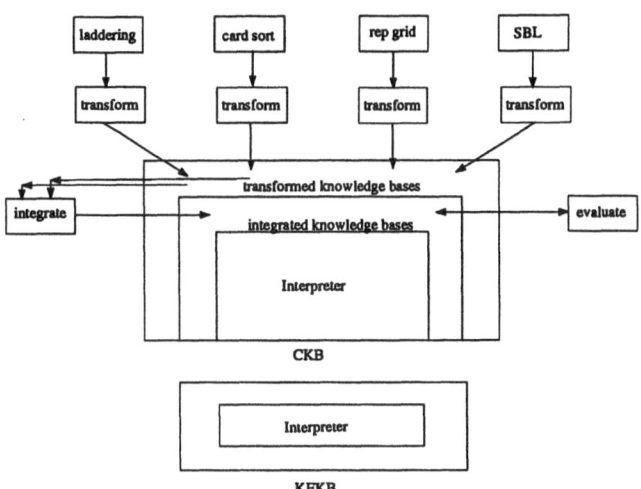

ProtoKEW makes a strict separation between "Knowledge Engineering Knowledge" and "Application Knowledge". The former refers to knowledge about knowledge engineering in general, and the KA activities performed so far. "Application Knowledge" refers to the domain and application knowledge acquired so far. The Knowledge Engineering Knowledge is stored in the Knowledge Engineering Knowledge Base (KEKB), while Application Knowledge is stored in the Common Knowledge Base (CKB). Both types of knowledge base have their own associated interpreters.

ProtoKEW contains a number of knowledge acquisition tools. Each tool typically uses its own knowledge representation language. The reasons for this are both pragmatic and theoretical. Pragmatics dictates that rather than building all tools from scratch we incorporate a number of existing tools. In section 6 we describe the kinds of theoretical considerations that led us to allocate tools their own KRLs.

Since the different tools in ProtoKEW can use different knowledge representation languages, ProtoKEW must allow for the transformation of knowledge from one formalism into the formalism used by the CKB. ProtoKEW contains a number of transformation tools. As we shall see in section 7, for some knowledge representation languages, transformation turns out to be impossible without further consultation with the domain expert. We regard this additional qualification of knowledge as an important extra phase of acquisition. We will refer to the outcome of the transformation process as a "Transformed Knowledge Base" (TKB).

Transformed knowledge bases are stored in the CKB. However, simply transforming tool-specific knowledge bases into the same knowledge representation language is not sufficient. One of the assumptions underlying ProtoKEW is the belief that integrating the results of different KA tools produces a KB more powerful than any produced by relying on a single KA method. ProtoKEW therefore contains a knowledge integration tool. Knowledge integration is discussed in more detail in section 8.

4 CONTROL IN PROTOKEW

As discussed in section 2 we are aiming to build an active and directive KA workbench. The evolution of such a system will be a gradual process. Initially we will use the knowledge engineer as the main controller of KEKB activity. Ultimately, we hope to encapsulate more and more knowledge about KA in the KEKB. At the moment control of ProtoKEW is very much in the hands of the knowledge engineer. Currently, the KEKB is restricted to a number of compiled knowledge structures along with limited reasoning about KA goals and activities.

Figure 3 shows the control interface to ProtoKEW.

Figure 3 Control Interface to ProtoKEW

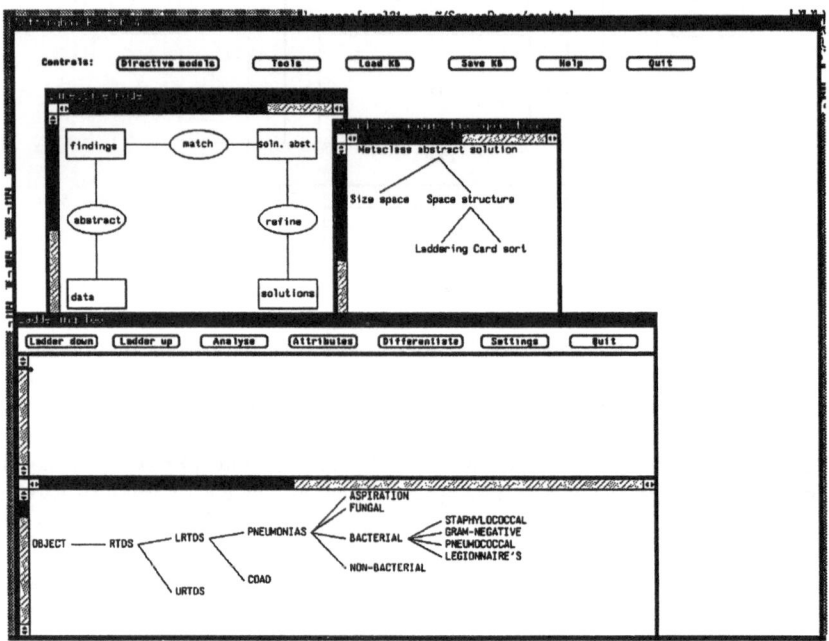

Control is exercised in the upper half of display whilst the detailed acquisition tools display their interfaces in the lower half. The control panel is a set of pull down menus and display windows. The first of these in the top left hand corner is used to display the *directive model* under consideration in the acquisition process. In this case it is displaying a library object resident in the KEKB which is the interpretation model for *heuristic classification*. Selection of this model of the problem solving underlying the application has been made by the knowledge engineer[2]. The thing to note about selection of this structure is that it sets the context for subsequent acquisition.

The directive model contains knowledge which can be used to inform acquisition. It shows the inputs and outputs of various processes that make up a generic type of problem solving[3]. There are four kinds of input/output class, or meta-class, for this model structure; data, findings, abstract solutions and solutions. The processes that operate on these meta-classes are; abstract, match and refine. Each of these processes is in turn associated with a set of methods for effecting the change from input to output. Thus refine is defined as a process of refining solution abstractions into more specific solutions; a method which can effect this is specialisation.

It is precisely this sort of knowledge that can generate acquisition goals. By looking more deeply into the heuristic classification structure we can establish goals and actions to take. In Figure 3 the meta-class *solution abstraction* has been selected and this has activated knowledge

---

2   In Shadbolt and Wielinga (1990) we describe how this selection might ultimately be automated.
3   Breuker and Wielinga (1987) give more details of the structure and content of Interpretation Models.

in the KEKB that shows us how to acquire knowledge about this part of the expertise space. This is shown as a knowledge acquisition goal tree.

The goal tree indicates that in this context we can use either laddering or a card sort to explore the structure of the solution space. It is this knowledge that leads the knowledge engineer to select an option off of the tools menu. We can see in figure 3 that the laddering elicitation tool has been selected and is actually present in the tool window. Should the knowledge engineer need extra information he can select objects on the knowledge acquisition goal tree. Thus selecting the *laddering* node would throw up a set of goals and actions to take in a laddering session.

5 THE COMMON KNOWLEDGE REPRESENTATION LANGUAGE

One of the central components in the architecture of any Knowledge Engineering Workbench is the module that stores the knowledge acquired. In section 3, we referred to this component as the Common Knowledge Base (CKB). In this section we discuss the KRL used in the CKB.

There is a trend among those building acquisition workbenches to use hybrid knowledge representation languages (e.g. Gaines and Linster, 1990). However, these systems give no guidelines as to when to use which of the different component representation languages. The knowledge engineer is often faced with a bewildering array of possibilities. This encourages an *ad hoc* style of programming and representation. This is exacerbated in the present context, where integration of knowledge from different sources becomes important. If knowledge is to be integrated we need to be made aware of inconsistencies that might result from the integration. If a piece of information can be represented in a large number of different ways, then this becomes at best tedious, at worst impossible.

Because of these difficulties ProtoKEW uses logic as its single CKB representation language. Logic confers substantial benefits when used as a knowledge representation language (see, e.g., Hayes, 1985). Logics have a model-theoretic semantics which allow one to determine the correctness (soundness) of the interpreter. Logics also provide considerable expressive power. Moreover, in the present context, the use of logic as the Common Knowledge Representation Language has the added advantage that it makes the problem of transformation and integration considerably easier, a point to which we return in sections 7 and 8.

The particular theorem prover that we are using is an implementation of a semantic tableaux proof theory for classical first-order predicate calculus. Its basic workings are explained in detail in Elfrink and Reichgelt (1989). However, we have improved the theorem prover in a number of ways. First, Elfrink and Reichgelt describe only a backward chainer. We have extended the theorem prover so that it can now also be used in a forward chaining fashion.

Second, the theorem prover described by Elfrink and Reichgelt contains hard-wired control heuristics. The theorem prover used in the CKB allows the user to change the heuristics used for conflict resolution, conjunct ordering, and backtracking.

A further improvement is that the CKB contains a partitioning mechanism which allows one to divide the logical axioms up into different partitions. In logical terms, each partition corresponds to a different theory. While the system will in general ensure consistency within a single partition, it does not ensure consistency between partitions. The partitioning mechanism therefore allows users to explore different theories simultaneously.

There are a number of ways to add a proposition to a partition in the CKB. These differ in the amount of testing that they do before a proposition is added. There are two types of test. First, the system tests whether a proposition is already entailed by the other propositions in the partition. If it is, then the proposition is not added to the knowledge base. Second, the system tests consistency — can we prove the negation of the proposition from the information that is already in the knowledge base? If a proposition fails this test, then the reason maintenance system is called on to ensure consistency. We discuss this in more detail in the section on integration, section 8. If both tests are performed, then the user is guaranteed that the set of propositions is minimal and consistent, at least within the limitations of the theorem prover.[4] Obviously, if we perform both tests during the construction of a partition, then constructing partitions is a relatively slow process. ProtoKEW therefore allows the user the option of not performing the tests.

As indicated the theorem prover has been interfaced to a McAllester style reason maintenance system (RMS) (McAllester, 1980). Before a theorem prover uses a particular proposition in its search for a proof, it will first consult the RMS to ensure that the proposition has support-status ''in''. The main reason for interfacing the theorem prover to an RMS is the fact that knowledge acquisition is often an iterative process in which previously accepted pieces of knowledge have to be rejected as more information becomes available, or as the expert changes his or her mind. In addition, an RMS turns out to be most useful when integrating knowledge from different sources. We return to this aspect of the CKB in section 8.

6 KNOWLEDGE ACQUISITION TOOLS IN PROTOKEW

Four KA tools were chosen for inclusion in the ProtoKEW. These were; ALTO an implementation of the laddered grid technique, a card sort program, an implementation of the repertory grid method, and a similarity based machine learning algorithm. We will discuss only one of these tools, ALTO, in detail. It raises most of the key issues about ProtoKEWs operation.

The ALTO system (Major and Reichgelt, 1990) implements the laddered grid method, described for example in Shadbolt and Burton (1990). In laddering, the expert and knowledge engineer construct a graphical representation of the relations between knowledge elements. The result is a two-dimensional graph whose nodes are connected by labelled arcs. In using the technique the elicitor enters the conceptual map at some point and, with a restricted set of prompts, attempts to move around it with the expert.

The laddering method can be used to elicit various types of knowledge. The use which ALTO embodies is to elicit what Clancey (1983) calls structural knowledge — knowledge about the types of entity present at the domain level.

Figure 3 showed ALTO as the KE tool in use in the domain of respiratory diseases. ALTO uses a simple object oriented language (CommonSloop, Reichgelt et al., 1990) as its tool-specific knowledge representation language. Each node in the laddered hierarchy is represented as an object in CommonSloop. An object can have user-defined slots which are properties of the item in the node hierarchy. CommonSloop supports multiple inheritance. Inheritance follows a default principle, and attributes associated with higher-level objects can be overridden in their children.

The use of the object-oriented style of representation for laddering is both natural and intuitive. In structured object representations we aim to bring together under a simple indexing method the associated properties of objects. The use of inheritance allows us to exploit taxonomic relations in an efficient way. Specialising objects by overwriting or adding attributes and their values provides for a means of discriminating between objects.

Another advantage of using a specialised KRL for each tool is the fact that it enables one to analyse the acquired knowledge in ways which would be very hard in logic. For example, an implicit assumption in object-oriented representations is that the children of a parent are distinct. Therefore, if the system finds two children that cannot be distinguished because they have exactly the same properties, it will ask the user if he/she wants to distinguish them, thus potentially engaging in a further round of KA. In a similar vein, if the system discovers that all

---

[4]   Within first-order predicate calculus there is, in general, no automatic method of determining the consistency of a set of first-order propositions. Any theorem prover needs to contain heuristics to cut off the search for a proof. Because these heuristics may terminate the search for a proof too early, it is possible that inconsistency remains undetected.

children of the same parent have a property in common, it will ask the user if he/she wants to associate it with the parent rather than the children. This reflects the assumption that properties should be stored as high up in the object hierarchy as possible.

As we shall see in section 7 the choice of this style of representation for ALTO has important consequences for the way in which the results of ALTO are transformed into the CKRL of ProtoKEW.

7 TRANSFORMATION

Each of the KA tools in ProtoKEW use its own representation language. In order to achieve the hoped-for synergy effects, the knowledge produced by the different tools needs to be transformed into the Common Knowledge Representation Language.

ProtoKEW contains different transformation algorithms for each acquisition tool. We will now describe the ALTO transformation algorithm in some detail.

Knowledge acquisition tools embody implicit assumptions about the type of knowledge to be acquired. The transformation algorithms rely on these assumptions. Various acquisition tools can be used to elicit different types of knowledge. Thus we could ladder the structural concepts of the domain level, or on another occasion ladder the structure of the task level. In the rest of this section we will assume elicitation at the domain level. However, as long as knowledge bases are kept distinct, the principles of transformation would be the same.

A knowledge base produced by ALTO will contain a number of frames with different slots. In ALTO, each object is actually treated as a class. The transformation algorithm will first establish for each leaf-node in the object hierarchy stored in the Sloop knowledge base whether it is an individual object, or a class of objects. However, this cannot be done automatically and therefore involves asking the user for each leaf node what the intended interpretation is. Individual objects are then translated as constants in the CKRL, whereas classes are translated as one-place predicates. Moreover, class leaf nodes are assumed to be non-empty, and we therefore add an axiom saying that there exists some object with the property denoted by the class-frame.

Once the translation of each frame is determined, other parts of the translation can be done automatically. For example, a super-link between a frame corresponding to a constant a and a frame corresponding to a predicate p is simply translated as $(p(a))$, whereas a super-link between two "predicate" frames p and q is translated as $((\forall x)(p(x) \rightarrow q(x)))$.

Slots can normally be translated automatically: a slot corresponds to a two-place predicate. A slot s with value v associated with a "constant" frame a is simply translated as $(s(a, v))$, whereas a slot s with value v associated with a "predicate" frame p translates as $((\forall x)(p(x) \rightarrow s(x, v)))$. This simple translation needs to be complicated in two ways.

First, the value of a slot may be a pointer to another frame. If the other frame is a constant frame, then it is simply translated as a constant in the logical language. Otherwise, interaction with the user is necessary to determine whether the intended interpretation is universal or existential.

1. $((\forall x)(p(x) \rightarrow treated(x, k)))$
2. $((\forall x)(p(x) \rightarrow ((\forall y)(drug(y) \rightarrow treated(x, y)))))$
3. $((\forall x)(p(x) \rightarrow (\exists y)(drug(y) \wedge treated(x, y))))$

A second complication in the translation of slots is necessary because of the fact that Sloop supports default inheritance. It is therefore possible that the value of a slot is overridden lower down in the hierarchy. An overly simple translation algorithm, might produce an inconsistent logical knowledge base, even though the input Sloop knowledge base was consistent under the intended interpretation. The translation algorithm takes care to avoid this by first determining whether any of the descendants of the frame have an incompatible slot value. If so, these are explicitly stored as exceptions in the antecedent of the rule.

In addition to generating axioms from super-links and slots, the Sloop translation algorithm also uses the sub-links to generate further axioms. This requires extensive interaction with the user. Two types of axiom are tried. First, the translation algorithm will ask the user if the children of some frame form an exhaustive list. If the answer is affirmative, it adds an axiom to the effect that any entity that is an instance of the parent frame must be an instance of at least one of the children as well. Second, the translation algorithm will try to establish whether the children of a parent are disjoint. In a number of cases, the algorithm can establish for itself that this is not the case, for example when two children have descendants in common. In other cases it will ask the user. If the user answers that they are, the translation algorithm will add an axiom to this effect. Negative responses by the users to either of these two types of check, exhaustiveness and disjointness, result in no addition of axioms to the knowledge base.

Figure 4 contains a very simple Sloop knowledge base, after which we give the translation into logic. We have assumed that the user has decided that all leaf nodes are classes. Moreover, as can be seen from axioms 10 to 13, the user has answered affirmatively to all questions concerning exhaustiveness and disjointness asked by the system.

Figure 4 A simple Sloop knowledge base

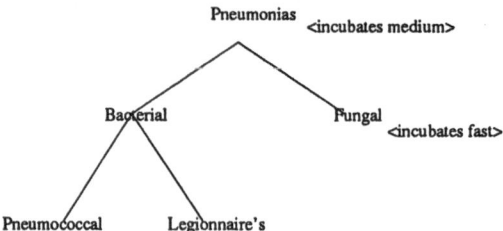

1. $((\exists x)(fungal(x)))$
2. $((\exists x)(pneumococcal(x)))$
3. $((\exists x)(legionnaire's(x)))$
4. $((\forall x)(fungal(x) \rightarrow pneumonia(x)))$
5. $((\forall x)(bacterial(x) \rightarrow pneumonia(x)))$
6. $((\forall x)(pneumococcal(x) \rightarrow bacterial(x)))$
7. $((\forall x)(legionnaire's(x) \rightarrow bacterial(x)))$
8. $((\forall x)((pneumonia(x) \& \neg fungal(x)) \rightarrow incubate(x, medium)))$
9. $((\forall x)(fungal(x) \rightarrow incubate(x, fast)))$
10. $((\forall x)(pneumonia(x) \rightarrow (fungal(x) \lor bacterial(x))))$
11. $((\forall x)(fungal(x) \rightarrow \neg bacterial(x)))$
12. $((\forall x)(bacterial(x) \rightarrow (pneumococcal(x) \lor legionnaire's(x))))$
13. $((\forall x)(pneumococcal(x) \rightarrow \neg legionnaire's(x)))$

The various translation algorithms have a number of features in common. In most cases, they have to be interactive. In general, tool-specific knowledge representation languages may leave the exact interpretation of some feature implicit, and in order to make these explicit one may need to consult the user. Moreover, most translation algorithms are straightforward to write once the interpretation of the basic entities in the tool-specific knowledge base and its use have been made explicit. Thus, to translate Sloop, we need to know whether a frame corresponds to a single entity in the world, or a class of entities. Similar considerations apply to our other acquisition tools.

8 INTEGRATION AND EVALUATION

In the previous section, we described the way in which ProtoKEW transforms knowledge formulated in a tool-specific knowledge base into logic, the language used by the Common Knowledge Base. However, simply transforming knowledge is not enough. ProtoKEW also needs to integrate knowledge from different sources. In this section, we briefly discuss the problems of integration.

The partitioning mechanism supported in the CKB is used when it comes to storing transformed tool-specific knowledge bases: each such knowledge base is stored in a separate partition. Since the CKRL interpreter can be instructed to try to prove a proposition using the information in more than one partition, or to forward chain on more than one partition, knowledge can be integrated in this simple way.

However, the danger is that even though the information in each single partition may be consistent, the combined information in the two partitions may be inconsistent. ProtoKEW supports integration via the merging of two partitions into a single partition. Merging is achieved by copying one partition into a new merged partition, and then incrementally trying to add the propositions from the other partition. While adding these new propositions, both tests discussed in section 5 are performed. Thus, we ensure that the new propositions are non-redundant and consistent.

If the theorem prover discovers a new proposition is inconsistent with the propositions stored already in the partition, the reason maintenance system takes over. We have slightly extended the RMS. Usually, a justification stored with a proposition is simply a list of propositions, which together allow one to prove the proposition in question, or an empty list, if the proposition is a premise. In ProtoKEW's CKRL, we also maintain pointers to the original partition from which the proposition originated. Because in general partitions will be created as the result of transforming a tool-specific knowledge base, this allows us to trace a piece of knowledge back to its source.

The information concerning the origin of a particular piece of information can be used by the RMS. In most RMSs, if the system discovers a contradiction, control is passed to the user who will then have to decide which of the contradictory propositions to withdraw. In ProtoKEW's RMS, if one source is believed to be more reliable than another, propositions originating from this source will always be retained in preference to those from a less reliable source. In general this approach may be too coarse grained. It is, however, a beginning.

Integration inevitably leads on to questions of evaluation — assessment of the *quality* of the knowledge in the CKB. A requirement on ProtoKEW must be the evaluation of the partitioned and integrated knowledge bases. For example, a knowledge base may be diagnosed *incorrect* in the sense that it gives the wrong answers to certain queries, or it may be diagnosed *incomplete* because it is unable to give the answers expected of it.

There are problems with a purely logical notion of consistency, and we are attempting to develop in addition an operational definition. The operational view requires the formulation of sets of propositions (pieces of knowledge) that the system must be able to deal with. The construction of such a set is itself a knowledge acquisition problem — the acquisition of validation knowledge. This might itself be driven by models of; problem solving, devices or procedures. A different approach to the testing of the CKB is via the re-presentation of knowledge using KA tools other than those originally used to acquire it. We cannot explore these issues in this paper, but they are major elements in our current work.

9 CONCLUSIONS AND FUTURE WORK

The attempt to produce software support for KA has led use to conceive of building a KBS for KA. We have described the basic ingredients of such a system. We have implemented a prototype based on the use of first order predicate calculus and partitioned knowledge bases. Individual KA tools produce their own intermediate representations which are then explicitly transformed into logic, and the output placed in partitions. Facilities for merging these partitions have been sketched.

Within this prototype we can observe the following important properties. Knowledge level models are used to establish acquisition goals and direct acquisition behaviour. Individual KA tools are able to use their own customised representation formalisms. Transformation from these representations into logic can be seen as an additional acquisition process. Integration of the results of various KA tools is an active process which makes use of RMS technology to help consistency management. The concept of consistency is understood both logically and operationally.

We are currently incorporating a number of additional KA tools within ProtoKEW. In the near term we are looking to make even more use of knowledge level structures, such as interpretation and task models. For example, we can imagine exploiting these structures when integrating and organising partitions into plausible application architectures. In the longer term we hope to increase the amount of explicit advice and guidance that ProtoKEW provides to the knowledge engineer regarding the acquisition process.

Bibliography

A. Anjewierden and J. Wielemaker. An Architecture for Portable Programming Environments. In *Proceedings NACLP'89 Workshop on Logic Programming Environments*, pages 10–16, Cleveland, Ohio, October 1989. Center for Advanced Computer Studies.

J. A. Breuker and B. J. Wielinga. Model driven knowledge acquisition. In P. Guida and G. Tasso, editors, *Topics in the design of expert systems*, Amsterdam, 1989. North Holland.

J.A. Breuker and B.J. Wielinga. Use of models in the interpretation of verbal data. In A.L. Kidd, editor, *Knowledge Acquisition for Expert Systems, a practical handbook*, New York, 1987. Plenum Press.

T. Bylander and B. Chandrasekaran. Generic tasks in knowledge-based reasoning: The 'right' level of abstraction for knowledge acquisition. In B. Gaines and J.Boose, editors, *Knowledge Acquisition for Knowledge Based Systems*, volume 1, pages 65–77. Academic Press, London, 1988.

W.J. Clancey. The epistemology of a rule based system -a framework for explanation. *Artificial Intelligence*, 20:215–251, 1983.

W.J. Clancey. Heuristic classification. *Artificial Intelligence*, 27:289–350, 1985.

B. Elfrink and H. Reichgelt. Assertion-time inference in logic-based systems. In P. Jackson, H. Reichgelt, and F. van Harmelen, editors, *Logic-based Knowledge Representation*. MIT Press, Boston, 1989.

L. Eshelman. MOLE: A knowledge-acquisition tool for cover-and-differentiate systems. In S. Marcus, editor, *Automating Knowledge Acquisition for Expert Systems*, pages 37–80. Kluwer Academic Publishers, The Netherlands, 1989.

B. Gaines and M. Linster. Development of second generation knowledge acquisition systems. In B. Wielinga et al, editor, *Current Trends in Knowledge Acquisition*, pages 143–160. IOS Press, 1990.

P.J. Hayes. The logic of frames. In R.J. Brachman H.J. Levesque, editor, *Reading in Knowledge Representation*, pages 287–295. Morgan Kaufmann, 1985.

N. Major and H. Reichgelt. Alto: An automated laddering tool. In B. Wielinga et al, editor, *Current Trends in Knowledge Acquisition*, pages 222–236. IOS Press, 1990.

S. Marcus. *Automatic knowledge acquisition for expert systems*. Kluwer, 1988.

D. McAllester. An outlook on truth maintenance. Technical report, MIT AI LAB, Cambridge, Mass, 1980.

A. Newell. The knowledge level. *Artificial Intelligence*, 1982:87–127, 1982.

H. Reichgelt, N. Major, and P. Jackson. Commonsloop: The manual. Technical report, AI Group, Dept Psychology, University of Nottingham, 1990.

H. Reichgelt and N. Shadbolt. Protokew: A knowledge-based system for knowledge acquisition. In D. Sleeman and O. Bernsen, editors, *Research directions in cognitive science vol 5: artificial intelligence*. Lawrence Erlbaum, In press.

N. Shadbolt and M. Burton. Knowledge elicitation. In J. Wilson and N Corlett, editors, *Evaluation of Human Work: A Practical Ergonomics Methodology*, pages 321–346. Taylor and Francis, 1990.

N. Shadbolt and B. Wielinga. Knowledge based knowledge acquisition: the next generation of support tools. In B. Wielinga et al, editor, *Current Trends in Knowledge Acquisition*, pages 313–338. IOS Press, 1990.

L. Steels. Components of expertise. *The AI Magazine*, 11:30–62, 1990.

Formalization of the KADS Interpretation Models

Thomas Wetter and Wolfram Schmidt[1]

ABSTRACT

For the KADS knowledge acquisition method, interpretation models are intended to guide and validate the transformation of verbal data into the conceptual model. Existing suggestions of interpretation models are limited in their usefulness due to lack of completeness, clarity, and precision. We present an attempt to denote interpretation models from KADS publications in a formal language, which we have formerly developed for notation of conceptual models. Formal notation guarantees an unambiguous meaning and enhances the usefulness of interpretation models for further formalization steps. We treat two distinct aspects of the problem, which may be understood as related to the expert's and the knowledge engineer's knowledge perspective: The first aspect is to provide a very concise and general notation to be readable for the expert. The second is to provide expansions of the terms in the concise language in variants of 1st order predicate logic (1stPL). Two important insights in the process of formalizing a considerable number of interpretation models were that one highly expressive intermediate sort model between the inference layer of KADS and the variety of possible domains could be created and that the number of knowledge sources seemed to converge when the number of interpretation models was getting larger.

keywords: KADS, Interpretation Models, Formalization

1.0 INTRODUCTION

After six years of ESPRIT funded research, KADS ([Wieli87]) has evolved into the most influential approach to knowledge engineering in Europe. Some of KADS' distinguishing features are that it aims at being domain independent (in contrast to domain related workbenches such as OPAL [Musen87] or KNACK [Klink88]) and independent of knowledge representation formalisms (in contrast to e.g. PRED [Xie88]).

It is central for the KADS approach that knowledge acquisition is a modelling activity. Concretely, different models serve different purposes in the process from scratch to executable code. Among the models used, the conceptual model plays a prominent role: From the perspective of knowledge acquisition as the first major phase, the conceptual model is the final document which is produced in a number of iterations and which fixes every identified item that was judged to be relevant for covering the contents of the application or the expertise

---

[1] IBM Germany, Scientific Center, Institute for Knowledge Based Systems, Wilckensstr. 1a, D-6900 Heidelberg, FRG, EARN: WETTER at DHDIBM1

to be modelled. From the perspective of system design i.e. the second major phase, the conceptual model is the mandatory input concerning the involved knowledge. In other words, the conceptual model is **the** interface between content related acquisition activities and artefact related design activities. (cf. [Wett90a]). This central role of the conceptual model has been acknowledged by the KADS researchers by providing interpretation models as specific support for constructing conceptual models. Just to give a first idea: Interpretation models exist for systematic diagnosis, monitoring, etc.

The material presented subsequently is one of a number of attempts of stabilizing the KADS method by formalizing and operationalizing its components and processes. We start with the description of the present state of conceptual models and interpretation models, which includes some more detail about the role of the latter during knowledge acquisition. From that we derive a number of criteria that a suggested formalization should satisfy. Then we present our suggestion in considerable breadth and depth on the example of a simple interpretation model and report, how this same formalization turned out to work in more complicated interpretation models that we tested and give some detail of repeated occurrence of elements such as knowledge sources.

2.0 ROLE AND STATUS OF INTERPRETATION MODELS

Interpretation Models (IM's) are intended to support the construction of conceptual models. A conceptual model is organized in four layers:

domain application specific static knowledge
inference elementary application independent methods
task major subproblems to be solved in the domain
strategy control of solution process

I.e. the conceptual model describes an application by its specific **domain** characteristics in a bottom layer and applies **processes** of the three higher levels to this domain knowledge. The **inference** and the **task** layer are assumed to reflect general characteristics of inferencing.[2] This gave rise to the idea to describe them independently of specific domains and to use such abstract descriptions in order to understand and structure new applications.

These abstract descriptions have been termed interpretation models. An assessment of interpretation models has already been attempted in an early stage of KADS by [Breuker]. The eleven authors of that text brought to bare their experiences from diverse fields of application and provided verbal, graphical, and semi-formal outlines of what they had arrived at as their abstractions of the encountered inferences. In this phase, a number of question marks still had to be placed in the text by the authors themselves, and readers found some more question marks. This may be one reason why the interpretation models have not been so much used in mainstream KADS experiments, whereas commercial users such as Bolesian [TM][3] have emphasized this aspect.

The additional question marks concern the aspect whether some details are meant conceptually or with regard to design, what role observable manifes-

---

[2] Some KADS researchers also take the position that the task layer is application specific.

[3] Bolesian is a trademark of Bolesian Systems Europe BV, Helmond, Netherlands

tations play etc. One reason for the question marks, in addition to the early stage of the whole endeavor, may have been that KADS did not at all prescribe a language for putting down the results from the phases. I.e. on one hand each knowledge engineer could develop his personal style for interpretation models as well as for conceptual models. But on the other hand interpretation of the interpretation models and the conceptual models was somewhat arbitrary. The disadvantages of this arbitrariness for the conceptual models have in the meantime been recognized by different groups ([Akker91; Wett90a]) and led to different attempts of providing a formal language for the conceptual model. In this paper we attempt to extend our approach of formalizing conceptual models towards formalizing interpretation models.

3.0 JUSTIFICATION AND STRATEGY OF THE APPROACH

Interpretation models play two significant roles in the KADS process of knowledge acquisition:

* They provide help and guidance to the knowledge engineer. When facing verbal protocols or any other documentation from knowledge elicitation sessions, he has to give all items some meaning. In other words: he has to interpret. As we have outlined in [Wett90b], expert utterances can have such a variety of meanings that arbitrary interpretation may lead to arbitrarily unpredictable system behavior. The KADS answer to this is that problem solving can be understood as executing one out of a small number of stereotypes and that in the course of solving an individual problem the expert produces utterances which refer to elementary steps of that stereotype process that he applies. The stereotypes are the interpretation models, i.e. they can be understood as kind of frames, which supply slots where to place expert utterances.

* If we assume that for an area of application it is known which interpretation model applies (and neglect the question how we could find that out), the interpretation model plays a second role of validation. An item from the expert protocols is judged to have been correctly interpreted when it has found its place in the interpretation model. Here comes one of the few places, where for our understanding KADS contains feedback: If a considerable number of items resist interpreting in the selected interpretation model, the interpretation model is put under question.

This should make absolutely clear that interpretation models don't allow arbitrariness. Hence we subsequently suggest a formal language for the interpretation models. We can then claim that what could be understood in terms of that formal language automatically inherits the semantics or meaning of that language. For such a language to be useful, we now introduce some criteria.

4.0 REQUIREMENTS FOR THE FORMAL LANGUAGE

Any such language, be it in the realm of KADS or as part of some other principled approach to knowledge acquisition, has to deal with two conflicting aims:

- It must have a well understood formal semantics for all of its expressions. No debate can be tolerated about what something means. A denotational semantics is not sufficient, since in the end we need formal interpreters of the results, i.e. we must also understand the procedural semantics of the expressions we use (cf. [Wett90a])

- On the other hand it has to be intelligible for human individuals. Some authors have called that a knowledge level representation ([Akker91]), but for reasons outlined in [Wett90c] we suggest a more precise use of the term. Nevertheless, such a formulation may involve highly comprehensive expression, i.e. short notations for eminently complex "words" of the above formal language. One could say that the intelligible notation is the tip, of which the detailed expansion in terms of a well understood language is the iceberg. This will be exemplified shortly.

The following requirements are specific for evolving a formal language for the KADS interpretation models.

- It has to cover the elements that can be found in the KADS documentation (in our case [Breuker]) of interpretation models. I.e. there is a concrete checklist of what has to be used (although, as outlined in "ROLE AND STATUS OF INTERPRETATION MODELS" the answers have to be provided for some of the q :estion marks.)

- As the interpretation models claim to be independent of the domain layer, it must be possible to arrive at a notation that does not make use of the domain layer. This is kind of writing algorithms without knowing to which data structures they are to apply. It may almost sound absurd to those who primarily understand KADS in terms of each layer being founded in the respective lower layer. This concept is deprived of its basement in the case of the interpretation models.

- On the other hand, an interpretation model has to allow natural linking to all such domain layers for whose problems it provides the appropriate solution processes.

The answer outlined in the next paragraph is that we provide a rather general and strong **sort model** as kind of an inserted ceiling which is "below" the inference layer and "above" the (future) domain layer and which allows for both: elegant formulation of tasks and knowledge sources and easy linking to different domain structures.

5.0 A GENERAL SYSTEM MODEL AS UNIVERSAL BASEMENT OF THE INFERENCES

We subsequently present a detailed outline of an abstract formal notation of a structure which is intended to allow both, use as "data structure" in knowledge sources and the other higher KADS layers and linking to domain concepts from structurally different domains, i.e. to the bottom layer. The notation draws upon a formalization of the KADS conceptual model by means of a KL-ONE like order-sorted logic ([Wett90a]), where sorts may have 1-place features and 2-place roles as a kind of T-box.

The graph is intended to make the abstract notation transparent. It uses terms which are domain independent. The linking to an example domain will be outlined below.

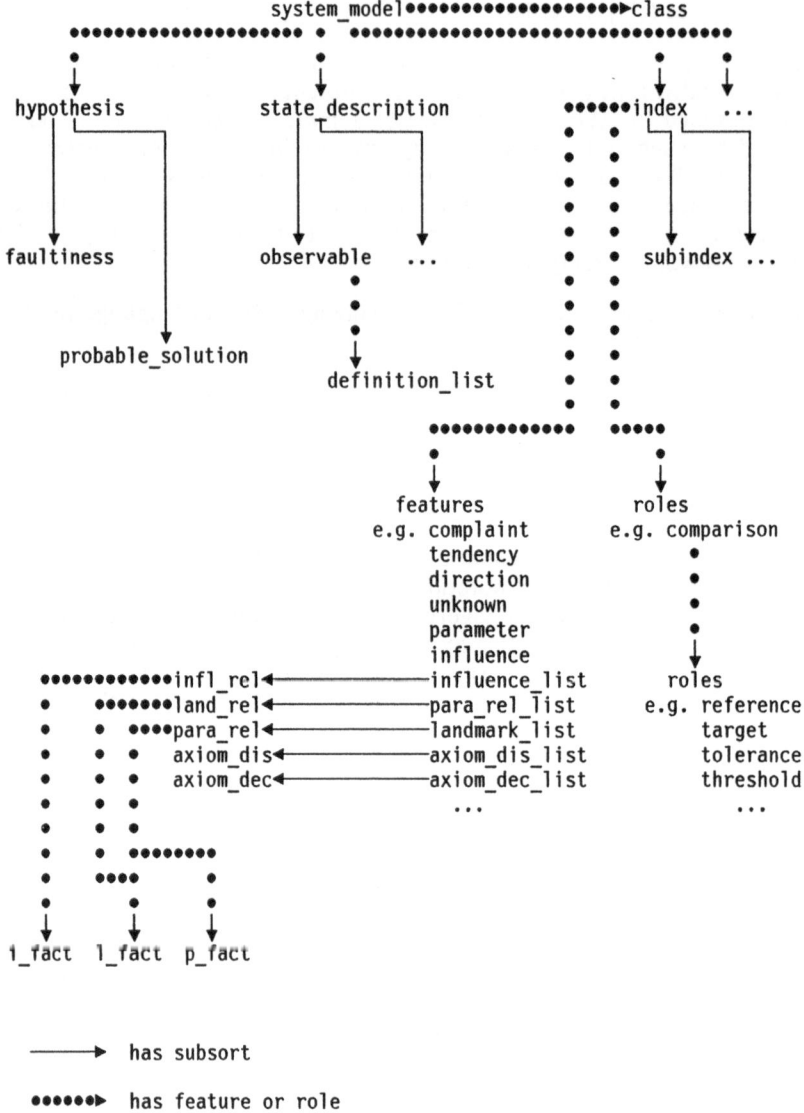

```
                                    ────────►  has subsort
                                    ●●●●●●●►  has feature or role
```

The **system_model** comprises structured knowledge, details of observation and status recording in its three roles:

- **Indices** respectively their subindices define the structured knowledge deemed to be general and in some form present in many applications. They are characterized by properties, formally denoted as *features*, and are connected to other items of structured knowledge; such a connection is formally denoted as a *role* which an item plays with respect to some other item in the structure. As an example in an economic application an index to indicate the performance of a company may have legal form and location as *features* and may be connected by a *role* to a standard with which to compare the actual indicator value.

Subindices inherit the *features* and *roles* from their superindices and may have additional features and roles. It will be described below, what is needed to connect this general sort model to specific sorts occurring in domains and what has to be added to cope with specific relations or dependencies of a given application.

- The **state-description** is composed of observables which can be transformed by adequate definitions into judgeable indices with their roles and features. This is necessary if the underlying observed values can't directly be integrated into the sort hierarchy. This may be due to a sort hierarchy written in abstract terms, which has to be applied to concrete, evtl. numeric values. The transformation process precedes the real examination in data driven tasks.
- Another possibility to guide a solution process is by giving a **hypothesis** which expresses a suspected faultiness or a suspected solution. As result we receive the confirmation or the rejection of hypothesis.

5.1 Example

In a banking application example where companies are judged whether they are still credit-worthy or not the sort model may have the following form:

System model is the *company*. Indices are relevant identifiers for judging the company e.g.*profitability of the company capital* with *profit-and-loss-account* as one possible subindex. The index might have the direction *falling*, an influence to another index, and other imaginable features. In a two step use of the structured knowledge, i.e. passing via the role *comparison* we find the role *target* pointing to the actual value and the role *reference* pointing to the standard value of the indices. Alternative references useful for other indices might be the value of the last year or a limit which has to be reached, etc.. The state-description could consist of parts of the balance sheet which are transformed into target values of indices or other observed facts about the company which, when transformed, give us some information about the features of the index. A hypothesis might be the statement that the company goes bankrupt or the company has to raise the company capital, etc..

   This example can only show one aspect of the possibilities which the sort model offers for describing real world applications. In order to be transparent for the domain expert, the sort model may be expressed in terms of the (in this case banking) application without changing it structurally. In this sense the sort model can be looked upon as the expert's knowledge perspective representation (for a differentiation of **one** knowledge level into **different** knowledge perspectives cf. [Wett90c]). It should then become an easily understandable and very expressive model for the expert, which allows the IM's to work without a domain-layer because they operate only with the given sorts. It plays the role of the connector between the specific domain knowledge and the general knowledge sources. Concrete domain specific knowledge to be linked to the sort model is written down as axioms (sometimes also called definitions or relations), which manifest e.g. in what way the specific observables of a domain are related to the domain independent sort model for reasoning support and vice versa. For this purpose we add to the above general sort model the general notion of a feature "list_of_axioms". The concrete axioms pointed to by such lists are part of a specific domain description. All the technical detail of influences, dependencies, landmarks, etc. of qualitative reasoning or other forms of describing the static contents of applications can be written in specific axioms and can be linked to IM's by the "list_of_axioms" construct of the latter.

5.2 Formalization of the Interpretation Model "Systematic Diagnosis"

In the following we present a short IM: Systematic Diagnosis. We have chosen this one because it is still possible to present it in its whole length in this paper, i.e. we can first present the easy to read tip of the iceberg and then still have place to argue in detail, what the iceberg looks like in terms of order-sorted logic. It can only give a small impression of the various IM's and their possibilities which can be found in [Breuker]. It does not make use of all features and roles introduced for the general sort model.

Systematic Diagnosis is a strategic reasoning task where we try to find the specific faulty component of a system model (the application oriented reader may think of the critical indicators of the performance of a company).

```
judgement_of_system_model(System_model,Index)
←
        a_select_index(in: System_model
                        out: Index)
    & examine(Index)


examine(Index)
←
        useall subsort(Index,Subindex)
          BEGIN
            (Chosen_reference := standard)
           & judge(Subindex,Difference,Chosen_reference)
           & IF(Difference<>0) THEN examine(Subindex) AND exitloop
          END


judge(Subindex,Difference,Chosen_reference)
←
        a_select_target_value(in: Subindex
                        out: Target_value)
    & a_select_reference_value(in: Subindex,Chosen_reference
                        out: Reference_value)
    & a_compute_difference(in: Target_value,Reference_value
                        out: Difference)
```

To increase the usefulness of such systematic notations of strategic reasoning tasks, the purpose of their expressions is subsequently explained for some of the examples. Such explanations can also be made available in possible implementations of our formal notation, hence providing additional help and guidance for both, selection of IM's and matching verbal data to an IM.

User's Guide:

examine

purpose stepwise proceed from unspecific indication to precise determination of fault (e.g. from large faulty component to small subcomponent causing the fault of the large component)

input the fault in the precision known in a given status of the inference process, starting with the first unspecific indication

output the fault in the highest precision supported by the attached domain description (i.e. a subindex, which can no longer be decomposed).

method for fault as identified on one level of precision check all candidates on the next level of precision until one exhibits indication of faultiness

subtasks judge

notes recursive deepening through the hierarchy of indices

judge

purpose determine whether a candidate subindex deviates from its respective norm

input
- subindex to be checked
- standard against which to compare

output resulting difference

method retrieval of the required data items by means of the sort model and computation of their difference

subtasks
- a_select_target_value
- a_select_reference_value
- a_compute_difference

notes the subtasks are closely linked to the sort model

Application oriented explication:
The operation of such subtasks can be made transparent for domain expert by rephrasing them in terms of their application. The formal meaning of this explication is provided in the following paragraph ("Complete Formal Expansion" on page 9).
First the faulty component of the system model is selected. In our example this is the index which has as complaint *degrade*. The rule "examine" is a recursive rule where the subindices of the faulty component are sequentially used as input for another rule "judge". In the example a subindex is e.g. *profit_and_loss_account*. Furthermore we determine from the index role *comparison* the reference *standard value* against which the *target value* (also determined from *comparison*) will have to be compared in the subtask "judge". If a difference is found the process of examinating subindices of the subindex is started again which means for the example that if the *profit-and-loss-account* has a differing value its subindices will be judged whether one of them deviates from the standard and so on. As result we receive the specific faulty components of the system model which in the example can be a statement about a deficient value of a specific index of the balance sheet.

Formally critical aspects:
Two apparently difficult points in this IM are the stop conditions of the "useall"-loop and of the recursion. The second one we can solve in a very easy

way because if we are at the bottom of the sort hierarchy there doesn't exist any more subindex of index and the "fail" causes the termination of the recursion. However in typical systematic diagnosis we have only one faulty component which makes it necessary to stop the iteration after the first faulty index is detected. These requirements introduce a variable *Found* which is assigned the value *true* if we have found the faulty index, so the following ones in the set of indices will not be judged any more.

5.3 Complete Formal Expansion

The solution of these and other problems is shown in the expansion of the IM Systematic Diagnosis. It is meant to be intelligible for a knowledge engineer with a background in KADS terminology and extensions of 1stPL, who has studied [Wett90a]. Most of the syntactic constructs should explain themselves on an intuitive level, i.e. they are within the knowledge perspective of a knowledge engineer as characterized above. Hence we only briefly describe three details:

- The *role_of* predicate has the form: role_of (domain_concept; sort_name) where sort_name refers to the general sort model. Concerning the KADS idea of describing basic inference in terms of knowledge sources operating on metaclasses, the sort_names play the role of metaclasses. This on one hand implies a tighter coupling between domain and inference layer then intended - elements of the sort model as a general image of a domain model **are** metaclasses instead of being temporarily identified with metaclasses-
  but the high generality of the sort model saves some of the generality claim of the knowledge source - metaclass notion.
  On the other hand, the tight coupling supports a comprehensive notation of the interpretation models which lends itself for tool implementation.
  For our general formal description this means that we have to use identifiers for the specific domain_concept, e.g. *SI* for *profit-and-loss-account*. Instead of using the sort-name we use expressions like *S_sort_name* to distinguish variable-name and sort-name.

- A *knowledge source* in [Breuker] usually corresponds to a *a_procedure_predicate*, but 1stPL predicates can in some places also be used.

- For solving some syntactic problems we have introduced assignment procedure predicates for *Found* and *Chosen_reference*. This is in accordance with the concept because such control expressions are required in KADS and in [Wett90a] their foundation has been supplied, i.e. they are part of the presented formalization.

```
judgement_of_system_model'(SM,IX)
←
   role_of(Chosen_company;S_system_model)
 & role_of(Selected_index;S_index)
 & a_select_index(in: S_system_model
                  out: S-index)
 & (Found := false)
 & examine(Selected_index)
```

```
examine(Selected_index)
←
  (Chosen_reference := standard)
  & WHILE (SI in (SI₁,...,SIₙ) of Selected_index)
        & (NOT Found) DO
      BEGIN
            judge(SI,Difference,Chosen_reference)
            & IF(Difference <> 0) THEN examine(SI)
            & (Found := true)
      END
```

```
judge(SI,Difference,Chosen_reference)
←
    role_of(SI;S_index)
  & role_of(Actual_value;S_target_value)
  & a_select_target_value(in: S_index
                          out: S_target_value)
  & role_of(SI,Chosen_reference;S_index,S_reference)
  & role_of(Standard_reference_value;S_reference_value)
  & a_select_reference_value(in: S_index,S_reference
                             out: S_reference_value)
  & role_of(Actual_value,Standard_reference_value;
            S_target_value,S_reference_value)
  & role_of(Difference;S_value)
  & a_compute_difference(in: S_target_value,S_reference_value
                         out: S_value)
```

In the following we present the expansion of the knowledge sources which back up our claim to formalize the ᴷADS IM's in a 1stPL language. In [Wett90a] one can find a detailed description of the procedure predicates of the form *a_predicate_name*. Furthermore for a better comprehension of the expansion it is necessary to know that a subsort of a sort inherits all features and roles of this sort, i.e. that a subindex has the same sorts as features and roles as the index.

selecting a faulty component of the system_model

```
∀ S_system_model : system_model
∃ S_index : index
    index(S_system_model,S_index)
  & (complaint(S_index) = degrade)
→ a_select_index(in: S_system_model
                 out: S_index)
```

selecting the target-value of the index

```
∀ S_index : index
∀ C : comparison
∀ T : target
∃ S_target_value : value
    comparison(S_index,C)
  & target_(C,T)
  & (S_target_value = value(T))
→ a_select_target_value(in: S_index
                        out: S_target_value)
```

selection of the referring value according to the special reference (here in the example: *S_reference* = *standard*)

```
∀ S_index : index
∀ S_reference : reference
∀ C : comparison
∀ R : reference
∃ S_reference_value : value
    comparison(S_index,C)
  & (reference_(C,R) = S_reference)
  & (S_reference_value = value(R))
→ a_select_reference_value(in: S_index,S_reference
                          out: S_reference_value)
```

computation of the difference

```
∀ S-target_value : value
∀ S-reference_value : value
∃ S_value : value
    (S_target_value - S_reference_value) = S_value
→ a_compute_difference(in: S_target_value,S_reference_value
                       out: S_value)
```

6.0 STATUS

In this way we have described seven different IM's of identification and classification tasks. As one result we found that their lengths vary between 25 and 50 lines, with expansion reaching up to more than 100 lines. The collection of our formalized knowledge sources is six pages long, so we decided to present only a short IM in this paper. But it was interesting to recognize that we can use nearly all knowledge sources in different IM's and it is very probable that the process of developing new knowledge sources that can satisfy the requirements of all possible IM's converges. It will be a further aim to formulate other patterns of problem solving found in the literature in the language used here.

REFERENCES

[Akker91] Akkermans, H., van Harmelen, F., Schreiber, G., Wielinga, B. *A Formalization of Knowledge-Level Models for Knowledge Acquisition* accepted for Int. J. Intelligent Systems

[Breuker] Breuker, J., Wielinga, B., van Someren, M., de Hoog, R., Schreiber, G., de Greef, P., Bredeweg, B., Wielemaker, J., Billault, J.-P., Davoodi, M., Hayward, S. *Model-Driven Knowledge Acquisition: Interpretation Models* ESPRIT Project 1098, Deliverable task A1, U. Amsterdam, Dept. Social Science Informatics

[Klink88] Klinker, G., Boyd, C., Dong, D., Maimann, J., McDermott, J., and Schnelbach, R. *Building Expert Systems with KNACK* in: Boose, J. and Gaines, B. (eds.); Proc. 3rd AAAI Knowledge Acquisition for Knowledge-Based Systems Workshop; Banff (Canada) Nov. 1988

183

[Musen87] Musen, M.A., Fagan, L.M., Combs, D.M., and Shortliffe, E.H. *Use of a Domain Model to Drive an Interactive Knowledge-Editing Tool* Int. J. Man-Machine Studies **26**, (1987), 105-121

[Wett90a] Wetter, Th. *First order logic foundation of the KADS conceptual model* in: Wielinga, B., Boose, J., Gaines, B., Schreiber, G., and Van Someren, M. (eds.), Current Trends in Knowledge Acquisition, Amsterdam: IOS Press (1990)

[Wett90b] Wetter, Th. and Nüse, R. *Use of Natural Language for Knowledge Acquisition - Strategies to Cope with Semantic and Pragmatic Variation* submitted for publication Sept. 90

[Wett90c] Wetter, Th. and W. odward, B. *Towards a Theoretical Framework for Knowledge Acquisition* in: Boose, J. and Gaines, B. (eds.) Proc. 5th AAAI Knowledge Acquisition for Knowledge Based-Systems Workshop, Banff (Canada) Nov. 1990

[Wieli87] Wielinga, B.J., Bredeweg, B., and Breuker, J.A. *Knowledge Acquisition for Expert Systems* Nossum, T. (ed.); Advanced Topics in Artificial Intelligence; Lecture Notes in Artificial Intelligence 345, Berlin 1987 (Springer), 96 - 124

[Xie88] Xie, S., Dumaresq, D.F., and Winne, P.H. *PRED: An Interface Development Tool for Editing Primitives in Knowledge Representation Languages* in: Boose, J. and Gaines, B. (eds.); Proc. 3rd AAAI Knowledge Acquisition for Knowledge-Based Systems Workshop; Banff (Canada) Nov. 1988

Qualitative Models for Simulation and Control of Dynamic Systems

Franz Lackinger

Christian Doppler Laboratory for Expert Systems

Alois Haselböck

Department of Computer Science

Technical University of Vienna
Paniglgasse 16
A-1040 Vienna/Austria
e-mail: lackinger@vexpert.dbai.tuwien.ac.at

ABSTRACT

In this work we discuss various issues of qualitative modelling for simulation and control (i.e. monitoring and diagnosis) of dynamic systems. We show how the choice of qualitative models has to be done according to different guiding rules for different inference tasks.

We point out the problems of current approaches to model-based diagnosis and monitoring based on such qualitative models. These approaches either concentrate on parts of the control task exclusively or are incomplete w.r.t. the detection of possible faults.

We introduce a general framework for integrated system control and clarify how these concepts are applied to real-world control problems. Our approach is based on the consistency-preserving paradigm of model-based diagnosis and uses a combined parameter-oriented and device-oriented qualitative representation language which is an extension of the QSIM-language [Kuipers,86]. We will show how such an integration of model-based monitoring and diagnosis based on qualitative models of correct dynamic behaviour improves the control process for dynamic systems.

1 INTRODUCTION

Monitoring and diagnosis of dynamic technical systems are key-applications of knowledge-based programming. They are used to overcome the shortcomings of traditional control systems which are mainly based on extensive numerical computations. Early knowledge-based approaches just used heuristically derived relations between faults and their causes to determine a technical system's faulty behaviour. Although many implemented expert systems which exclusively follow these concepts offer a high runtime performance, they suffer from severe disadvantages like incompleteness (w.r.t possible faults) and inflexibility (w.r.t knowledge maintenance).

We follow the model-based reasoning paradigm instead and use qualitative, hierarchical device-models of correct behaviour to determine a device's dynamic faulty behaviour.

In the field of model-based diagnosis previous research has typically concentrated on static technical systems (i.e. mechanisms which do not significantly change their behaviour over time). Many diagnostic systems have been introduced in the past which use models of static correct (and sometimes static faulty) behaviour to predict the possible system behaviour. Some well-known examples are XDE [Hamscher,90] and SHERLOCK [deKleer,89].

Although these systems have been successfully applied to the static diagnosis of digital circuits, they are usually incapable of dealing with dynamic mechanisms which perform time-dependent behaviour and which are therefore characterized by means of time-varying parameters.

Only a few approaches to monitoring and diagnosis of dynamic physical systems have been published in the past [Dvorak,89, Hayes,89].

They all concentrate either on monitoring (i.e. fault detection) or diagnosis (i.e. fault localization) exclusively, and therefore miss important aspects of effective system control.

In this paper we concentrate on the modelling aspects of our approach. A full discussion of the implemented qualitative reasoner **DIAMON**[1], including algorithmic details, notes on terminology and implementation and more examples can be found in [Lackinger,90].

In the following we start with a discussion of various aspects of qualitative modelling in Section 2. In a next step we introduce our integrated framework for model-based monitoring and diagnosis in Section 3. An example will show how we apply our implemented framework to the control of a central heating. In Section 4 we discuss related research work and finally present topics for future work in Section 5.

2 ASPECTS OF QUALITATIVE MODELLING

We start with a discussion of various issues concerning qualitative modelling. We show that we have to design models that are used for simulation and control tasks by following different guidelines. The discussion is mainly concentrated to QSIM-models [Kuipers,86], nevertheless the conclusions are valid for other qualitative representation languages as well.

Figure 1 shows the world of all possible behaviour patterns which are derivable from qualitative models and motivates the following discussion.[2]. The notion *behaviour pattern* refers to a partial envisionment.

---

[1]DIAMON means **DIA**gnosis and **MON**itoring Tool

[2]B_a ... all behaviour patterns, B_c ... patterns of correct behaviour, B_f ... patterns of faulty behaviour, $B_u = B_a - B_c - B_f$ ... behaviour patterns which are physically impossible (see [Kuipers,85]), B_s ... behaviour patterns derivable from simulation models, B_d ... behaviour patterns derivable from diagnosis models, B_m ... behaviour patterns derivable from monitoring models

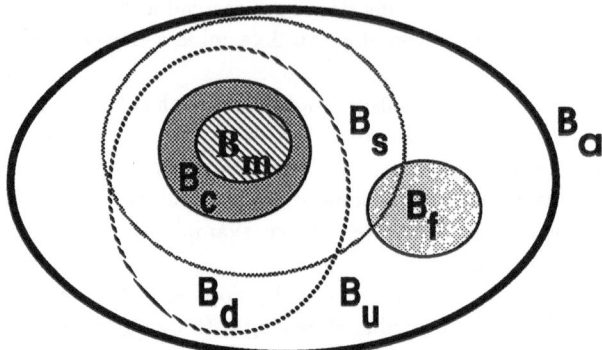

Figure 1: A Taxonomy of Behaviour Patterns

2.1 Simulation Models vs. Diagnosis Models

A QSIM-model is *a priori* designed for qualitative simulation. Starting with an initial state the simulation procedure recursively derives possible successor states. Conversely, diagnosis typically requires a kind of *backward chaining*-inference, i.e. detecting the causal relation between observed fault symptoms and physical component faults.

Consequently a diagnosis model has to contain relations between constraints and components which are not necessarily needed for simulation.

Simulation usually does not use hierarchical models. Although [Franke,89] have introduced component-connection (CC) models which allow hierarchical modelling at an abstract level, their QSIM-constraints again use only one level and are therefore *flat*. Diagnosis, instead, often requires the use of hierarchical models. Complex real-world technical systems consist of intrinsic hierarchies which are related to the modularity or the purpose of the mechanism.

Another aspect lies in the notion of a *component*. Doing simulation, we are mainly interested in the behaviour of the mechanism over time. This behaviour is optimally derived from a structural model which uses time-varying parameters as its model primitives (i.e.components). Usually the device-components (i.e. the physical subsystems) do not change over time (in technical systems), only their associated parameters are time-varying.

This parameter-oriented view, however, is not sufficient for diagnosis. Parameters can represent fault symptoms (e.g. the exceeding of thresholds), but physical components are to be blamed for the fault. We claim that the main aspect of diagnosis is *to provide information for repair*, and only mechanical devices (and not parameters) can be repaired. [3] This is a main reason why we compose an integrated approach out of monitoring (which concentrates on parameters similar to simulation) and diagnosis.

It is well-known that simulation of a qualitative model is ambiguous and produces behaviour patterns which are physically impossible [Kuipers,85]. These behaviour patterns do not cause problems for a diagnostic engine as they are physically impossible and can never be observed in reality.

---

[3]The adjustment of parameters is a struggle against fault symptoms, not against the fault causes.

On the other hand, there is a third class of behaviour patterns (in addition to correct and physically impossible behaviours), faulty behaviours, which can lead to diagnostic problems. It is at first glance surprising (and has not yet been explicitly stated in the literature to our knowledge) that the simulation of a model of correct behaviour may result in behaviour patterns which could stem from a fault model as well.

Let us give an example to clarify this important point.

Example 1 Imagine a simple bathtub which contains a certain amount of water and which is filled.

This dynamic system can obviously perform 3 qualitative distinct behaviour patterns:

1. **OVERFLOW:** The amount of inflow is greater than the amount of outflow.

2. **EQUILIBRIUM:** The amount of inflow is equal to the amount of outflow.

3. **DEPLETION:** The amount of inflow is smaller than the amount of outflow.

Imagine now that we have a fault model which expresses

1. the OVERFLOW-behaviour and

2. the fact that the bathtub is perforated and that

3. the amount of lost water is equal to the difference between inflow and outflow.

Simulation of this fault model will obviously result in a behaviour pattern which is qualitatively equivalent to the EQUILIBRIUM-behaviour. □

What we need to solve this ambiguity is, of course, an additional relation between inflow and outflow which can even be quantitative.

This example shows that the careless choice of a qualitative diagnostic model can cause grave problems for the diagnostic engine. A diagnostic algorithm will overlook inconsistencies which indicate faulty behaviour patterns that could have been derived from the model of correct behaviour. This is due to the underlying *theorem prover*, [4] if it is used for behaviour derivation and consistency checking both. Table 1 summarizes the main differences between simulation and diagnosis models.

SIMULATION MODELS	DIAGNOSIS MODELS
used for forward inference	used for backward inference
may contain faulty behaviours	must not contain faulty behaviours
typically parameter-oriented	typically device-oriented
typically flat models	typically hierarchical models

Table 1: Simulation vs. Diagnosis Models

---

[4] e.g. the constraint-propagator of QSIM

2.2 Monitoring Models vs. Diagnosis Models

Both qualitative models for simulation and diagnosis use structural knowledge about the technical system. Monitoring, on the other hand, uses behavioural and teleologic models to detect fault symptoms in the system.

A monitoring model usually contains only a few parameters and constraints. The main task of this type of model is to provide the representation of the mechanism's purpose in terms of parameters which can then be efficiently monitored. As monitoring is *per definitionem* an on-line task, its success greatly depends on the size of the underlying qualitative system model. Consequently we will use models which are *minimal* w.r.t. the amount of included parameters and constraints in order to achieve an optimal runtime performance.

Diagnosis models, instead, have to contain many parameters to guarantee an optimal distinction between various fault hypotheses. In most cases the diagnosis process does not have to work under hard real-time constraints and can therefore use as many observations as it needs to localize faults within the mechanism.

Another obvious distinction lies in the kind of information that the two model classes express.

Monitoring models express the purpose of the mechanism, the function that the mechanism has to fulfill and that has to be monitored. In consequence such a model will usually be flat and contain no hierarchies. [5]

Conversely, diagnosis models include component-connection information and are typically hierarchically structured. It is obvious that the lowest-level model has to contain only components which can be repaired. [6] This kind of layered structure is clearly most important for an effective control of real-world mechanisms which are complex and hierarchically designed.

We can finally distinguish between monitoring- and diagnosis models when we consider the degree of completeness of the observations which is required.

Monitoring typically requires a full set of observations to guarantee that all possible fault symptoms can be detected.

Diagnosis, however, can work well enough with subsets of the measured variables if we accept a set of fault hypotheses. We view diagnosis as a *stepwise-refinement-*process which uses models of different granularity to determine more or less exact diagnoses.

Note that not only a device-oriented structural model can be hierarchical; we use hierarchical, parameter-oriented structural models as well to represent decomposable physical quantities.

The above mentioned distinctions express the different purposes of monitoring and diagnosis according to our interpretation of system control as the integration of monitoring, diagnosis and repair.

Table 2 summarizes some of the differences between monitoring and diagnosis models.

---

[5] Although it sometimes might be useful to express a kind of sub-purpose of sub-mechanisms.

[6] We will denote these components *Smallest Replaceable Units (SRU)*

MONITORING MODELS	DIAGNOSIS MODELS
contain a few important parameters	contain many parameters
express purpose of mechanism	express SRUs of mechanism
require complete sets of measurements	allow partial sets of measurements
flat models	hierarchical models
simultaneously measurable parameters	incrementally measurable parameters

Table 2: Monitoring vs. Diagnosis Models

2.3 Correct Models vs. Fault Models

In the approach of [Dvorak,89], which present MIMIC, a model-based monitoring system, the use of fault models is essential for the control procedures. MIMIC can detect fault symptoms only if they match with the predictions for at least one fault model. A decision tree for fault hypotheses which is off-line constructed allows quick generation of hypotheses.

Unfortunately, the use of fault models introduces several problems. One such problem, concerning the *unknown fault mode*, is well-known from static diagnosis. Fault models are *per se* incomplete as it is impossible to guarantee that the whole range of possible faults is covered by a certain set of fault models. As a consequence more or less possible faults can not be detected. We have already shown how we can restrict the unknown fault mode in static systems in [Friedrich,90].

Another problem is the process of modelling faulty behaviour. Similarly to models of correct behaviour it is not straightforward to model time-dependent faulty component behaviour by means of parameters and constraints.

This task is comparatively easy in static mechanisms. One can, for example, express an adder's faulty behaviour with a simple inequality (i.e. output(adder) $\neq$ input1(adder) + input2(adder)) by means of symbolic values as presented in [Friedrich,90].

Nevertheless, we claim that it is not necessary to model a system's faulty behaviour explicitly by means of fault models.

Instead, we associate (parameter-oriented) constraints which describe the system's correct behaviour to (device-oriented) components and use a consistency-preserving approach for monitoring and diagnosis both.

3   THE BASIC CONCEPTS OF DIAMON

In the following we briefly describe the basic concepts of DIAMON (a more detailed discussion can be found in [Lackinger,90]).

DIAMON is a model-based reasoner which uses qualitative, teleologic (i.e. purposive) parameter models for monitoring and device-oriented component models for diagnosis. Thus it combines two important tasks of dynamic system control (fault detection and fault localization).

3.1   Example

To give a realistic example we will demonstrate how DIAMON applies to the control of a complex technical device - a central heating.

3.1.1 Qualitative Model

Figure 2 shows the constraint-network of the central heating and its associated observable parameters at the SRU-level. The central heating consists of a boiler (consisting of two heating elements H1 and H2, an insulation and a switch), the pipe-system (consisting of the pipes and the pump) and the room (consisting of a radiator, its switch and a thermostat). The thermostat is connected to the boiler via a feedback-line.

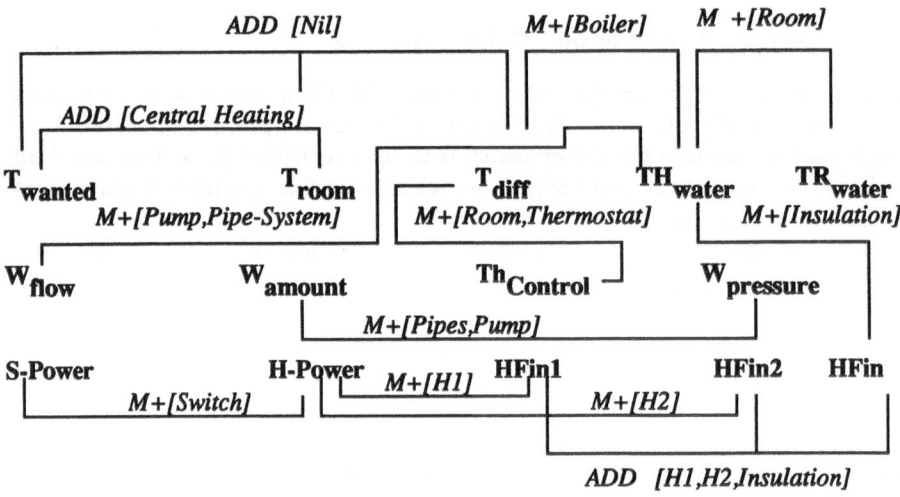

Figure 2: Constraint Network for the Central Heating

We use a flat monitoring model and a hierarchical diagnosis model which contains two levels of abstraction. The monitoring model consists of one constraint and two parameters, the diagnosis models use 7 (resp. 16) parameters and 5 (resp. 13) constraints.

3.2 Extended Constraint Models

We extend the QSIM-language [Kuipers,86] to integrate component-oriented information (which is represented in relations between constraints and physical components). According to this extension, we distinguish between four classes of constraints which are described in the following section.

Teleologic Constraints: A teleologic constraint includes parameters which are measured during the monitoring cycle in order to detect a first inconsistency. It is quite obvious that the device itself (at its highest level of abstraction) is the device-oriented part in such a constraint. Teleologic constraints are therefore used to express the *purpose* of a device and build up a teleological model.

Example 2 In our example, we use the following teleologic constraint which connects the intended and the observed room temperature:

- $T_{wanted} = T_{Room}$

Tautologic Constraints: These constraints denote relations between parameters which can not become inconsistent, due to a component fault. We use them, too, to denote laws of nature, for example energy-conservation. Clearly such a constraint is not associated to any component as it can not provide any diagnostic information.

Example 3 We use tautologic constraints to relate observable parameters with computation parameters like

- $T_{diff} = T_{wanted} - T_{Room}$

Singleton Constraints: Some constraints are explicitly related to only one component. They mean restrictions concerning internal operations of the component which do not affect its surroundings. An inconsistency between such a constraint and the observed parameter values is therefore explained by a single fault in the concerned physical component.

Example 4 We associate a constraint that expresses a certain qualitative state of the radiator-signal to the radiator:

- $RADIATOR : R_{Control} = ON$

Set Constraints: This class of constraints connects at least two components. Although the concerned components are usually situated at the same level of abstraction, some set constraints might connect components at different levels of abstractions as well. This is a useful strategy for sophisticated focussing techniques. Clearly, an inconsistency between a set constraint and the observed parameter values is explained by the assumption that not all concerned components can behave correctly (i.e. they form a conflict set).

Example 5 The monotonic functional relation (expressed by an $M^+ - constraint$ (see [Kuipers,86])) between the amount of water in the pipe-system and the pressure of water concerns the pipes and the pump both:

- $PIPES, PUMP : M^+(W_{Pressure}, W_{Amount})$

In contrast to [Franke,89], we do not consider the component-oriented approach to be at a higher level of abstraction than parameter-oriented models are. Instead, we use different levels of abstraction for the integrated modelling language which concerns component-oriented and parameter-oriented aspects simultaneously.

As we have already stated, we have to choose our qualitative models w.r.t. the control task. In consequence we perform qualitative simulation to verify our models *before* they are used for monitoring and diagnosis to detect whether they allow the derivation of faulty behaviour patterns.

3.3   The Algorithmic Part of DIAMON

DIAMON uses the *HS-DAG*-algorithm [Greiner,89] which is a corrected version of
the original Reiter-algorithm [Reiter,87] for model-based diagnosis. The included
correction now guarantees that no conflict sets can be missed due to the application
of pruning strategies. We extended the basic algorithm to deal with dynamic systems
similarly to the algorithm presented in [Ng,90].

However, due to the above mentioned correction our algorithm is more complete
than [Ng,90].

Example 6 In [Lackinger,90], we have simulated a triple-fault in the water-heater
example of [Ng,90].

We have applied the algorithm of [Ng,90] and DIAMON both to localize this
multiple fault which is observed as a loss of heating power in the heating-system.

While DIAMON correctly detected the responsible triple fault $[H1, H2, S]$, the
Reiter/Ng-algorithm, however, didn't find any conflict set and consequently no diagnoses which is due to an incorrect pruning step. □

Consistency Preservation: Related approaches to monitoring usually concentrate
on the surveillance of predefined thresholds. We, instead, view monitoring from the
consistency-preserving point of view which shows its close relation to diagnosis. Therefore, we use parameter-oriented constraints for our monitoring-model and define a
fault symptom to be an inconsistency between the monitoring model and the observations. Similarly, we rely on the consistency-preserving approach for diagnosis and
use the traditional notion of a diagnosis (e.g. [Reiter,87]) to be a minimal hitting set
among the conflict sets.

Dynamic Model Zooming: Hierarchical modelling as presented in [Hamscher,90]
results in discrete model layers. Different levels of abstraction are predefined and during diagnosis the algorithm performs discrete shifts between the qualitatively different
layers.

We, on the other hand, have developed a continuous strategy of dynamic model
zooming. According to the diagnosis progress, constraints and parameters are zoomed
in and used for the refinement of the already computed diagnoses.

In consequence we can easily focus on important parts of the mechanism and thus
perform diagnosis efficiently and quickly.

Note that we use full sets of measurements at each level of abstraction. This is
due to the fact that otherwise possible diagnoses could be missed (for an example see
[Lackinger,90]).

3.3.1   Notes on Implementation

DIAMON has been implemented in Common LISP and currently runs on SUN
SPARC-workstations. We use the constraint propagator of QSIM as the theorem
prover for the *HS-DAG*-algorithm. In the current implementation, we apply a *breadth-
first*-zooming strategy for the dynamic refinement of our diagnosis-models. However,
we plan to integrate a *best-first*-zooming strategy in the future which will allow us to

focus on more important parts of the model w.r.t. additional heuristic information (e.g. fault probabilities).

3.4 Example: Diagnosing Multiple Faults

We continue our example and consider a typical fault scenario - a double fault. Let us assume that the radiator is switched off and one heating element (H2) is faulty. This fault is recognized as the deviation of the intended room-temperature T_{wanted} from the measured room-temperature T_{Room}. [7]

Table 3 shows how the monitoring-cycle of DIAMON switches over to the diagnostic part after fault detection. The two diagnosis models are incrementally *zoomed-in* and diagnosis continues until the SRU-level is reached.

Parameters/States:	s0	s1	s2	s3
T_{wanted}	T_{Room} std	T_{Room} std	T_{Room} std	T_{Room} std
T_{Room}	T_{Room} std	$(Cold, T_{Room})$ dec	*Cold* std	*Cold* std
TB_{Water}			$(Cold, HOT)$ dec	$(Cold, HOT)$ dec
TR_{Water}			*Cold* std	*Cold* std
$Th_{Control}$			ON std	ON std
$R_{Control}$				0 std
Switch				*CLOSED* std
H_{Power}				*ON* nil
HF_{in1}				*ON* std
HF_{in2}				0 std
Hierarchy:	Monitoring	Monitoring	Diagnosis-1	Diagnosis-2 (SRU)
Actual Diagnoses	nil	{Central-Heating}	{ROOM}, {BOILER}	{RADIATOR,H2}

Table 3: Double-Fault-Diagnosis

4 RELATED WORK

Our work is closely related to [Dvorak,89] and [Ng,90]. However, we differ from both approaches in some important ways.

First, we use a combined approach which integrates monitoring and diagnosis. This results in a more powerful and complete control procedure.

Second, the algorithms of [Dvorak,89] and [Ng,90] are both incomplete w.r.t. possible faults. In [Dvorak,89] this is due to the use of fault models, in [Ng,90] this results from the use of the original Reiter-algorithm and the heuristic choice of initial parameter subsets. In [Lackinger,90] we show how faults are missed due to such a heuristic choice.

In contrast to [Ng,90], we allow many-to-one relations between components and constraints and thus, achieve more expressiveness in our qualitative modelling language. We are able, for example, to relate components at different levels of abstraction.

---

[7]A qualitative state s of a parameter is a pair (*qval qdir*) where *qval* denotes a qualitative value (or an interval) and *qdir* denotes the qualitative direction-of-change (std = steady, inc = increasing, dec = decreasing, nil = undetermined) - see [Kuipers,86]

We differ from [Dvorak,89] in that we do not use fault models and inductively derived fault hypotheses for monitoring. We rather rely on the behaviour discrepancies to the correct behaviour model, which allows us to handle unanticipated faults, too. Additionally we do not have to simulate a sometimes large set of fault hypotheses.

In [Dvorak,89], qualitative simulation is used to predict possible behavioural patterns of fault models. However, we have shown before that qualitative simulation can derive faulty behaviour from the model of correct behaviour. Due to this fact, *MIMIC* can miss faults if the model of correct behaviour is not chosen carefully. We have recognized this problem and perform qualitative simulation of the correct model for model-verification before using the model for diagnosis and monitoring.

5 CONCLUSIONS AND FUTURE WORK

In this work we have discussed several aspects of qualitative modelling for dynamic system control. We have shown how the use of integrated parameter- and component-oriented models for monitoring and diagnosis improves these tasks.

Nevertheless, a lot of work remains for future research.

DIAMON (and most of the other currently known knowledge-based control systems) can currently only deal with permanent faults. Faults which once occur remain in the system, and mechanisms are not allowed to perform *periodic faulty* behaviour. However, a wide class of faults (so-called *transient or intermittent faults*) remain undetectable under this assumption. In the future we will need concepts to handle these probabilistic faults if we apply our algorithms to safety-critical technical systems.

Measurement selection and interpretation in dynamic systems has to be addressed in the future. Many static diagnosis systems rely on information theory (e.g. [deKleer,89]) to determine optimal measurements. However, the fixation of the optimal measurement points is essentially more complicated in dynamic systems where measurements are time-dependent.

In contrast to the well understood control algorithms, qualitative modelling has not yet reached a satisfying level. We decided to use the QSIM-language for our system because it is quite expressive. Nevertheless, the restrictions of this language are a temptation to develop more powerful modelling concepts in the future.

Acknowledgements

We especially thank Benjamin Kuipers who provided the Common LISP implementation of QSIM (Q2) and several new research reports of his research group. The contents of this paper have benefitted from many discussions with Wolfgang Nejdl.

References

[Dvorak,89] Daniel Dvorak and Benjamin Kuipers. Model-Based Monitoring of Dynamic Systems. In *Proceedings of the International Joint Conference on Artificial Intelligence*, pages 1238–1243, Detroit, August 1989. Morgan Kaufmann Publishers, Inc.

[deKleer,89] Johan de Kleer and Brian C. Williams. Diagnosis with Behavioral Modes. In *Proceedings of the International Joint Conference on Artificial Intelligence*, pages 1324–1330, Detroit, August 1989. Morgan Kaufmann Publishers, Inc.

[Franke,89] David W. Franke and Daniel L. Dvorak. Component Connection Models. In *Proceedings of the Workshop on Model Based Reasoning*, pages 97–101, Detroit, 1989.

[Friedrich,90] Gerhard Friedrich, Franz Lackinger, and Wolfgang Nejdl. Redefining the Candidate Space in Model-based Diagnosis. In *Proceedings of the European Conference on Artificial Intelligence*, pages 277–282, Stockholm, August 1990. Pitman Publishing. also appeared as Technical Report CD-TR 90/1.

[Greiner,89] Russell Greiner, Barbara A. Smith, and Ralph W. Wilkerson. A Correction to the Algorithm in Reiter's Theory of Diagnosis. *Artificial Intelligence*, 41(1):79–88, 1989/90.

[Hamscher,90] Walter Hamscher. XDE: Diagnosing Devices with Hierarchic Structure and Known Component Failure Modes. In *Proceedings of the IEEE Conference on Artificial Intelligence Applications*, pages 48–54, Santa Barbara, March 1990.

[Hayes,89] Barbara Hayes-Roth, Richard Washington, Rattikorn Hewett, Michael Hewett, and Adam Seiver. Intelligent Monitoring and Control. In *Proceedings of the International Joint Conference on Artificial Intelligence*, pages 243–249, Detroit, August 1989. Morgan Kaufmann Publishers, Inc.

[Kuipers,85] Benjamin Kuipers. The Limits of Qualitative Simulation. In *Proceedings of the International Joint Conference on Artificial Intelligence*, pages 129–136, 1985.

[Kuipers,86] Benjamin Kuipers. Qualitative Simulation. *Artificial Intelligence*, 29:289–388, 1986.

[Lackinger,90] Franz Lackinger, Wolfgang Nejdl, and Alois Haselböck. On Model-based Monitoring and Diagnosis of Dynamic Systems. Technical Report CD-TR 90/14, Christian Doppler Laboratory for Expert Systems, Technical University of Vienna, July 1990.

[Ng,90] Hwee Tou Ng. Model-Based, Multiple Fault Diagnosis of Time-Varying, Continuous Physical Systems. In *Proceedings of the IEEE Conference on Artificial Intelligence Applications*, pages 9–15. IEEE Computer Society Press, 1990.

[Reiter,87] Raymond Reiter. A Theory of Diagnosis from First Principles. *Artificial Intelligence*, 32:57–95, 1987.

TRACTABLE RATIONALITY AT THE KNOWLEDGE LEVEL

*Walter Van de Velde**

Artificial Intelligence Laboratory
Vrije Universiteit Brussel
Pleinlaan 2, B-1050 Brussels, Belgium
WALTER@ARTI.VUB.AC.BE

ABSTRACT

The notion of knowledge level is an attempt to resolve some confusions in the usage of the terms "representation" and "knowledge" in Artificial Intelligence. The value of the idea will be ultimately determined by the extent in which it can be turned into a practically useful tool for the analysis, description, specification and construction of (software) systems, and of knowledge based systems in particular. In this note an interpretation of Newell's original notion of knowledge level and some new ideas are put together to indicate a possible road toward this goal. The discussion centers around two closely related issues namely a re-interpretation of the principle of rationality, and the knowledge level representation of problem solving methods, competence and control. Other aspects of intelligence like behavior, memory and learning are not ignored but beyond the scope of the paper and the panel.

1. INTRODUCTION

The notion of knowledge level was introduced by Allan Newell (82) in an attempt to resolve some confusions in the usage of the terms "representation" and "knowledge" in Artificial Intelligence. The value of the idea will be ultimately determined by the extent to which it can be turned into a practically useful tool for the analysis, description, specification and construction of (software) systems, and of knowledge based systems in particular. This is the goal of much of current research in knowledge based systems (Clancey 85,89; Chandrasekaran 86; McDermott 88; Steels 90; Wielinga, Schreiber and Breuker 90)[1]. Sticklen (89) has pointed at some problems (see also (Schreiber, Akkermans and Wielinga 90)) and proposed a departure from some of the basic ideas, in particular with

---

* This research has been supported by Dirección General de Investigatión Científica y Técnica (DGICYT), Spain. Currently it is supported by ESPRIT project P5248, KADS-II. The views expressed in this paper are not necessarilly those adopted within the KADS-II project.

[1] For most of these the knowledge level was not the original motivation. It is only in retrospect that one can now view and unify some of them from a knowledge level perspective.

respect to structure of and communication patterns at the knowledge level. In this note an interpretation of Newell's original notion of knowledge level and some new ideas are put together to indicate another possible road. Briefly stated, these are the main ingredients collected from (Steels 90), (Van de Velde 88) and (Van de Velde 90):

*   The application of Newell's Principle of Rationality is decomposed into a two step process. The first step, called "configuration", makes explicit the role of "task features" at the knowledge level and separates out concerns of pragmatics.
*   Configuration results in a "task model", a temporary structure imposed on the knowledge level, and described in terms of tasks, domain models, and methods. Within an appropriate task model the principle of rationality is practically applicable.
*   The "competence theory" of a method distinguishes the explanation structure of a reasoning process from the derivation structure. It is the major knowledge level feature of a method and the primary source of rationalization (explanation).
*   The general principle of rationality is reformulated for specific methods, serving as a knowledge level specification of control.
*   Method specific principles of rationality are operationalized by means of so called "handlers", a class of tasks that enable the competence theory of a method to do its work.

This work contributes to a more ambitious research program, currently underway in a number of projects, in which the knowledge level idea is used as the basis for a comprehensive methodology for integrated KBS development both in a general way (ESPRIT P5248, KADS-II), more specifically for construction tasks (ESPRIT P5477, CONSTRUCT), and as the basis for a general architecture for intelligence (Plaza and Van de Velde 90; Van de Velde 90). This note only treats the approach as it relates to reasoning and problem solving and leaves other important aspects of intelligence, such as memory and learning, untouched.

1.1. The Knowledge Level

The knowledge level (Newell 82) provides the means to "rationalize" the behavior of a system from the standpoint of an external observer. This observer maintains that the agent acts "as if" it possesses certain knowledge and uses this knowledge in a perfectly rational way. The behavior of the agent thus results from it using its knowledge. The emphasis on knowledge instead of on representation and implementation issues is the major source of power of the knowledge level idea. It allows one to make meaningful statements about an agent's behavior without reference to the structures and mechanisms within the agent that realize that behavior.

In more detail a knowledge level description is based on the following model of an agent (Dietterich 86):

> The agent possesses knowledge
> Some of this knowledge constitutes the goals of the agent
> The agent has the ability to perform a set of actions
> The agent chooses actions according to the principle of rationality:
>> The agent will select an action to perform next which according to its knowledge leads to the achievement of one of its goals.

The knowledge level is a level of description above the symbol level (Newell 82). The symbol level provides a means to "mechanize" a behavior. At the symbol level a system is described as a mechanism over symbols or representations (structures of symbols). Neither type of description makes a claim about the real nature of the agent. It is only assumed that the agent acts "as if" it has such knowledge or mechanisms. Moreover, both knowledge and symbol level models describe approximations of the actual behavior. For example, at the symbol level, the exact effect of certain functions may be unknown (e.g. sort in LISP with a non-total ordering predicate scrambles the elements in an unpredictable way) which may lead to diverging behaviors. Also at the knowledge level the whole of behavior usually can not be rationalized. Several behaviors may be rational, or none. Nevertheless there is one actual behavior. More fundamentally, the agent is realized through a physical (mechanistic) substratum, the details of which may lead to aspects of behavior which can not be rationally accounted for. The agent may be (and usually is) subject to various limitations (time, resources, memory, precision) which prevent it from taking fully rational decisions. Finally, many details of action are the result of adaptation to agent and environment constraints and hardly explicable in terms of knowledge. In all but trivial cases the knowledge level description is inherently an approximation, and much more so than the symbol level description.

1.2. Criticisms on the Knowledge Level

The notion of knowledge level is believed to provide one with the right perspective to understand much of current research in knowledge based systems (Clancey 85,89; Chandrasekaran 86; McDermott 88; Steels 90; Wielinga, Schreiber and Breuker 90). As explained before, the emphasis on knowledge instead of on representation is the major source of power of the idea. But knowledge is not an end, but a means to generate behavior through the principle of rationality. But then, how can rational behavior practically emerge out of an enormous soup of knowledge? Real systems are not perfectly rational, and computing a deductive closure is clearly explosive. It seems that we have to conclude that, within this model at least, the knowledge level is not "heuristically adequate".

Other criticisms to the knowledge level idea have been formulated. Among these are the inability to represent control, the lack of predictive power (due to the inherent incompleteness of a knowledge level description) (Sticklen 89), a potential computational inadequacy (supra) and the non-operational character (how to design a KBS starting from a knowledge level model) (Schreiber, Akkermans and Wielinga 90). Another problem is pointed out by Steels (90) who emphasizes that practical problem solving is interesting exactly because it is subject to many limitations of knowledge and its use. Omiting these limitations from the knowledge level (i.e. sticking to perfect rationality) misses the point of much interesting reasoning patterns (Newell does not rule out knowledge about these things, but they are no fundamental ingredient of his knowledge level framework). Another problem is the lack of any criteria to select among various possible knowledge level models, even though some are clearly better than others (for example, because they have more predictive power). Finally, the knowledge level notion has not been adequately related to other aspects of intelligence, such as learning (Van de Velde 90).

2. TWO STEP RATIONALITY AND CONFIGURATION

The principle of rationality relates knowledge to behavior in a single step:

It serves as a global interpreter for the knowledge of the agent. Given the enormous size of the agent's knowledge, its likely inconsistency and the existence of multiple viewpoints on a task it is hard to imagine how exactly this may work. Two step rationality views this process as consisting of two steps:

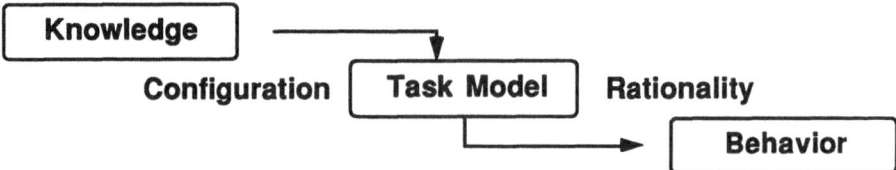

In the first step, called "configuration", knowledge is configured into a model of the actual task set to the agent (called the "task instance"). In this step the agent is thought of as imposing a structure on selected pieces of its knowledge, and assigning roles to these in its reasoning. This structure is what we will refer to as the knowledge level model of the task instance or the "task model" for short.[2] The task model, which will be detailed shortly, is the way in which the agent frames a task instance, and expresses the current state of knowledge about the task instance within that frame. The ability to appropriately configure a task model is probably at the hart of excellence in problem solving and rational behavior. The goal of configuration is to enable the practical application of the principle of rationality within the boundaries of the task model. This is the second step in two step rationality. To the extent that the task model is adequatly configured this can be practically done and leads to a satisfactory solution. Adequacy of the task model is determined by the compliance of the possible behaviors with the so called task features of the task instance. These are desicribed in the following subsection.

2.1. Task features

What makes every task instance different from the other one are the specific circumstances in which it is to be solved. These circumstances may be related to the characteristics of the environment (critical, static or highly dynamic, size and complexity) and the agent's interaction with it (accessibility and reliability), or may impose additional restrictions on the task (quality or specificity of solution, limited resources). These aspects of a task instance are called the "task features". Task features play a fundamental role in configuring the task model:

---

[2] Task models have been situated by Steels (90) on a so called "knowledge use level". In this perspective the knowledge use level is simply a structure temporarily imposed on the knowledge level.

The agent must configure the task model so that the behavior resulting from the application of the principle of rationality within the boundaries of the task model complies with the task features of the task instance.

For example an agent should only rely on information which is accessible; if the information is uncertain then it should take this into account; if memory is limited and the task instance highly complex then certain ways to perform the task will not be considered. An important class of task features are what Steels (90) called the epistemological problems (i.e. problems with the knowledge) and the pragmatic problems (i.e. problems with the pragmatics of using the knowledge) (Steels 90). Epistemological problems arise because we are dealing with models of a real and open-ended world. Problems of pragmatics are forced upon us by the reality of the task environment. They follow from the practical limitations of the complete system of the agent and its environment.

The decomposition of the principle of rationality reflects the fact that there is more to rationality than just being logical. The task features of a task instance determine what behavior is practical, i.e. feasible and appropriate within the actual agent-task-environment combination. Once a task model has been configured to comply with these practical constraints the principle of rationality can freely explore possibilities.[3] The pragmatic concerns are thus taken care of in configuration, the rational concerns by the application of the principle of rationality within the task model.

2.2. Rationalizing Configuration

In two-step rationality it is the role of configuration to come up with a task model that will comply with the task features of the task instance. Within the boundaries of the task model then, there is no problem to use the principle of rationality. For configuration the knowledge of the agent plays the role of a disposition, a frame of mind, to approach a task (implosive role of memory). It indicates how the agent can perform a task instance in such a way that it complies with the task features of the task instance. This configuration is the organization of knowledge items in a structure, referred to as the task model. In this structure it is determined what knowledge will be brought to bear on the task and in what role. Configuration is thus a deliberate (and revokable) restriction of rationality. This is, however, the only way to achieve practical rationality during reasoning. Within an appropriately configured task model the principle of rationality is applied. Here knowledge selected during configuration serves as a store of possibilities (expansive role of memory).

A configuration will always represent a trade-off so that, even when it can be rationally explained in retrospect, the decision process itself may be hard to rationalize. This is where the criticism of non-predictive power of the knowledge level (Sticklen 89) may be partially justified. The process of configuration must be partly non-deductive, any result representing a compromise between task features. Thus it is anticipated that much of configuration would be an emergent functionality of a reinforcement dynamics over

---

[3]Re-configuations are not excluded of course. In fact they are necessary to keep the system really rational. however it is seen as an important capacity to be able to temporarilly limit the knowledge horizon for tractable reasoning.

configuration fragments (Steels; personal communication). It is, of course, possible to provide a knowledge level model of an agent using any such mechanism, but this model would be necessarily a very crude one. Another important factor is that the agent is likely to be disposed to select certain configurations and others not. For example in a fastly evolving environment it should rely a lot on interaction; an agent with a "bad memory" will simply not have memory intensive methods; depending on its architecture an agent will use operations that are easy to do. Finally, elaborating the configuration task may open up the way for an infinite regress. In as far as configuration can be rationalized, it may be based on a selection method that uses "cliches", mappings between classes of task instances, described by task features, and classes or fragments of task models (McDermott 88; Steels 90; Plaza and Van de Velde 90).

3. TASK MODELS

Configuration comes up with a task model of a task instance. What does such a model look like? There are a variety of approaches to knowledge level modelling (Clancey 85,89; Chandrasekaran 86; Marcus 88; Steels 90; Wielinga, Schreiber and Breuker 90). The basis of the analysis in this section are the "Components of Expertise" (Steels 90) and the work on inference structure for problem solving (Van de Velde 88). "Components of Expertise" is an informal framework for describing knowledge level models of problem solving. It provides a vocabulary in which problem solving knowledge can be expressed in a systematic and coherent way. In this vocabulary there are three basic types of components: tasks, problem solving methods, and domain models.

3.1. Tasks and Task Instances

Task refers to the general goal of an agent. Task instance refers to the goal to accomplish a task in a specific environment (an environment is the whole of the agent-world combination).

A task can be identified with a triple (P,S,Solution) consisting of a set of *problems* P, a set of *solutions* S and a *task relation* Solution between problems and solutions. The task is to relate a problem p to a solution s, such that Solution(p,s) holds. A task instance is specified in addition by a case and an acceptability relation (Van de Velde 88). The case is a body of knowledge about a problem-solution pair. The acceptability relation is a subset of the task relation. The task instance is solved if, from what is known about the case, the problem-solution pair is necessarily in the acceptability relation.

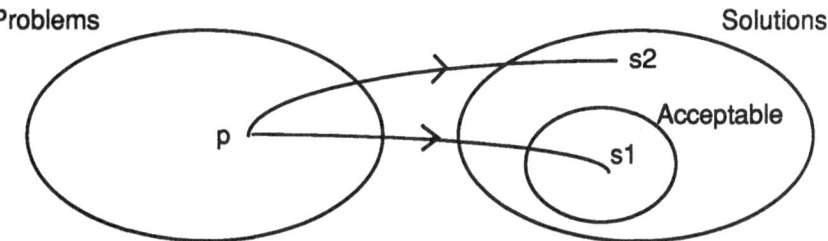

202

Figure 1: Tasks and task instances are modelled as relations. For a given task instance only some of the solutions are acceptable.

Repair is an example of a task. The task of repair is to relate malfunctioning devices to repairs, such that the repair remedies the malfunction. Repairing a specific car in a specific garage and keeping the bill below $500 is an example of a task instance. The task instance is solved if such a repair is found.

3.2. Problem Solving Methods

A method models how new information about a case is inferred in order to solve a task instance. At the knowledge level it is specified by three components: a *task decomposition* (Steels 90), a *competence theory* and a *specialized principle of rationality* (Van de Velde 88). A task decomposition is a list of task instances, called sub-tasks. The task relations of the sub-tasks decompose the task relation of the top-task. This decomposition is called the *inference structure* of the method (Clancey 85; Van de Velde 88; Wielinga, Schreiber and Breuker 90). The inference structure links problems and solutions of the top-task by means of other task-relations and inference primitives (e.g. problem abstractions, sets of solutions,...). The competence theory of the method is a logical theory that relates the relations in the inference structure to the task relation of the top-task (Van de Velde 88). Its role is to specify exactly what the solutions of the sub-tasks contribute to the solution of the top-task. When the sub-tasks are solved the competence theory infers new information from the corresponding instances of the task relations of the sub-tasks. This information is then considered to be part of the case model of the top-task. The definition of the top-task then determines whether the task instance is solved or not. The specialized principle of rationality is a knowledge level specification of control. It will be explained in the following section.

3.3. Domain Models

The domain for a task instance is the whole of information and knowledge to which that task instance relates. During configuration the agent constructs domain models of the domain. A domain model expresses or imposes a structure on the domain. The hierarchies of problem and solution abstractions in heuristic classification are examples of domain models. Other examples are causal models or structure and function models. Basically, the domain models play two closely related roles. First, they are required for the definition of a task instance. For example, the meaning of repairing a non-starting car requires a domain model in which at least the notions of car, its properties (e.g. starting), malfunction and repair are related. The task instance of finding a cheap repair requires a domain model about costs of repairs. The second role of domain models is in the construction of the task models themselves. Many of the task relations in a task model will correspond to the relations within a domain model. For example the task relation of a sub-task to find the cause of a malfunction will be derived from the "causes" relation in a causal model.

4. METHOD SPECIFIC RATIONALITY AND CONTROL

The application of the principle of rationality has been decomposed in two steps. The different concerns of practicality (compliance with the task features) and rationality are taken care of in each of these. It was already explained how configuration must come up with a task model in which the possible behaviors are compliant with the task features. In this section we take a closer look at how the principle of rationality is applied within a task model and, more specifically, as component of a method. It may appear as a surprise that methods could be formalized at the knowledge level and an example may clarify what this exactly amounts to.

4.1. Task decomposition

The method of heuristic classification is a well known and versatile problem solving method (Clancey 85). Instead of directly relating a problem to a solution heuristic classification decomposes a task into three sub-tasks: abstraction, match and refinement (figure 2).

The abstraction sub-task links a problem to a most specific class to which that problem is known to belong. These classes or abstractions are typically organized in an abstraction hierarchy. So, let $(\Delta_P, \leq_P)$ denote such an abstraction hierarchy on P with generalization relation $\leq_P$ (from specific to general).

The refinement sub-task relates solution abstractions to solutions. The goal is to select a solution which is described by a given set of solution descriptions. Like the problem abstraction, the solution abstractions are typically organized in an abstraction hierarchy $(\Delta_S, \leq_S)$ on S.

The match sub-task relates problem abstractions to solution abstractions. The task relation of this sub-task is a set of associations which we call 'Experience'. An association is an element of $\Delta = \Delta_P \times \Delta_S$. Associations are denoted with small Greek letters and their components indicated with subscripts: $\alpha = (\alpha_P, \alpha_S)$.

4.2. Competence Theory

How do the sub-tasks relate to the original task, or what is the exact role of an inference relation in relating a problem to a solution? Clearly not every path through an inference structure will link a problem to one of its solutions. Additional problem solving knowledge is needed to distinguish paths in the inference structure that lead to a solution. This knowledge is the second component of a method, namely the *competence theory*. The competence theory specifies what exactly it is that is concluded about a problem solution pair. Heuristic classification is based on the following assumptions:

whenever a problem p can be abstracted to a description α_P that matches a description α_S, then α_S can be refined to a solution for p. Moreover it is (usually) assumed that evidence from multiple associations can be combined (which is not necessarily true): if $\alpha_P(p)$ and $\beta_P(p)$ then Solution(p,s) for some s for which $\alpha_S(s)$ and $\beta_S(s)$.

Thus, the competence theory is a theory relating the task relation of the top-task to the task relations of the sub-tasks. It may be possible to prove from this theory that Solution(p,s) holds but the conclusion need not be so strong. For example, in heuristic classification the conclusion is at most that a solution abstraction describes a solution but it is not known exactly which one. The competence theory thus determines the competence of the method, i.e. exactly what information it derives about the solution to a problem.

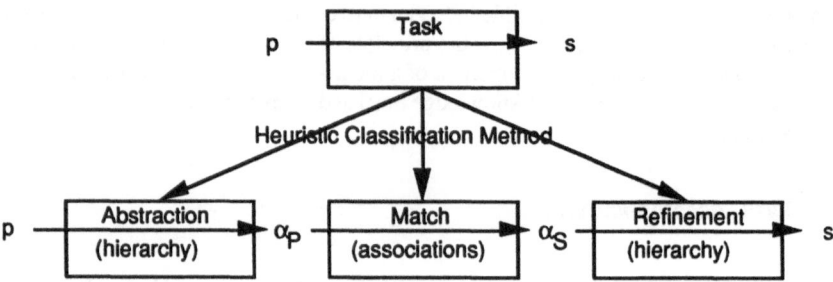

Figure 2: The heuristic classification method decomposes a task Task in three sub-tasks. Abstraction, Match and Refinement. The competence theory relates the task relations of the sub-tasks to the task relation of the top-task.

The competence theory is the major knowledge level ingredient of a method. It formulates the inference making competence and not the performance aspect of the method, the way in which the inference is achieved. Thus, no matter how complex the process in which a method finally arrives at a solution, the explanation or rationalization of the solution will always take the form of the competence theory of the method. For example, the heuristic classification method may have needed several steps abstraction steps, possibly actions to collect new information and so forth, to reach the right problem abstraction. Nevertheless the rationalization will contain no more than "since the problem is an instance of this particular problem abstraction...".

4.3. Principle of Rationality

The principle of rationality is of course still applicable to the deliberately restricted set of knowledge items. Moreover, however, it can be reformulated in a method specific way. For example, the method of heuristic classification is based on the following principle of rationality:

A problem solver that uses the method of heuristic classification uses its knowledge to minimize the size of the differential.

Note that for every application of the method to a specific task instance this principle can be phrased in domain terms. It is thus a rationalization of method specific control, and as such a knowledge level specification of control.

The specialized principle of rationality can be operationalized in a number of ways. This is done by means of so called "handler tasks" or handlers for short. Handlers are tasks executed by an agent to enable the competence theory to infer information about the case. Its rationale is to enable reasoning, guided by the method specific principle of rationality. Repair handlers for heuristic classification will thus implement the various ways to achieve a reduction of the differential. One possible handler for this problem will change the instantiation of the abstraction sub-task to a more specific one. When this is done, the inference path that links the problem to the solution abstraction is broken. A handler for this problem looks for a new instantiation of the match sub-task. After this is handled the competence theory of the heuristic classification method can do its work and infer a more specific differential. It is checked whether this new one is acceptable. If so, the task is solved. If not the handlers will try further repairs.

Task Model

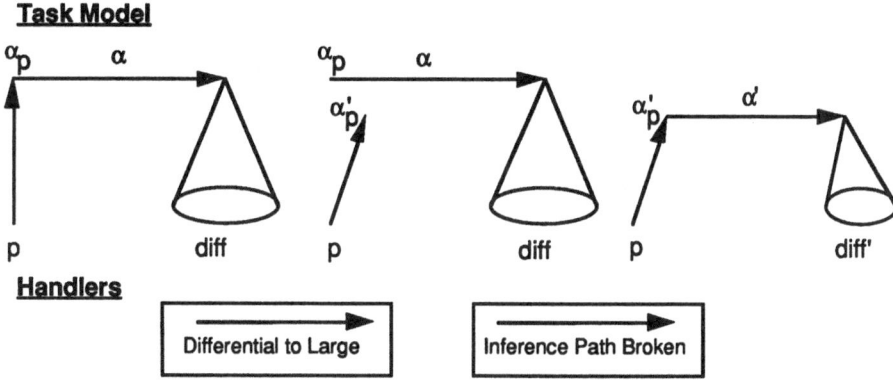

Handlers

Figure 3: Two repair handlers for heuristic classification at work. The first handler is specific for the heuristic classification method, the second one is more general.

This is in a nutshell how methods are defined at the knowledge level. Using the notions of *task decomposition, competence theory* and a *specialized principle of rationality* a method can be formulated in terms of knowledge. Sub-tasks are of course genuine tasks and the full arsenal of problem solving methods can be applied to solve them. In addition methods can be combined in various ways. This corresponds to the expansion, chaining and combination of inference structures and competence theories, leading to methods with different competences. For example, two methods, called construction and classification, and their combination are analyzed in (Van de Velde 88). Handlers for a method are genuine tasks as well, and may lead to complex task models themselves (e.g. for finding a more specific problem abstraction).

It must be clear from all this that the knowledge level model of an agent which is solving a task consists of much more than just the task model. In addition other task models are around of the tasks associated with handlers[4]. Handlers are not considered to be part of the task model of the agent, but to operationalize it need to be configured as well. Handlers will often lead to new lines of reasoning. The associated task models however do not become decompositions in the model from which the handler was called (thus keeping the explanations neatly detached from eachother).

---

[4]Learning tasks are another class of dissociated task models. They are modelled through the same handler mechanism as those that implement method specific control. Configuration, itself is also done by handlers.

5. FINAL REMARKS AND CONCLUSION

In this note a few concepts were proposed that serve as ingredients for a genuine knowledge level treatment of knowledge based problem solving. A few final remarks:

*   The knowledge level model of an agent consists of much more than just the model of the application task instance. In addition other models are around, for example of the tasks associated with the method specific handlers.

*   Subtasks spawned by a method are genuine tasks and the full arsenal of methods may be applied to it. Further decomposition leads to a more complex competence theory, and therefore a more elaborate rationalization of the behavior.

*   The difference between task and handler is a relative one. Both are modelled using the same knowledge level terminology. The point is that the task model of a handler does not lead to a rationalization of the method for which the handler is appropriate. It just enables that method, but adds no explanatory power to it.

*   Finally, it must be mentioned that learning within the framework is modelled at the knowledge level through handlers as well, and that both tasks and handlers must be configured by the agent (Van de Velde 90).

To summarize, in this paper it is attempted to add to the original idea of the knowledge level a number of features to turn it into a practical tool for describing, analyzing, specifying and constructing knowledge based systems. In particular we have emphasized here the idea of two-step rationality and method specific principles of rationality. These and other ideas are currently being worked out in a number of ongoing projects, in particular in ESPRIT P5248 KADS-II, more specifically for construction tasks in ESPRIT P5477 CONSTRUCT, and as the basis for a general architecture for intelligence (Plaza and Van de Velde 90; Van de Velde 90).

ACKNOWLEDGEMENT

The author acknowledges the influence of the members of the Knowledge Based Systems and Machine Learning groups at CEAB and VUB AI-Lab, and in particular of Luc Steels. Jaume Agosti, Philip Rademakers, Carlos Sierra, Pedro Meseguer, Enric Plaza, Kris Van Marcke and Johan Vanwelkenhuysen contributed useful insights. This work has been supported by Dirección General de Investigatión Científica y Técnica (DGICYT), Spain. Currently this work is continued within ESPRIT project P5248, KADS-II. Thanks to the KADS-team at the University of Amsterdam, and in particular to Bob Wielinga for stimulating discussions.

REFERENCES

Chandrasekaran, B. (1986) Generic Tasks in Knowledge-Based Reasoning: High Level Building Blocks for Expert System Design. In *IEEE Expert*, Vol 1.

Chandrasekaran, B. (1990) Limitations of the generic task toolkit idea. Proposal for an architecture that integrates different types of problem solving. In Steels, L. and McDermott, J. (Eds.) *Expert System Foundations* (forthcoming).

Clancey, W.J. (1985) Heuristic Classification. In *Artificial Intelligence* Vol 27(4) p289-350.

Clancey, W.J. (1989) Viewing Knowledge Bases as Qualitative Models. In *IEEE-Expert* Vol 4 p9-23.

Dietterich, T.G. (1986) Learning at the Knowledge Level. In *Machine Learning* Vol 1(3) p287-316. Kluwer Academic Publishers. Boston.

Marcus, S. (1988) *Automating Knowledge Acquisition for Expert Systems*. Kluwer Academic Publishers. Boston.

McDermott, J. (1988) Preliminary Steps towards a Taxonomy of Problem Solving Methods. In Marcus, S. (Ed.) *Automating Knowledge Acquisition for Expert Systems*. Kluwer Academic Publishers. Boston.

Newell, A. (1982) The Knowledge Level. In *Artificial Intelligence Vol 18 p87-127*.

Plaza, E. and Van de Velde, W. (1990) *The MMP project: a massive memory architecture*. Research proposal, Dirección General de Investigatión Científica y Técnica (DGICYT), Spain.

Schreiber, G., Akkermans, H., and Wielinga, B. (1990) On Problems with the Knowledge Level Perspective. In *Proceedings of the Banff 90 Knowledge Acquisition Workshop*.

Steels, L. (1990) Components of Expertise. *AI Magazine*, Summer 1990. Also as AI-Memo 89-2, VUB, Brussels.

Sticklen, J. (1989) Problem solving architecture at the knowledge level. In *Journal of Experimental and Theoretical Artificial Intelligence*.

Van de Velde, W. (1988) *Learning from Experience*. Ph.D. Thesis. Vrije Universiteit Brussel. Brussels. (also as VUB AI-Lab TR-88-1).

Van de Velde, W. (1990) Reasoning, Behavior and Learning: A Knowledge Level Perspective. In *Proceedings of COGNITIVA-90*. Madrid, Spain.

Wielinga, B., Schreiber, G., and Breuker, J. (1990) *KADS: A modelling approach to KBS development*. Technical report, University of Amsterdam.

On Problems with the Knowledge Level Perspective*

Guus Schreiber *   Hans Akkermans †   Bob Wielinga *

*Department of Social Science Informatics, University of Amsterdam
Roetersstraat 15, NL-1018 WB Amsterdam, The Netherlands
Electronic mail: guussc/wielinga@swi.psy.uva.nl
†Netherlands Energy Research Foundation ECN
P.O. Box 1, NL-1755 ZG Petten, The Netherlands
Electronic mail: hans@ecn.UUCP

ABSTRACT

In this paper some points of criticism on Newell's Knowledge Level Hypothesis are investigated. Among those are: the inability to represent control, the potential computational inadequacy, the lack of predictive power and the non-operational character (the problem of 'how to build it'). We discuss Sticklen's Knowledge Level Architecture Hypothesis in which he tries to overcome these problems. On the basis of general arguments as well as specific insights from our KADS knowledge level modelling approach we reject the points of criticism. We also argue that the extension Sticklen proposes is not necessary and partly also unwanted.

1 Introduction

The introduction by Newell of the *knowledge level hypothesis* has attracted considerable attention and stimulated new lines of research. It claims that there exists a distinct computer systems level that lies immediately above the symbol or program level. This knowledge level characterises the behaviour of problem solving agents in terms of their goals and actions, with knowledge serving as the medium, on the basis

---

*The research reported here was carried out in the course of the REFLECT project. This project is partially funded by the Esprit Basic Research Programme of the Commission of the European Communities as project number 3178. The partners in this project are the University of Amsterdam (Amsterdam, The Netherlands), the Netherlands Energy Research Foundation ECN (Petten, The Netherlands), the National German Research Centre for Computer Science GMD (St. Augustin, West-Germany) and BSR Consulting (Munich, West-Germany).

of a simple principle of rationality saying that an agent will carry out a certain action if it has knowledge that one of its goals can be achieved by that action [Newell, 1982].

It was Clancey who first showed the importance of this idea for the theory of knowledge-based reasoning [Clancey, 1983; Clancey, 1985b]. Since then, a variety of authors has elaborated the viewpoint that the knowledge level is the right level of abstraction for knowledge acquisition and engineering [Wielinga et al., 1989; Bylander and Chandrasekaran, 1988; McDermott, 1989; Alexander et al., 1988; Musen et al., 1988; Steels, 1988]. This research has focused on the conceptual, implementation-independent aspects of knowledge and, on this basis, has contributed to generic models of problem solving and to more solid methodologies for KBS development.

Evidently, the knowledge level hypothesis has been a very fruitful one. On the other hand, it has also attracted strong criticism. This is well exemplified in a recent paper by Sticklen and the associated commentaries [Sticklen, 1989]. In brief, from discussions like these we single out as basic problems related to the knowledge level hypothesis:

1. *Computational inadequacy*: Due to the high level conceptual bias of knowledge level models, a very real danger is their potential computational inadequacy.

2. *Non-operational character*: Knowledge level models do describe knowledge that is necessary for problem solving, but give no clue as to how to build computational systems embodying and exploiting that knowledge.

3. *Inability to represent control*: Knowledge level models capture knowledge used in problem solving actions, but they do not provide ways to express the control of problem solving.

4. *Lack of predictive power*: Knowledge level models are useful to explain —from hindsight— the behaviour of certain problem solving agents (such as AI programs), but are unable to generate empirically testable predictions about that behaviour.

Interestingly, most of this criticism on the knowledge level hypothesis appears to be inspired by what is seen by some as its greatest advantage: moving away from implementational issues in favour of the conceptual aspects of knowledge. In the present work, which is basically a *position paper*, the knowledge level hypothesis and its problems will be investigated in some detail. On the basis of general arguments as well as specific insights from our KADS knowledge level approach to KBS development [Wielinga et al., 1989], we will consider —and reject— the points of criticism raised above.

2   The Knowledge Level Hypothesis Debate

2.1   The Knowledge Level Hypothesis

The Knowledge Level Hypothesis (KLH) was put forward by Newell in his presidential address to AAAI-80 [Newell, 1982]. Newell discusses in this address the notions of *knowledge* and *representation* which is his view are central to AI. Newell signals that most of the work in AI is centred on representation. Representation refers here to the actual data structures and processes in an (AI) program. He suggests that the confusing issues in AI research on representation may (partly) be due to the limited attention the research community is giving to the study of the nature of knowledge. The Knowledge Level Hypothesis is aimed at providing a platform for studying knowledge independent of its representation in a programming language. Newell phrases the KLH as follows:

> "There exists a distinct computer systems level, lying immediately above the symbol level, which is characterised by knowledge as the medium and the principle of rationality as the law of behaviour."

Representations (data structures and processes) are part of the the symbol level, whereas knowledge is the prime ingredient (the medium) at the knowledge level. Newell sketches the structure of the knowledge level as an agent that has a physical body (consisting of a set of actions), a body of knowledge, and a set of goals (goals are bodies of knowledge about the state of the environment). The principle of rationality that governs the behaviour of the agent is formulated as follows:

> If an agent has knowledge that one of its actions will lead to one of its goals, then the agent will select this action.

The central issue now becomes: what is the nature of the knowledge the agent has? Newell characterises knowledge as a "competence-like notion, being a potential for generating action" and as "entirely *functionally* in terms of what it does, not *structurally* in terms of physical objects". A representation is defined as a "symbol system that encodes a body of knowledge".

As an example of the usefulness of a distinction between knowledge level and symbol level, Newell points to the work of Schank on conceptual dependency structures [Schank, 1975]. He argues that the main contribution of this work is at the knowledge level – namely by providing a quite general way of describing knowledge of the world. Although AI researchers felt that this work was incomplete without an implementation, the actual program added little to the theoretical work: it was just a large AI program with the usual ad hoc constructions.

2.2   Knowledge Level Modelling in Knowledge Acquisition

One of the areas where the knowledge level hypothesis has received considerable attention is the field of knowledge acquisition. Experience with the first generation of knowledge-based systems (MYCIN and its derivatives) showed that the *transfer approach* to knowledge acquisition was simply inadequate. In the transfer approach the knowledge engineer tries to extract knowledge from a domain expert in the form of the representation in the system (e.g. as production rules). The problems with this approach are manifold: the mapping from elicited expertise-data onto the required representation is difficult and often not possible; systems with a large knowledge base become difficult to maintain; explanation facilities are poor; etc. The main reason for this is that the gap between the observed problem solving behaviour and the target application is just too wide. What is needed is an intermediate description of the expertise in a task domain at a more abstract level. The knowledge level provides precisely this intermediate level of description.

Broadly speaking, two approaches can be identified to the use of the idea of a knowledge level description in knowledge acquisition, In the first approach the starting point is an implementation of (parts of) a problem solver. Here, knowledge level notions are introduced by providing abstract, implementation-free, descriptions of the knowledge elements required by the problem solver. Examples of this approach are the Generic Task approach [Bylander and Chandrasekaran, 1988] and the work of McDermott et al. on MOLE, SALT and other systems [McDermott, 1989]. In the second approach, exemplified in the KADS methodology [Wielinga et al., 1990], the knowledge level descriptions are part of a conceptual model of a task domain. The conceptual model serves as a specification of the (knowledge) requirements for a particular knowledge-based application. The conceptual model is not directly linked with the actual implementation.

2.3   Criticism of the Knowledge Level Hypothesis

The introduction of the KLH has led to criticism both of the KLH itself and also of the application of knowledge level descriptions in the development of knowledge-based systems. In a recent article, Sticklen [Sticklen, 1989] phrases these points of criticism in the form of an extension of the Knowledge Level Hypothesis: the "Knowledge Level Architecture Hypothesis". We will go through his argument in some detail, as his discussion is in a sense typical for critics of the KLH.

First, Sticklen acknowledges that the notion of a knowledge level description is a useful one. He points to the work of Clancey on Heuristic Classification [Clancey, 1985b] as a prototypical example of a knowledge level description of a problem solving agent (process). In his article, Sticklen apparently views the "horse shoe" inference structure of heuristic classification as a complete knowledge level description. He then concludes that this type of description is unable to yield verifiable predictions of the problem solving behaviour of an agent and that thus the knowledge level hypothesis is incomplete. This conclusion is based on the assumption that a scientific theory has two necessary components: (i) the theory must account for known phenomena and (ii) the theory must make (verifiable) predictions about phenomena that will be observed in the future. He argues that the lack of predictive power of knowledge level descriptions is due the fact that there is no way in Newell's knowledge level to specify problem solving control. In his Knowledge Level Architecture Hypothesis he proposes to extend the KLH with the possibility of decomposing an agent (task) into sub-agents (sub-tasks) and allow specification of ordering among sub-agents. This extension seems harmless enough. Newell himself is not very clear whether decomposition of agents is allowed. A requirement for the decomposition is that the resulting sub-agents are 'knowledgeable', i.e. that they can be described in knowledge level terms. Sticklen is however not very clear on how this can be ensured.

Given a decomposition of an agent into sub-agents, Sticklen defines the corresponding knowledge level architecture through two ingredients: (i) a specification of the communication paths between sub-agents, and (ii) the specification of the message protocols for inter-agent communication.

Sticklen claims that a knowledge level architecture description provides a

> "*blueprint* for how to build a problem solver that may be used as a simulator."[1]

The simulator provides the required predictive part of the theory, The role of the simulator can be compared with the role of numeric simulations in physics.

In his article, Sticklen tries to cope with some –highly interrelated– points of criticism of the knowledge level approach,. He mentions two points explicitly: the *inability to represent control* and the *lack of predictive power*. Two other points of criticism are:

computational inadequacy:
When a knowledge level description is transformed into a symbol level description, what kind of guarantees does one to have that the resulting system is computationally adequate?

non-operational character:
A knowledge level model gives no clues about how to build an operational system. I.e. it does not solve the 'design problem'.

These last two points are also covered by the knowledge level architecture hypothesis through the blueprint for building a simulator (i.e. a knowledge-based application).

In the rest of this article we discuss the various points of criticism. We will argue that the extension that Sticklen proposes is not necessary and partly also unwanted.

3   Representing   Control   in   Knowledge   Level   Models

Sticklen's Knowledge Level Architecture Hypothesis encompasses an extension of the knowledge level with respect to the description of problem solving control. In our view knowledge about task (agent) decompositions and dependencies is indeed just

---

[1]italicisation by the authors

another type of knowledge with its own specific characteristics that should —and can— be described in a knowledge level model. The description in [Clancey, 1985a] of the diagnostic strategy developed for NEOMYCIN is a good example of what we would call a knowledge level description of problem solving control. Clancey calls this a "competence model" of diagnostic strategy, which already indicates that the description has the knowledge level flavour Newell is aiming at in his KLH.

In our opinion, the question whether this type of (competence-like) control knowledge is or is not present in the Knowledge Level Hypothesis, as originally stated by Newell, is not very important or interesting. From our experience it is clear that the above-mentioned type of control knowledge is a necessary and important ingredient of a practical knowledge level theory of problem solving. In addition to the task decompositions and inter-dependencies (the task knowledge in the KADS model, see [Wielinga et al., 1989]) we would also add meta-knowledge about a problem solving agent as a separate kind of control knowledge (somewhat confusingly termed 'strategic knowledge' in KADS). This strategic or tactical knowledge is an important ingredient for building more flexible knowledge-based systems.

The problem of ensuring that the decomposition results in 'knowledgeable' sub-agents can be handled by providing a knowledge level typology of canonical inferences (the lowest level of sub-agents), thereby ensuring that such agents can indeed be described in knowledge level terms. Examples of canonical inferences are the three steps in the Heuristic Classification inference structure (abstraction, association and refinement) [Clancey, 1985a] and the set of knowledge sources defined in KADS [Breuker and Wielinga, 1989]. Clearly, much work still needs to be done in this area to arrive at a coherent and more or less complete typology.

What worries us in the Knowledge Level Architecture idea is that it should provide a blueprint for building a simulator. Whereas we think that it is very well possible to define structured ways of building a knowledge-based system from a knowledge-level specification (see Sec. 6), we do not believe, that a knowledge level model should –and can– contain all information necessary for building the implementation. In fact, by nature it should not! In the process of implementing a system it will always be necessary to add specific information. The design process is constrained by the knowledge level specification, but a large number of design decisions concern issues that are not relevant at the knowledge level.

We think that the confusion arises from the way in which the word "control" is used. There is a difference between what we would call respectively *knowledge level control* and *symbol level control*. The description of the diagnostic strategy of NEOMYCIN in [Clancey, 1985a] is a clear example of knowledge level control. This type of knowledge concerns task decompositions of and orderings between knowledgeable agents and possibly also meta-knowledge about agents. Symbol level control is concerned with the control issues that arise when a particular representation or AI technique is selected to realise a problem solving agent. A similar distinction between these two types of control is made by Gruber [Gruber, 1989; page 5].

Although symbol level control is not an issue at the knowledge level, it does pose several problems that have to have solved in the implementation of a particular application. One only has to look at the vast amount of ' 'symbol level" AI research to conclude that these problems are by no means trivial. Thus, specification of knowledge level control does *not* provide a blueprint for building a simulator.

4 Epistemological and Computational Adequacy

Knowledge level models give a high level description of the knowledge as it is utilised in problem-solving reasoning. Although terminology is different, a common view appears to be emerging in the literature based on the idea that the knowledge level is constituted by different types and components of knowledge, and that these forms of knowledge play different roles in the reasoning process and have inherently different structuring principles. In addition, the knowledge level approach attempts to demonstrate that many of these knowledge types and components have a generic character, *i.e.*, they are applicable to a broad class of tasks and/or domains. In this sense, generic knowledge components can be viewed as intermediate in the continuum from weak to strong methods.

The use of knowledge level models lies in yielding a high level and intuitive *explanation of reasoning behaviour*. Moreover, generic models at the knowledge level are important vehicles for knowledge acquisition, because they provide the knowledge engineer with *reusable interpretation 'templates'* that guide the analysis and organisation of elicitation data.

As a consequence of the high-level conceptual nature, a major objection to the use of knowledge level models in the KBS development process is their potential computational inadequacy. Since knowledge level models do not specify the operational control regime in full detail they are apt to potential combinatorial explosion behaviour. The generic task approach by Chandrasekaran *et al.* takes the view that the knowledge level description and the operational problem-solving method as employed in the computational system cannot be separated. In contrast, the choice of computational techniques to realise a certain knowledge level function is seen in KADS as part of the design activity in knowledge engineering (further discussed in Sec. 6). An important criticism of the KADS-type of conceptual models is therefore that — although they are very useful from a practical epistemological viewpoint— they do not guarantee computational tractability.

4.1 The knowledge level: role limitations

In this very broad and general way of speaking, the criticism above is correct: knowledge level models do not make statements about computational adequacy as such. However, we claim that the *structure* of knowledge level models as outlined previously provides important safeguards against the computational inadequacy. The combinatorial complexity at the computational level is caused in our view by the unrestricted applicability of and access to knowledge as present in the knowledge base. The underlying principle of knowledge level modelling is *imposing structure through knowledge differentiation*. This is achieved by distinguishing within the involved body of knowledge different types and components that play specialised roles in the totality of the problem-solving process.

An example is the cover-and-differentiate method [Eshelman et al., 1988] for diagnosis which takes the following steps:

1. Determine events (hypotheses) that potentially explain symptoms.

2. Identify information that can differentiate between candidate explanations by ruling out, providing support for candidates, providing preferences.

3. Get this differentiating information and apply it.

4. If new symptoms become available, go to step 1.

In this example, several types of knowledge are specified in an informal way. First, the domain should provide concepts like: event, symptom, explanation link, preference, rule-out relations etc. Second, a number of basic inference types (similar to KADS knowledge sources [Breuker and Wielinga, 1989]) are defined: generating a hypothesis, matching a hypothesis to the available data, selection or ordering, compute preferences. In addition there is control knowledge that indicates that all possible candidates are generated given a set of symptoms, and that differentiating information is obtained in a backward manner. These aspects of knowledge would be categorised as task knowledge in KADS.

The differentiating requirements and constraints as laid down in the knowledge model express the specific role that the considered knowledge plays in the problem-solving process. This limits the use that can be made of that knowledge. For instance, a logical implication sentence of a certain type can be specified to be usable only for matching inferences, and not for other types of inference steps (like, say, a selection). KADS notions such as knowledge sources, metaclasses and task structures [Breuker and Wielinga, 1989] generally yield the possibility of selecting specific rules or theories needed to produce a certain inference. In this way the knowledge level model provides *role-limiting constraints* [McDermott, 1989] to the use of knowledge.

4.2 The computational level: access limitations

Thus, an essential epistemological feature of knowledge level models is that they specify role limitations of knowledge. The corresponding notion at the computational level is that of access limitations[2]. The knowledge that is specified in a KADS conceptual model cannot be used in arbitrary ways: it has to fulfill certain typing requirements and can only be applied in accordance with the constraints specified by the model. Given that knowledge components can only be selectively used due to specified role-limiting constraints, the consequence will be a restricted access to the computational representation of those components in a knowledge-based system. Assuming that (as said) the computational complexity results from unrestricted applicability of and access to knowledge, the structure of a knowledge model has a profound effect on the computational adequacy. If the knowledge model sufficiently refines the various

---

[2]Cf. Newell's slogan: *representation = knowledge + access*

knowledge types and explicitly indicates what inferences access what domain structures, the computational complexity will be greatly reduced.

Our position is supported by experiences from AI. Here, a common method to achieve computational tractability is to introduce structural differentiations that at the knowledge level can be characterised as adding new role specialisations and limitations of knowledge. As a matter of fact, this attitude is quite clearly exemplified in the work on generic tasks. Also heuristic classification is a good specimen: if direct association between data and solutions results in a computationally inadequate model, a possible method to obtain a more tractable model is the introduction of additional inference steps, *viz.*, abstraction and refinement. The associated knowledge can now be specified to be accessible only in a restricted part of the 'horse-shoe' inference structure, whereas this is impossible in a simple direct-association model. Yet another interesting example is provided by the work of Patil on medical diagnosis [Patil, 1988], showing that complicated forms of diagnosis can be gradually built up by starting from a simple generate-and-test method and subsequently introducing new elements of knowledge differentiation, so as to preserve the computational adequacy with increasing task complexity.

In conclusion, we suggest that *epistemological role limitations as described by a knowledge level model are connected to computational access limitations.* Computational adequacy cannot be strictly guaranteed, but the knowledge level approach does provide significant handles on the computational tractability by means of the role and access limitations ensuing from knowledge differentiation.

5   Do Knowledge Level Models Yield Predictions?

Sticklen puts forward as a central objection to the knowledge level hypothesis in its current form its lack of predictive power. In his view, knowledge level models are capable of explanatory analysis of the reasoning behaviour of intelligent systems in retrospect, but the do not generate empirically verifiable predictions. He discusses this in the context of the broad question whether AI can be considered to be a science when it does not contain a predictive component.

First of all, Sticklen's equation of science with predictive power needs some qualification. On this score, we basically agree with the critical commentaries on his position. Restricting ourselves to physics —Sticklen's favourite example of an 'established science'— it is clear that explanatory and predictive power constitute much more subtle ingredients of science than he suggests. Especially in branches of physics that are close to engineering we encounter phenomenological models that have strong predictive power but no explanatory status. This is the case if such models numerically express important regularities of experimental data without referring to more fundamental laws of physics (this may be achieved by, simply speaking, a linear regression analysis of a certain large amount of data that happens to be successful in the general case). Conversely, there are models that are based upon basic physical principles (and so are felt to be relevant in providing a physically intuitive picture of a process) but refer to phenomena that are far beyond any experimental test (such as processes on time scales that are orders-of-magnitude shorter than can be measured)[3]. In general, physical theory is an iceberg of which only a tiny part is visible for empirical verification. An important aspect is that physical theories only yield predictions at a certain level and within a certain regime. For instance, macro-physical theories such as hydrodynamics do make predictions about, say, fluid pressure and waves, but not about microphysical entities like atomic interaction potentials within water molecules. The latter notions have even no existence at the macro-physical level, whereas in the microphysical theory there is no place for concepts like fluid, waves and pressure. Thus, each level of physical description generates its own type of predictions.

This parallel carries over to modelling for knowledge-based systems. A knowledge level model describes what types of reasoning steps an agent that is being modelled is expected to take in performing a certain task. In addition it makes certain claims about the structure of the domain-specific knowledge involved, and it specifies the strategic elements of the reasoning. For example, the cover-and-differentiate knowledge model outlined earlier tells us that certain hypotheses will be discarded in a *rule-out* inference step. How such an inference will operationally manifest itself depends on the system under investigation. An AI program may print out the removal of a hypothesis from the list of current candidates, while a human expert may utter a natural language sentence implying that the hypothesis is no longer considered. Although the operational form may differ, in both cases the ruling-out of a hypothesis is in principle empirically verifiable. Similarly, the heuristic-classification model would predict that much of the reasoning effort would be concentrated in data reduction and not in hypothesis handling, as is the case in the cover-and-differentiate method.

Thus, a knowledge level model may be applied to both human and artificial problem solvers. In either case, however, it is hard to see why knowledge models as we have sketched them possess no predictive power, as seems to be Sticklen's complaint. But it has to be acknowledged that the corresponding predictions are of a certain kind only, namely, on the level of the reasoning steps —which type, under what knowledge conditions— that we expect an agent to perform. No predictions are made concerning the detailed, operational or symbol, level of observation. As corroborated by much of the literature concerning the philosophy of science, testing a theory requires an interpretation of the observations that we make concerning the real world. Evidently, the regime of prediction (and, thus, of validity) of knowledge level models is limited — in this case to the type of and the conditions for inference steps to be carried out by an intelligent agent. Nevertheless, as pointed out, a limited regime or level at which predictions can be made is standard not only in AI but also in physics. Consequently, we disagree with Sticklen's criticism on the predictive power of knowledge level models.

---

[3]Our examples are based upon personal experience in mainstream nuclear physics and engineering. If we accept as a simple operational definition of what may count as science: the publication of work in refereed international journals on a regular basis (the latter to rule out incidental mistakes of reviewers), all these examples must be accepted as science. We can provide the interested reader with pertinent references to the literature.

6 System Building on the Basis of Knowledge Level Models

Knowledge level models do not contain all information necessary for the implementation of a system. In the KADS approach to developing knowledge-based systems, a separate *design model* is introduced [Schreiber et al., 1988]. In this design model appropriate AI techniques and representations are selected to realise the problem solving behaviour specified in the knowledge level model. The design model is thus a specification of the symbol level notions such as data structures and processes. The design model is also the place where additional, *symbol level*, control (cf. Sec. 3) is specified.

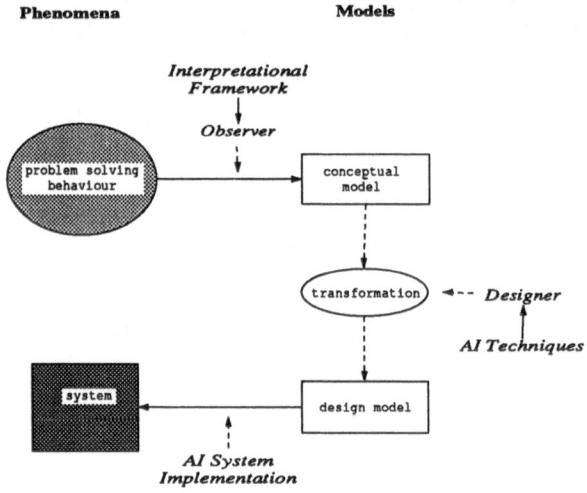

Figure 1: Role of the conceptual (knowledge level) model and of the design (symbol level) model in the development of knowledge-based systems

Fig. 1 provides a graphical representation of the different roles that the knowledge level model and the design model in our view play in the development process of a knowledge-based system. The knowledge level model is constructed by an observer of problem solving phenomena (e.g. human expertise). The observer (knowledge analyst) is aided in this task by an interpretational framework, that should consist of two parts: (i) a vocabulary for describing various knowledge types, such as the categorisations in the KADS conceptual model, and (ii) generic knowledge components. These generic components are partial instantiations of knowledge reoccurring in a class of tasks and/or domains. Heuristic classification, cover-and-differentiate and the interpretation models in KADS [Breuker et al., 1987] are examples of such generic components.

The design model is constructed by transforming the knowledge-level descriptions into symbol-level descriptions through the selection of appropriate AI techniques and representations, that realise the specified problem solving behaviour. The design model provides the basis for implementing the physical system. Although the designer is in principle free to develop any design model that meets the requirements of the knowledge level model, we are strongly in favour of a *structure-preserving* design. With this we mean that there is a structural correspondence between knowledge level elements and symbol level elements. This approach is in line with Pylyshyn's "cognitive penetrability" requirement for programs simulating cognitive behaviour [Pylyshyn, 1986]. Structural correspondence paves also the way for explaining the computation of a program at various levels of abstraction (physical, symbol/functional, knowledge). To support this structure-preserving design we have developed a *design description language* [Schreiber et al., 1989]. This language is a notational device that enables a design in which the transformation is basically a process of *adding* symbol level information, such as operational control, to the knowledge level model. We are currently embarking on an ESPRIT-II endeavour in which this approach will be explored further, for example by providing a catalogue of AI techniques and representations together with corresponding shellifications. Given the state of the art, such a catalogue will however for the time being remain incomplete.

7   Conclusions

In this paper we have investigated some points of criticism on Newell's Knowledge Level Hypothesis: the inability to represent control, the potential computational inadequacy, the lack of predictive power and the non-operational character (the problem of 'how to build it').

We have pointed at a possible confusion between two types of control. We have indicated that in our view there is a need to model in a practical knowledge theory of problem solving a particular type of control knowledge with a strong knowledge level flavour as for example decompositions of knowledgeable agents and meta-knowledge about agents. If this type of knowledge level control was not part of Newell's original hypothesis, we feel that it should be extended in this respect. We disagree with an extension such as Sticklen's Knowledge Level Architecture Hypothesis, as it requires a type of control specification that inherently belongs to the symbol level. We have argued that the role-limitations in knowledge level descriptions give rise to access limitations at the symbol level. Together they provide important safe-guards against potential computational inadequacy. We have also explained that knowledge level models as we propose them allow limited forms of prediction – namely at the level of the type of and the conditions for inference steps carried out by an intelligent agent. We have shown that this is not different from the role of formal theories in predicting physical phenomena. Finally, we have argued that in the process of system building there is a place for a separate design model. We view design as a process of adding symbol level information to a knowledge level model. Notational devices, catalogues, and shellifications can support the design and implementation, but by nature these activities are open-ended, i.e. the solution space is large.

Although we feel that the original Knowledge Level Hypothesis still stands, much work still needs to be done to 'make it work': to arrive at a practical knowledge level theory of problem solving. Looking at the various approaches to knowledge level modelling it is clear that the terminology used to describe the knowledge level is confusing and ambiguous. In our opinion there is a clear need for a *formal* framework for describing knowledge level models. We fully agree with Newell [Newell, 1982; p. 121-122] that the major role of logic in AI should be to support the analysis of the knowledge level. In [Akkermans et al., 1990] a first effort is made to devise a logical framework for knowledge level analysis. Although this work can only be seen as a first start, we feel that this is one important research direction for improving the state of the art in knowledge acquisition.

Acknowledgement   Frank van Harmelen provided useful comments on an earlier version of this paper.

References

Akkermans, H., van Harmelen, F., Schreiber, G., and Wielinga, B. (1990).   A formalisation of knowledge-level models for knowledge acquistion. *International Journal of Intelligent Systems*. Forthcoming.

Alexander, J., Freiling, M., Shulman, S., Rehfuss, S., and Messick, S. (1988). Ontological analysis: an ongoing experiment. In Boose, J. and Gaines, B., editors, *Knowledge-Based Systems, Volume 2: Knowledge Acquisition Tools for Expert Systems*, pages 25–37. Academic Press, London.

Breuker, J., Wielinga, B., van Someren, M., de Hoog, R., Schreiber, G., de Greef, P., Bredeweg, B., Wielemaker, J., Billault, J.-P., Davoodi, M., and Hayward, S. (1987). Model Driven Knowledge Acquisition: Interpretation Models. ESPRIT Project P1098 Deliverable D1 (task A1), University of Amsterdam and STL Ltd,.

Breuker, J. A. and Wielinga, B. J. (1989). Model Driven Knowledge Acquisition. In Guida, P. and Tasso, G., editors, *Topics in the Design of Expert Systems*, pages 265–296, Amsterdam. North Holland.

Bylander, T. and Chandrasekaran, B. (1988).   Generic tasks in knowledge-based reasoning: The 'right' level of abstraction for knowledge acquisition. In Gaines, B. and J.Boose, editors, *Knowledge Acquisition for Knowledge Based Systems*, volume 1, pages 65–77. Academic Press, London.

Clancey, W. (1983). The epistemology of a rule based system -a framework for explanation. *Artificial Intelligence*, 20:215–251. Also: Stanford Heuristic Programming Project, Memo HPP-81-17, November 1981, also numbered STAN-CS-81-896.

Clancey, W. (1985a). Acquiring, representing and evaluating a competence model of diagnostic strategy. In Chi, Glaser, and Far, editors, *Contributions to the Nature of Expertise*.

Clancey, W. (1985b). Heuristic classification. *Artificial Intelligence*, 27:289–350.

Eshelman, L., Ehret, D., McDermott, J., and Tan, M. (1988). MOLE: a tenacious knowledge acquisition tool. In Boose, J. and Gaines, B., editors, *Knowledge Based Systems, Volume 2: Knowledge Acquisition Tools for Expert Systems*, pages 95–108, London. Academic Press.

Gruber, T. (1989). *The Acquisition of Strategic Knowledge*. Perspectives in Artificial Intelligence, Volume 4. Academic Press, San Diego.

McDermott, J. (1989).   Preliminary steps towards a taxonomy of problem-solving methods. In Marcus, S., editor, *Automating Knowledge Acquisition for Expert*

Systems, pages 225–255. Kluwer Academic Publishers, The Netherlands.

Musen, M., Fagan, L., Combs, D., and Shortliffe, E. (1988). Use of a domain model to drive an interactive knowledge editing tool. In Boose, J. and Gaines, B., editors, *Knowledge-Based Systems, Volume 2: Knowledge Acquisition Tools for Expert Systems*, pages 257–273, London. Academic Press.

Newell, A. (1982). The knowledge level. *Artificial Intelligence*, 1982:87–127.

Patil, R. (1988). Artificial intelligence techniques for diagnostic reasoning in medicine. In Shobe, H. and AAAI, editors, *Exploring Artificial Intelligence: Survey Talks from the National Conferences on Artificial Intelligence*, pages 347–379. Morgan Kaufmann, San Mateo, California.

Pylyshyn, Z. (1986). *Computation and Cognition: Toward a Foundation for Cognitive Science*. MIT Press, Cambridge, USA.

Schank, R. (1975). *Conceptual information processing*. North Holland, Amsterdam.

Schreiber, G., Breuker, J., Bredeweg, B., and Wielinga, B. (1988). Modelling in KBS development. In *Proc. 2th European Knowledge Acquisition Workshop, Bonn*, pages 7.1– 7.15, St. Augustin. GMD. GMD-Studien 143.

Schreiber, G., Wielinga, B., Hesketh, P., and Lewis, A. (1989). A KADS design description language. ESPRIT Project 1098, deliverable B7 UvA-B7-PR-007, University of Amsterdam.

Steels, L. (1988). Components of expertise. AI Memo 88-16, AI Lab, Vrije Universiteit Brussel. Published in *AI Magazine*, summer 1990.

Sticklen, J. (1989). Problem solving architecture at the knowledge level. *Journal of Experimental and Theoretical Artificial Intelligence*.

Wielinga, B., Akkermans, H., Schreiber, G., and Balder, J. (1989). A knowledge acquisition perspective on knowledge-level models. In Boose, J. H. and Gaines, B. R., editors, *Proceedings Knowledge Acquisition Workshop KAW'89, Banff*, pages 36-1 – 36-22, University of Calgary. SRDG Publications.

Wielinga, B., Boose, J., Gaines, B., Schreiber, A., and van Someren, M., editors (1990). *Current Trends in Knowledge Acquisition*. IOS, Amsterdam.

THEOREM PROVING

Using Abstraction*

Fausto Giunchiglia
IRST, Trento and
DIST, Genova, Italy
fausto@irst.uucp

Toby Walsh
Department of AI,
Edinburgh, Scotland
T.Walsh@ed.ac.uk

KEYWORDS: abstraction, automated reasoning, theorem proving

ABSTRACT

This paper uses the theory of abstraction presented in [Giunchiglia & Walsh, 1989a] to consider how an abstract proof can be "mapped back" onto a proof of the unabstracted theorem. This analysis naturally suggests the architecture of a generic abstract theorem prover. We have implemented this theorem prover, and begun to investigate its properties; our results agree favourably with a computational model we have developed for analysing the benefits of abstraction.

1 INTRODUCTION

Abstraction has been proposed as a powerful heuristic for theorem proving (for example [Plaisted, 1981, Plaisted, 1986, Tenenberg, 1988, Giunchiglia & Walsh, 1989b]). Usually, the structure of an abstract proof is used to help construct an unabstracted, or "ground" proof. This process of using an abstract proof to guide the construction of a ground proof is the **mapping back** problem.

In this paper, we will look at this problem using the *theory of abstraction* presented in [Giunchiglia & Walsh, 1989a]. This requires us to make precise a notion of similarity between the structure of proofs. The property we want, called **tree subsumption** is one of monotonicity: for any node in the abstract proof tree there must be a corresponding node in the ground proof tree. The idea is that the ground proof tree can be obtained by adding nodes to an "unabstraction" of the abstract proof tree; no abstract nodes need to be thrown away.

We begin by describing some essential aspects of our theory of abstraction (section 2). We then introduce a general notion of similarity between ground and abstract

---

*This work was begun when the first author was working at the Department of Artificial Intelligence at Edinburgh University, supported by SERC grant GR/E/4459.8. Currently the first author's research at IRST is founded by ITC (Istituto Trentino di Cultura). The second author was originally supported by a SERC studentship; he is now a SERC Postdoctoral Research Fellow. All the members of the Mathematical Reasoning group in Edinburgh and the Mechanized Reasoning group in Trento are thanked for their contributions to this work. Both authors especially thank Alan Bundy, Caroline Talcott and Colin Williams for their discussions on this topic, and Paul Brna for his LaTeX advice.

proof trees (section 3). We show how this notion naturally suggests the architecture of a *generic* abstract theorem prover (section 4). We describe some results of using this theorem prover (section 5), comparing them with a computational model (section 6). We end with a description of related work (section 7), and some conclusions (section 8).

2 A THEORY OF ABSTRACTION

Abstraction can be described as the mapping of one representation of a problem, the **ground** representation onto a new but simpler representation, the **abstract** representation. To define abstraction formally, we therefore need to decide how to represent problems; one very general method is with a **formal system**, Σ in which we specify a **language** for describing the problem and (some way of generating) a set of true statements, the **theorems** of Σ or $TH(\Sigma)$. An **abstraction** is then simply a mapping from one formal system to another.

> **Definition 1 (Abstraction)** : *An abstraction, written $f : \Sigma_1 \Rightarrow \Sigma_2$ is a pair of formal systems $\langle \Sigma_1, \Sigma_2 \rangle$ with languages Λ_1 and Λ_2 respectively, and a function, $f_\Lambda : \Lambda_1 \mapsto \Lambda_2$.*

Note that it is not sufficient just to give the two formal systems, we also need some way of relating what we say in them; this is the purpose of the function for mapping between their languages. Following historical convention, Σ_1 is called the **ground space** and Σ_2 the **abstract space**. Where it is not ambiguous, we use $f(\varphi)$ to stand for $f_\Lambda(\varphi)$.

This is a very general definition of abstraction. If an abstraction is to be of any use, there must also be a relationship between the properties of the ground space and those of the abstract space. Since our focus is on proving theorems, an interesting restriction is to abstractions that preserve provability. In [Giunchiglia & Walsh, 1989a] we identified the very important and common class of **TI-abstractions**[1].

> **Definition 2 (TI-abstraction)** : *The abstraction $f : \Sigma_1 \Rightarrow \Sigma_2$ is a TI-abstraction iff, for any wff φ, if $\varphi \in TH(\Sigma_1)$ then $f(\varphi) \in TH(\Sigma_2)$.*

TI-abstractions are complete (the abstraction of any ground theorem is a theorem in the abstract space) but may not be correct (there may be theorems in the abstract space which do not correspond to any theorem in the ground space). This is why the mapping back problem must be solved.

3 MAPPING BACK

Preserving provability is only a very weak property to demand; we also want abstractions to preserve the *structure* of proofs. Abstract proofs can then be used to guide a theorem prover in finding ground proofs. We begin, first, by defining some notions for describing proofs.

A **formulae tree**, Π is either a wff φ, or:

$$\frac{\Pi_1 ... \Pi_n}{\varphi}$$

---

[1] "T" stands for theorem and "I" for increasing.

where $\Pi_1, ...\Pi_n$ are themselves formulae trees. In both cases, φ is the **root** formula. For the sake of brevity we will write "tree" to mean "formulae tree". The trees $\Pi, \Pi_1, ...\Pi_n$ are called **subtrees** of Π; any subtree of $\Pi,...\Pi_n$ is also a subtree of Π. If Π is a subtree of Γ then Γ is a **supertree** of Π. A **strict** subtree of Π is any subtree not equal to Π. A **proof tree** is a tree in which every wff is derived from the wffs directly above by the application of an inference rule and the top most formulae are either discharged assumptions or axioms. If $f : \Sigma_1 \Rightarrow \Sigma_2$ is an abstraction and Π a tree in Σ_1, the **abstraction of** Π, written $f(\Pi)$, is the tree constructed by applying $f_\Lambda : \Lambda_1 \mapsto \Lambda_2$ to every wff in Π.

One notion of similarity between a ground proof tree, Π_1 and an abstract proof tree, Π_2 is that Π_2 can be obtained by deleting some formula occurrences from $f(\Pi_1)$; this deletion can occur anywhere within the proof tree, either at the top, in the middle or at the bottom of the tree. In such a situation we say that Π_2 **subsumes** $f(\Pi_1)$, or in symbols $\Pi_2 \subseteq f(\Pi_1)$. Formally:

Definition 3 (Tree subsumption) : $\Pi_1 \subseteq \Pi_2$ *iff*

- $\Pi_1 = \varphi$ *and* φ *is the root formulae of a subtree of* Π_2;
-

$$\Pi_1 = \frac{\Gamma_1...\Gamma_n}{\varphi}$$

and φ *is the root formula of a subtree,* Γ *of* Π_2 *and for every* i, $1 \leq i \leq n$ *there exists a strict and distinct subtree of* Γ, Γ'_i *such that* $\Gamma_i \subseteq \Gamma'_i$.

By distinct, we mean that if Γ'_i is a *subtree* of Γ'_j then $i = j$. Note that the subtree relation is stronger than tree subsumption (if Π_1 is a subtree of Π_2 then $\Pi_1 \subseteq \Pi_2$ but not vice versa). There is, however, a close similarity between tree subsumption and the subtree relation. Both are **monotonic**; wffs which appear in one tree appear in the same order in the other tree. In [Giunchiglia & Walsh, 1990] we demonstrate (by means of an equivalent but less computational definition) why tree subsumption is exactly the relationship between the structure of tress that we need – it is as strong a relation as is possible that captures our intuitive idea of mapping back. There are two main differences between tree subsumption and the subtree relation. With tree subsumption, wffs anywhere in the subsuming tree can be skipped and the ordering of trees is ignored, whilst with the subtree relation, only wffs in the supertree beneath the subtree are skipped and the ordering of the trees is fixed.

As an example of tree subsumption, consider the propositional TI-abstraction used in [Giunchiglia & Walsh, 1989b] to plan the unfolding of definitions; this abstraction maps first order wffs onto propositional wffs by throwing away their quantifiers and arguments, but keeps their connective structure. For example, $\exists x . x \subseteq_{set} a \lor a =_{set} 0$ abstracts onto the proposition, "$\subseteq_{set} \lor =_{set}$" where "$\subseteq_{set}$" and "$=_{set}$" are propositional sentence letters. Consider the theorem that if two sets are equal then one is a subset of the other. This has an abstract proof:

$$\frac{\dfrac{=_{set} \qquad =_{set} \leftrightarrow (\in \leftrightarrow \in)}{\dfrac{\in \leftrightarrow \in}{\dfrac{(\in \rightarrow \in)\&(\in \rightarrow \in)}{\dfrac{\in \rightarrow \in \qquad \subseteq_{set} \leftrightarrow (\in \rightarrow \in)}{\subseteq_{set}}}}}{=_{set} \rightarrow \subseteq_{set}}$$

This abstract proof subsumes the *abstraction* of the ground proof tree:

$$
\dfrac{
\dfrac{
\dfrac{
\dfrac{a =_{set} b \qquad \dfrac{\forall y, z. y =_{set} z \;\leftrightarrow\; x \in y \leftrightarrow x \in z}{a =_{set} b \;\leftrightarrow\; x \in a \leftrightarrow x \in b}}
{x \in a \leftrightarrow x \in b}
}
{\dfrac{(x \in a \rightarrow x \in b)\&(x \in b \rightarrow x \in a) \qquad \dfrac{\forall y, z. y \subseteq_{set} z \;\leftrightarrow\; x \in y \rightarrow x \in z}{a \subseteq_{set} b \;\leftrightarrow\; x \in a \rightarrow x \in b}}{x \in a \rightarrow x \in b}}
}
{a \subseteq_{set} b}
}
{\dfrac{a =_{set} b \rightarrow a \subseteq_{set} b}{\forall y, z. y =_{set} z \rightarrow y \subseteq_{set} z}}
$$

We use the notion of tree subsumption to define a very general class of abstractions called **PI-abstractions**[2] which preserve the structure of proofs:

Definition 4 (PI-abstraction) : *An abstraction $f : \Sigma_1 \Rightarrow \Sigma_2$ is a **PI-abstraction** iff, for any proof Π_1 of φ in Σ_1, there exists a proof Π_2 of $f(\varphi)$ in Σ_2 with $\Pi_2 \subseteq f(\Pi_1)$.*

It follows trivially that a PI-abstraction is a TI-abstraction. Note that the reverse is not true; not all TI-abstractions are PI-abstractions. There are, of course, many other ways for two proof trees to be similar. However, this notion of similarity holds for most abstractions of which we are aware. For example, the propositional abstraction described earlier in this section is a PI-abstraction. As a second example, consider the abstraction used in ABSTRIPS [Sacerdoti, 1974] where preconditions to an operator are thrown away. If we use a situation calculus to describe a STRIPS system, this mapping can be described as a PI-abstraction which maps between two situation calculi abstracting hypotheses of an implication (representing an operator) onto true, $\top$.

4 USING ABSTRACTIONS

This notion of an abstraction which preserve the structure of proofs naturally suggests a general method for using abstractions. The intuitive idea is that of **jumping between islands**. To prove a theorem with the aid of abstraction:

1. we abstract the problem;

2. we find an abstract proof;

3. we "unabstract" the abstract proof; this gives us a plan that provides the major steps (or islands) we will jump between in the ground proof. To make this more concrete, we define an **abstract proof plan** as any tree whose abstraction is subsumed by the abstract proof. In fact, we build a **minimal** abstract proof plan whose abstraction equals the abstract proof.

4. we refine the abstract proof plan by filling in the gaps between the islands. We define a **refinement** of an abstract proof plan as any tree that subsumes the abstract proof plan but is larger than the plan. By definition, a refinement is

---

[2] "P" stands for proof, and "I" for increasing. Note that it is the number of proofs in the abstract space and not their weight or depth that is increasing.

itself an abstract proof plan. It is a tree formed by inserting wffs (or, more strictly, trees) into the abstract proof plan. We search through the refinements till we find a ground proof.

Abstraction thereby save us time by "dividing-and-conquering" the search; we will explore this point in more detail in section 6. Note that we only perform theorem proving in steps 2 and 4, and not in step 3; this separation is purely for conceptual clarity. This procedure will be **complete** for PI-abstractions; that is, it will eventually find us a proof of any theorem of the ground space.

We have implemented such an abstract theorem proving procedure in Prolog that works with any user-defined PI-abstraction or hierarchy of PI-abstractions. A simple depth first iterative deepening resolution theorem prover is used to find proofs in the strongest abstract space, and to refine abstract proof plans. For horn clause problems, the prover uses LUSH resolution. For non-horn problems, the input restriction is weakened to ancestor resolution; this guarantees completeness. We perform our own explicit unification with an occurs check; this guarantees soundness. One extra heuristic is that, since lots of clauses in the abstract space factor together which would not factor in the ground space, proofs without factoring are favoured over those proofs with factoring.

5 RESULTS

We have tested our abstract theorem prover on various examples. Here we give some results for McCarthy's famous "Monkey and Bananas" problem where a monkey gets some bananas by standing on a box. We use the situation calculus axiomatisation of the problem given in [Green, 1969]). Our results for a hierarchy of Abstrips and propositional abstractions are given in fig. 1. To apply a hierarchy of Abstrips abstractions, we needed to decide upon some criticalities for the preconditions to the operators. Those preconditions most difficult to achieve (like being in reach of the bananas) were given the greatest criticality, those less difficult (like being on the box) were given a lower criticality, whilst those easiest to achieve (like being at a location in the room) were given the lowest criticality. We deal with the very important problem of automatically building abstractions in [Bundy et al., 1990].

We will make some general observations about these results. Abstraction definitely seems to offer the possibility of great savings, reducing the time to prove this problem by a factor of 10^3. Interestingly, the greatest saving was not produced by using the most levels of abstractions; compare, for example, the 6th abstraction against the 9th. Nor was the greatest saving produced by using the least number of abstraction levels; consider, for example, the 2nd and the 6th abstractions. This suggests that there is an optimum number of levels of abstraction. Sometimes, using a stronger abstraction worsened the theorem prover's performance; consider, for example, the 10th and the 11th abstractions. This suggests that there is an optimal strength for an abstraction. Finally, the more evenly spaced the abstract spaces (or, more precisely, the lengths of the proofs in the various abstract spaces), the greater the savings; see, for example, the 3rd and the 11th abstractions.

	Abstraction	No. of inferences	Total no. of inferences	Length of Proofs	Time / t_0
1	s	4450280	4450280	11	1.00000
2	s⇒al	75,390	465	11,7	0.00197
3	s⇒al⇒a2	76,221,6	303	11,7,3	0.00122
4	s⇒al⇒a2⇒a3	76,221,3,3	303	11,7,3,2	0.00120
5	s⇒al⇒a2⇒a3⇒a4	76,221,3,2,1	303	11,7,3,2,1	0.00118
6	s⇒al⇒pl	75,202,267	544	11,7,7	0.00087
7	s⇒al⇒a2⇒p2	76,221,3,6	306	11,7,3,3	0.00118
8	s⇒al⇒a2⇒a3⇒p3	76,221,3,2,3	305	11,7,3,2,2	0.00118
9	s⇒al⇒a2⇒a3⇒a4⇒p4	76,221,3,2,1,1	304	11,7,3,2,1,1	0.00118
10	s⇒al⇒a3	75,379,3	457	11,7,2	0.00183
11	s⇒al⇒a4	75,384,1	460	11,7,1	0.00188

Figure 1: Summary of results for the Monkey and Bananas problem.

Notes.

1. Some abbreviations: "s" stands for the STRIPS representation of the problem, "p" for the propositional abstraction of "s", "an" for the Abstrips representation that abstract all preconditions of criticality n or less, and "pn" for the propositional abstraction of "an". "$x \Rightarrow y$" means solving the problem in the space "x" using the abstraction (or space) "y".

2. For the number of inferences (length of proofs) the figures are given for the number of inferences (length of proofs) in each of the spaces in turn going from the ground to the most abstract.

6 A COMPUTATIONAL MODEL

The procedure for mapping back naturally suggest a "simplified" computational model for the cost of theorem proving with multiple levels of abstraction. This model considers four factors:

1. the time to abstract the problem;

2. the time spent theorem proving in the (most) abstract space searching for an abstract proof;

3. the time to build the abstract proof plans;

4. the time spent theorem proving whilst trying to refine the abstract proof plans.

To compute the cost of theorem proving (items 2 and 4), we consider three parameters: the branching rate b, the length of proof l and the time t to perform one inference. Since we must explore $b + b^2 + ... + b^{l-1} = \sum_{i=1}^{l-1} b^i$ nodes, the **cost function** (the time to find a proof of length l) is:

$$c(b, l, t) = \sum_{i=1}^{l-1} b^i t = \frac{b}{b-1}(b^{l-1} - 1)t$$

Although we assume, a constant branching rate and thus a search exponential in the length of the proof, similar results would be obtained for a variable branching rate (*eg.* a super-exponential search) or indeed any other cost function provided its boundary conditions and derivatives were similarly behaved. To consider the costs of inference in the different spaces, we will index b, l, and t with the number of the level (using "0" for the ground space).

We will use τ_n to represent the time to prove a theorem using n levels of abstraction. To compute this, we introduce $\tau(m, n)$, the time to prove the theorem at the m-th level using the levels m to n. Clearly, $\tau_n = \tau(0, n)$. We can define $\tau(m, n)$ recursively on m. Because of the way we map back, the recursion "runs backwards" from $m = n$ to $m = 0$ having its base case at $\tau(n, n)$. The base case is simply the time to prove the theorem in the most abstract space (that is, $c(b_n, l_n, t_n)$). The step case gives the time to prove the theorem in the m-th space in terms of the time to abstract the wff (represented by a_m), the time to prove the theorem in the $m + 1$-th space (that is $\tau(m + 1, n)$), the time to unabstract the l_{m+1} wffs of this abstract proof (given by $l_{m+1}u_m$), and the time to refine the abstract proof plan. The time to refine the plan depends on the size of each of the $(l_{m+1} - 1)$ gaps in the plan; we can show using the method of Lagrange multipliers that $\tau(m, n)$ is minimised for any convex cost function if the abstract proof plans have steps that need an equal amount of refining. We will therefore assume that the size of each gap is of uniform size, g_m where $g_m = \frac{l_m - 1}{l_{m+1} - 1} + 1$. Thus the time to refine the abstract proof plan is $(l_{m+1} - 1)c(b_m, g_m, t_m)$. Note that we assume a constant time to abstract and unabstract wffs. We also ignore **mapping failures**, abstract proofs which cannot be mapped back. In this sense, our model is optimistic; it computes the best possible savings an abstraction can provide. Thus, we define $\tau(m, n)$ as follows:

$$\tau(n, n) = c(b_n, l_n, t_n)$$
$$\tau(m, n) = a_m + \tau(m + 1, n) + l_{m+1}u_m + (l_{m+1} - 1)c(b_m, g_m, t_m)$$

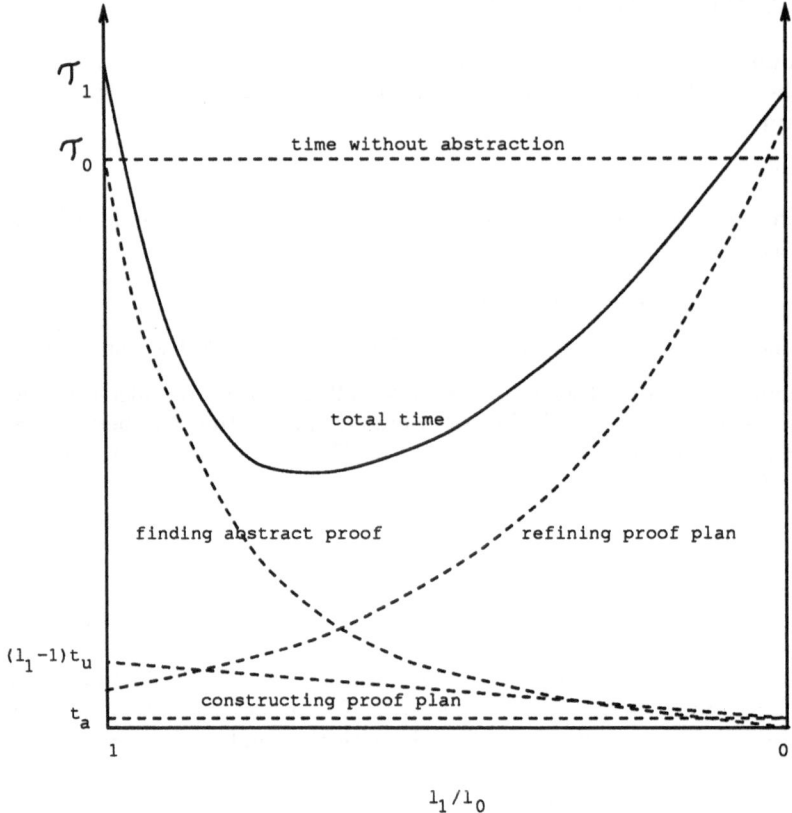

Figure 2: The time taken to prove a theorem using one level of abstraction, τ_1 plotted against the length of the abstract proof, l_1.

We now compare the time to prove the theorem without abstraction, τ_0 against the time with one level of abstraction, τ_1:

- $\tau_0 = c(b_0, l_0, t_0)$ as required;

- $\tau_1 = a_0 + c(b_1, l_1, t_1) + l_1 u_1 + (l_1 - 1)c(b_0, g_0, t_0)$

τ_1 consists of essentially two competing cost functions: the cost of proving the abstract theorem and the cost of refining the gaps. As we increase the strength of the abstraction, l_1 decreases, the cost of proving the abstract theorem decreases but the cost of refining the gaps increases. The result is that τ_1 is **convex**. We can see the exact behaviour of τ_1 in figure 2.

The various partial derivatives of τ_n offer interesting information about the benefits of abstraction. In particular:

- by considering $\frac{\partial \tau_n}{\partial l_i}$, we can prove that the greatest benefits arise when the levels are evenly spaced;

- by considering $\frac{\partial \tau_n}{\partial l_n}$, we can prove there is an optimum strength for the most abstract space, neither too strong (when refining the abstract proof plan is too difficult) nor too weak (when proving the abstract theorem is too difficult);

- and by considering $\frac{\partial \tau_n}{\partial n}$, we can prove that if the spacing between abstraction levels is fixed, then there is an optimum number of abstraction levels.

Every one of these results is in exact agreement with our empirical observations at the end of section 5.

7 RELATED WORK

Various other researchers have given theoretical, computational and empirical analyses of the mapping back problem. As far as we are aware, this is the first paper to give all three. We have used our theoretical framework to suggest a procedure for mapping back; this procedure in turn naturally suggested a computational model; the properties of this model are in good agreement with our empirical observations.

Closest in spirit to our theoretical analysis is the analysis provided by Plaisted in [Plaisted, 1981]. He gives various mapping back strategies for abstractions between resolution systems. Our work generalises Plaisted even if we restrict ourselves just to mappings between resolution systems; all of Plaisted's abstractions are PI-abstractions but not all PI-abstractions between resolution systems can be captured by Plaisted.

Korf [Korf, 1979] provides a similar computational analysis of the benefits of abstraction for state space search. This analysis is essentially restricted to Abstrips abstractions as it ignores the cost of building abstract proof plans. Like us, Korf assumes no mapping failures, and a constant branching rate.

Finally, in [Giunchiglia & Walsh, 1989b] we analysed the theoretical and empirical properties of using a propositional abstraction to determine which definitions to unfold in a proof. However, we did not exploit most of the information in the structure of the abstract proof, only the sequence of definitions that were unfolded.

8 CONCLUSIONS

We have used our theory of abstraction to consider the problem of how an abstract proof can be "mapped back" onto a proof of the original theorem. This analysis has naturally suggested the architecture of a general purpose abstract theorem prover. We have implemented this theorem prover, and begun to investigate its properties. Its behaviour agrees with a simple computational model we have devised for calculating the benefits of abstraction. This provides us with a very *complete* picture of the theoretical, computational and empirical properties of mapping back.

REFERENCES

[Bundy et al., 1990] A. Bundy, F. Giunchiglia, and T. Walsh. Building abstractions. In *Proceedings of the AAAI-90 Workshop on Automatic Generation of Approximations and Abstractions*, pages 221–232. American Association for Artificial Intelligence, 1990. Also available as DAI Research Paper No 506, Dept. of Artificial Intelligence, Edinburgh.

[Green, 1969] C. Green. Application of theorem proving to problem solving. In *Proceedings of the 1st IJCAI*, pages 219–239. International Joint Conference on Artificial Intelligence, 1969.

[Giunchiglia & Walsh, 1989a] F. Giunchiglia and T. Walsh. Abstract Theorem Proving. In *Proceedings of the 11th IJCAI*. International Joint Conference on Artificial Intelligence, 1989. Also available as DAI Research Paper No 430, Dept. of Artificial Intelligence, Edinburgh.

[Giunchiglia & Walsh, 1989b] F. Giunchiglia and T. Walsh. Theorem Proving with Definitions. In *Proceedings of AISB 89*. Society for the Study of Artificial Intelligence and Simulation of Behaviour, 1989. Also available as DAI Research Paper No 429, Dept. of Artificial Intelligence, Edinburgh.

[Giunchiglia & Walsh, 1990] F. Giunchiglia and T. Walsh. Abstract theorem proving: mapping back. Forthcoming research paper, Dept. of Artificial Intelligence, University of Edinburgh, 1990.

[Korf, 1979] R.E. Korf. Planning as search: A quantitative approach. *Artificial Intelligence*, 33:65–88, 1979.

[Plaisted, 1981] D.A. Plaisted. Theorem proving with abstraction. *Artificial Intelligence*, 16:47–108, 1981.

[Plaisted, 1986] D.A. Plaisted. Abstraction using generalization functions. In *8th Conference on Automated Deduction*, pages 365–376. 8th Conference on Automated Deduction, 1986.

[Sacerdoti, 1974] E.D. Sacerdoti. Planning in a hierarchy of abstraction spaces. *Artificial Intelligence*, 5:115–135, 1974.

[Tenenberg, 1988] J.D. Tenenberg. *Abstraction in Planning*. PhD thesis, Computer Science Department, University of Rochster, 1988. Also TR 250.

Sound substitution into modal contexts

Sam Steel
Dept Computer Science, University of Essex Colchester CO4 3SQ, UK

Abstract:

I review the problems involved in substituting into modal contexts, and state a rule which permits this to be done soundly. Such a rule justifies a expanded substitution process for modal logic. The process is syntactic but incurs proof obligations. I show constructs that permit the naming of objects outside the current modal contexts. These devices were motivated by problems found while using modal logic in planning.

1: INTRODUCTION: THE PROBLEMS

I have recently been working on planning, using modal logic, rather than situation calculus, as my representation language. My reason for doing this is that I am particularly interested in the interaction of action and knowledge, and both of these have a modal logic: dynamic logic in one case, epistemic logic in the other. (I assume an acquaintance with both.) It is then very easy to define a language with a respectable Kripke semantics that includes both and lets one say such things as

    [dip(litmus)in(liquid)] K acid(liquid) v K -acid(liquid)

Nevertheless there are problems, particularly to do with the interaction of terms and modals. This turns up in three ways; the first is fairly novel, the two last are standard.

I shall assume that all modals are "necessity" type. Like $\vdash$, they make a claim about all accessible worlds. "possibility" type modals are then defined in the usual way.

Problem 1. Modals may contain terms. The semantics of modal logic has to be revised to permit this. Usually modals are atoms interpreted straight off as relations on indices. But if they contain terms, the relation denoted must depend on what the terms denote. The (as yet unexplained) action modal

    [dip(litmus)in(liquid)]

is one example. Another would be the representation of "Tom believes" and "Fred knows" not by separate atomic modals K, K' but by the structured items K(tom), K(fred). Because such modals contain terms, whose denotation will vary from index to index, their denotation will vary too. This needs a semantics.

Problem 2. Substituting identical terms for the same variable in different modal contexts is unsound. A classic (and classical) example is this: if B is the modal corresponding to "Oedipus believes" then this inference is invalid.

$$\text{jocasta} = \text{wife(oedipus)}$$

$$B \text{ mother(oedipus)} = \text{jocasta} \equiv B \text{ mother(oedipus)} = \text{wife(oedipus)}$$

But is is a difficult inference to evade. Here is the ordinary equality rule.

$$\text{Term1} = \text{Term2}$$

$$S \{x:=\text{Term1}\} \equiv S \{x:=\text{Term2}\}$$

An instance of it is

$$\text{jocasta} = \text{wife(oedipus)}$$

$$(B \text{ mother(oedipus)}=x) \{x:=\text{jocasta}\} \equiv$$
$$(B \text{ mother(oedipus)}=x) \{x:=\text{wife(oedipus)}\}$$

which is apparently the invalid inference about what Oedipus believes. What has gone wrong is the notion of substitution.

Problem 3. Quantifier rules involving modals are unsound. One source of problems is that different indices may have different domains, but that is not what concerns me here: I shall assume that all indices have the same domain. What concerns me is that

$$\forall x. \text{ Modal } P(x) \vdash \text{ Modal } P(t)$$

is invalid, even if the domains at all indices are the same. For example, suppose giving gifts does not affect one's sex.

$$\forall x. \forall y. \forall z. \quad \text{male}(x) \equiv [(x)\text{gives}(y)\text{to}(z)] \text{ male}(x)$$
$$\forall x. \forall y. \forall z. \; -\text{male}(z) \equiv [(x)\text{gives}(y)\text{to}(z)] \; -\text{male}(z)$$
$$\forall x. \forall y. \forall z. \qquad\qquad [(x)\text{gives}(y)\text{to}(z)] \text{ owner}(y) = z$$

But suppose

$$\text{male(owner(fido))}$$
$$-\text{male(mary)}$$

Then it is easy to show that

$$[(\text{owner(fido)})\text{gives(fido)to(mary)}] \text{ male(owner(fido))}$$
$$[(\text{owner(fido)})\text{gives(fido)to(mary)}] \; -\text{male(mary)}$$
$$[(\text{owner(fido)})\text{gives(fido)to(mary)}] \text{ owner(fido)} = \text{mary}$$

There is nothing wrong with the axioms. It is the rule of universal elimination which is the problem. Quantification over such modals is all right, since, given an assignment function, a variable has the same denotation at all indices and therefore in all modal contexts. But that is not true for constant terms, which are interpreted by different interpretations at each index and in each modal context.

2: FIX FOR PROBLEM 1

Here is a semantics that lets terms occur in modals. It is biased towards dynamic logic, but that is not necessary. An interpretation is

< Indices, Domain, Valuation, ModalDomain, Modalizer >

Indices is a set of indices; Domain, a set of objects to quantify
over, shared by all indices; Valuation takes an index and an atom
(predicate or function) and assigns a set of tuples from Domain in the
usual way to that atom at that index. Constants are nullary functions.

ModalDomain is a subset of Domain. It is that subset of things that
are actions or events or changes, rather than jugs or numbers or
rabbits. Modalizer is a function from ModalDomain to relations on
Indices. Given an action object, it returns the state transitions that
will be produced by that action.

The syntax will make clear which terms denote objects in ModalDomain
by assigning grammatical types to atoms and variables and demanding that
applications respect those types.

Now to give the semantics of a dynamic logic that includes
predication but not quantification (I shall return to quantifiers
later). Most of such a semantics is utterly routine, so I just give the
important clauses, for Modals. i is an index, g is an assignment
function. Ordinarily the clauses would be

    Sentence ::= Modal Sentence

      i g |= Modal Sentence iff

        all i1 (<i,i1> e (|[Modal]|, i1 g |= Sentence)

  Modal ::= ... some atom such as K ...

    |[Modal]| = some fixed relation on Indices

But now the denotation of a modal depends on where it is evaluated.

    Sentence ::= Modal Sentence

      i g |= Modal Sentence iff

        all i1 (<i,i1> e |[Modal]| i g), i1 g |= Sentence)

  Modal ::= [Term]

    (if Term is of the type that denotes an object in ModalDomain)

    |[Modal]| i g = Modalizer(|[Term]| i g)

  Modal ::= ... some atom such as K ...

    |[Modal]| i g = some fixed relation on Indices

An example biased to epistemic rather than dynamic logic would allow
modals such as K(Knower). Then ModalDomain would be the subset of the
domain that could have beliefs; people, or possibly animals or computers
too.

3: FIX FOR PROBLEM 2

To fix the problem about equality, one needs two things.

238

* An equality across modals, that ensures that two terms in different modal contexts denote the same object.

* A way of making sure substitution is sensitive to such equalities.

To get the first, add a new construct to the language

    Term1 =[Modal]= Term2

to mean "the object denoted by Term1 at the current index is denoted by Term2 at all Modal-accessible indices". For instance, if the modal is an action, one can say

    mary =[(john)gives(fido)to(mary)]= owner(fido)

for "Mary is the owner of Fido after John has given Fido to Mary". It can also be used with other modals. Eg

    certain-shepherds-wife =[B]= mother(oedipus)

is "Oedipus thinks his mother is certain-shepherds-wife". Of course, if Oedipus is uncertain about his mother, there is no such term that can go on the left-hand side to make a true sentence. Formally,

  i |= Term1 =[Modal]= Term2 iff

    all i1. (<i,i1> e |[Modal]| i, |[Term1]| i = |[Term2]| i1)

Say Modal is "empty" if there is no index Modal-accessible from the current index. If Modal is empty, then "Term1 =[Modal]= Term2" is trivially true.

I shall now suggest how this can let one adjust substitution so that it applies to modal contexts. The ordinary definition of substitution in logic is given as a recursion over the structure of expressions. It will include such clauses as

    (P & Q) {x:=t} = (P {x:=t}) & (Q {x:=t})

    P(A1,...,An) {x:=t} = (P {x:=t}) (A1 {x:=t}, ..., An {x:=t})

    ....

plus tedious restrictions to avoid clashes of variables, which I assume. Anyhow, if modals are admitted to the syntax, substitution will go straight through them.

    (Modal S) {x:=t} = Modal{x:=t} S{x:=t}

An alternative is to use the definition of substitution from lambda calculus used in defining beta-reduction.

    (λx. P) t = P{x:=t}

First one must apply Church's device, and see the syntax of 1PC as lambda calculus with certain useful constants. Eg "P & Q" is a sugared version of the straightforward function application "&(P,Q)" in principle just like "dead(fred)" except that the denotation of "&" is fixed in the semantics. Church's device fixes quantifiers too. "∀ x. P" is taken as a sugared version of "∀ (λx. Q)".

Extra semantic clauses for lambda abstraction and application are needed, but then are standard.

┊[λx . P]┊ i g = LAMBDA d e Domain . ┊[P]┊ i g<x <- d >

┊[F(A)]┊ i g = ┊[F]┊ i g (┊[A]┊ i g)

The clauses for logical constants are eg

┊[&]┊ i g = LAMBDA x. LAMBDA y. x and y

┊[∀]┊ i g = LAMBDA P. all d e Domain. P(d) = truth

Once that is done, substitution in logic is just the ordinary lambda calculus substitution. The only exception is for modals. The expression "Modal S" is syntactic sugar for nothing - it is a new sort of expression. This is useful. Suppose John owns Fido. One might think one could beta-reduce

(λx. [(x)gives(fido)to(mary)] male(x))(owner(fido))

which seems to denote a true sentence, to

[(owner(fido))gives(fido)to(mary)] male(owner(fido))

which does not. Something seems to have gone wrong. But I am denying that that there is any clause in the definition of substitution for handling

(Modal S) {x:=t}

so the invalid reduction is impossible.

Look back at the rule for equality. It can now be written as

$$\frac{\text{Term1 = Term2}}{((\lambda x. \ S) \ \text{Term1}) \equiv ((\lambda x. \ S) \ \text{Term2})}$$

In that case the Oedipus instance is

$$\frac{\text{jocasta = wife(oedipus)}}{((\lambda x. \ B \ \text{mother(oedipus)=x)} \ \text{jocasta}) \equiv} $$
$$((\lambda x. \ B \ \text{mother(oedipus)=x)} \ \text{wife(oedipus)})$$

But that is as far as it goes. If one tries beta-reduction, it jams. Certainly

((λx. B mother(oedipus)=x) jocasta) = (B mother(oedipus)) {x:=jocasta}

but the right side is undefined. If however one had

jocasta =[B]= wife(oedipus)

so that one could infer that Oedipus knew he had married his mother, how would one use it? With a new rule. I give a simple form of the proposed rule first, where Modal is an atom, such as K or B or [].

$$\text{Term1 =[Modal]= Term2}$$

$$\overline{((\lambda x. [Modal] S) Term1) \equiv [Modal] ((\lambda x. S) Term2)}$$

The intuition behind the new rule is that as the process of substitution of Term1 for x "crosses" the modal, a new name for Term1, appropriate "on the the other side of" the modal, is used instead. The condition of the rule guarantees that the two terms mean the same thing.
The rule needs to be complicated slightly because "x" may occur free in the modal. The full version is

$$\text{Term1 =[Modal']= Term2}$$

$$\overline{((\lambda x. [Modal] S) Term1) \equiv [Modal'] ((\lambda x. S) Term2)}$$

where Modal' is ((λx. Modal) Term1).

Proof of soundness: Expand the semantic definition of the two sides of the consequent until then are the same. At one point one needs to use the equality provided by expanding the semantic definition of the antecedent. ▊

One might worry about whether one could use lambda calculus equalities in modal contexts. Fortunately any theorem of the system is valid in any modal context. Alpha-conversion across modals is sound, because

$$\overline{\text{Var =[Modal]= Var}}$$

is sound if Var is a variable.

Proof. Look at the definition of Term1 =[Modal]= Term2. Remember i ¦= S abbreviates

        all g. i g ¦= S

where g is an assigment function.

        ¦[Var]¦ i g = ¦[Var]¦ i1 g = g(Var)

for all i, i1. ▊

4: FIX FOR PROBLEM 3.

The essence of the problem is, how to block the troublesome inference

$$\forall x. \; male(x) \equiv [(x)gives(fido)to(mary)] \; male(x)$$

$$\overline{male(owner(fido)) \equiv \\ [(owner(fido))gives(fido)to(mary)] \; male(owner(fido))}$$

To do this requires a less usual, though still standard, way of looking at universal elimination. Usually it is stated as

$$\forall\ x.\ P\ |-\ P\ \{x := t\}$$

With Church's device, one can state it as

$$\forall(P)\ |-\ P(t)$$

and P(t) will usually simplify via beta-reduction - but not across modals. The attempted proof goes

$$\forall\ (\ \lambda x.\ male(x) \equiv [(x)gives(fido)to(mary)]\ male(x)\ )$$

$$(\ \lambda x.\ male(x) \equiv [(x)gives(fido)to(mary)]\ male(x)\ )\ (owner(fido))$$

$$............$$

$$male(owner(fido)) \equiv$$
$$(\ \lambda x.\ [(x)gives(fido)to(mary)]\ male(x)\ )\ (owner(fido))$$

But the right side can go no further without the false premise

$$owner(fido) =[\ (owner(fido))gives(fido)to(mary)\ ]= owner(fido)$$

Here is an example where one can "substitute". From

$$(\forall\ \lambda x.\ P(x)\ ->\ (\ [A(x)]\ (\ Q(x)\ \&\ [B(x)]\ R(x)\ )\ )$$

one can derive

$$P(fred)\ ->\ ((\ \lambda x.\ [A(x)]\ (\ Q(x)\ \&\ [B(x)]\ R(x)\ )\ fred\ )$$

straight away. With

$$fred =[\ A(fred)\ ]= bert$$

one gets to

$$P(fred)\ ->\ [A(fred)]\ (\ Q(bert)\ \&\ ((\ \lambda x.\ [B(x)]\ R(x)\ )\ bert\ )$$

and with

$$[\ A(fred)\ ]\ bert =[\ B(bert)\ ]= tom$$

one finishes at

$$P(fred)\ ->\ [A(fred)]\ (\ Q(bert)\ \&\ [B(bert)]\ R(tom)\ )$$

5: A SUBSTITUTION PROCESS

In fact that process needs many, trivial, steps. A better approach is to define a revised substitution process that incurs a proof obligation when it goes through modals. Such a process can be based on this fact.

If   Γ   !-   S {v:=T2} ≡   S'

then   M{v:=T1} Γ, T1 =[M{v:=T1}]= T2 !- (M S){v:=T1} ≡ M{v:=T1} S'

where M is a modal; Γ is a set of sentences; Modal Γ is
{ Modal g ¦ g e Γ }.

Proof:

$$
\cfrac{
  \cfrac{
    M\{v:=T1\}\ \Gamma \qquad
    \cfrac{\cfrac{}{\Gamma}\ 1 \quad S\{v:=T2\}\ \equiv S'}{M\{v:=T1\}\ (S\{v:=T2\}\ \equiv S')}\ R
  }{
    \begin{array}{cc}
      \text{T1 =[M\{v:=T1\}]= T2} & M\{v:=T1\}\ (S\{v:=T2\}) \\
      (M\ S)\{v:=T1\} \equiv M\{v:=T1\}\ (S\{v:=T2\}) & M\{v:=T1\}\ (S\{v:=T2\}) \equiv M\{v:=T1\}\ S'
    \end{array}
  }\ 1
}{
  (M\ S)\{v:=T1\} \equiv M\{v:=T1\}\ S'
}
$$

Rule R is the natural deduction form of

Modal(A -> B) !- (Modal A -> Modal B) |

Then given an expression of the form

M S{v:=T1}

to reduce, one first takes a fresh variable, T2 say, and recursively
reduces

S{v:=T2}

to S', say, perhaps thereby incurring a proof obligation Γ. Then one
knows that the original expression reduces to

M{v:=T1} S'

with the proof obligation

M{v:=T1} Γ, T1 =[M{v:=T1}]= T2

Because this process is essentially the finding of a particularly
convenient derived proof rule, its product can contain meta-variables -
syntactic variables over arbitrary terms. For instance, the process
yields the derived rule

T1 =[A(T1)]= T2,   [A(T1)] T2 =[A(T2)]= T3   !-

     ((λx. P(x) -> ([A(x)] (Q(x) & [B(x)] R(x))) T1) ≡

         P(T1) -> [A(T1)] (Q(T2) & [B(T2)] R(T3))

Now concrete terms (eg fred, bert, tom) can be immediately textually
substituted for T1, T2 and T3. Any proof obligations that arose are
explicit in the antecedent.

6: RELATED WORK

I know only two pieces of related work, by Moore and by Konolige. Both are concerned with naming objects in different modal contexts.

Moore proposes that any object d should have a "standard name", ∂d. One then considers only frames in which

    all i. all i1. |[∂d]| i1 = |[∂d]| i2

Then

$$\forall x. P \mid- P \{x:=\partial d\}$$

is sound. The terms d and ∂d, a meta language name and a name, can be in the same language since Moore works permanently in the meta language in which object language names are terms.

Konolige proposes a bullet operator o D, which in all contexts names the object named by D in the current context. (More accurately, suppose D names d. Then in modal context M, o D names the constant E which in modal context M names d. The effect is the same.) Then

$$\forall x. P \mid- P \{x:= o D\}$$

is sound.

Both of these are perfectly workable. Consider an object d. Konolige's approach works by letting one use the name one uses for d in the "home" context in the "distant" context too. Moore's approach works by generating a name for d that is the same in both the "home" and the "distant" context. My approach works by finding separate names for d in both the "home" and the "distant" context, and using them in parallel.

Konolige, K: 1986
        A deduction model of belief
        Pitman/Morgan Kaufman
Moore, RC: 1985
        A formal theory of Knowledge and Action
        in: Hobb, J; Moore, RC (eds): 1985
                Formal theories of the commonsense world
                Ablex

MACHINE LEARNING

Modelling Representations of Device Knowledge in Soar

Elizabeth F. Churchill and Richard M. Young

ABSTRACT

This paper presents two simulation models which address the effect of alternative instruction types on the development of skilled performance when using a device. Two instruction types are considered: (i) "how-to-do-the-task" or "operational" knowledge, which provides step-by-step action sequences specifying how to perform typical tasks, and (ii) "conceptual device model", "how-the-device-works" or "figurative" knowledge, which specifies the effects of users' actions on the device. Performance differences between groups presented with these alternative instruction types suggest that presenting users with a conceptual model facilitates the development of robust skilled performance. Using Soar, a theoretically committed cognitive architecture, the impact of instruction type on the development of skilled performance is addressed through simulation modelling. Skilled performance is assumed to result from the execution of automatised solution methods which specify procedures for accomplishing goals. It is demonstrated with these simulation models that even where observed performance may be identical, the knowledge that underlies skilled performance may differ considerably given alternative instruction types.

INTRODUCTION

With practice, people become skilled at the things they do. The development of skill is demonstrated in performance by an increase in the efficiency with which the task is carried out, resulting in a decrease in the total time taken to complete the task (Snoddy, 1926). In studying the development of efficiency two issues are of interest: the initial reasoning process that is involved in determining a set of appropriate actions to achieve the task, and the changes in the underlying knowledge that are responsible for the observed speed-up in task performance after practice (Anderson, 1983; Laird, Rosenbloom and Newell, 1986).

For example, faced with the task of solving even simple calculations on an unfamiliar device, like a postfix or "reverse polish notation" (RPN) calculator, users typically spend some time searching and reasoning with their knowledge about the device (the calculator) and the task (solving the arithmetic problem) to determine the appropriate keypresses (Halasz, 1984). This reasoning or "problem solving" process is dependent upon the availability of appropriate information and the relevance of the information that is available. Users may try various problem solving strategies: remembering examples presented in the instructions, imagining the effects of actions they could perform on the calculator, using analogies to similar devices, or trial-and error application of possible keystrokes. Whatever the strategy employed to determine the appropriate keystrokes, after successfully problem solving and determining the required action sequence once, if the task is re-presented, it will usually take considerably less time for successful completion. This speed-up in performance continues with re-presentation (practice) of the task until a plateau of performance is reached.

The kind of instructions which best support the transition to skilled performance has been addressed at the group level by observing performance differences between groups given alternative instruction sets. Typically, two types of knowledge about a device are contrasted: "how-to-do-the-task" or "operational" knowledge, and "how-the-device-works" or "figurative" knowledge (Halasz and Moran, 1983; Kieras and Bovair, 1984). This work has to some extent supported the intuitive view that teaching users a conceptual model of the device facilitates the development of expert performance, particularly on complex and novel tasks.

The knowledge underlying performance in such tasks has been analysed and described at the level of individual users in formal models such as the GOMS model presented by Card, Moran and Newell (1983). It is proposed by Card et al that people's knowledge of how to do tasks can be broken down into Goals (and sub-goals) of the whole task, Operators which may be used to achieve those goals, Methods which are operators that achieve a goal or a sub-goal, and Selection rules which specify the conditions under which a particular method is chosen for application. Novice performance is predominantly made up of problem solving. Skilled performance is made up of methods which are determined through repeated problem solving. Performance changes in an individual at different levels of expertise may be accounted for by changes in the ratio of problem solving to automatised method application. Performance differences between individuals may also be described in this way. The methodology does not, however, explicitly address the issue of learning and the development of the methods themselves as an individual moves from novice to expert (Card, Moran and Newell, 1983).

The simulation models presented in this paper address the development of methods from problem solving experience on a given task. As methods develop from the knowledge that is searched in problem solving, it is proposed that the knowledge content of the methods differs given alternative instructions for performing a task, even if the observable behaviour does not reflect this. In order to compare the effect of alternative instruction sets on method development and content, two simulation models are discussed: one embodies operational knowledge about a device and the other figurative knowledge about the same device. The task or goal is to produce a solution to a binary calculation on an RPN calculator. Before describing the models I shall try to illustrate more clearly the differences between these types of instruction.

Different Types of Instruction

To illustrate the difference between operational and figurative knowledge, imagine solving a binary calculation on the RPN calculator. RPN calculators have an internal memory stack that is used to store operands and intermediate results. Numbers can be stored in this stack and manipulated using the commands provided. Operational instructions for solving a binary calculation of the form N1 + N2, for example 3 + 5, would be something like those presented in Figure 1.

Figure 1: Operational Instructions

To complete a binary calculation, N1 + N2, do the following actions:

1. Key in the number N1
2. Press the key marked ENTER
3. Key in the number N2
4. Press the key marked with a +

These instructions offer a task-oriented, ordered, recipe-like list of actions providing a solution method that can be applied one step at a time. The task is completed when all the steps are done. This "recipe" can be applied to any binary calculation.

Figurative instructions are not solely task-oriented, but offer conceptual information about the device itself. Figure 2 shows instructions that refer to the internal memory stack with a diagrammatic representation of the display cell and the memory stack before and after the specified action (shown in bold) has been carried out .

Figure 2: Figurative Instructions

---

1. Pressing a number key (or keys): the number(s) appear in the display
    of the device

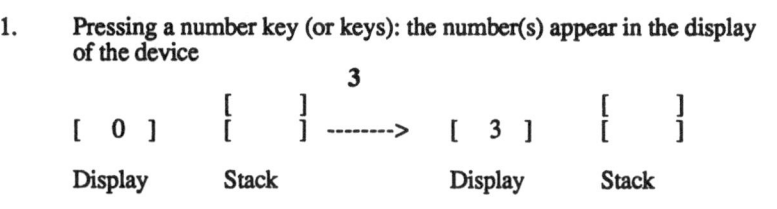

Display   Stack   Display   Stack

---

2. Pressing the key marked ENTER: stores the number shown in the
    display in the first cell of memory stack of the device.

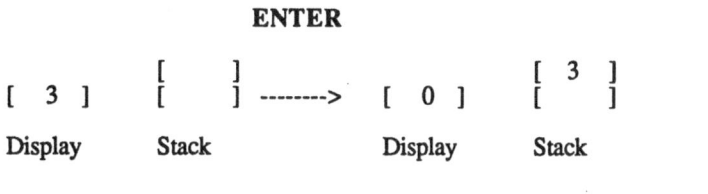

Display   Stack   Display   Stack

---

3. Pressing an arithmetic operator: performs an arithmetic calculation.
    The number at the top of the stack is used as the first operand and the
    number in the display as the second operand. The product is shown in
    the display, and the number in the top cell of the stack is deleted.
    Although only two stack cells are shown here, the stack is assumed to
    be infinite

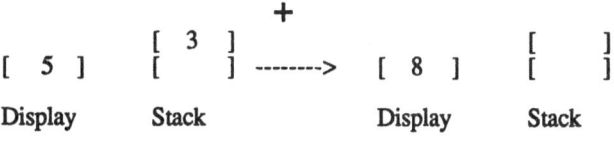

Display   Stack   Display   Stack

Using such figurative knowledge, it is possible to determine correct action sequences for producing task solutions by imagining the effects that individual actions will have on the device state (Young, 1981; Mayer and Bayman, 1981; Gentner and Stevens, 1983; Payne, 1989).

MODELLING USERS' KNOWLEDGE

Two simulation models are presented. The models are built in the Soar cognitive architecture, so before describing the models in detail, I shall give a brief introduction to Soar.

Soar

Soar is a cognitive architecture, which incorporates a learning mechanism, "chunking" (Laird, Rosenbloom and Newell, 1986). Soar specifies a relatively fixed set of mechanisms that permit goals and knowledge of the task environment to be encoded in memory and brought to bear to produce problem solving behaviour. This problem solving behaviour is realised in a nested series of problem spaces each of which has states and legal operators. Tasks are formulated in these problem spaces and long term knowledge is held in "recognition memory", realised as productions. Processing proceeds by a sequence of cycles (called "decision cycles") that accumulate knowledge about what spaces, states and operators to select. If decision-making knowledge is insufficient or conflicting, an "impasse" occurs and sub-goals are generated in an attempt to resolve the impasse. With the generation of a sub-goal, a new problem space is invoked. This sub-problem space may be a copy of the main space, may be specialised domain knowledge or may even embody knowledge from another domain (as is the case in analogical reasoning). The impasse will be resolved if some appropriate information which enables the problem solving in the higher problem space to continue is located by problem solving in a sub-space. As soon as the uncertainty is resolved, the information relating to the sub-goal is removed from working memory, and the sub-goal effectively "disappears". The solution path that led to the resolution is traced back, to determine what knowledge was relevant to the resolution (i.e. the circumstances under which the impasse arose, the knowledge that led to the resolution and the resulting state). This knowledge is represented in a new production, a "chunk". Problem-solving resumes in the main space and the new chunk fires, creating a new state. If this new state matches the goal state, problem solving halts as the task has been successfully completed. If the new state does not match the goal state, problem solving continues. As the chunk is retained in recognition memory with other productions, if the same situation arises in the main problem space, this chunk will fire automatically in the main space. There will be no impasse and no sub-space search. This method of learning from experience is similar to that embodied in ACT* (Anderson, 1983, 1984, 1985) and in Explanation Based Learning (Mitchell, 1982; Mitchell et al, 1984).

So how does this relate to human behaviour? As stated above, the knowledge that underlies performance of novel tasks may be information which must be searched and reasoned with. Thus novel tasks take considerably longer to perform than familiar ones, and a correct solution may not be found. Similarly, Soar proceeds in new domains by searching through the knowledge available to find the relevant operations for problem solutions. If the knowledge is insufficient to determine a correct solution, Soar cannot proceed but must sub-goal to find sufficient knowledge to proceed. If this search fails, Soar must halt or "give up". As users practice tasks, their performance speeds-up. Efficient performance on familiar, practised tasks is assumed to result from the existence of automatised solution methods in the user's task knowledge. In Soar, performance changes through practice are accounted for by the development of new productions, "chunks" as described above. The chunks lead to a decrease in the time taken to complete the task, observed in Soar as fewer decision cycles - as a result of a decrease in the number of impasses, sub-goaling and search. It is proposed that the chunks that develop through practice on a task in Soar may be equivalent to users methods. It is also proposed that as methods develop from task knowledge that is searched, users presented with different instructions will develop different methods. These differences may not be discernible in observed performance on the familiar tasks, but may result in differential transfer to novel tasks. Methods may be more or less specific to the task for which they were developed. The simulation models described address this issue, investigating performance changes through practice, given operational and figurative task knowledge.

Models of Device Knowledge in Soar

The knowledge necessary to perform a simple binary calculation on the RPN calculator was analysed in terms of the two instruction types outlined above, operational and figurative. This knowledge was then represented in Soar in terms of the goal (to complete a binary calculation), the problem spaces required, the initial states and the relevant operators.

The Representation. In the simulation models two kinds of problem space are represented, distinguishing between actions that would be executed in the external world from problem solving and imaginary actions. The "main" or "top" problem space has as its goal the completion of the binary calculation and contains operators that represent the actions that can be executed in the external world. There are four possible operators, for the four actions involved in completing the binary calculation: inputting the two operands, pressing the ENTER command key on the calculator, and inputting an arithmetic operator. The second kind of problem space contains knowledge about the device for specifying when the actions are applicable. These device knowledge spaces correspond to what the user knows, so problem solving in these spaces corresponds to thinking about the device and not actually carrying the actions out in the world. These knowledge spaces differentiate the two simulation models, one offering operational device knowledge and the other figurative device knowledge, and are described below.

Device Knowledge Spaces: Operational. Operational instructions are ordered sequences of actions that must be carried out in order to perform tasks. In the Soar model, this solution recipe is represented as a datastructure. Each step in the "recipe" is marked as having been done or not. Figure 3 shows a diagram of part of the datastructure; here, the first two actions in the recipe are shown. The value associated with the attribute "been-done" specifies whether or not an item has been inputted. A set of operators scan over the datastructure to determine how much of the recipe has been executed (e.g. whether the first operand has been inputted, the ENTER key has been pressed yet, etc). If the attribute "been-done" has the value "yes" the scanning goes on to the "next" action in the list. The first action that has the value "No" to the "been-done" attribute is selected as the next thing to do.

Figure 3: Recipe datastructure

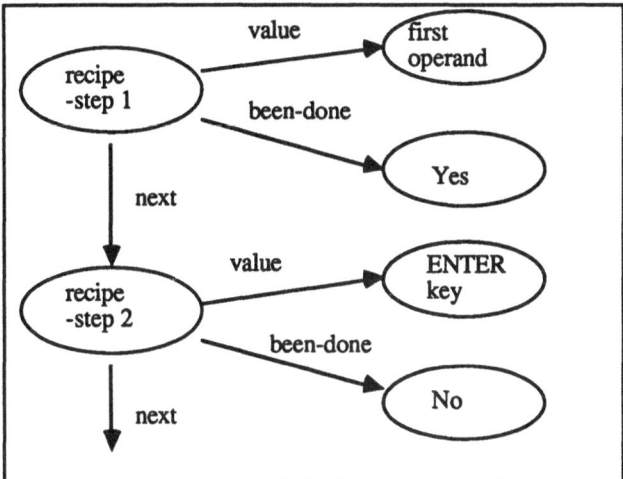

The datastructure and the scanning process correspond to remembering a set of actions and then mentally running through them one by one, "ticking them off" as having been completed when each one is done. When the next action needs to be selected the recipe structure must be inspected again.

Device Knowledge Spaces: Figurative. The figurative instructions focus on the imagined state of the calculator's internal memory stack and the effect of actions on the stack. To correspond to this, the device model sub-problem space is represented as productions that match the current state of the device. These device states are imagined ones and do not necessarily correspond to those of the device in the real world. Figure 4 shows part of one production. Here, the conditions specify that when there is assumed to be an internal stack memory and the display cell of the stack has a number in it, then the result of pressing the ENTER key will be to place the number from the display into the top cell of the internal stack and to leave the display with a zero in it.

Figure 4.   Representation of Figurative Device Knowledge

IF

there is a stack
and
there is a display which has number in it
and
you press the ENTER key

THEN

the top cell of the stack will contain the number that was in
the display
and
the display will have a 0 in it

To determine the next appropriate action, the current state of the device is matched to the preconditions for the known actions. The appropriate action is applied, leading to a new device state. This cycle continues, as if the device state were being altered from the start state to the desired goal state. This corresponds to the user's behaviour as imagining the effects of one's action on the device before actually carrying them out in the "real" world.

Program Behaviour

Problem solving starts in the top space and the initial state ("S1"), with no actions having been performed and the goal being to complete the presented binary calculation. The initial state for the operationally conceived task is that no action has yet been executed and nothing had been yet been inputted to the calculator, and for the figurative representation of the task that the device stack and the display cell are currently empty. Initially, there is insufficient knowledge available to determine the next appropriate action, and the four possible operators tie (denoted by the arrows in Figure 5) resulting in an "impasse".

Figure 5: Tie Impasse and sub-goaling

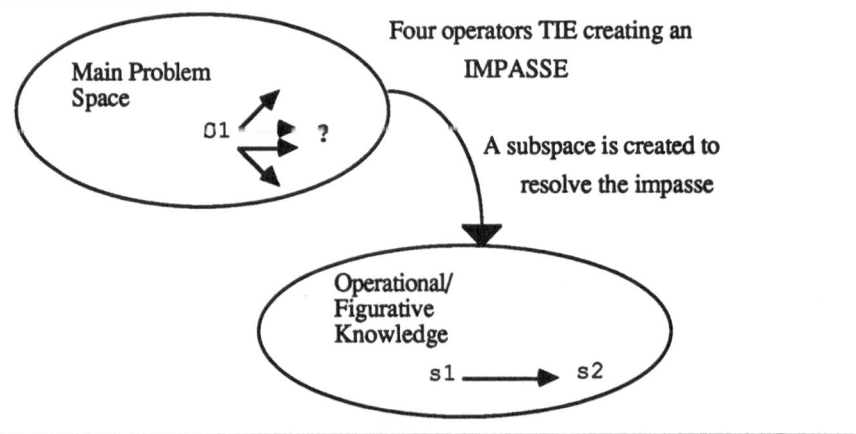

Main Problem Space

01   ?

Four operators TIE creating an
IMPASSE

A subspace is created to
resolve the impasse

Operational/
Figurative
Knowledge

s1 ⟶ s2

Had there been sufficient knowledge available, one action would have been selected in the main space. This immediate selection would correspond to the invocation of a known or skilled solution method, resulting in the swift execution of actions characteristic of skilled performance. However in this instance a sub-space is generated, the aim (goal) of which is find out which of the actions is most appropriate, thereby resolving the tie. The sub-space that is invoked is the operational or figurative one described above. In both models, on the generation of the sub-space, the knowledge of the current situation (represented in the state, S1) is copied into the new sub-problem space, and the specialised operational or figurative knowledge is applied to the copied current state. This has the effect of creating a new state, s2. As this processing is in the sub-space, this corresponds to imagining the effects of the actions rather than actually doing them.

Once the goal to resolve the tie is achieved in the sub-space, the impasse is resolved and the sub-space "disappears", i.e. the contents of working memory relating to the sub-space is removed. The features relating to this action selection are compiled into a new production, a "chunk". The conditions of the chunk are the features that led to the impasse. The action that was determined to be appropriate from the problem solving in the sub-space is applied in the main problem space and a new "real" state results. This process continues until the goal of the top space (to complete the binary calculation) has been achieved.

Performance Changes and "Chunks"

For users performing the task above, a decrease in the time taken to perform the task is observed after practice. This speed-up can be accounted for by a shift from problem solving to the selection and implementation of compiled methods. Similarly, the two simulation models initially problem solve to determine the correct actions to perform in order to complete the task. On the first trial, for each step in the task solution, there is a tie between the actions available; this results in an impasse and the generation of the operational knowledge sub-space or the figurative knowledge sub-space. Search in the sub-space produces the next appropriate action resolving the tie impasse, and problem solving in the main space resumes. The features of the task that caused the impasse and the knowledge discovered in the sub-space that led to the resolution of the impasse are compiled into a chunk. This process occurs for the selection of each action in the solution. The chunks that are built are applied in the main space on re-presentation of the task, enabling the task to be executed without any impasses being encountered, and thus circumventing the need to generate and search sub-spaces. The chunks thus account for a substantial reduction in the amount of processing required to produce the problem solution. In Soar, this decrease in problem solving is reflected in the reduced number of decision cycles taken to achieve the goal.

After several trials, both models reach a stable number of decision cycles to complete the task. The observed performance of the two models is comparable, taking the same number of decision cycles and producing the same sequence of actions. Although the task performance of both models at this point is identical, the knowledge content of the chunks that underlie the performance differ.

The chunks that develop from the operational knowledge have as conditions of application the knowledge of the last action performed. In order to be selected for application, the knowledge of the last action performed is required. This is illustrated in Figure 6.

Figure 6. Example chunk derived from Operational knowledge

Content of Operational chunk:

IF

      the first operand has been inputted
          and
      ENTER hasn't been inputted

THEN

      press the ENTER key

Each of the chunks built from this knowledge forms part of an ordered sequence of actions. The chunks are reliant on knowing the last action performed in the sequence in order to be applicable, and thus would not be applicable if the task were, for example, to complete an already partially solved binary calculation. In this situation, a sub-space would be generated in order to try out the actions available to discover the next appropriate action. In Soar, this sub-space search would result in more decision cycles, corresponding to extra time problem solving by users. The lack of association between the possible actions and the device display and stack in the "recipe" solution is thus reflected in the chunks that develop.

By contrast, the chunks from the figurative knowledge refer to the current imagined state of the device and do not rely on knowledge of past actions. Their conditions of applicability refer to the display and the imagined state of the stack (Figure 7).

Figure 7.   Example chunk derived from Figurative knowledge

Content of Figurative chunk:

IF

　　　the display has a number in it
　　　　　　　and
　　　that number corresponds to the first operand

THEN

　　　press the ENTER key

These chunks form units that locally specify the conditions for actions in the top space and which are not reliant on knowing the last action performed. If the current state of the display can be determined, these chunks can be transferred to produce solutions to related tasks, for example partially completed problems. The relationship between the actions and the device is exploited to enable the actions in the solution to be applied separately.

To relate this difference to users' performance, imagine the task of completing a partially solved binary calculation. The operational chunks would not be applicable in this situation as the last action performed could not be inferred. The chunks require that the known recipe sequence be followed, with each action being part of the sequence and thus linked to the actions that have already been performed. The chunks therefore support only the solution of a complete binary calculation. By contrast, the figurative chunks could be applied by visual confirmation of the correspondence between the calculation operands and the contents of the display. The actions are not linked specifically to the preceding actions. This is in accord with the experimental results, where the differentiation between groups presented with either operational or figurative instructions is with respect to novel problems but not familiar problems.

DISCUSSION

The models have demonstrated that the chunking mechanism of Soar offers a way to model the development of skill as a reduction in the amount of problem solving required to produce task solutions. The models have also demonstrated that identical task performance may derive from automatised methods which embody different task knowledge. The operational chunks form a chained sequence which can only be applied to complete a binary calculation. Each action requires that the preceding action in the sequence has been performed. Thus the task of completing a partially completed binary calculation for example could not be performed. The figurative chunks do not form an ordered sequence in this way and could be applied to produce solutions to problems which which do not require precisely the same complete action sequence.

These models have raised a number of questions that are currently being addressed through experimental work and further modelling. The experimental work aims to chart the development of skilled methods in individual users at a more detailed level than that reported in the experimental work cited above. This is done by analysing the time taken to produce individual keystrokes in task solutions using the metrics specified in the Keystroke Level Model (Card, Moran and Newell, 1983). By using these time metrics it is possible to determine which keystrokes can be grouped, reflecting the application of automatised methods. Differences in these methods should account for the user group differences observed in the experimental work cited above (Halasz and Moran, 1983; Kieras and Bovair, 1984). To complement this analysis, further Soar models are being developed to analyse the effects of alternative knowledge types and search strategies on the development of solution methods.

REFERENCES

Anderson, JR (1983) *The Architecture of Cognition*. Cambridge, Mass: Harvard
    University Press
Anderson JR (1984) Acquisition of proof skills in geometry. In R Michalski, JG
    Carbonnell and TM Mitchell (Eds) *Machine Learning, An Artificial Intelligence
    Approach,* Springer-Verlag
Anderson JR (1985) The Geometry Tutor, *Proceedings of IJCAI-85*, Los Angeles, Calif.
Card SK, Moran TP and Newell A (1983) *The Psychology of Human Computer
    Interaction*, Hillsdale, N.J.: Erlbaum
Gentner D and Stevens AL (Eds) (1983) *Mental Models*, Hillsdale, NJ: Erlbaum
Halasz FG and Moran TP (1983) Mental Models and Problem Solving in Using a
    Calculator, *Proceedings of ACM SIGCHI*, Boston, M.A
Halasz FG (1984) *Mental Models and Problem Solving in Using a Calculator*,
    Unpublished Doctoral Dissertation, Stanford University, U.S.A.
Kieras D and Bovair S (1984) The Role of a Mental Model in Learning to Operate a
    Device, *Cognitive Science, 8*, 255-273
Laird J and Newell A (1983) A Universal Weak Method, Dept. of Computer Science
    Report, CMU-CS-83-141, Carnegie-Mellon University
Laird J, Rosenbloom P and Newell A (1986) *Universal Sub-goaling and Chunking: the
    Automatic Generation and Learning of Goal Hierarchies*, Kluwer, Hingham, MA
Mayer RE and Bayman P (1981) Psychology of Calculator Languages: A Framework for
    Describing Differences in Users' Knowledge, *Communications of the ACM, 24,
    No. 8,* 511 - 520
Mitchell TM (1982) Generalization as search. *Artificial Intelligence, 18,* 203 - 226
Mitchell TM, Utgoff PE and Banerji R (1984) Learning by experimentation: Acquiring
    and refining problem-solving heuristics. In R Michalski, JG Carbonnell and TM
    Mitchell (Eds) *Machine Learning, An Artificial Intelligence Approach,* Springer-
    Verlag
Payne, S (1989) A notation for reasoning about learning. In J Long and A Whitefield
    (Eds), *Cognitive Ergonomics and Human Computer Interaction*, Cambridge University
    Press, Cambridge
Snoddy GS (1926) Learning and stability. *Journal of Applied Psychology, 10,* 1 - 36
Young RM (1981) The machine inside the machine: users' models of pocket calculators.
    International Journal of Man-Machine Studies, 15, 51 - 85

Instance-Based and Generalization-Based Learning Procedures Applied To Solving Integration Problems.

Terry Elliott & Paul D. Scott, Dept of Computer Science, University of Essex

ABSTRACT

The majority of machine learning systems produce representations that contain generalizations derived from training examples but recent research has led to the development of instance-based methods that produce representations composed of sets of examples. Instance-based methods are believed to offer advantages both in the resources required for learning and the power of the resulting representation. However there has been little experimental evidence to support the view that instance-based learning can produce better representations than generalization-based approaches. In this paper we describe a comparative study of instance-based and generalization-based learning applied to the domain of symbolic integration. This domain differs from those chosen for earlier research in instance based methods in that examples cannot be described as N-tuples of feature values and the significance of individual features is highly context sensitive. We describe two types of similarity functions which can be used for this type of example. The results obtained demonstrate that instance-based learning produces a better representation and it is shown that this is a consequence of the inability of generalizations to adequately represent the complexities of the domain. We conclude that complex highly structured domains might prove to be one of the most profitable areas for application of instance-based methods.

INTRODUCTION

One of the most interesting recent developments in machine learning research has been the emergence of *instance-based learning methods*. The majority of machine learning systems are *generalization-based*: that is, they use inductive or deductive reasoning to derive generalizations from sets of training examples. These generalizations may then be used to categorize subsequent examples. In contrast, instance-based methods do not attempt to construct generalizations: they simply store training examples in *exemplar sets*. Such systems categorize an example encountered after learning by finding the most similar stored example. Thus generalization-based methods construct intensional representations of concepts while instance-based methods acquire extensional representations. The earliest instance-based machine learning procedures appears to have been Samuel's (1963) rote learning but little research was carried out until the mid 1980's. Successful instance-based systems have been described by Stanfill & Waltz (1986), Bareiss, Porter & Weir (1987), Bareiss (1989), Bradshaw (1987), Kibler & Aha (1987,1988), Kibler, Aha & Albert (1989), Kurtzberg (1987), Connell & Utgoff (1987), Jabbour, Riveros, Landsbergen & Meyer (1987), Aha (1989), and Aha & Kibler (1989).

Advantages of Instance-Based Learning

Instance-based methods offer several potential advantages over generalization-based techniques. The representations produced are simple since they are merely lists of examples. The incremental learning costs are small because there is no process of deriving a good generalization to be performed. Provided the system is selective in its acquisition of examples, storage costs will be modest. However, their greatest advantage may lie in the representational power of exemplar sets. Generalization-based methods attempt to represent concepts as expressions, in some representation language, that specify the necessary and sufficient conditions for category membership. Such systems are thus inherently limited to those concepts that can be defined in the representation language, and are typically further restricted to those relatively simple expressions which may be readily derived by the learning procedure. Hence generalization-based systems are likely to have difficulty in learning complicated concepts. In contrast, exemplar sets can be used to represent concepts of any complexity: all that is needed to handle greater complexity is to add more examples. The difference between the two approaches is analogous to that between approximating a mathematical function with a polynomial and with a series of straight line segments. The main disadvantage of instance-based methods is the time taken to find the most similar stored example when categorizing novel examples. However, this can be reduced both by selectivity in adding examples to exemplar sets and by developing indexing schemes.

A further reason for the current interest in instance-based representations is an increasing body of evidence suggesting that human category representation does not take the form of necessary and sufficient conditions for category membership (Smith & Medin, 1981). In particular, human categories have clear typical examples and somewhat vague boundary conditions. Such a continuum of degree of membership cannot be expressed in terms of membership predicates but is characteristic of the form of representation used in instance-based methods.

Evaluating Instance-Based Learning

Research on instance-based learning has so far concentrated on discovering ways of making it work effectively and efficiently. The work reported in this paper had a different objective. Since both generalization-based and instance-based methods have been successful, it is pertinent to ask under what circumstances, if any, and in what way, one approach is preferable to the other. There have been very few comparative studies of generalization-based and instance-based learning. The most systematic that we are aware of are those of Aha & Kibler (Kibler & Aha, 1988; Aha, 1989; Aha & Kibler, 1989) who compared the performance of various instance-based methods with Quinlan's (1986) C4 decision tree algorithm. They found that the better instance-based methods were more economical in time and space but neither approach showed a clear advantage in accuracy of the resulting representation. Thus the notion that the representational power of instance-based methods provides a significant advantage remains a plausible belief unsupported by experimental evidence. One goal of the work described in this paper was to investigate whether such an advantage does exist.

Most of the work on instance-based learning has been concerned with two types of problem domain: relatively simple artificial domains, which are easy to modify and hence very useful for systematic experimentation, and natural domains, such as medical databases, that typically contain a large number of features. We know of no work on the use of instance-based methods to learn to solve problems in a domain for which a sound domain theory exists. This type of learning requires the system to learn rules for selecting the most appropriate operator to apply at each stage of problem solving. Inductive generalization-based methods have had only very limited success in such domains, and this has been one of the reasons for the growth of interest in deductive (explanation-based) learning. Our second goal was therefore to investigate how successfully instance-based learning could be applied to learning this type of problem solving.

Overview

In this paper we describe experiments in which we compare the performance of a generalization-based learning system, LEX (Mitchell, Utgoff & Banerji, 1983), with two instance-based methods, applied to solving symbolic integration problems. Section 2 provides a brief account of LEX and a discussion of its limitations, while section 3 contains descriptions of the instance-based systems we implemented. In section 4 we describe the results obtained by running all three systems on the same problems. These show that instance-based learning is, on average, very much more effective. Finally, section 5 contains some general conclusions.

LEARNING TO INTEGRATE - LEX AND ITS LIMITATIONS

We chose the domain of symbolic integration because it enabled us to achieve both the goals of this investigation. LEX (Mitchell et al, 1983) is a program that uses a generalization-based approach to learning to solve integration problems. The program was successful but is known to suffer from limitations that arise, at least in part, from limitations in representational power. Thus attempting the same learning task with an instance-based method could provide evidence for the conjecture that instance-based systems can acquire better representations. Furthermore, symbolic integration is a highly structured formal domain, and hence is a suitable vehicle for investigating whether instance-based methods can be successfully applied to such domains.

An Overview of LEX

LEX has been described in detail elsewhere (Mitchell et al, 1983): we confine ourselves to a brief account of how the program works. Given a mathematical expression containing an integral sign, and a set of operators for transforming mathematical expressions, integration can be accomplished, in principle, by a blind search for a sequence of operators which will produce a mathematical expression containing no integral sign. Unfortunately the search space implicit in this approach is vast and so an effective system will require some guidance in selecting operators. This can take the form of heuristics which indicate which operators are likely to be successful for particular expressions. Both LEX and the instance-based systems described later improve their performance at performing integrations by acquiring such heuristics as a result of experience in solving integration problems.

LEX learns heuristics by application of the candidate elimination algorithm (Mitchell, 1982) to examples that comprise successful and unsuccessful applications of operators to expressions. This attempts to construct generalized descriptions for expressions which may be successfully integrated through the application of particular operators. These descriptions are couched in a representation language which thus determines the representational power of the system. In LEX these descriptions take the form of mathematical expressions in which elements may have been replaced by more general forms. Thus $3x \cdot cos(x)$ may be generalized to $poly(x) \cdot trig(x)$ or even $fun_1(x) \cdot fun_2(x)$. These generalizations are based on a hierarchy of function types which is supplied to LEX as a priori domain knowledge. This type hierarchy determines which heuristics can be represented: the candidate elimination algorithm determines which of these can be discovered.

Limitations of LEX

Although LEX was successful, it nevertheless suffered from serious limitations. Some of these are a consequence of using the candidate elimination algorithm, which is extremely costly in both time and space, but others were apparent even on problems small enough to be solved by the program. Mitchell et al (1983) suggest that the inability to discover some heuristics arose in part from limitations in LEX's representation language, and suggest that refining the type hierarchy used to build generalizations would enable the system to discover more heuristics. They also argue that analysis of why operators succeed would be a better way of finding good general heuristics: a line of thought which has subsequently been developed into explanation-based approaches to learning (Mitchell, Kellar, & Kedar-Cabelli, 1986).

However, analysis of the way LEX behaves suggests that the real source of its limitations is that the program is directed towards seeking generalizations. If a concept can only be expressed disjunctively in the representation language employed, the program often fails to discover a good heuristic. This happens because LEX is biased towards generalizing rather than admitting disjunctive concepts. Consequently the program may fail to discover important disjunctive concepts. An example of this kind of behaviour is described in section 4. This kind of problem is not a consequence of the particular type hierarchy used to guide generalization and would not be eliminated simply by extensions to the representation language.

Instance-based representations could be regarded as an extreme form of disjunctive representation. Furthermore, they are not limited by the representation language since any expression can form part of the exemplar set representation. Hence it seems plausible that instance-based learning might overcome at least some of the limitations encountered by LEX. We therefore now describe two alternative instance-based systems for learning to solve integration problems.

TWO INSTANCE-BASED LEARNING SYSTEMS

Instance-based learning systems are comprised of three major components (Aha & Kibler, 1989): the *similarity function* that provides a numerical measure of how closely two examples resemble one another; a *classification function* that uses the similarity of an example to members of the exemplar sets to assign that example to a specific class; and a *memory updating procedure* that determines which examples should be saved in exemplar sets and maintains pertinent statistical information. In this section we describe how we implemented each of these in a system which learns to solve symbolic integration problems.

The Similarity Functions

Many instance-based learning systems operate in domains in which instances have a fixed number of attributes. In such domains instances can be described as N-tuples of feature values, and similarity can then be defined as the Euclidean distance in an N-dimensional space. This approach is not possible in the symbolic integration domain because mathematical expressions have a nested structure and may be of arbitrary length, and hence cannot be represented in any reasonable way as N-tuples of feature values.

Furthermore, the Euclidian distance approach implies that each feature makes an independent contribution to the similarity. In contrast, the significance of features of mathematical expressions may depend on the context in which they appear. For example, x^n and x^{n+1} may be treated in the same way for most mathematical purposes. In particular, they are integrated in the same way and so one would expect a reasonable similarity metric to indicate that they have high similarity. Now consider e^x, which is trivially integrable, and e^{x^2}, which has no closed-form integral. The only difference between these expressions lies in the exponent of x yet they are manifestly dissimilar with respect to integration.

We developed two alternative methods for determining the similarity of mathematical expressions. The first was a rule-based system, while the second made use of the same type hierarchy of mathematical functions that is used by LEX.

The Rule-Based Similarity Function. The apparent need for context sensitivity in similarity measurement suggested that a set of production rules, which would allow premises of arbitrary complexity, would be the most effective way of defining a good similarity function. Furthermore, this approach is amenable to refinement should the initial set of rules prove inadequate.

After some experiment, a system of 14 rules was produced which calculated the similarity of any two expressions. These were somewhat ad hoc, and their only justification is that they appear reasonable and seem to work. The similarity of two monomials is calculated by a mathematical formula based on their coefficients and exponents; the similarity of two transcendental functions is found by reference to a table of similarities; and the similarity of more complex expressions is derived from the similarities of their constituents. The full set of rules, together with some justification, may be found in Elliot (1990).

The Type Hierarchy Similarity Function. The rule-based similarity function could be criticised in two respects. First, the similarity function embodies a priori knowledge about the relationships between entities in the domain. It thus plays the same role as the type hierarchy used for generalization in LEX. Hence it could be argued that any difference in performance between LEX and the instance-based method could be due to a difference in a priori domain knowledge rather than the learning procedures employed. The second potential criticism stems from the fact that it would be possible to build a great deal of knowledge pertaining to integration methods into the rule-based similarity function. Hence it could be argued that in creating the rules we have solved most of the problem in advance.

In order to counter both these objections we implemented an alternative similarity function that uses exactly the same a priori domain knowledge as LEX. This employed LEX's type hierarchy in order to determine the similarity of two example expressions, f and g. The type hierarchy is used to find the maximally specific common generalization of f and g. Let M be the number of steps needed to reach this generalization. Then the similarity of f and g can be defined as 2^{-M}. As the results described later show, this proved to be an effective but computationally expensive similarity function.

The Classification Function and the Memory Updating Procedure

The instance-based systems builds exemplar sets for each operator. When an expression, is to be integrated, the most similar example is found in the exemplar set of each applicable operator. The operators are then tried in turn, in the order generated by similarity ranking. Operators for which no examples are found are tried last.

The examples saved in each exemplar set comprise, the expression to which the operator is applied, the variable bindings made, and counts of the number of times that the operator has been used successfully and unsuccessfully. Only examples with more successes than failures are considered by the classification function.

When an operator, O, is applied, either successfully or unsuccessfully, to an expression, e, the most similar stored example, f, is found. If f is in the exemplar set of an operator other than O, or if the similarity between e and f is below a threshold, then the example is added to the exemplar set of O. If e is not saved, then the success or failure count of f is incremented appropriately.

EXPERIMENTAL RESULTS

Three learning procedures were implemented in C-Prolog on a Sun 3/50: LEX, which was a reimplementation following published accounts; Instance-Based R, which used the rule-based similarity function; and Instance-Based T, which used the type hierarchy based similarity function. All three shared the same blind integration and critic components. Further details of the implementations are given in Elliott (1990).

Experimental Procedure

Each of the three learning procedures was trained through solving the six problems in the training set. The performance of each was then evaluated through solving a further four problems in the evaluation set set, but no further learning took place during the evaluation phase. The problem sets used were as follows:

Training Set: $e^x x^2$; $\cos x . x$; $2\cos x$; $x^4 - 3x + 2$; $\ln x . x$; $(1+x^2)^3 . x$

Evaluation Set: x^5+3x^3+5x+2 ; $\sin x . x^2$; $4e^x x$; $(1+x^3)^2 . x^2$

Both problem sets were chosen to present a variety of integration problems to the learning system. It should be noted that in the course of integrating a single expression a number of operators will be applied and hence the effective number of training examples is considerably larger than six. It was not possible to do comparative runs using more complex expressions because the version space constructed by LEX grew intractably large.

During evaluation, counts were made of the number of operators selected by means of heuristics, the number of operators selected blindly, and the amount of cpu time used. The results obtained, along with the corresponding results obtained by an untrained system, are given in Table 1. All three training sessions were repeated twice with the training examples re-ordered: essentially identical final evaluation results were produced. More detailed results, including evaluations carried out during learning, are presented in Elliott (1990).

Table 1: Performance of Learning Procedures on Entire Evaluation Set

	Untrained	LEX	Instance-Based R	Instance-Based T
Heuristically Selected Ops	0	27	20	22
Blindly Selected Ops	949	108	6	0
Total Ops	949	135	26	22
Time (cpu seconds)	63	160	44	414

Discussion

The most obvious conclusion which can be drawn from these results is that, after learning, the instance-based systems required far fewer operator applications in order to solve the evaluation examples. Furthermore, heuristics determine most of the instance-based systems' operator selections, whereas most of LEX's choices are blind. In order to understand why this occurred it is necessary to consider the performance of the systems on individual members of the evaluation set. Table 2 shows the results obtained in integrating $\sin x \cdot x^2$, LEX's least successful performance.

Table 2: Performance of Learning Procedures on $\sin x \cdot x^2$.

	Untrained	LEX	Instance-Based R	Instance-Based T
Heuristically Selected Ops	0	11	6	6
Blindly Selected Ops	653	72	0	0
Total Ops	653	83	6	6
Time (cpu seconds)	32	72	12	137

This example took LEX 83 operations, mainly through blind search, while the instance based systems solved it with 6 heuristically chosen operations. Clearly LEX has failed to acquire heuristics appropriate for this example. Because the type hierarchy instance-based method did as well as the rule-based counterpart it appears that the problem lies in the process of generalization rather than the information used to guide generalization. To integrate this expression, it is necessary to apply integration by parts, using the substitution $\int u \, dv = uv - \int v \, du$ with the appropriate substitution for u and v, which in this case is $u = x^2$ and $dv = \sin x \, dx$. The instance-based methods have no difficulty because the problem is very similar to one of the training examples, $\cos x \cdot x$, and hence the correct operator and substitution are chosen. LEX chose the wrong substitution and hence wasted much effort on a path that was doomed to failure. However, immediately after being presented with the $\cos x \cdot x$ training example, LEX's performance was just as good as that of the instance-based methods. In fact, LEX's dismal final performance only arose as a result of a collapse after the training example $\ln x \cdot x$ had been given. The reason for this is as follows.

Like $\cos x \cdot x$, $\ln x \cdot x$ is integrated by parts, but the substitutions made are different. To integrate $\ln x \cdot x$ it is necessary to choose $u = \ln x$ and $dv = x \, dx$.

When LEX attempts to find a generalized form which encompasses both these examples the only possibility is one asserting that $fun_1(x).fun_{2(x)}$ can be integrated by parts making the substitution $u = fun_2(x)$ and $dv = fun_1(x)dx$, where fun_1 and fun_2 are any functions. This rule is correct but useless as it is too general, amounting to no more than the preconditions for integration by parts to be applicable. Thus a valuable heuristic that was acquired through integrating cos x . x is destroyed by overgeneralization and the choices of substitution become blind. No amount of training will enable LEX to recover from this error because the candidate elimination algorithm cannot backtrack and re-specialize a generalization. In contrast, the instance-based methods saved both examples and hence were not disrupted by the occurrence of an expression requiring a different substitution.

There are however circumstances in which LEX did as well or better than the instance-based methods. Table 3 shows the results obtained when integrating the polynomial in the evaluation set, x^5+3x^3+5x+2.

Table 3: Performance of Learning Procedures on x^5+3x^3+5x+2.

	Untrained	LEX	Instance-Based R	Instance-Based T
Heuristically Selected Ops	0	9	7	9
Blindly Selected Ops	47	0	6	0
Total Ops	47	9	13	9
Time (cpu seconds)	13	26	17	55

For this example, LEX required fewer operations than the instance-based system that used a rule-based similarity function, and the same number as the type hierarchy instance-based method. This suggests that the a priori knowledge embodied in LEX's type hierarchy is well suited to characterizing polynomial expressions and that LEX's generalization procedure is able to learn how to integrate any polynomial after just one training example.

The figures given for time taken to solve problems do not correlate well with the number of operators applied. In particular the type hierarchy instance-based system, which is the most economical in terms of operator applications, requires a large amount of cpu time. The reason for this is that finding the most specific common generalization in the type hierarchy is a computationally expensive procedure. The type hierarchy instance-based system must do this a number of times in finding the most similar example. LEX incurs a similar cost, though not so often, in finding which generalizations match a candidate expression. In contrast, the rule-based similarity function is much cheaper to compute and hence this system is always faster than the other two. However, even this system incurs a significant time cost in selecting operators and hence the untrained system is actually faster for the polynomial example.

CONCLUSIONS

This investigation was designed to answer two questions. The first was whether, as has been argued but not demonstrated, instance-based methods have greater representational power than their generalization-based counterparts. The results show that both instance-based methods are, on average, very much more effective than LEX at learning to solve problems in symbolic integration. In particular the results show that instance-based methods are better able to represent the rules needed to determine when and how to apply the integration by parts operator. This we regard as a convincing demonstration that, under some circumstances, instance-based methods do indeed have greater representational power.

The second question was whether instance-based methods could be successfully applied to learning to solve problems in domains for which a sound domain theory exists. The success of both the systems we implemented demonstrates that they can. This is the more surprising result. Instance-based methods have usually been advocated as a method for dealing with the problems that arise in natural domains in which concepts are typically polymorphous (Bareiss et al, 1987). Consequently several workers have suggested that they are not appropriate for learning mathematical domains (eg Kibler & Aha, 1987; Bareiss et al, 1987). Hence our results imply that the scope of instance-based methods may be wider than has hitherto been believed.

Acknowledgements

We thank the SERC for support of Terry Elliot through Advanced Course Studentship 89402711, and Kingsley Sage for useful discussions in the early stages of this project.

References

Aha DW (1989) Incremental Instance-Based Learning of Independent and Graded Concept Descriptions. Proceedings Sixth International Workshop on Machine Learning, Ithaca, NY, June 1989, Morgan Kaufmann, Los Altos California.

Aha DW & Kibler D (1989) Noise-Tolerant Instance-Based Learning Algorithms. Proceedings of the Eleventh International Joint Conference on Artificial Intelligence, Detroit, Michigan, August 1989, Morgan Kaufmann, Los Altos, California.

Bareiss RE, Porter BW & Weir CC (1987) Protos: An Exemplar-Based Learning Apprentice. Proceedings Fourth International Workshop on Machine Learning, Irvine, Calif. June 1987, Morgan Kaufmann, Los Altos California.

Bareiss RE (1989) Exemplar-Based Knowledge Acquisition. Academic Press.

Bradshaw G (1987) Learning About Speech Sounds: The NEXUS Project. Proceedings Fourth International Workshop on Machine Learning, Irvine, Calif. June 1987, Morgan Kaufmann, Los Altos California.

Connell ME & Utgoff PE (1987) Learning to Control a Dynamic Physical System. Proceedings AAAI-87, the Sixth National Conference on Artificial Intelligence, Seattle, WA, August 1987, Morgan Kaufmann, Los Altos, California.

Elliott T (1990) Instance-Based Learning and Integration: An Exploration. M.Sc. Dissertation, Department of Computer Science, University of Essex, Colchester, UK.

Jabbour K, Riveros JFV, Landsbergen D & Meyer W (1987) ALFA, Automated Load Forecasting Assistant. Proceedings of the 1987 IEEE Power Engineering Society Summer Meeting, San Francisco,

Kibler D & Aha DW (1987) Learning Representative Exemplars of Concepts: An Initial Case Study. Proceedings Fourth International Workshop on Machine Learning, Irvine, Calif. June 1987, Morgan Kaufmann, Los Altos California.

Kibler D & Aha DW (1988) Comparing Instance-Averaging With Instance Filtering Learning Algorithms. Proceedings Third European Working Session Learning, Glasgow, Scotland, Oct 1988, Pitman Publishing, London.

Kibler D, Aha DW & Albert M (1988) Instance-Based Prediction of Real-Valued Attributes. Computational Intelligence, May 1989.

Kurtzberg JM (1987) Feature Analysis for Symbol Recognition By Elastic Matching. IBM Journal of Research and Development 31:91-95.

Mitchell TM (1982) Generalization as Search. Artificial Intelligence 18:203-226.

Mitchell TM (1986) Explanation-Based Generalization: A Unifying View. Machine Learning 1:47-80.

Mitchell TM, Utgoff PE & Banerji R (1983) Learning by Experimentation: Acquiring and Refining Problem Solving Heuristics. In Machine Learning: An Artificial Intelligence Approach, RS Michalski, JG Carbonell & TM Mitchell (eds), Morgan Kaufmann, Los Altos, California.

Quinlan JR (1986) Induction of Decision Trees. Machine Learning 1:81-106.

Samuel A (1959) Some Studies in Machine Learning Using the Game of Checkers. IBM Journal of Research and Development 3:211-229.

Smith EE & Medin D (1981) Categories and Concepts. Harvard University Press, Cambridge, Massachusetts.

Stanfill C & Waltz D. (1986) Toward Memory-Based Reasoning. Communications of the Association for Computing Machinery 29:1213-1228.